GRAND DRAGON

GRAND DRAGON

D. C. Stephenson and the Ku Klux Klan in Indiana

M. William Lutholtz

Purdue University Press
West Lafayette, Indiana

97   96   95   94   93   5   4   3   2   1

The paper used in this book meets the minimum requirements of
American National Standard for Information Sciences—Permanence of
Paper for Printed Library Materials, ANSI Z39.48-1984.

Printed in the United States of America
Designed by Anita Noble

First paperbound printing 1993

Library of Congress Cataloging-in-Publication Data
Lutholtz, M. William, 1954–
    Grand dragon : D. C. Stephenson and the Ku Klux Klan in
Indiana / M. William Lutholtz
        p.   cm.
    Includes bibliographical references and index.
    ISBN 1-55753-046-7
    1. Ku Klux Klan (1915–)—Indiana—History. 2. Stephenson, David
Curtis, 1891–1966. 3. Murder—Indiana—Case studies. I. Title.
HS 2330.K63187 1991
322.4'2'092—dc20   90-20132
[B]   CIP

To Kate

There at the beginning and there at the end

Contents

Preface

I first heard about D. C. Stephenson and the Ku Klux Klan in Indiana in the summer of 1974. I was in my sophomore year of college and helping some friends—nursing students—move into a rented house on the east side of Indianapolis, in a neighborhood called Irvington. I had grown up on the city's north side and had never spent any time in Irvington. After we finished with the heavy lifting, three of the women invited me to take a quick tour of the neighborhood. One had grown up near Irvington and knew the area well. It was summer—a bright sunny day—with light streaming down through the trees and birds singing all around the neighborhood.

Irvington had started its life as a small town east of Indianapolis in the late 1800s. Gradually, as Indianapolis pushed outward, the town was swallowed up by the city and was no longer considered a suburb. The narrow winding streets, however, were a reminder that this was not really part of the city, that this had once been a separate place of its own. The streets bore the names of authors—Emerson, Hawthorne, Whittier—in fact, the town had taken its name from Washington Irving. The town had been, for thirty years or so, the home of Butler College, before the school had moved to new land on the far north side of the city. The former football field had sprouted several blocks of bungalow houses. But some of the old campus buildings still stood—reminders of where the college had stood.

As we came around a corner on University Avenue, my friends pointed out a magnificent ruin of a house. On first glance, it looked like a back lot set from *Gone With the Wind*—a perfect southern mansion with a huge, two-story porch and massive white columns. The lot was overgrown with weeds and small trees. The house, once white, was badly in need of paint.

". . . And that's the house where the leader of the Ku Klux Klan lived," one of the women said. "He killed a girl in that house, and they sent him to prison. When I was in high school, my friends used to believe that her ghost was here." Then she laughed, half-embarrassed at sharing such a story.

Ku Klux Klan? In Indiana? This was news to me. I had grown up and lived all my life in Indianapolis and never heard much about the Ku Klux Klan. I could not recall having ever heard or read anything about the Ku Klux Klan in my grade-school Indiana history classes. There had been an incident with some modern-day klansmen, and William Chaney, who had once been the grand dragon of the Klan in the 1960s, went to prison for attempted murder with a pipe bomb. But those were recent happenings—something I had always dismissed as the activities of a radical fringe.

A murderer? In my mind, I imagined an old lunatic in a Confederate soldier's uniform with the Stars and Bars of Dixie hanging on his wall. The Klan was something I had grown up associating only with the South. Indiana had been a Union state—what would the Klan be doing this far north?

I decided that the story must have been the work of some overactive high-school imaginations. I dismissed the story and thought no more about it.

Four years later, in 1978, now holding a degree and a few years of newspaper and magazine editing experience, I was working as editor of the *Indac* magazine. This was a monthly publication for the Indianapolis Athletic Club, one of the city's two downtown, prestigious private clubs. The other club, the Columbia Club, had its roots in the Republican party. Housed on Monument Circle, the Columbia Club had started out as a group of supporters of then–presidential candidate Benjamin Harrison. The Athletic Club was created later to give the Democrats a place of their own. Now, I was editing its magazine, a publication that dated back to 1921 and had once carried the by-lines of the state's best writers—Booth Tarkington, George Ade, Kin Hubbard, and Meredith Nicholson. My office was on the top floor of the building, with windows overlooking the downtown and its parks and memorial plazas. A stack of old magazines, bound in hardcovers, occupied a bookshelf at the end of the room, and I frequently took down copies to study my predecessors' works.

One of my first projects was to write a piece on some club members who were restoring old homes. In doing research to prepare for the story, I bought a small paperback book, the *Indiana Almanac & Fact Book,* by local writer and historian Ed Leary. It included an "Indiana chronology," which I studied to get information on the periods when the old homes of our club's members were being built. As I read, I found myself learning about the history of my state—something that I had not studied since the fourth grade.

Suddenly, on pages 19 and 20 of Leary's book, these three terse entries leapt out at me:

> 1922—David Curtis Stephenson is appointed Grand Dragon of KKK for Indiana and begins climb to power in Hoosier political and economic life.
> 1925—Stephenson arrested and charged with murder. His trial results in startling expose of corrupt role KKK played in Indiana politics. Several officials, including mayor of Indianapolis, are sentenced to jail. . . .
> 1928—*Indianapolis Times* wins Pulitzer Prize for its campaign against KKK.

So it was true after all! As I read that chronology, my mind raced back to that summer drive through Irvington and the old faded mansion. It must have been the same man! And the story must have been true! I decided to drop everything and start studying this story to find out what more I could learn.

The *Indianapolis Times* had folded in the 1960s, but I knew that some of the paper's former reporters still wrote for the city's two other dailies, the *Indianapolis News* and the *Indianapolis Star.* I began by calling one of them, Gerry LaFollette with the *News,* to ask him what he knew about the story. Of course he had heard about D. C. Stephenson—didn't everybody know about Stephenson? Yes, the paper had won a Pulitzer, and LaFollette had remembered hearing old-timers talk about it. He suggested that I start by reading a book by former *Times* managing editor, Irving Leibowitz, which had a good chapter on the Stephenson story.

That night, with a library copy of Leibowitz's *My Indiana* at home, I began to steep myself in the legend of D. C. Stephenson—grand dragon, political power broker, super salesman, rapist, and murderer. Leibowitz's story was written in 1964, shortly before the demise of his newspaper. The eighth chapter of his book was titled "The Klan in Indiana." Directly beneath the chapter title was this quotation:

> "I am the law in Indiana."
> —D. C. Stephenson

Part of the chapter reprinted, in full, an incredible document: the deathbed testimony of Madge Oberholtzer as she told it to her lawyer, attorney Asa Smith.

In the deathbed statement, the twenty-eight-year-old state-house secretary told how she had met Stephenson at the inaugural ball for Governor Ed Jackson (which had been held in the fourth floor ballroom of the Athletic Club—directly below my office!). She told how she was abducted from her home in Irvington and taken by Stephenson and two of his men to the train station. She described how one of the men slept in one compartment of the Pullman car on the trip to Hammond, Indiana, while Stephenson attacked and raped her. To frighten him into releasing her, she took poison in Hammond. Stephenson immediately rushed her back to Indianapolis. Almost a month later, she died, either from the side effects of the poison or from the horrible bites she suffered from Stephenson during the rape.

The statement was used in court to convict Stephenson, who spent the next thirty-one years in the Indiana State Prison at Michigan City, Indiana, on a charge of second-degree murder—the longest imprisonment ever in the state for such a crime.

Leibowitz told the story in only thirty-six pages. It was a fast-paced narrative written only eight years after Stephenson was finally released from prison in 1956. The story highlighted the role that Leibowitz's predecessors at the newspaper played in bringing down the grand dragon and how the paper earned a Pulitzer prize for its reporting on the Klan.

But Leibowitz's story also dangled some unresolved mysteries:

• The 2,347-page transcript of the trial was missing. As Leibowitz told it, "The official court record of Madge's dying declaration is mysteriously missing, along with the historic trial transcript. Alice Whitecotton, former clerk of the Indiana Supreme Court, says she discovered it was missing when someone asked to see it. Indiana Attorney General Edwin K. Steers sent two deputies searching through the vaults of the Statehouse in March 1963 trying to locate the complete Stephenson trial transcript. They reported they could not find it." And no one ever has.

• Stephenson himself disappeared from Indiana after his release from prison. No one (at the time Leibowitz was writing) knew where he had gone.

• Stephenson and his lawyers had argued that he had been framed, that he was not guilty. Leibowitz did not seem to give much credence to this argument. Was there any overlooked evidence that might suggest that Stephenson had been framed?

When I finished reading Leibowitz's version of the story, I was deeply puzzled. Had I really been such a bad listener in my grade-school classes? Could I have read or heard such an incredible story and simply forgotten it? I started searching through old Indiana history grade-school textbooks. I found the text that had been used in my classes in the 1960s. Sure enough, the Klan was mentioned—with less than two sentences and no reference to Stephenson at all. I checked other textbooks. Again, the same treatment. The Klan period, squeezed in between World War I and the Great Depression, was covered in less than a paragraph and dismissed. It was as if most of the school textbook writers deliberately wanted to blot the story from the history of the state.

Even more amazing was the fact that Stephenson had been sentenced in the circuit courtroom in Noblesville, Indiana. As a reporter for the nearby *Carmel News Journal* I had spent a good deal of time in that courtroom. In 1976, I had spent several days covering a murder trial in Noblesville. Not once, however, had I ever heard any of the story of D. C. Stephenson and the trial of 1925 that took place in the same courtroom.

I began to dig further—the first steps of a twelve-year effort. I read more books on Stephenson and the Klan. I interviewed several older newspaper reporters, including a couple who had actually interviewed Stephenson while he was in prison. I began to feed dimes (later, quarters) into the newspaper microfilm copying machines at the Indiana State Library and the Indianapolis–Marion County Public Library, taking the sixty-year-old newspaper stories home to digest slowly. Later, I talked with Butler College classmates of Madge Oberholtzer's about her school days. I tracked down one of Stephenson's former mistresses, who threatened to have her lawyers after me in a minute if I revealed her name. I also had two luncheon interviews with a distinguished-looking old gentleman, a former klansman who had worked for Stephenson. He was fond of arranging cloak-and-dagger-style meetings and only allowed me to know him by the title of "Mister X." He eventually agreed to look over some of the early chapters of the book and commented on their legitimacy, pointing out some errors, and offering suggestions of where to look for more information.

Old assumptions on my part died hard. The first was my notion that the Klan had always been a southern problem. My image of the Ku Klux Klan was of two periods: the post–Civil War period of the 1860s, when the Klan was a group of night-riding southern vigilantes who were fond of hanging blacks and wayward Yankees, and the pre–civil rights era of the 1960s, when the Klan had been active in church bombings and the shootings of blacks and meddling Yankees. I had never associated the Klan with the northern states.

The second assumption I had to lose was that the Klan had been aimed only against blacks. What I discovered was that, at least in the Indiana of the 1920s, there had been very little effort spent terrorizing blacks. Most of the Klan's hatred in my state had been directed against other whites—those who were Catholic, Jewish, or foreign-born.

In Indiana, the Klan was closely linked to the Republican party. At that time, most blacks in Indiana were staunch Republicans (they were still of a generation that honored the memory of the Great Emancipator and threw their votes to "Mr. Lincoln's party"). As such, the blacks posed no threat to the northern Klan. Jews and Catholics, on the other hand, tended to be Democrats, and thus, the conflict was met, most often, on the political battlefield.

Using recently discovered Klan membership documents, Leonard Moore from the University of California has carefully analyzed the Klan membership of Indiana. Incredible as it may seem, he discovered that roughly two hundred fifty thousand men—about 30 percent of all native-born white men in Indiana—joined the Klan in the early 1920s.

As I studied, interviewed, and read, I found conflicting sets of voices—most of them long dead—arguing whether or not Stephenson actually committed the crime for which he served thirty-one years in prison. One book, brazenly titled *So They Framed Stephenson*, put the issue very bluntly: Stephenson had been framed by politicians who feared his power and who wanted him locked away, shut off from his supporters. He might have been guilty of abusing political power, so the argument went, but he was not guilty of murder.

Was it possible that the trial court of 1925 had delivered Stephenson unjustly to prison? Was it possible that he had, as he always claimed, committed no murder, driven no one to suicide?

To uncover the truth, I reasoned, it would be necessary to reconstruct the trial. This I did by rebuilding the missing trial transcript out of the copious newspaper reports from the trial.

I found many questions that were left unanswered by the trial. In some cases, I found answers—or at least possible answers. In others, I was left with conflicting facts, some of which suggested that Stephenson might have been framed, others that suggested he got the justice he deserved.

Eventually, I uncovered a second murder that may have been linked to the Klan trial. It was a second young woman, who may have tried to help Stephenson. She was found along a Hamilton County roadside after a brutal beating. The police never made an arrest in connection with her death. Did her story—as Stephenson himself insisted—have anything to do with Stephenson's long imprisonment?

To think that Stephenson had plotted to become president of the United States may sound farfetched today. But in 1923, it was also farfetched to believe that either Hitler or Mussolini—both contemporaries of Stephenson—might one day seriously threaten most of Western civilization with their own dictatorships. The murder trial in Noblesville, Indiana, in 1925 ended Stephenson's quest for power. Up until that trial, there were thousands of people across America who supported Stephenson and the things he stood for. Would our history have turned out differently if Stephenson's story had taken a slightly different turn?

As I started to work on the early drafts of this book, I also noticed the incredible present-day parallels to the sixty-year-old material I was studying. Throughout the late 1970s and early 1980s, there was continued talk of a "new Klan" movement in America. There were marches and violence in the South. The Klan was also resurgent in the North—even in Indiana. A former klansman, David Duke—equally as charismatic as Stephenson—was elected as a state representative in Louisiana and even ran (unsuccessfully) for election to the United States Congress. The same old rallying calls, the same old speeches about the supremacy of the white race. Not only were the events of the 1920s forgotten, but the entire cycle seemed, at times, to be on the verge of repeating itself.

Through it all, Stephenson remained an enigma. Before his arrest in 1925, he was a man of mystery. Little was known about him or where he had come from. Even most of his supporters knew him only by his nicknames, "Steve" or "The Old Man." After his conviction, Stephenson became almost loquacious—giving interviews, trying to win back his freedom. Several times, I backtracked over his claims to reporters and discovered that he was a liar. Other times, however, it appeared that he sometimes told the truth about his political maneuvers. The difficulties came in knowing when to believe him and when to understand that he was lying to protect himself. He would not be, as I soon came to realize, a cooperative subject . . .

Acknowledgments

The difficult thing about writing acknowledgments is knowing that you are likely to leave someone important out of the list. If I have done that, it is not by intention.

My first and greatest debt is to my librarian wife, Kate, and our children, Ann Marie and Tom. For them, this book has carried a price tag of having either my mind elsewhere—usually 1925—or my body elsewhere—usually the library. Their patience and endurance have helped greatly.

In the line of information sources, no one even comes close to the late John L. Niblack, reporter, attorney, and judge, who saved his own notes as well as the notes of prosecutor Will Remy and attorney Asa Smith. This incredible store of information, donated to the Indiana Historical Society, formed much of the starting ground for this book. Niblack's memoirs, *The Life and Times of a Hoosier Judge*, provide one of the clearest accounts of the Klan times—and a startling eyewitness account of the great Kokomo Klonvocation of 1923. Had he not saved his material and his memories, this book would probably not have been written.

Attorney Asa Smith, a man I'm sorry I never met, deserves deep thanks as well. If not for his deft legal footwork in 1925, Madge Oberholtzer's deathbed testimony might never have been recorded. If not for that, Stephenson probably would not have been convicted. And if not for that, this book would be considerably different.

Irving Leibowitz is another person I'm sorry I never met. Leibowitz wrote the brief, spine-tingling account of Stephenson's rise and fall that first made me believe there might be a book somewhere in all this. His book, *My Indiana*, is worth recommending for its other chapters, but my debt is specifically to him for the chapter on Stephenson and the Klan.

Thanks also to the late John Bartlow Martin, whose work, *Indiana: An Interpretation*, was one of the most cogent explanations of Stephenson's rise. It still stands as an excellent piece of historical writing about the Hoosier state.

Thanks to Ed Leary for including mention of Stephenson in his book, *Indiana Almanac & Fact Book*, the work that triggered my first research. His was the first printed reference I saw to Stephenson and the Klan in Indiana.

Alan Nolan, attorney and author, was able to give me leads on some of the more elusive parts of this book and point me to sources and answers.

Librarian Eric Pomeroy, formerly of the Indiana Historical Society, and newspaper archivist John Selch were both extremely helpful during my research at the Indiana State Library. Marybelle Burch of the Indiana Division pointed me to oral histories and manuscript sources. Justin Walsh shared his notes on the 1925 General Assembly with me. Their help was truly appreciated.

Dr. Ralph D. Gray and Wanda Lou Willis of the Marion County/Indianapolis Historical Society both offered advice and encouragement during the project.

The Catholic Archdiocese of Indianapolis was most cooperative in sharing its library and its photocopying machine for my research.

Attorney John Martin Smith was quite generous in sharing his research on the Horse Thief Detective Association, which shed some light on Stephenson's involvement with that organization.

Thanks to my many friends at the office who listened patiently when I needed to talk about the project, especially Jim Hetherington, Bill Earl, and Don Nelson. They were the ones who for years most often asked me, "Say, how's that book of yours coming along?" Without their gentle nagging, I believe, this book might not have gotten done.

Thanks also to my friends of the Indianapolis Writers Roundtable, a group that has no officers, no dues, and no newsletter. Nancy Kriplen, Vesle Fenstermaker, Val Gregory, Jean Glick, Bill Carr, Mary Beth Moster, Judy Keene, Skip Berry, Susan Neville, and Barb Shoup—more folks who nudged me. And thanks to my editors at *Indianapolis Magazine*, Pegg Kennedy and Nancy Comiskey, who often asked me about the project—more nudges.

Bob Van Buskirk, the current owner and restorer of Stephenson's house and a fellow hunter of Stephenson lore, frequently commented on the work in progress.

Kenton Broyles of Pennsylvania, historian and antiquarian, provided some commentary and helped in other ways.

Thanks also to the mysterious Mr. X, whoever he was. A close ally of Stephenson's, he examined several chapters of the book and made comments on accuracies and inaccuracies that he noticed.

Thanks to Jim Ware of Books Unlimited (an aptly named store), who used his book-buying intelligence to come up with some truly unique historical pieces that I could not find even in libraries . . . and at prices that didn't break my limited budget.

Thanks to attorney Jim Foster, nephew of Judge Sparks of Rushville, who provided help in looking up biographical material on the judge; Richard Morris, a relative of Asa Smith's, who pointed me to some documents that I used; and Jim Farmer, who also shared some of his Asa Smith and D. C. Stephenson stories with me.

Thanks especially to the people who read early drafts of the manuscript and offered many helpful suggestions, questions, and edits: Gary G. Taylor, Esq.; William R. Coffey, Esq.; Judge Edward P. Madinger; Roseanne Huckleberry; Patrick Traub; and William Meitzler.

Special thanks to Shirley Smith Hill and Sheila Connerty Kaufman, who were along for the ride through Irvington when one of their friends pointed out the Stephenson house in Irvington to me for the very first time.

Sincere thanks to the people of Kaypro Corporation, makers of a fine computer at a price even a writer can afford. And, in the same vein, thanks to the people who created the word processing program WordStar. Without the Kaypro and WordStar, I would probably still be typing.

Thanks also to the staff of the Purdue University Press—William Whalen, Margaret Hunt, Carolyn McGrew, and Anita Noble—who worked diligently to bring this book to completion.

I must also offer my thanks to all the many reporters and photographers who covered the trials and later events, especially Horace Coats, Tubby Toms, John Niblack (again), Walter Watson, Frank Prince, Mary Bostwick, Harold Feightner, and the many others who received no by-lines. Their careful notes provided the only means of restoring the lost transcript of the trial.

Usually at this point, the author of a biography is expected to make a general disclaimer, something to the effect that he and he alone is responsible for all the errors that occur in the book. Well, I'd love to make a statement like that, too. Certainly, none of the people that I have acknowledged here have any responsibility for errors. But I can't help feeling that at least a little responsibility for any errors needs to be shared with D. C. Stephenson, who did as much as anyone could to cover up the details of his life. For those errors, if any, I apologize, but I ask the reader to consider that my subject wasn't exactly the most cooperative soul on earth.

—M. William Lutholtz

Chapter One

The Closing Door

November 14, 1925

The smell of cheap cigars saturated the clothing of the reporters who worked in the cramped "pressroom" of the Hamilton County Circuit Court. The town of Noblesville, Indiana, rarely played host to celebrity murder trials, so the town fathers had never bothered to build a proper pressroom in the courthouse. Now that they had a sensational trial with reporters sent to cover it from as far away as Chicago and New York, the townsmen scrambled to install some tables, a few typewriters, and some "candlestick" telephones in a restroom adjacent to the courtroom. The smell of cigars, which several of the reporters smoked, soon clogged the air of the tiny pressroom.

The trial involved no less a figure than D. C. Stephenson, the mysterious man who had once been grand dragon of the Ku Klux Klan in Indiana and one of the state's most colorful political power brokers. He had been the man in charge when the Klan had recruited 30 percent of the state's white, native-born male population. Now he was charged in the death of a twenty-eight-year-old woman, Madge Oberholtzer. The newspapers had been filled with stories of how Stephenson viciously attacked her in a Pullman car during a train ride to Hammond, Indiana, and how she eventually took poison in hopes of frightening him into letting her go. When she died in April, the charge shifted from abduction to murder, and the stage was set for the trial that had just ended.

Reporters milled around the courthouse in the late November afternoon waiting for word of the jury's verdict. Earlier that morning, more than a thousand people had crushed their way into the courthouse, filling the tiny courtroom and spilling out into the hallways. They were anxious to catch sight of the former grand dragon or his two henchmen, Earl Klinck and Earl Gentry, who were also named in the murder charges.

Most of the crowd stayed through the morning while Ralph Kane, one of the prosecuting attorneys, delivered a long tirade against Stephenson demanding that the twelve jurors find him and his partners guilty of Oberholtzer's murder. "We can't bring Madge Oberholtzer back to life and restore her to her bereaved parents," Kane shouted, "but we can make an example of them for the protection of other daughters!"[1]

Judge Will Sparks had given his instructions to the jury, then declared a one-hour recess for lunch. Most of the crowd remained in the courtroom during the recess, unwilling to risk losing their seats. Many had brought their lunches with them; others bought their food from a makeshift lunch stand that was set up in the hallway by the Women's Relief Corps. People ate and talked in the courtroom, waiting for the jury to return.

At 12:25 P.M., the jurors were ushered back into the courtroom briefly, then sent to the jury room to deliberate the case. Judge Sparks took his hat and coat and went to his room at the Houston Hotel to rest.

Over the course of the next five hours, the crowd slowly dwindled. A rumor circulated that the jurors might well take all night or might go to bed and continue their discussions the next day. More people trickled out of the courtroom. Some stood outside the courthouse on the square, talking in the late-autumn afternoon. Several reporters escaped their smoke-filled restroom to hunt up dinner at one of the local Noblesville restaurants.

Suddenly, just before five o'clock, there was a flurry of activity around the courthouse. A deputy sheriff went hustling down the street to the hotel to get the judge. The jury had reached its verdict. At 5:15 P.M., Sheriff Charles Gooding escorted the three prisoners back from the jail to the courthouse. Reporters scrambled back from nearby restaurants.

Stephenson, overweight and dressed in a business suit, looked more like a prosperous banker than a murder suspect. He certainly did not look like someone who might have—as the papers all said he had—once declared himself "the law in Indiana." He tried now to affect a nonchalant air, chatting casually with the sheriff, as if he were attending a horse race instead of a murder trial. Klinck and Gentry were more subdued—and obviously worried—as they were led into the courtroom.

The crowd was much smaller than it had been at any time during the trial when, at 5:21 P.M., the jurors, carrying their hats and coats, were led up the marble staircase and into the second-floor courtroom. They had appointed farmer W. A. Johnson as their foreman.

Judge Sparks seated himself at the bench and asked, "Gentlemen, have you agreed upon a verdict?" Johnson replied, "We have." He handed the jury's verdict to Ingram Mallery, the bailiff, who handed the note to Judge Sparks. Not one of the jurors looked in Stephenson's direction.

The judge opened the sheet and read the verdict in an even, calm voice: "We, the Jury, find the defendant David C. Stephenson guilty of murder in the second degree, as charged in the first count of the indictment and that he be imprisoned in the Indiana State Prison for and during his natural life. We, the Jury, find the defendant Earl Gentry not guilty. We, the Jury, find the defendant Earl Klinck not guilty."[2]

Judge Sparks asked the defense attorneys if they wished to have the jury polled. Floyd Christian replied that they did. Slowly, deliberately, each of the twelve jurors was asked if that was his verdict. Ten Hamilton County farmers, a truck driver, and a manager of the local gas company all replied that it was their verdict.

Then the judge dismissed the jury, banged his gavel, and declared the court adjourned. Judge Sparks quickly left the courtroom without taking any questions from reporters, who quickly knotted around the defense and prosecution benches.

On the prosecution side, there were handshakes and congratulations for the young Marion County prosecutor, Will Remy, and the rest of his team.

On the defense side, Stephenson smiled smugly and tried to sound defiant as he snorted to a reporter, "Surrender? Hell, we've only begun to fight!"

Gentry and Klinck rushed to defend their former boss. "Why acquit me and convict Steve?" Gentry demanded.

Klinck said, "It is the most ridiculous verdict I ever heard of. It should be a notice to the public that it is not a vindication of any law but persecution of the best man that ever lived. He has been the best friend thousands of Indiana people ever had."

Christian's statement was more terse: "Of course we will appeal." Then the reporters rushed to the telephones to file their stories.[3]

It came out later that the jurors had pronounced Stephenson guilty on their first ballot. Some had doubted that the jury would find him guilty. This was Noblesville, a town where the Ku Klux Klan had been extremely powerful for the past three years and where Stephenson, as its leader, had many loyal followers. But the prosecutors had been quite convincing in presenting the story of Stephenson's brutal attack on Oberholtzer.

Most of the afternoon's debate among the jurors centered on what punishment to give him. Some argued for first-degree murder—a possible death sentence. Others held out for second-degree murder—life imprisonment. A few had considered manslaughter. Finally, they agreed upon second-degree murder.

As for Klinck and Gentry, most felt that Gentry should be punished for his role in the crime, but they could not agree on the degree. No one believed that Klinck had played a decisive role in the case. Finally, the jurors agreed to acquit both of the bodyguards. The entire matter took only eleven ballots over five hours and thirty-five minutes.[4]

―――――――――

As prosecutor Will Remy was driving his Oakland automobile home to Indianapolis, Indiana, that evening, he noticed a black sedan with four men in it pull up behind his car. As he headed south on Allisonville Road, the sedan continued to follow him.

Remy pulled to the side to let the other car pass. Instead, the car stayed just behind him.

As Remy drove on, he noticed another vehicle—a police car—draw up alongside the black sedan. Remy recognized the officers in the police car. He pulled his Oakland over to the side of the road. As he did, the four men in the black sedan sped past him. The two police officers followed Remy the rest of the way home.

When Remy reached his home, his wife met him at the door with the news that he had a long-distance telephone caller who was waiting for him. Remy picked up the telephone. On the other end of the line was Stephenson's attorney, Floyd Christian, his voice full of worry. "Bill? Are you all right?" he asked.

"Of course, I'm all right, Floyd," Remy replied. "What's the matter?"

"Thank God," said Christian, and hung up.

Remy went back outside where the police officers were waiting and asked them what was going on. They told him how, just after Remy left the courtroom, Christian had asked to speak with Remy. Told that Remy had already left for home, Christian immediately found two Indianapolis police detectives and instructed them to follow Remy's car home. "I can't tell you why," Christian told them. "Just do as I say and get to him as quickly as you can."

Remy later learned from another person that Stephenson had whispered instructions to some of his men just after the verdict was announced. Christian had overheard the conversation and quickly moved to get the police officers to go after Remy.

Remy said that Christian "never told me what he had heard and I never asked him," but Remy was certain "that afternoon one more attempt was to be made upon my life." The quick actions of one of Stephenson's own attorneys and two police officers, Remy believed, were the only things that saved him.[5]

The sentencing was immediately set for Monday, November 16. Judge Sparks did not require much time to consider the matter.

At 1:25 P.M., Sheriff Gooding escorted Stephenson into the courtroom. A few of Stephenson's friends sat in the seats behind the attorneys' tables, and he waved and smiled to them. Then he sat down, flanked by his attorneys.

Judge Sparks looked up from a stack of papers on the bench and asked, "Gentlemen, has the defendant any legal reason why judgment should not be pronounced?"

Then Stephenson stood and spoke the only words he uttered to the judge during the entire trial: "Yes, Your Honor." He walked around the table to face the bench. "I am not guilty of murder or any lesser degree of homicide. It has always been my understanding that no man should be deprived of his liberty without due process of law. I believe the opinion is universal that in this case there was not due process of law."

Stephenson went on to describe the outbursts of applause and hissing that came from the audience whenever things were said against him. "These people represented no opinion except their own. Other action rendered it impossible for this jury to give me a fair trial. Time will unfold the cold white light of truth and this court and the world will know that D. C. Stephenson is not guilty of murder or any other degree of homicide." He then turned and marched back to his seat.

Judge Sparks commended Stephenson for his "gentlemanly statement" and apologized for not having been aware of any hissing in the audience: "If I had heard that, I would not have tolerated it for one moment."

Floyd Christian then told the judge that several times during his closing arguments he had heard hissing from the audience. "I hope that what the defendant has just said—that time will tell—will be true," said the judge. "I regret very much the hissing, but in a case like this, with the large crowds, the crowds are hard to handle. The hissing doesn't speak very well for the county where it happened."

Stephenson rose and said that he did not believe the hissing came from the people of Hamilton County "but from the scum and scurvy of the whole state of Indiana."

Then Judge Sparks read his verdict: "Under the direction of the jury, I find you guilty of second-degree murder and sentence you to the Indiana State Prison during life."[6]

———————————

Early on Saturday, November 21, at about three o'clock in the morning, Sheriff Gooding and two of his deputies woke Stephenson and told him to get ready for his ride to the Indiana State Prison.

Outside the jail, reporters who had been tipped that the prisoner would be moved sometime during the night went up to the jail and asked to be let in. They found the other prisoners in Stephenson's cell block awake and talking with him. One of the other prisoners threw his arms around Stephenson and cried; others shook his hand and wished him good luck. Sheriff Gooding's wife came to see Stephenson off. "You've been mighty good to me," he told her. She was unable to reply.

The trip was made in two cars—one with the prisoner and the sheriff, the other carrying a carload of reporters. Along the way, Stephenson suggested the best directions to take to reach Michigan City, Indiana, where the prison was located, and told stories about his political triumphs and the celebrated elections he had helped win in the counties that they drove through on their way north.

The caravan stopped at a diner for breakfast in Kokomo, Indiana, the town where Stephenson had been named grand dragon of Indiana only two and a half years earlier in the largest Klan rally ever held in the United States. As Stephenson ate breakfast surrounded by sheriff's deputies and reporters, he had time to think about the difference between this morning and that hot July afternoon in 1923 when he had held the crowd at Melfalfa Park in the palm of his hand.

Eventually, the deputies led Stephenson out of the diner and back to the cars. The morning was now cloudy and overcast with traces of snow turning to a light rain during the drive.

The entire trip lasted seven hours. Along the way, Stephenson told Horace Coats of the *Indianapolis Star*, "God, if I could only get the people of Indiana together so I could talk to them, I would not stay in this penitentiary long." He fell asleep in the car as they drove through Plymouth, Indiana, and slept most of the remainder of the trip.

Shortly before 11:00 A.M., they arrived at the gates of the state prison. John Moorman, a member of the prison's board of trustees, was there to receive the prisoner. Stephenson was ushered to a prison clerk's desk, where he was asked to empty his pockets. The former millionaire's possessions included a persimmon, several almonds, a white-gold watch and chain, two combs, a nail file, two magazines, a book, and $26.37 in cash.

"Have you any cuff buttons and collar buttons?" the clerk asked him. "Yes, sir," Stephenson answered. "I must have them, too," said the clerk.

Stephenson had brought a portable typewriter, an extension cord, and a light bulb. These were taken away from him, but he was allowed to keep his handkerchiefs and his toothbrush.

Accompanied by an orderly, he was then taken to the inner area of the prison, and the gates clanged shut behind him. D. C. Stephenson was now Indiana State Prisoner Number 11148.

Back in Indianapolis, several important politicians no doubt breathed an audible sigh of relief. Stephenson was finally out of the political picture and behind bars—a convicted murderer.

But if the politicians relaxed just a bit, lit their cigars, and congratulated each other, they did so prematurely. Stephenson might be in prison. They might be through with him. But he was definitely not through with them.[7]

Chapter Two

A Nobody from Nowhere

1891–1920

Who was D. C. Stephenson? Where did he come from, and how had he risen with such swiftness to the top of the Republican party in Indiana and to the top of the Ku Klux Klan organization nationally?

At the time of his conviction in 1925, few people in the state could answer those questions. Even those closest to Stephenson knew very little about him. To many inside the Ku Klux Klan, he was known only by his nickname, "The Old Man"—although he was only thirty-four years old when he was sent to prison.

"I'm a nobody from nowhere, really—but I've got the brains," Stephenson told his friends. "I'm going to be the biggest man in the United States!"[1]

He had appeared suddenly in Indiana in 1920. A year later, he ran for the U.S. Congress as a Democrat and lost. The following year, he moved to Indianapolis and became a Republican.

In 1923, he was named grand dragon of the Klan in Indiana, in charge of more than two hundred thousand Hoosier klansmen. At the same time, he was placed in charge of Klan operations in twenty-two other northern states. He became friends with most of the Republican politicians in the state and would later claim to have helped elect many of them, including Mayor John Duvall of Indianapolis and Governor Ed Jackson.

At the time of his arrest, Stephenson had been working on a plan that might have resulted in an appointment for him to fill a vacancy in the United States Senate. His ultimate goal was nothing less than the White House.

In spite of all these accomplishments, there were still very few people who seemed to know anything about the heavyset, blond power broker.

He told some reporters that he was the son of a wealthy businessman from South Bend, Indiana. According to Stephenson, his father had sent him off to college, but he had decided to strike off on his own. He had gone to Evansville, Indiana, at the southwest tip of the state and had worked in the coal business there. When America declared war in 1917, Stephenson said, he had volunteered to join the army, had risen to the rank of lieutenant, and had been decorated for fighting the Germans in France. When he returned from the war, he had discovered that some modest stocks he purchased before the war had skyrocketed in value, making him a millionaire in his own right. He now owned more than sixty thousand acres of prime coal lands, operated a wholesale coal business and a wholesale automobile accessory business, and was a director of an Evansville bank. Active in Evansville politics for more than ten years, he had joined the Klan in 1921 to help a patriotic men's organization get started in Indiana. His leadership abilities became known to the Klan organizers in Atlanta, Georgia, and they had appointed him to head the Klan in Indiana.[2]

The story was good. But like so many of Stephenson's stories, it was mostly lies.

The real account of his early life was even more incredible than the fictional biography he created. "It's no one's business where I was born or who my folks were," he would snap later on.[3]

His father was not a millionaire business owner but a poor sharecropper. David Curtis Stephenson was born August 21, 1891, probably in Houston, Texas.[4] His father, Andrew Monroe Stephenson, was fifty-two when D. C. was born; his mother was forty-two.[5] He had at least one older brother, Arizona, and a sister, Clara. In Houston, the Stephensons sent their young children to a Catholic grade school to be educated.

The family pulled up stakes and moved to Oklahoma in 1901, settling near a newly established town called Maysville. Like most new families in the area, the Stephensons set up their first living quarters in a dugout house—simply a large hole in the ground covered by a pole roof.

D. C.'s formal education was delayed by the move to Maysville because there was no school in the new town. The arrival of a rail line nearby eventually brought more people to the town, including a teacher who began holding school in the newly constructed Methodist church. D. C.'s education continued, and he became an avid reader with an interest in history, politics, and oratory. The adventures of Caesar and Napoleon enthralled him.[6]

Aside from history and politics, D. C.'s other interest was girls. Among the neighborhood boys, he had a reputation as a "lovebird" with the town's young ladies. His romantic pursuits may even have been at the root of a teenage rivalry that led to one of his earliest-recorded strange performances. Years later, people in Maysville would still recall how young David Stephenson had come running into the town drugstore one afternoon, pale and out of breath. He was nervous and kept talking about being pursued by enemies. Whether the enemies were real or imagined, D. C. spent half the day hiding out in the drugstore, not daring to go outside. The incident might have been forgotten, like so many other teenage stories, except from that day on, D. C. always walked through town with a revolver strapped around his waist.

In the spring of 1907, D. C. graduated from eighth grade at age sixteen. Beyond eighth grade, Maysville had nothing more to offer. The town had no high school, and the nearest one was several miles away. In any case, an eighth-grade education was considered enough schooling in Oklahoma at that time to qualify for an elementary teaching job, so it would have been enough to allow D. C. to enter politics.

The territory was on the verge of statehood in 1907. Like most settlers, D. C. probably followed the arguments in the town's weekly newspaper, the *Maysville News*.[7] After a long dispute over whether the Indian Territory and the Oklahoma Territory should enter as separate states, the two sections were combined under the name Oklahoma to become the forty-sixth state. Politics and statehood dominated the talk that year.

In the meantime, however, there was the mundane business of earning a living. For a year or two, D. C. went to the shops and farms around Maysville, doing odd jobs and chores for anyone who would pay him. His older brother, Arizona, had already found a job learning to operate the typesetting equipment for the *News*.

After two years of waiting, D. C. was no richer than when he started. In 1910, his brother came home one day with the news that John Cooper, a farmer who lived on the hill just outside the town, was buying into the newspaper. Cooper was a stocky fellow with a bushy mustache who called himself a Socialist. He loved to talk politics almost as much as he loved farming—a man who would fit in as a newspaper publisher in a small town. Owning the paper would give him a soapbox to air his political opinions. He would need more help with the paper, and Arizona encouraged his younger brother to apply. Finally D. C. went to see Cooper about a job and was quickly hired.[8]

From Cooper, D. C. learned about the business of publishing a newspaper and got involved in Socialist politics. Young

Stephenson soon found himself paying close attention to the things that were being said in the newspaper office about politics.

The Socialists were plotting a course to the governor's office. They had tried it before in 1907, the state's first election, and they had lost miserably. The Socialists had improved their position in the 1910 governor's race. They still lost, but this time they more than doubled their support, earning more than twenty-four thousand votes. These efforts proved to the Socialists that they could draw votes away from the two major parties and might one day be the victors on election day.[9]

One of the leading Socialists in Oklahoma at that time deliberately used an entertainer's approach to sell politics to the people. Oscar Ameringer hoped that socialism might appeal to the same instincts that had drawn people to William Jennings Bryan's populism twenty years earlier. Ameringer, in his mid-thirties, was a German immigrant and a crafty observer of human nature. He discovered that farmers would only listen to his speeches out of idle curiosity, not from any avid political interest. So he traveled around the Oklahoma countryside with a troupe of musicians and singers, first drawing a crowd to hear the music, then giving them his Socialist pitch.[10]

It is easy to see why the comparative glamour of this life would appeal to Stephenson. As Ameringer wrote in his autobiography, "These meetings were usually better than self-supporting. Expenses were low: there was no rent to pay; advertising was done by giving general ring calls over the party lines, which were free; the speaker was boarded and bedded by one of the comrades. The salary of the preacher was catch as catch can. Speakers and organizers of the Party, as strong advocates of unionism, had organized a union of their own, providing a sliding scale of from twelve to eighteen dollars a week. As one of the stars, I received the top. Any money left over the union scale went to the cause."[11]

Twelve to eighteen dollars a week! This was a good wage for someone like Stephenson, who was recruited to travel the countryside, like Ameringer, delivering speeches and drumming up support for the Socialist party. It was a lost crusade from the start, but Stephenson took his responsibilities seriously.

Later, he would use some of the ideas he learned at these Socialist rallies to shape the course of his own Klan rallies. He learned that crowds would not stand around to listen to a man who talked without conviction, but they would pay rapt attention to a man who spoke from the heart. The people enjoyed speakers like Ameringer who had a bit of the showman in them, the ones who knew how to entertain and educate. Stephenson watched, listened, and studied these things, learning the art of controlling an audience with words and glances.

Eventually, the party leaders sent Stephenson out to campaign for their newest gubernatorial candidate, Fred Holt, who had been tapped to run in the 1914 elections. For the first time in his life, Stephenson was traveling on his own, away from his family and home.

As the Socialist candidate for governor, Holt had a difficult race to run. True, the public had been warming to the views of the Socialists in the last years before America's entry into the brewing European war. But Oklahoma was, and would continue to be for some time, a Democratic state with Republicans running a strong but consistent second place, and the Socialists, a distant third.

After the Socialists lost, D. C. drifted. Never close to his family, he simply left them behind and never looked back. His sister, Clara, married a man named Churchill and moved to Tulsa, Oklahoma. His brother, Arizona, decided to strike out for California. The only other ties D. C. had to Maysville were the Socialists. Soon, he would drift away from them, wandering aimlessly in search of a future.[12]

His knowledge of newspaper work would help him find jobs wherever he traveled: in Purcell, Oklahoma, where he worked on the *Register* for a few weeks; and in Pauls Valley, Oklahoma, where he worked on the *Democrat*. In Byars, Oklahoma, a barber was left with a shaving mug with Stephenson's name printed on it and a picture of a typesetter as the only settlement for a $6.50 bill.[13]

The spring of 1915 found Stephenson working for a newspaper in Hugo, a small town in southeastern Oklahoma, just a few miles north of the Red River and the state of Texas. By this time, he was serving double-duty as both typesetter and reporter, writing news in the morning and setting type in the afternoon. Evenings he spent drinking and talking politics.

He was also spending time with an attractive young woman, Nettie Hamilton, a girl just a few years younger than himself. Little had changed about Stephenson since his school days; he still imagined himself as a ladies' man whose blond hair and blue eyes made him irresistible to women. Perhaps he was right. It wasn't long before Stephenson was a regular caller for Nettie, and not long afterward her picture appeared in the paper under the headline "THE MOST BEAUTIFUL GIRL IN OKLAHOMA." The tactic was as obvious as it was successful.

Nettie became his wife on Friday, March 26, 1915, in Tishomingo, Oklahoma. It was not a church wedding. Charles S. Fenwick, a county judge, performed the ceremony in his offices. One Stephenson trait that would later become more developed was already present: On the day the couple applied for their marriage license, D. C. gave his age as twenty-two. He was really twenty-four.[14]

The newlyweds moved to the town of Madill, Oklahoma, on Lake Texoma, to begin their married life. Things were happening quickly for D. C. He landed a job on the *Madill Record* as a reporter. A bit of luck blew his way, and he quickly became editor. Then his young bride announced that a baby was on the way. For a moment, it seemed that the young drifter was going to set down permanent roots.

Instead, he soon lost his job and abandoned his wife. He left town, saying that he would send for her when he found work.

He began drifting through Oklahoma again, north to the town of Sulphur, then on to Ada, and from there to Cushing. The pattern was always the same: a few weeks of work, a bout of drinking or a fight with the publisher, then it was on to another town.

In Cushing, he went to work for the *Citizen*, setting type by day and carousing by night. It was here word reached him that he was a father. Nettie's parents had taken her to Oklahoma City, where she delivered their daughter, Florence Catherine, May 16, 1916. When Nettie wrote to him in Cushing, she asked for money to help pay the doctor's bills. He replied that he was unable to send money or even to travel the sixty miles to visit his wife and baby.

Stephenson developed a reputation in Cushing as a rogue who enjoyed squiring the young ladies around town. He talked one woman into what the townsfolk later described politely as "intimate relations," convincing her that he was still single. The ploy worked well until the day Nettie Stephenson arrived in Cushing with her baby, looking for her stray husband. D. C. quickly dealt with this dilemma. He left suddenly, taking eight hundred dollars of the publisher's money with him. He struck out for the northeast corner of the state and a small town called Miami.

It was only a few months before Nettie had again tracked him down. He knew she would pursue him relentlessly with their child unless he could outdistance her. He fled again, this time across Missouri and into Iowa, north of Des Moines. This time Nettie did not try to follow him. With an infant daughter in the middle of winter, the pursuit was simply too much for her to continue. On February 10, 1917, she filed for a divorce.[15]

D. C. managed to find a job with a printer in Boone, Iowa, and spent the winter of 1916 there. In the spring, he left and took a job with another printer a few miles away in Story. By now, he was notorious as a drinker and general hell-raiser. He was nearly at the bottom of the social ladder, far from his grandiose dreams of political power. At twenty-five, he had failed at everything: failed as a Socialist, as a newspaperman, as a husband, and as a father.

Stephenson was floundering in April 1917, and so was the rest of the world. On April 6, America entered World War I in Europe. Eleven days later, Stephenson walked down to the post office in Story, Iowa, and volunteered to serve in the U.S. Army. He enlisted in the Iowa National Guard and received orders to report to Fort Des Moines for training.[16]

If Stephenson had any romantic notions about a gallant death on the battlefields of Europe, those hopes were soon dashed. After three months of training, he entered active service in July. On August 5, he received his orders: report to the armory in Boone, Iowa. He was promoted to corporal, but it appeared that he might never face the German enemy. Instead, he was made a recruiter for the army.

He was told to report to Capt. Walter L. Anderson, a regular army officer stationed in Boone. Years later, Anderson remembered Corporal Stephenson as a loud talker and a heavy drinker.[17] Stephenson bunked at the armory most of the time, but he kept a room in town for his sexual adventures with the local girls. He was a discipline problem, suspected as the man behind a mysterious break-in of the armory's private stocks. He also ran up several loans with other men in the outfit, failing to pay back any of them. Within a few weeks of his arrival, Stephenson had managed to alienate most of the company. In a desperate move, the officers decided to put in for Stephenson to receive a commission as a second lieutenant; according to Anderson, they did it to get Stephenson out of Boone. The papers came through in November, and Stephenson was off to Fort Snelling, Minnesota, to join the 36th Infantry, Company D, Officers Reserve Corps.

Officers' training did not get him any closer to the front lines. Instead, he was sent to Camp Devens, Massachusetts. This was as close to Europe as he would ever get. The only heroics he knew about were the ones he read about in the newspapers. He spent the rest of the war waiting for overseas orders that never came. On November 7, the New York newspapers prematurely announced that the war had ended, and crowds jammed the streets to celebrate, only to learn they were wrong. Four days later, on November 11, the real armistice was signed. The war was over.

Stephenson received his honorable discharge papers at Camp Devens on February 4, 1919. Having nowhere else to go, he boarded a train to Iowa. He returned to Boone, this time taking a job with a wholesale grocer.

In midyear, he took a job as a traveling salesman for a manufacturing company that made and sold typesetting machines and printing equipment. The job meant more money, better clothes, and an opportunity to travel the Midwest.

Soon he was calling on newspapers and print shops in Ohio and Indiana, writing orders for new typesetting machines. He was able to wear three-piece suits with a golden watch fob, looking as much like a banker as a salesman. His drinking had given him a paunchy stomach, but the extra weight seemed only to enhance his prosperous image. Donning a pressed suit, a fresh white shirt with a new collar, and a four-in-hand tie transformed him. With this new image, he was now using the same techniques he had once employed to bring socialism to the prairie farmers of Oklahoma. The only difference was that he was now selling printing equipment instead of politics.

One of the towns on his sales route was Akron, Ohio, in the north central section of the Buckeye state. It was there that he met a young secretary named Violet Carroll. She was quite taken with the fancy-talking salesman in the flashy new suit. He was a man who always brought a girl flowers. They met late in the year, but they became engaged by Christmas with a hastily set wedding date of January 7.[18] Everything was done in a flurry of activity, and suddenly Stephenson had a new wife. Violet had spent her life in Akron, but now D. C. was talking about a new job waiting for him in Evansville, Indiana. She quickly bundled her things, and they boarded a train for southern Indiana.

Chapter Three

The Early Days in Evansville

1920

Two important newcomers arrived in Indiana in 1920. The first was an unknown typesetting salesman, D. C. Stephenson, and the second was a secret fraternal order, the Ku Klux Klan. They arrived separately, eight months apart. But curiously, they both entered the state through the Ohio River city of Evansville, Indiana. For Stephenson, Evansville represented a new start with a new bride and a new job. For the Ku Klux Klan, Evansville was the beginning of a serious push into the northern states west of the Allegheny Mountains.

Evansville was the largest city in the state south of the capital, Indianapolis. About 90,000 people lived in this bustling river town with its thriving industrial and shipping center. Coal was big business in the city. More than 150 coal mines nestled in the hills around Evansville, providing a natural supply of coal to fire the furnaces of more than 200 Evansville factories. Seven railroads connected overland freight traffic with the Ohio River.

This was a gathering place for aggressive young business-men, a mecca for fast-talking hustlers like Stephenson, all anxious to make a quick fortune selling pieces of the postwar American dream. With railroad cars and river barges carrying coal in every direction, Stephenson quickly saw that there was money to be made here.[1]

Thanks to the business boom, Evansville had several hotels that catered to newly arrived businessmen. Stephenson and his young bride chose the Vendome, a brick-and-limestone hotel that faced South Third Street in the heart of town and featured one of the best restaurants in the city. Its lobby was filled with other young salesmen who, like Stephenson, were waiting to strike pay dirt with the right money-making scheme. The Vendome also happened to be a popular gathering place for the leaders of the city's ruling Democratic party—not surprising, since the hotel was managed by Elmer Bosse, a nephew of the city's powerful leader, Mayor Benjamin Bosse. The Vendome was the right place for someone in a hurry to make connections.[2]

As a typesetting equipment salesman, Stephenson was in great luck. Evansville boasted three daily newspapers and a spacious press club where the right insider introductions could be made. There was enough work here to keep a new printing equipment salesman busy.

D. C. and Violet Stephenson arrived in Evansville in January 1920 to find the city buzzing with all kinds of news and rumors. The town was caught up in a Red Scare, with headlines screaming about a suspected revolutionary plot by Bolsheviks living in the United States to take over the government (U.S. Attorney General A. Mitchell Palmer and his investigation of aliens triggered the scare). There was also plenty of talk about Prohibition. Cartoons depicting the "death of John Barleycorn" noted that "his spirit will live on in hip flasks and bathtubs." And Mayor Bosse, in his first speech of the new year, told the town: "The enforcement of the prohibition laws in the coming year depends upon the patriotism of the people. The prohibition statute is now part of the United States constitution and anyone violating this state law is violating the constitution of the United States."[3] (The following week a former Evansville mayor pleaded guilty to a charge of transporting liquor into Indiana and received a fine of $300 plus costs.)

People were also reading about the resignations of two county commissioners charged with political improprieties. And they followed the case of Ernest G. Tidrington, a black politician whose efforts to become a lawyer were opposed in court by the members of the Vanderburgh County Bar Association.

Most of the town's reporters gathered at the Evansville Press Club in the Carmody Building, not far from Stephenson's hotel rooms. With his past newspaper connections, Stephenson was quickly drawn into this circle. There, in a place where no one knew his name, simple stories could grow, and small events could turn into bigger ones. An ex-serviceman could move his war service from Massachusetts to France. A second lieutenant's rank could be self-promoted. Fights in the Iowa armory could become battles against the Germans in the heartland of Europe. As long as no one could dispute him, Stephenson's stories of personal heroism did not hurt anyone, and they helped him make a new circle of friends and admirers.[4]

It did not take long for this bright fellow with stories of his bravery to catch the eye of a local entrepreneur. L. G. Julian was the president, secretary, and manager of the Citizens Coal

Company, a local coal brokerage firm.[5] A man with too many hats to wear, Julian needed a partner like Stephenson. Julian arranged a meeting with Stephenson and offered to bring him into the coal business as a stock salesman. With his knack for talking a fast line, Stephenson found it simple to draw smart investors into the coal market. It was a no-strings-attached offer. If Stephenson found he did not like the business, he could quit tomorrow. If the work appealed to him, he and Julian might seriously talk about a regular partnership.

Coal was a much-needed commodity for industry. Plentiful and cheap, it heated buildings and powered factories. Being in the coal business also meant that Stephenson would be in contact with other local business and community leaders. This was his chance to meet the town's movers and shakers and talk with them as an equal.

Stephenson quickly developed into a man others would remember as a "super-salesman," an aggressive, likable man who always appeared in public well-dressed and physically impressive. He could talk business and politics with well-read citizens, usually holding a strong opinion of his own to share with them. But he could also talk with average people on their own terms without seeming to patronize them. Newspapers, business, or politics—wherever Stephenson turned, he managed to build new friendships without apparent effort.

Perhaps it was also natural then that a group of young army veterans talking about forming a local organization would turn to this friendly "Major" Stephenson for advice.[6] Given any group of men, most of them would quickly find an excuse to either start or join a fraternal society. Already in Evansville there were groups representing the Knights of Pythias, the Knights of St. John, the Royal Arcanum Lodge, the Order of Red Men, the Order of Chosen Friends, and the Order of Foresters, not to mention a smattering of Druids, Elks, and other fraternal groups.[7] The Civil War veterans had their Grand Army of the Republic, and now the veterans from World War I in Europe wanted their own society. So Stephenson volunteered to help canvass around Evansville and Vanderburgh County to assemble an organization for veterans of the 36th U.S. Infantry.

With the coal business, the veterans, and his new bride, Stephenson was a very busy man by the summer of 1920. Coal was earning him a good income, and organizing the veterans group promised to help him make even more money. Fraternal orders were not only a way for nostalgic veterans to get together but were also a lucrative form of business. Each fraternal group levied its own dues—part of which went to the organizers—and sold books and manuals, caps, ribbons, certificates, or jewelry. The profits were limited only by the organizers' imaginations.

A wave of patriotic hysteria sweeping the country made it easier to organize a veterans group. The U.S. attorney general's investigation of a communist plot to overthrow the government was stirring up anti-foreigner sentiments in the country. Ministers preached against the threat of communism. Newspapers used the Red Scare to sell papers. The hysteria even reached Evansville, where the *Journal-News* printed an editorial under the headline "WIPE OUT THE COMMUNISTS": "It looks very much like a revolution had been nipped in the bud in our country. How far the conspirators would have been able to go with their wild scheme is doubtful, of course, but that there was a plot to overthrow the constitution is perfectly evident. . . . It is a damnable outrage that our government should have permitted such doctrine to be preached in the United States. . . . Ours is a free country, but it isn't free to Jacobins and Soviets." With this feeling in the air, practically any flag-waving organization was assured of success.

While Stephenson worked to start his veterans organization, another group in Atlanta, Georgia, was working on a similar scheme. In June, two promoters—Edward Young Clarke and Elizabeth Tyler—were completing an agreement with another fraternal organizer, "Colonel" William J. Simmons. (His colonelcy had been granted not by the military but by the Woodmen of the World.[8]) Their idea was to promote the Knights of the Ku Klux Klan into a national organization. Simmons had tried for five years to make the Klan grow beyond the South, but now he finally recognized the need for expert advice to make his dream come true. The plan for a northern invasion was underway.[9]

To spearhead the Indiana operations, the Klan leaders picked an organizer from Houston, Texas: Joe Huffington. In the late summer of 1920, Huffington moved to Evansville and began the Klan's first recruiting drive north of the Mason-Dixon Line. He set up his office a few blocks east of the courthouse in a small, two-story building that had once housed a bakery. It did not take him long to scout out the territory and decide that this was fertile ground to start his operation. Evansville had more than seventy churches, most of them Protestant denominations. Catholics accounted for only a handful of the local churches. Two Jewish synagogues served all the town's Jewish population.

Thus, the "alien" population was small enough to be controllable but just large enough to plant the seeds of doubt in the minds of their "100 percent American" neighbors.

Sometime in early fall, probably September, Huffington introduced himself to the sharp, young coal salesman who was going around Evansville organizing the veterans. Stephenson had not heard much about the Klan before. Like most, he may have simply dismissed them as a wild bunch of southerners parading around in bed sheets. As he later described the situation to a reporter from the *New York World*: "I was in Evansville in the fall of 1921, where my friends were a crowd of fine young men. Nearly all of them had joined the Ku Klux Klan. I was against it. . . . They kept after me, tho, and explained to me that the Klan was not an organization which took negroes out, cut off their noses, and threw them into the fire, nor did they tar and feather people or oppress them in any way. I was told that the Klan was a strictly patriotic organization. . . . They finally convinced me the Klan was a good thing and I joined."[10]

Huffington and Stephenson were both attempting to accomplish similar goals. Both were trying to find good, solid Americans to join an organization that would capitalize on patriotism. Most of the veterans that Stephenson knew would also be likely candidates for membership in the Klan. Many of them had just returned from Europe, where they had fought the same forces they believed were now threatening America at home. With Stephenson's business connections, he and Huffington would be able to approach the local business leaders who would support an organization that stood against Socialist labor agitators. Stephenson's course obviously overlapped Huffington's.

But there was one great difference: Stephenson was trying to start a new group, while Huffington represented a group that was already part of a national machine. With only a little imagination, one could see that the Klan might eventually develop political power. When bands of klansmen joined across the nation, there was the possibility of raising a new political voice that could be heard all the way to Washington. Unlike the Socialists' policies Stephenson encountered in Oklahoma, the Klan's policies were firmly entrenched in the values of white, mainstream America. It did not take Stephenson long to realize that his best chance in politics would be in working for the Klan.

Accounts vary about how Stephenson got involved in the Klan. One version claims the Evansville Klan was having troubles with the Imperial Palace in Atlanta, and a representative from Simmons was sent north to clear up the problem. An

Evansville klansman who knew Stephenson and who had heard him speak asked him to join the Klan to help deal with the representative from Atlanta.

"When the night arrived, Stephenson and W. Lee Smith, who later became Grand Dragon of Indiana, . . . were at the Klavern [a meeting of the local Klan organization] to question the Atlanta representative, a man named Mahoney. Stephenson held the spotlight in the verbal combat which took place. Not only did he do this, but he was delegated to go to Chicago and have the matter out with E. Y. Clarke, who was then head of the Klan propagation and a close advisor of Colonel Simmons who was at that time Imperial Wizard."[11]

No more details are given about the exact nature of the dispute between Evansville and Atlanta, nor is any mention made of the outcome. But some agreement was soon reached, because Stephenson's reputation began to soar as a result of the encounter. His meeting with Clarke, one of the most powerful men in the organization, would soon provide a startling payoff.

Chapter Four

The Klan Reborn

1920

To understand the world Stephenson was about to enter, it is necessary to first understand some of the history of the Ku Klux Klan. Most people today have only one or two mental images of the Klan. The first is the Klan as a gang of post–Civil War night riders with torches, galloping through the Deep South, chasing carpetbaggers and lynching blacks. The second image of the Klan stems from the attacks on civil rights activists during the 1950s and 1960s—the image of southern racists wielding baseball bats and axe handles. In these popular mental images, the Klan is always southern and always violent, an organization scented with magnolia blossoms and blood.

The Klan has had at least four distinct and separate incarnations. It is a recurring nightmare in America's history, half-remembered and half-forgotten. In its various lives, the Klan has not been entirely southern. White supremacy has always been its goal, but its anger has been targeted against more groups than just black Americans.

The first Ku Klux Klan was a short-lived but spectacular organization that flourished in the South for only seven years, from 1865 to 1872.[1] The group was started by six men in Pulaski, Tennessee, mainly as an elaborate game for grown men who like to wear eerie costumes and ride at night on horseback. It did not take long before the Ku Klux Klan (the name supposedly came from the Greek word *kuklos* for "circle") was turned from a fraternal group into a vigilante organization. An ex-Confederate, General Nathan Bedford Forrest, was chosen to head the Klan. A secret society was drawn up with bizarre and elaborate titles: grand wizard, grand dragon, titans, and cyclops. The membership was drawn from the men who had recently filled the ranks of the rebel army. The klansmen's aim was three-fold: to strike back at the federal Reconstruction government, to put the blacks "back in their place," and to chase the white carpetbaggers back North. The southern establishment had been left out of the plans to rebuild the war-torn states. To them, it seemed that the Yankees were anxious to turn everything south of the Mason-Dixon Line over to illiterate blacks, so the Klan became a way for the upper-class southern whites to strike back.

The first Klan attacked with great vengeance. During its short reign, the Klan set the tone for the future organization. Its trademark was violent death meted out to anyone, black or white, who was foolish enough to stand in its way. Lynchings, shootings, whippings, and stabbings were the klansmen's tools. They saw themselves as defenders of the white man's way of life, protectors of their women, and saviors of their land and property. The government saw them as bloodthirsty bandits.

Finally, the federal government stepped in to order the Klan disbanded. Forrest reluctantly gave the order for his Klan to dissolve in 1869. Even after the Ku Klux Klan officially disbanded, the torture of blacks continued with whippings and lynchings throughout both the South and the North, carried out by groups known as night riders. But the Klan, at least as an organization, was temporarily "dead."

Disbanded, the Klan might have been forgotten. But a popular novelist, Thomas Dixon, Jr., writing more than thirty years after the Klan's demise, produced a romanticized version of the hooded order's history. Two of his books, *The Leopard's Spots* and *The Clansman,* depicted the Klan as a group of rightly angered gentlemen defending their honor from wild blacks and evil white scalawags. Dixon claimed the Klan was fighting for a just cause—a gathering of virtuous knights who might have easily sprung from the pages of Sir Walter Scott's *Ivanhoe* into the American South.[2]

In 1915, a decade after Dixon's *Clansman* appeared, filmmaker D. W. Griffith used the novel as the basis for his *Birth of a Nation.* The film was honored in the South and damned in the North. Southerners saw it as the true story of the South's betrayal and a stirring defense of white supremacy; Northerners decried the film for its old-style southern racism. But when President Woodrow Wilson, a southerner himself, went on record saying that the film was "all too terribly true," the film suddenly gained acceptability. People flocked to see this epic melodrama, and a new generation discovered the appeal of the night riders.

It was no coincidence then that on December 7, 1915, the evening that *Birth of a Nation* premiered in Atlanta, Georgia, there appeared an advertisement in the *Atlanta Journal* for "The World's Greatest Secret Social, Patriotic, Fraternal, Beneficiary

Order"—the Knights of the Ku Klux Klan. The ad appeared on the same page as the ad for the movie. The Klan's ad featured a crudely drawn image of a klansman with a flaming torch mounted astride a rearing stallion. The ad described the Klan as "A High Class Order for Men of Intelligence and Character." It announced that the group had been chartered by the state of Georgia, December 6, 1915 (the day before), and that interested parties could contact "Col. W. J. Simmons, Founder & Imperial Wizard, 85 West Peachtree Place, Atlanta, Ga." Thus, the Klan began its second life.

The second coming of the Klan was far different from the first. The horrors of the Reconstruction period were long behind the South. If the first Klan had been formed to save the South from Yankee treachery, there was little of that motive left to account for its second appearance. The first Klan was a "law-and-order" society. The second Klan, at least in the beginning, was basically a social club for white supremacists.

William J. Simmons was a bespectacled former Methodist minister who was both a compulsive joiner and organizer. As the Klan's self-proclaimed imperial wizard, he was not of the same stock as Nathan Bedford Forrest—even though Simmons's father had once been a member of the old Klan. William Simmons had started a career as a circuit-riding preacher but was turned out by the Methodists as "inefficient." So Simmons put his oratorical talents to work recruiting members for various fraternal organizations. He had worked for the Masons, the Woodmen of the World, and similar groups before turning to his major work, the reorganization of the Ku Klux Klan. He was thirty-five years old, too young to even remember the first Klan, but he took on the job enthusiastically.[3]

Why would someone like Simmons want to rebuild the Klan? Why would other people be willing to join it? These questions were in William G. Shepherd's mind when he interviewed Simmons in 1928 for a series of articles in *Collier's* magazine. Simmons told him:

> I went around Atlanta talking to men who belonged to other lodges about the new Ku Klux Klan. The Negroes were getting pretty uppity in the South along about that time. The North was sending down for them to take good jobs. Lots of Southerners were feeling worried about conditions. Thirty-four men belonging to various other lodges, promised to attend a meeting in [attorney E. R.] Clarkson's office. And on the night of October 26, 1915, we met. They were all there. Two of them were men who had belonged to the old Klan.

John W. Bale, speaker of the Georgia legislature, called the meeting to order. He was the first man in America to wield a Klan gavel. I talked for an hour and we all decided that the idea would grow. We voted to apply for a state charter.

A month later, Simmons and his fellow klansmen held their first swearing-in ceremony and cross burning. It was a windy evening, the night of Thanksgiving Day, 1915, and the party of fifteen men climbed to the top of Stone Mountain. Simmons had arranged an elaborate oath, then struck a match to the pine cross, which was soaked with a half-and-half mixture of gasoline and kerosene. The cross blazed on the windswept mountaintop. In less than two weeks, *Birth of a Nation* would be playing to packed theater houses, providing free advertising for Simmons and the reborn order. Selling memberships, booklets, robes, and even insurance, Simmons soon found himself at the head of a thriving organization.

But why were people joining the group? Surely there was more to the Klan's rebirth than the problem, as Simmons called it, of "uppity Negroes." Perhaps it was the great popularity that fraternal orders were enjoying at that time. Simmons himself claimed to be a member of twenty-three degrees of seven fraternal groups besides the Klan. Fraternal groups provided business and social contacts for their members. The groups appealed mostly to patriotic themes and "good, clean living." Simmons's Klan was no different, talking about the importance of "100 percent Americanism" and other flag-waving slogans. This was a time when people wanted something to belong to, and the Klan, with all its mystery, pomp, and pageant, offered them their money's worth.

When the United States entered World War I in 1917, the Klan gained even more strength. Already aligned to patriotism, the Klan was now in its element. America now had to be protected from the "evil" Germans and a host of others: Catholics, Jews, Socialists, blacks, and union leaders. The Klan, at the center of a strong nativist movement, was ready to protect the nation. Membership in the Klan was one way for Americans at home to help win the war in Europe. The Klan began to move into other states as membership grew. It was fast becoming more than just a southern phenomenon.

The United States' involvement in the war lasted only a short time, ending with Germany's surrender in November 1918. Americans had been stirred to fight, but who was left to oppose? The Europeans may have had their fighting spirit subdued by four years of a bloody conflict, but America was still spoiling for action. With no one left to fight, the nation's aggression turned inward.

The defeated Germans would eventually place the blame for their nation's problems on the Jews. The Klan—in a way remarkably similar to the Nazis—would try to blame the problems of the United States on the Catholics and blacks as well as the Jews.

Both the Catholics and the Jews made logical targets for the Klan. Both groups were comprised mostly of first- and second-generation immigrants, many of whom spoke with thick accents and dressed differently from "normal" Americans. Both groups practiced religions that differed greatly in outward appearances from mainstream Protestantism. Jewish rabbis and Catholic priests and nuns dressed so distinctly that they stood out plainly in their communities as "different." Catholics were said to owe their first allegiance to the pope in Rome; their priests still said the Mass in Latin, a language few Protestants understood. Jews were seen as part of an international financial plot to take over the world through their shrewd business dealings. These differences aroused suspicion—and fear—among their Protestant neighbors.

Blacks continued to be a target for violence. During the summer of 1919, the nation was rocked by a series of explosive racial riots in Illinois, Nebraska, Arkansas, and Texas. One riot on Chicago's South Side began when a black youth was caught swimming in a restricted "white" swimming area on a Lake Michigan beach. He had apparently drifted up from the "colored" beach into the restricted area and was promptly attacked by a gang of angry white swimmers. They stoned him while he was still in the water, and he was drowned. The boy's death on July 27 sparked thirteen days of fighting, during which 537 people were injured and 37 died. More than a thousand homes on the city's South Side were destroyed in the fire bombings that accompanied the riots.[4]

The Chicago riot was not an isolated incident. Across the country, more than 70 blacks were lynched and 14 were publicly burned, all in the bloody year of 1919. The newspapers were full of stories about riots, and even people who lived in towns with no significant black population began to worry about race riots.

White America had more than just the "Negro problem" to worry about. There was also much talk about plots by the Socialists and Communists. Late in the year, U.S. Attorney General A. Mitchell Palmer organized his federal anti-Red raids, arresting people who were suspected of being Communists, anarchists, or labor organizers. Palmer's attack was partly in response to strikes that had paralyzed the police force in Boston, Massachusetts, and the steel mills of the U.S. Steel Corporation earlier in the year. In January 1920, Palmer's agents arrested more than 2,700 "Reds" and rounded them up for questioning. Before the scare was over, approximately 250 aliens would be deported from the country.[5]

History and the times were conspiring to lay a solid groundwork for the Klan's quick rise to power.

Simmons realized that for his Klan to grow into a national organization, it would need more promotion and development than he alone could give it. He needed others who could spur its growth in the northern and western states. He turned to Edward Young Clarke and Elizabeth Tyler to serve as his chief promoters and organizers.

Their agreement was quite lucrative. As Simmons later told it, "I had watched Clarke, and I wanted him. In order to get him, I had to sign a contract with him giving him 80 percent of all he took in from new members. That meant that every new member brought him in $8. Of course, he had to pay all expenses. He put an army of 1,100 paid organizers in the field; hundreds of smart men were working for him. They made things hum all over America."[6]

At first, Clarke protested that the Klan's philosophy would cost him many valuable friends who happened to be either Catholic or Jewish. But the 80 percent enticement was enough to make him forget his moral problems with the Klan. In June 1920, Clarke signed the contract with Simmons to become the imperial wizard's chief of staff.

The results of Clarke's efforts were almost immediate. That fall, a national membership drive began to create the first klaverns, or local Klan organizations, in the northern states. Areas that had not been considered traditional strongholds for the Klan became the targets of this organizing effort: Indiana, Ohio, Pennsylvania, New Jersey, New York, and Maine. Within a year, the Klan would have a national membership of more than one hundred twenty-five thousand.

Joe Huffington, the man the Klan leaders picked to start the operation in Indiana, chose Evansville, Indiana, as his base of operations. He started his work in the late summer of 1920, and it was not long before he met a young man named D. C. Stephenson.

Stephenson was a busy man in 1921. He was selling stock for
L. G. Julian's coal company. He was also helping Huffington sell
memberships for the Klan. In both jobs, he was making very
good wages, better than most of his Evansville neighbors.

It took time for Stephenson to learn the Klan's special language. He had dealt with political parties, newspapers, and the
U.S. Army, but never before had he run into anything like the
Klan. As a secret society, the Klan had developed a complicated
scheme of code words and officers' titles, all playing on the allit-
erative sound of "Ku Klux Klan." Huffington, for instance, was
known as the king kleagle, a title which meant he was in charge
of recruiting members in Indiana. Simmons was known as the
imperial wizard, the highest office in the organization. Other officers were called such fanciful names as kligrapp, kludd, nighthawk, and cyclops. Meetings were known as klonvocations. The
membership dues were called klecktoken.[7]

Like other new recruits, Stephenson had to swear an oath
of allegiance to the Klan and a vow of secrecy. Newcomers were
asked nine questions: "Is the motive prompting your ambition to
be a Klansman serious and unselfish? Are you native born,
white, Gentile, American citizens? Are you absolutely opposed to
and free of any allegiance of any nature to cause, government,
people, sect, or ruler that is foreign to the United States of America? Do you esteem the United States of America and its institutions above any other government, civil, political, or ecclesiastical
in the whole world? Will you, without mental reservations, take
a solemn oath to defend, preserve, and enforce these same? Do
you believe in Klannishness and will you faithfully practice same
toward your fellow Klansmen?"

The universal answer to all these questions was a re-
sounding yes or else the new member would be refused. There
were still more questions to be asked in the initiation ritual:
"Do you believe in and will you faithfully strive for the eternal
maintenance of White Supremacy? Will you faithfully obey our
constitutions and laws, and conform willingly to all our us-
ages, requirements, and regulations? Can you always be de-
pended on?"

Providing the correct answer to all these questions, the
new klansmen would be told that their oath could only be broken
by "death and the call of your Eternal Maker." The options were,
at best, threatening.

How seriously Stephenson took all these oaths no one can say. He does not appear to have been the stereotypical racist klansman; comparatively few hate messages showed up in his public speeches. He usually left the hatemongering to the fanatics who truly believed it and who were, therefore, more convincing. But there could be no doubt that he paid close attention to the other business of the organization—especially the recruiting and the money.

To join and be "naturalized" as a member of the Klan, new recruits had to pay a ten dollar klecktoken. From this amount, four dollars went to the kleagle who brought in the recruit; another dollar to the king kleagle of that particular realm, or region; and fifty cents to the local grand goblin, or sales manager. The remaining $4.50 was mailed to the national office in Atlanta to be divided among the imperial wizard and his imperial promoters.

There was money to be made in the "Invisible Empire." The Klan's money-making potential probably appealed to Stephenson more than any hatred of Catholics, blacks, or Jews. As the local kleagle in Evansville and Huffington's assistant, Stephenson had a chance to make money as he had never done before. To do this, they had only to go out waving the flag and scaring the local rubes with tales of Catholic plots and scheming foreigners. Inborn fears and suspicions took care of the rest. At four dollars per head for his efforts, he would—and did—become a rich man overnight.

Huffington soon realized that Stephenson was a potential gold mine. Memberships were selling faster than ever, and Stephenson had only begun. Huffington was anxious to show off his best recruiter to the Atlanta leadership. He arranged for Stephenson to travel by train with him down to Atlanta, where he would be introduced to Imperial Wizard Simmons, Ed Clarke, and Elizabeth Tyler. Huffington probably thought this introduction would serve a dual purpose, impressing both Stephenson and the national office.

Atlanta might have been impressed with Stephenson, but he was not impressed with them. Facing the leaders he had heard Huffington talk so much about, Stephenson discovered that they were hardly cast in the mold of anything wizardly or imperial. Like himself, they were just well-heeled hucksters. Simmons, Clarke, and Tyler did not have any grand design that went beyond selling more and more memberships while crusading under the banner of white supremacy. They talked about holding Klan parades without any particular reason other than for giving families a chance to dress up in their robes and march

down Main Street. They made plans for a big national klonvocation, but only to get the klansmen together, not to call them
to action.[8]

When Stephenson first met the Atlanta leaders in the
summer of 1921, they stood at the head of more than eighty
thousand klansmen across the nation with hundreds of new
ones joining every day. Yet to Stephenson, it seemed these people
did not realize their own power. They had managed to assemble
a host of frightened, angry citizens, all joined in a common
cause that reached down to the grass roots of the country. But
the leaders failed to see anything beyond more meetings, more
cross burnings, and more speeches and parades. They lacked a
long-range plan of action.

Wisely, Stephenson kept his thoughts to himself. He
played the part of the awed recruit in the Imperial Palace. If he
had doubts about the leadership, he was careful not to show it.

When he left, Stephenson had thoroughly impressed the
top leadership. They recognized that the Indiana Klan was growing more through the young coal salesman's efforts than
through Huffington's work. The Evansville klavern had not begun to catch fire until Stephenson came on the scene. Now, less
than a year old, the Indiana Klan was one of the fastest-growing
organizations in the country.

The Hoosier state group was exploding in size and popularity. Offices had been opened in the capital, Indianapolis, and
recruiting operations were started in central Indiana. C. W. Love
had been named grand goblin for this northern outpost with a
kleagle named J. S. Engleerth. They had set up headquarters in
the Lemcke Building, one of the most prestigious addresses in
the city.[9] No sooner had their offices opened in March than they
began to receive hundreds of new recruits. By midsummer 1921,
their list of new klansmen included the names of some important bank officials in the city. On August 13, Grand Goblin Love
applied for a state incorporation charter for the Ku Klux Klan.
The man who carried out the state's authorization was the
then–Secretary of State Ed Jackson, an amiable politician
whose career was on the rise. Jackson would soon play a cornerstone role in Stephenson's plans for the state.

The Klan was growing, not just in Indiana, but all over the
country. Klaverns were forming in western states and in the industrial northeastern states. The Klan was no longer just a
southern phenomenon.

In September 1921, the *New York World* ran an exposé of
the Klan aimed at uncovering what the paper called "Bigotry in

Bedsheets." The series of twenty-one articles ran with a task force of reporters supplying material that revealed the seamy underside of the secret society. *World* reporters managed to infiltrate a New Jersey klavern, and one reporter even covered a Klan rally. The paper also ran a roster of local Klan officers and their addresses.[10]

Instead of shaming the organization, the *World*'s detailed coverage merely gave the Klan more publicity than it could ever have hoped to purchase. The Klan leaders were astonished. Recruiting was no longer a problem. The newspapers were "recruiting" for the Klan, on the front page, free of charge![11]

If the newspapers were unconsciously helping promote the Klan, so was the national economy. A postwar production slump was cutting into American industry. Without the war demand, industrial plants were cutting back on everything. Workers across the nation were being asked to accept drastic wage cuts. In September 1921, the Department of Labor reported that five million Americans were out of work—nearly 20 percent of the country![12] In rural areas, farmers were also feeling the bite of the failing economy. Cattle producers were finding the market prices of beef would not even cover the cost of taking their animals to the slaughterhouse.

Politicians did not have answers for what was ailing the country. But the Klan was there to provide an answer: It was because Socialist labor agitators were undermining the country. The ministers could not explain why the whole country seemed to be falling apart morally and spiritually, but the Klan knew it was because the Jews and Catholics had pulled Americans away from God. If these weren't the right answers, at least they were answers that people could listen to, talk about, and ponder. What the Klan had to say made sense to many people.

The Klan relied on the flag and the Bible to help bring new members into the fold. It took time, but gradually the ministers began to believe that the Klan was on their side. Most preachers were after the same things the Klan wanted: cleaning up morals and virtues, a general return to God and piety. If the klansmen wanted to dress up in white robes to deliver their message, what difference did that make? If the newspapers back East said that the Klan was no good, well, weren't most of those papers being run by Jews and Catholics?

The sermon preached by the Reverend William Forney Harris in February 1922 at the Grand Avenue Methodist Church in Indianapolis was typical of what many Protestants were hearing on Sundays. In normal times, Harris told his congregation, secret societies like the Ku Klux Klan would not get his support.

But these were times of "moral decay," and as such, any organization that stood for decency and order ought not be spurned. Soon, other clergymen would find themselves offering similar sentiments to their congregations and receiving more support from the Klan.[13]

Memberships were selling all over Indiana. Stephenson found himself becoming something of a civic leader in Evansville. Important people were asking him for his opinions about the affairs of the day. Some were even talking about his chances of getting into the state legislature. An election was coming up in 1922, and the First Congressional District seat from Evansville would be on the ticket. Why should he settle for just the state legislature when he could easily run for the United States Congress? At last, Stephenson was standing on the brink of his lifelong dream: to run for a national political office. And this was only the beginning.

Chapter Five

The Klansman and the Mayor

1921–22

"I first learned about politics from Ben Bosse of Evansville, where I had my first coal business," D. C. Stephenson once told his friend, Court Asher.[1]

Did he mean that he had learned about politics by simply observing the Evansville mayor and studying his technique? Or was Stephenson suggesting that he had an even closer connection with Mayor Bosse?

The question of how Stephenson, an outsider with no roots or connections in the state, got as far as he did in such a few years is a puzzle. It seems only logical that he must have had more going for him than mere salesmanship.

Today, Benjamin Bosse's name has all but slipped from the pages of the Indiana history books. But in the early 1920s, his name was synonymous with wealth and political power. He was mayor of his city, leader of the state's Democratic party, a remarkable businessman who ran a wide range of successful companies, and a philanthropist whose many contributions left a lasting mark on the city. Most importantly, Bosse was a self-made man. At his death, the *Evansville Courier*, which he owned, eulogized him: "His interests were so diversified, his activities so numerous, his sphere of influence so all-embracing that one approaches the task of discussing the man and his work with no small degree of trepidation. In his case, superlatives are essential, naught else will suffice. His genius for finance was amazing. His business vision seemed to border closely on the supernatural. No man grasped the details of a proposition more readily nor pursued its logic more unerringly."[2]

On paper, Bosse's life sounds like the life that Stephenson would have dreamed of for his own. Bosse was born in 1871, an immigrant German farmer's son in Vanderburgh County and the sixth of twelve children. In 1886, Ben went to work at age fifteen with his eldest brother, William, in a grocery business.

He attended night school to complete his education. A few years later, Ben and another of his older brothers, Henry, started their own grocery.

In 1899, Benjamin Bosse took the step that would eventually make him a millionaire: he entered a partnership in the Globe Furniture Company. Under his management, the company prospered and became a leader in the industry. Bosse carefully turned his profits into speculative investments. He became president of a dozen businesses and sat on the boards of many more. His holdings ranged from banks to real estate, insurance, newspapers, coal, and furniture. Not satisfied with his business success alone, Bosse went into politics as a member of the Board of Public Safety in 1906. He ran for mayor of Evansville in 1913 and went on to win that office for three successive four-year terms.

He developed a reputation as a selfless politician by refusing to accept his salary as mayor. Instead, he turned the money over to philanthropic purposes and bought swimming pools and playground equipment for the city's parks. He led drives to improve the parks, schools, libraries, and hospitals of Evansville. Two new city parks were developed under his leadership. He pushed for a new YMCA building, a new coliseum, two new high schools, and additions to local hospitals.

But for all his benevolence, Bosse was also a man who enjoyed power and knew how to use it, as demonstrated by a story of how he came to control the *Evansville Courier*.[3] Henry Murphy, one of the owners of the paper, had a son who was attending high school in Evansville. Murphy got word that high school boys were involved in petty gambling in the town's pool halls. Murphy decided to turn the matter into an editorial issue, declaring Bosse responsible for failing to curb this activity.

Not long afterward, in the spring of 1920, Henry Marshall, publisher of the Lafayette, Indiana, *Courier-Journal*, made an accepted offer to buy the *Evansville Courier* from Murphy and his partners. Marshall held onto the paper less than a year before selling it to Bosse. While no one could prove that Marshall and Bosse had hatched the plan to take over the paper, the rapid transaction seemed planned. With the purchase, the mayor gained a newspaper and effectively silenced one of his most vocal critics. Soon, the *Courier* was running front-page cartoons depicting the mayor welcoming new businesses to Evansville.

Bosse was also chairman of the Indiana Democratic State Committee, leader of the party, in the early 1920s. The post gave him statewide and even national prominence. While the Republicans held tight control over most of Indiana, the Democrats were still a force to be reckoned with and, by extension, so was Bosse.

Bosse would have been attracted to Stephenson's public manner, so much like his own. Both were self-educated, self-made men. Every political organization needs people with organizing ability—self-starters who can spur others to action. Had Bosse noticed this quality in Stephenson, he would have probably tried to quickly find some use for it in his own organization.

In addition to Stephenson's comment to Court Asher, there are at least three separate accounts of the Bosse-Stephenson connection. The first account of their meeting appears in the article "There's Mud on Indiana's White Robes" in the July 27, 1927, *The Nation*.[4] In that piece, writer Louis Francis Budenz describes Stephenson's trip to meet with the Klan leadership in Atlanta:

> About this time murmurings of the Klan could be heard in southern Indiana. Benjamin Bosse, Democratic mayor of Evansville and State chairman of his party, looked upon it with some favor as a possible means of curbing the growing Negro vote in his district and as a possible stepping-stone to the Governorship. He dispatched the busy Stephenson to Atlanta to look into the prospects of the Invisible Empire. "Steve" went, saw, and conquered—for he returned not as Bosse's agent, but as an important unit in the national Klan machine.

Another reference to a connection between Bosse and Stephenson is in Harold Zink's "A Case Study of a Political Boss."[5] While the piece does not mention Bosse by name, there can be no question that he is the subject of the passage:

> Through a fortunate association with the leading Democratic politician of Evansville, Stephenson was appointed to visit the South where the Ku Klux Klan flourished and see what could be done about transplanting the Klan to Indiana for political purposes. By 1922 the Klan organization was well underway in Indiana. Then the friend died and Stephenson decided to transfer himself and the Klan to the Republican party. Within a few months, the State of Indiana was organized until it stood out as the most powerful Klan in the entire United States.

A third reference to a connection between Stephenson and the mayor comes from Stephenson himself. It appeared in a statement to his attorneys published in a 1940 pamphlet, "The Stephenson Case."[6] In it, Stephenson says:

> In 1922 I was again approached by a group of Evansville citizens and was requested to revive the klan for use in the 1922 election. Shortly thereafter a national officer of the klan came

to Evansville and called on me, with a committee of local citizens, and again they urged me to take over the leadership of
the Evansville klan, revive its political interest, rebuild its
voting power, and throw the organization's political strength
behind a slate of candidates in which the local committee was
interested. I agreed to the plan and again took over the job of
directing the Evansville klan, in politics.

The three statements each describe the same transaction:
Bosse's plan to use Stephenson and the Klan as part of his own
political machine. In each case, the story is the same: Stephenson goes to Atlanta to investigate the Klan at Bosse's request or,
at the very least, with Bosse's knowledge and approval; Stephenson returns and takes over the leadership of the local Klan.

Early in 1922, Stephenson courted the leaders of the
Evansville Democratic party with the result that he entered his
name in the running for the U.S. First Congressional District
seat. He apparently entered with the understanding that the
party would support his candidacy if William Wilson, former
county clerk and the Democratic candidate for Congress in
1920, decided not to run. Wilson had done well in the last election, winning even the support of many Republicans, but there
was talk that Wilson might not run in 1922. Then Stephenson
would have a clear signal to join the Democratic primary race.

In Stephenson's bid for office, a "nobody from nowhere"—
his own description of himself—was entering the race for one of
the highest political offices in the state. He had, after all, only
lived in Indiana a little more than a year. Few people even knew
who he was, yet he would be running against two well-known
candidates, Will Carleton and Judge Herdis Clements. Why
would a newcomer like Stephenson even entertain the idea of
running for office under these circumstances—unless he was
counting on support from a very high source within the party,
perhaps even an endorsement from Bosse? Again, the evidence
seems to point overwhelmingly toward a close personal connection between the two men.

But fate crushed Stephenson's plans. On March 25, 1922,
the Democrats of Vanderburgh County met to set their strategy
for the May primary. Bosse, suffering from rheumatism, was unable to attend. With much concern focused on the sheriff's and
coroner's races, the party leaders suddenly discovered they had
still not reached a consensus on the important congressional
race. Wilson had finally announced his intention to run again
for office, but there was still the field of declared candidates to
deal with, Stephenson among them. As the day wore on, Wilson

emerged as the man who would most likely attract a crossover Republican vote, thus helping the rest of the ticket. Stephenson's boat appeared to be sunk before it was truly launched.

Next day, the Sunday edition of the *Evansville Journal* carried Stephenson's announcement that he would not run:

> Inasmuch as it has come to my attention today from an authoritative source, that William E. Wilson will be a candidate for the Democratic nomination for the office of representative to the United States congress from the First district of Indiana, I cannot and will not be a candidate.
>
> In the beginning, I was given to understand that Mr. Wilson would not be a candidate, but recently, he has changed his mind and in a conference Friday, assured me it was his intention to make the race. In view of the fact that Mr. Wilson was the Democratic standard bearer during a campaign when it was obvious public sentiment would swing the district into the Republican column, it is unfair in the extreme for either myself or any other candidate to cause Mr. Wilson to make a campaign in the primary or oppose him.
>
> He is entitled to the nomination without opposition, and in view of my belief in the old adage, "only the good die young," I will have plenty of opportunity in the future to make the race for this office, if I desire to do so. He is the only man entitled properly to make the race on the Democratic ticket at this time. Therefore, I cannot be at ease with my own conscience and cannot be in absolute harmony with what I know to be right and oppose him for the nomination, if no other aspirants announce. Consequently, I am making this announcement of my withdrawal from the race.[7]

The evening after Stephenson's withdrawal appeared in the local papers, the Ku Klux Klan paid a visit to the Central Methodist Episcopal Church. A silent parade of twenty men wearing white hoods and robes marched into the church. They walked up to the altar, knelt for a few minutes in silent prayer, then handed the Reverend A. M. Couchman twenty-five dollars and left. Contacted by the newspapers, Klan organizer Joe Huffington claimed he knew nothing of the display. He told reporters, however, "That is the first public appearance of the klan here, but it won't be the last."[8]

Stephenson seemed to be out of the political race, but the party still had some doubts. A few days after his withdrawal, the paper carried a statement from a group calling itself the Labor Political Support Association, which declared its interest in Stephenson. The statement read:

> All other candidates are using the same old camouflage by saying that they favor the farmer and working men and

women, but do not at the same time put forward any real statements as to what they stand for. Mr. Stephenson advises that if the machine wishes to support him, well and good; but it will be on Mr. Stephenson's principles and not those of the machine. . . . Therefore, we chose Mr. Stephenson on his past record and his platform for the future, and if the machine sees fit to place another nominee in the field, we suggest that the public judge the candidate by the history both machines have made during the past eight years, and assist us in placing a man in congress that has no ties except to the farmer and other working men and women.[9] [Note the similarities between the rhetorical style of the Labor Political Support Association and some of Stephenson's writings. It appears he may have drafted the "association's" statement himself.]

Rumors were flying. Stephenson had left town for Chicago. Some said he would appear in Indianapolis on Friday to file for office. Next day, however, the *Journal* reporters talked to Stephenson by phone, and he repeated his statement that he would not run against Wilson. "I told Mr. Wilson I would not run against him," Stephenson said. "In all my life, I have never violated a confidence and will not be put in the position of breaking faith."

By the weekend, however, the furor over the congressional race was all but forgotten. Bosse's illness had suddenly grown worse. Through the week, the *Courier* carried updates on the forty-six-year-old mayor's fading health. An infection had spread to his lungs, and it seemed that it might take him several weeks to recover. After a brief rally, his condition became critical. Oxygen was administered, but to no avail. On Tuesday, April 4, the *Courier* ran an extra edition with the banner headline: "MAYOR IS DEAD; BENJAMIN BOSSE PASSES ON AT 6:31 O'CLOCK THIS MORNING."

The following morning, the *Courier* printed a long list of messages of condolences from national, state, and local leaders. At the bottom of the first column was the following message: "Grand Rapids, Mich. April 4 Accept my deep and sincere sympathy for grief you must feel over the death of Mayor Bosse. Observation of the mayor compelled me to honor and respect his personal honesty, business integrity, and masterful executive ability. Evansville will long mourn the man who gave his best to her advancement.—D. C. Stephenson."

On election day, Stephenson's name still appeared on the ballot, but the wind was out of his sails. Wilson did have an opponent, Edward Meyer, in the Democratic primary. In the early returns, it even appeared that Meyer, with a substantial lead, might defeat Wilson. Stephenson trailed the ticket in every county in the district. In the final count, Wilson won with 9,681 votes, while Meyer ran second with 7,879. Stephenson, officially withdrawn from the race, still managed to earn 1,598 votes.[10]

After the primary, Stephenson and Huffington consulted with the Atlanta offices to map a new development strategy for the Indiana Klan. Since Stephenson wouldn't be going to Washington, there was still much organizing work to be done for the Klan. Evansville was well on its way to becoming a solid unit. The Klan offices were now located in a two-story brick building at the corner of Edgar and Division streets on the north side of the business district. The new klavern in Indianapolis was pulling in new members every month, but the organizers needed help.

The Atlanta office had probably heard by now about the problems that Stephenson and his wife were having.[11] Everyone knew that he was a heavy drinker, but now the word was filtering out that he had been abusing his wife. Even worse, Violet was telling her troubles to other people. It simply would not do to have a would-be congressman with stories like that floating around Evansville. Perhaps a change of scenery would be in order.

For whatever reason, the Atlanta office picked Stephenson, not Huffington, to go north to Indianapolis and work with the Klan office in the state capital. For Stephenson, the new office would mark an advancement. For Huffington, it was a snub, notice from his superiors that he had been passed over for a very honored and lucrative job. In a short time, this selection would become a matter of fierce rivalry between the two Klan organizers.[12]

Stephenson's coal partner, L. G. Julian, wasn't against the idea. Stephenson was now manager of their newly formed Vulcan Coal Company. A move to Indianapolis would allow them to start an upstate office and maybe even a new company. If politics was the unofficial religion of Indiana, then Indianapolis was its Mecca. A coal company with offices near the statehouse would put them within arm's reach of the top public officials and all the rich, state contract jobs. So Stephenson and his wife packed up their things and headed for Indianapolis.

Chapter Six

Citizens of No Mean City

1922

In 1922, Indianapolis was a city basking in the smug glow of its accomplishments. It was a major agricultural center with rail lines from across the nation converging on the city's stockyards. It was also a manufacturing hub with at least fourteen different car builders in the city. Most of the residents were white, Protestant, and Republican—three qualities that seemed to create an aura of thrice-blessed prosperity. The city leaders took this sign of divine approval quite seriously. For the cornerstone of the City Hall, they had chosen the words of St. Luke—Acts 21:39—to sum up their feelings for Indianapolis: "I am myself a citizen of no mean city."

No mean city, indeed. In other parts of the country, youngsters were going wild with the birth of what would later be called the Jazz Age. In Chicago, mobsters like Al Capone and his gang were running the new bootleg whiskey industry under the approving eyes of the local politicians. Down in Florida, a few speculators were beginning to take another look at the unfarmable beaches and swamplands with an eye toward the real estate boom of the century. But in Indianapolis, things were quieter, more stately, and above all else, proud.

In 1922, Indianapolis was a city of entrepreneurs and pragmatic business leaders, not romantics. Novelist Booth Tarkington had taken an accurate poke at the city fathers in his Pulitzer prizewinning novel, *The Magnificent Ambersons*: "The idealists . . . had one supreme theory: that the perfect beauty and happiness of cities and of human life was to be brought about by more factories; they had a mania for factories; there was nothing they would not do to cajole a factory away from another city; they were never more piteously embittered than when another city cajoled one away from them."[1]

The city was still a melting pot with pockets of ethnic neighborhoods: Irish on the southeast and near west side, Italians and Greeks to the east, Jews immediately south of downtown, and Germans—the most assimilated ethnic group—on all sides. Most blacks lived on the northwest side, anchored to the diagonal strip known as Indiana Avenue.

Behind the Christian zeal of the white majority was a sense of ethnic and racial superiority. Among the most enlightened, there was a sense of duty, of responsibility to lead the "weaker" races to a better way of life. Farther down the social ladder, there was a simple fear that blacks, Catholics, and Jews should not be allowed to get away with too much.

Stephenson could pursue his coal business in a city that offered an unlimited chance to promote the organization, his company, and most importantly, himself.

Those early summer months of 1922 should have been almost perfect for Stephenson. But the drinking and the wild swings in his temper were causing the rift between D. C. and Violet to widen. They had just settled into one of the neat, new apartment houses on East Seventeenth Street, only a few blocks north of downtown. But as D. C.'s rages grew more frequent and more violent, Violet found it impossible to continue living with him. At one point, he struck her in the face, giving her a black eye. Another time, as Violet described it later, he "scratched my face and kicked me several times, and he took off my dress and scratched me here, and pulled my hair."[2]

The marriage finally fell apart on August 7, 1922. Some friends of the Stephensons, a Mr. and Mrs. Schorr, had come up from Evansville for a visit. Edith Schorr later told how she found the couple in the apartment along with Stephenson's secretary and Violet's sister from Ohio. It was obvious that there had been an argument.

With his wife still sobbing in the adjoining room, D. C. roared that he would "give his right arm" if Violet would divorce him. He told the Schorrs he didn't think he should be a married man, that he didn't care for the responsibility of married life.

Violet did not have to be told twice. Next morning, she packed her things and returned with her sister to Akron. A year and a half later, her divorce from D. C. was granted.

Even if D. C. ever suffered second thoughts about his treatment of Violet—which seems most unlikely—he did not have long to brood. The Klan increasingly demanded his time and energy. He was busy traveling back and forth between Klan offices in Indianapolis and Columbus, Ohio. In September, he received from the Atlanta office his official imperial passport, a Klan identification card, signed by Simmons. (Even his imperial bosses in Georgia apparently had a difficult time keeping up with him; the passport was mailed to the Vendome Hotel in Evansville.)

He moved into a pair of rooms on the thirteenth floor of the Hotel Washington in downtown Indianapolis, which served as his main living quarters and also as offices for the Klan. He also set up a floor of offices for the Central States Coal Company directly across the street in the Kresge Building.

Of these two operating centers, the most important would be the coal company offices in the Kresge Building. Located on the third floor, these offices were lavishly decorated, designed to strike awe and respect into anyone who entered them. Ultimately, the guests in these offices would be some of the most influential men in the state. An office staff of several secretaries—at least three at one time—handled Stephenson's correspondence. Over the main entryway Stephenson hung a sign: "To the ox that draws the cart goes the fodder." In his private office, another sign warned, "Bearers of Evil Tidings Shall Be Slain." Eight telephones rang in the suite of offices—an extravagant number especially in that day. Later, Stephenson would install a dummy telephone in his office which served as a fake hot line to the White House. At the height of his power, he would interrupt politicians and lobbyists in midconversation to "take calls from the president." Books lined the walls. On his desk stood a bust of the man he considered his equal: the Emperor Napoleon Bonaparte. Stephenson built his offices carefully, realizing that he was building his own legend with them.[3]

What made Stephenson think he could sell the Klan in Indianapolis? Was there anything unique about Indiana in the 1920s that made the state ripe for the phenomenal impact of the Ku Klux Klan? Stephenson might have been just as successful in some other state. But the fact remains that he found his greatest success in Indiana.

The natural disposition of so many Hoosiers of that period to be joiners contributed to Stephenson's success. Hoosiers in the 1920s were eager to become part of some organization, any organization. The Klan satisfied that need, and Stephenson simply happened to be in the right place at the right time.

Stephenson also benefited from the fact that Indianapolis, unlike the eastern seaboard and New England cities, was not an "old money" city with a wealthy establishment in power. Many of the state's wealthiest people in the 1920s were "first-generation money," having pulled themselves up by their own bootstraps. This meant that the city was more open to newcomers and less likely to lock someone like Stephenson out of the power circles. He probably would not have moved up the political ladder as rapidly in Boston, Massachusetts, or Richmond, Virginia.

Another key to Stephenson's success was the fact that some Hoosiers harbored strong nativist fears about foreign ethnic groups and religions. This made Hoosiers susceptible to the Klan's appeal. Part of this may have stemmed from Indiana's relatively insulated location in the Midwest. The European ways of the Jewish community and the Roman Catholic trappings of the Irish, Polish, and Italians made them stand out as "different" in Hoosier communities. This difference, coupled with rough economic times, fed the fears of the native-born American population.

In his 1966 history of the Indiana Klan, John A. Davis concluded, "The Knights were successful in recruiting members in Indiana because they found fertile soil in this rurally-oriented, native American, white and Protestant stronghold. . . . It found ready acceptance among Hoosiers who were confused by change and angry over what they felt to be a breakdown of authority."[4]

Leonard Moore offers the opinion that the real appeal of the Klan was fear and resentment of social changes, rather than ethnic or religious groups. "The real source of popular dissatisfaction," Moore writes, "could be traced to the complex social changes which had eroded the cohesiveness of community life, undermined traditional values, and made average citizens feel more estranged from the major institutions which governed their lives."[5]

Grand Goblin C. W. Love had already managed to recruit a few hundred Klan members out of the 314,000 people who lived in the city. The Klan was not recruiting lower-class whites; it was selling itself to the middle- and upper middle-class, white, Protestant Americans as a new fraternal order. Fear of blacks did not provide the strong incentive to join in Indianapolis that it did in the South. There were only about 30,000 blacks in Indianapolis at the time, most of them peaceful and most of them Republican (the honor of belonging to "Mr. Lincoln's party" still carried some weight in the black community).

Foreigners were suspect in Indianapolis. And about sixty thousand residents were either first- or second-generation Americans. There were also about 32,000 Catholics in the city. It was commonly believed that Catholics owed their first loyalty to the pope in Rome, not the president of the United States. Many midwesterners lived in genuine fear that one day the pope would send out his orders for the Catholics in America to revolt and claim the country for the church of Rome.

Writer Lowell Mellett described the depth of anti-Catholic feeling in his article "Klan and Church" in the November 1923 issue of the *Atlantic Monthly*:

> Very clearly, the crux of the Klan problem in Indiana is the Catholic Church. The Klan is feeding on a revival of anti-Catholic feeling and renewed circulation of Catholic goblin stories. Men actually join the Klan because they believe that a magnificent home (a multi-million dollar palace, is the term usually used) is being built in Washington, D.C., to house the Pope, and that the Vatican is soon to be moved to the American capital![6]

Against the foreigners and the Catholics, the Klan represented what was "good" and "right" in America. It was not surprising that the Klan should have attracted some influential citizens. It is easier to see why such men as the president of the Commercial National Bank, Brandt C. Downey, and the cashier of the National City Bank, Chester A. Jones, should have paid their membership dues to the organization.[7]

Many others, however, were not drawn to the Klan. The mayor of Indianapolis, Samuel Lewis "Lew" Shank, was one who would eventually become one of the Klan's strongest and most vocal opponents. Shank was a big, blustery, cigar-smoking, card-playing mayor who made friends—and enemies—with ease. An auctioneer by trade and an ex-vaudevillian, he was a popular mayor, twice elected by the people to serve nonconsecutive terms.

Ironically, Shank's career as mayor during his first term, from 1910 to 1913, had hinged on the city's strong anti-Catholic feelings. In the 1909 elections, when a Democratic victory seemed assured, it came to light that the Democratic slate was entirely Catholic except for two candidates. Suddenly the race was no longer a matter of Republicans against Democrats but a race between Protestants and Catholics. In the general election, Shank, a Protestant Republican, polled 27,038 votes, while his opponent received 25,403. Shank, who would later fight the anti-Catholic Klan, had won on the strength of the public's fear of "papists."[8]

Like Stephenson, Shank gave rousing talks on a variety of topics using a strong declamatory style and every inch of his towering frame to capture and hold his audience. His ability to deliver strong speeches, a talent he first acquired as an auctioneer, earned him the nicknames "Leather-Lung Lew" and "Limber-Lung Lew." At the podium, he was easily a match for Stephenson.

Shank had a reputation for making snap decisions. When he won the 1921 election, he began studying appointments for offices. Stuck on the question of who he should pick for fire chief, he asked a friend who was the best man on the department. "John O'Brien," was the answer, "but you can't make him chief. He's a Democrat and, besides, he can't do you any good in politics." Shank ignored the party differences and hired O'Brien on the spot. He later had to call on O'Brien and his men to help quell the Klan riots in the city, and the favor was more than repaid.[9]

Why Shank opposed the Klan is unclear. Perhaps it was the result of his strong personal beliefs, or because the Klan provided a convenient political punching bag, or even a combination of the two. He often said that people who had to hide their faces behind bed sheets must be cowards. On the other hand, Shank was known as a mayor who occasionally liked to stir things up. Fighting the Klan may have only been another outlet for his gamesmanship.

Whatever the reasons, during the next two years, Shank attacked the Klan with all the power he could muster. In the end, Shank's opposition to the Klan would cost him his office, his chances for the governorship, and his entire political career.

At the opposite end of the spectrum from Shank were men such as the Honorable Judge Charles J. Orbison. A former Democratic Marion County judge, Orbison was one of the thousands who joined the Klan as a patriotic fraternal order.

Orbison brought an impressive array of credentials with him when he joined the Ku Klux Klan. He had served from 1901 to 1903 as general counsel for the Indiana Anti-Saloon League, a politically strong temperance group. From 1910 to 1914, he sat on the bench of Marion County Superior Court, room 1. From 1915 to 1919, he was general counsel for the Indiana State Tax Board and a member of the State Board of Charities. In 1922, he had just resigned as the federal prohibition director of Indiana and returned to private practice. His credentials, however, were slightly blemished. His resignation from the prohibition job was linked to charges of illegal possession of liquor.

As with so many men of his day, Orbison was a great joiner. Like Simmons, the judge strongly believed in the need for fraternal groups. Orbison was very active in the Masons, having served as deputy grand master and grand master of the Grand Lodge of Masons; he was also granted the honorary thirty-third degree. He was active in Irvington Lodge Number 666 and all the York and Scottish rite bodies of Masonry in Indianapolis.

He also belonged to the Independent Order of Odd Fellows, the Knights of Pythias, the Improved Order of Red Men, the Elks, and the Shrine.[10]

Orbison was extremely active in the Klan as a public speaker and lecturer for the Klan, making appearances around the state and even around the country. Through his friendship with Stephenson, Orbison would be elected to the Imperial Kloncilium, the highest governing body of the national Klan organization. And Orbison would remain active in the Klan's work long after its eventual fall from grace in Indiana.

Today it is difficult to understand why a man of Orbison's stature would have connected himself to the Klan. Orbison himself provided the answer when he was invited to speak—apparently as a last-minute stand-in for Stephenson—at the July 1923 first annual meeting of the national Knights of the Ku Klux Klan in Asheville, North Carolina. Orbison said, "With all of its teeming millions, the [eastern states] have fewer native-born American citizens in proportion to the total population than any other section of the country. The time is coming when the Americans of the West, South, and Middle West must Americanize the East and it can't be done by putting the supreme power in the hands of a foreign-made section of our country. . . . The enemies of the constitution are within our gates."[11]

Orbison was only one among many lawyers, doctors, college professors, and ministers who saw in the Klan a chance to stand up for his country against an evil foreign tide. To their eyes, the well-intentioned but misguided men like Shank were the ones who had failed to grasp the problem, who did not see the imminent danger. Orbison and others like him felt that they had been given a sacred mission: to educate and warn their fellow citizens. With men like this working for him, how could Stephenson fail?

Chapter Seven

The Art of the Double-cross

1922

On October 3 and 4, a "Curtis Stephenson" appeared on the list as a delegate to the sixty-second annual session of a most unusual group: the National Horse Thief Detective Association, in Logansport, Indiana. Under the auspices of this organization, Stephenson was beginning to organize the enforcement brigades that he called his "military machine."[1]

The National Horse Thief Detective Association, a peculiar anachronism which dated back to 1852, had been created to allow citizens to band together legally to pursue horse thieves. These "Horse Thief Detective Companies" operated like posses. The state empowered members of the association to "pursue and arrest horse thieves and all other criminals against the laws of the State of Indiana, and to serve papers relating to the same, and to follow and pursue such criminals in and through any part of the State of Indiana; and in the absence of warrant, members shall have power to arrest and hold in custody without warrant and for such time as may be necessary to procure a warrant."

Most of the horse thief detectives were older men who enjoyed the thrill of playing police officer after a week's work as grocers, farmers, and factory workers. Once a year, the detectives held their annual meeting in cities around the state. Each meeting was a two-day affair, featuring a street parade of officers and delegates, the marching band from the local American Legion post, and all the town's regular police force; a welcome from the mayor of the city; and an evening program of singing and entertainment. The songs included "Onward, Christian Soldiers" (the song which would later become the unofficial anthem of the Ku Klux Klan), "There's a Long, Long, Trail A-Winding," and "Back Home Again In Indiana." The detectives even had their own song:

> We're the guys who catch the horse thief,
> We're the guys who catch the horse thief,

47

> We're the guys who catch the horse thief,
> If he stays inside the old barn lot.

The tune, unfortunately, has not survived.

Of course, horse thieves had all but disappeared from Indiana by 1922 (the association's operating report notes for the
year: Horses stolen, four; Horses recovered, four). But the detective association had somehow managed to survive without horse
thieves. Adapting to modern times, members continued to operate as legalized vigilantes, chasing car thieves and bootleggers,
and patrolling country roads where immoral young people might
be found "parking" in automobiles. In these efforts, the detectives
were more successful. Their annual report credits them with 98
car thieves captured and convicted, and the recovery of 26 out of
28 stolen automobiles. (They did not report on their success at
chasing bootleggers and patrolling roads, but local newspapers
often ran stories about their achievements in these areas.)

The detective association seems to have evolved into a fraternal order with the unique distinction of having the power to
arrest people, a point which, no doubt, caught Stephenson's attention. Seventy years after their start, the horse thief detectives
still had enormous power granted to them by the broadly worded
state law that governed their actions. If the Klan was going to
make good on its claims of defending America against foreigners
and subversives, then it too would need the power of the law behind it. It would be almost impossible to convince the state to
give the Klan such powers of its own. But what if enough klansmen joined the horse thief detective association? Then they
would be able to share its police powers simply by participating.

Starting a company of horse thief detectives was a simple
matter. Any company or member in good standing could organize a new company. A form had to be filled out and sent along
with a $6.50 filing fee to the secretary of state's office. The com-
pany could be any size. The smallest company had six members;
the largest one, in Cass County, had 576 members. After filing
with the state, the company needed only to follow the vague
rules laid down by the state, and it was in operation.

With Stephenson already organizing klaverns for the Klan,
it would not take much more effort to organize new companies of
horse thief detectives—so he did.

Before the 1920s, the horse thief detectives had nearly
died out as membership around the state sagged. But in the period from 1922 to 1923, new klaverns were forming all over the
state. During the same period, the number of horse thief detec-

tive companies grew from 258 to 345. The number of detectives in the state rose from 11,578 to 14,314.

With little effort, Stephenson had managed to develop the fighting force that could become his tool for intimidation and the enforcement of his decrees. No longer a gang of folksy, would-be cops, the Klan-organized detective companies would become vigilantes and prove to the people that the Klan meant serious business.

William E. Wilson, son of the congressman from Evansville, Indiana, was a college student away at Harvard at the time, but he always came home to Indiana during the summers. He kept up on the news from home in his correspondence with his parents: "I had read and heard the stories of what the Horse Thief Detective Association was doing to others. They entered homes without search warrants and flogged errant husbands and wives. They tarred and feathered drunks. They raided stills and burned barns. They caught couples in parked cars and tried to blackmail the girls, or worse. On occasion, they branded the three K's on the bodies of people who were particularly offensive to them. And over in Illinois there had even been a couple of murders."[2]

In other states, the Klan organized gangs of night riders who often committed the kind of violent acts that came to be associated with the Klan. As historian John Davis described them, "They were the 'bully boys,' the sadists who enjoyed the terrorizing and flogging parties, the Klansmen who would have found the regular routine of Klan fraternalism a little on the dull side."[3]

The "peaceful" days of the Klan were nearly over.

———

Trouble was also brewing around the Imperial Palace in Atlanta. Signs of weak leadership were leading to a struggle for control of the organization.

The problems started in May 1922, when William Simmons unwisely decided to take a long vacation from his duties as imperial wizard. (This coincided with the period after the Indiana primary when Stephenson was moving to Indianapolis.) After seven years of organizing and ruling the Klan, Simmons felt he had earned a rest. His timing could not have been worse.[4]

Apparently blind to the bad reputation his partner, Edward Y. Clarke, had been developing, Simmons left the Imperial Palace in Clarke's willing hands. In 1910, Clarke was charged with embezzling church funds. In 1919, he and his associate, Elizabeth Tyler, were arrested for disorderly conduct, both of them drunk and partially clad. In June 1922, shortly after addressing a Klan gathering in Muncie, Indiana, on the topic of law enforcement, Clarke had been arrested for possession of liquor. (The liquor was found in his suitcase, and in light of later events, it is not impossible that Stephenson himself might have engineered the entire event.)[5]

No sooner had Simmons started his six-month vacation than Clarke began to issue orders in the name of the imperial wizard to all Klan organizers in the field. Problems developed immediately. There were charges and countercharges over mismanagement of funds. Weeks dragged by, and matters grew worse. Simmons did not decide to cut short his vacation. In October, a federal grand jury in Atlanta indicted Clarke for "misuse of the mails." On October 4, bowing to pressure, Clarke announced to the Klan that he would resign his position.

But instead of improving the situation, this only made matters worse. Now the organization was running completely without a leader. At last, Simmons returned to his office on November 10. "The Klan was seven years old on Thanksgiving Day, 1922," Simmons later recalled. "I had never called a national convention of Klansmen, but I decided that the time had come to have a national gathering, or a 'Klonvocation.' I fixed the date for Monday, November 27th, the Thanksgiving season."

Once again, Simmons's timing could not have been worse. There were scattered rumblings throughout the organization questioning his inept leadership. Yet Simmons was now calling the klansmen to meet in one place, where they could unite to work against him. There was less than three weeks to plan for the event with an office staff in Atlanta that was already badly demoralized.

To provide security and keep the meetings secret, Simmons picked the imperial klaliff—or vice president—Fred L. Savage, a balding, hawk-nosed man who had once worked as a strikebreaker on the New York City docks. Savage was responsible for organizing a group of klansmen to keep prying reporters and other undesirables out of the meeting. Simmons did not realize that a plot was already brewing to unseat him from the imperial wizard's throne and that Savage was one of the plotters.

On opening day of the klonvocation, Simmons was still blind to the plans being made against him. He reviewed the opening parade of hooded klansmen, who marched across the old battlefield with their flags waving, banners flying, and bands blaring martial music. At the Klan's newly built Peachtree Creek auditorium, he led the throng in prayer and in singing "Onward, Christian Soldiers." Then he delivered his speech, a long and flowery oration about how the angels were surely looking down from "the battlefield of the eternal city" and how the angels must feel "a kind of envy of you, in your position and in the work you have to do." Simmons did not realize he had less than one day left as leader of his beloved Klan.[6]

The plot to oust Simmons centered on a Texas dentist, Dr. Hiram Wesley Evans, the exalted cyclops of Dallas Klavern Number 66. Evans was a pudgy, bespectacled man whose soft exterior concealed a ruthless mind. A growing number of klansmen saw in Evans the type of man needed to consolidate the organization and build its strength. Besides Fred Savage, Evans had the support of H. C. "Kyle" Ramsey, Louisiana Klan secretary and a bartender from New Orleans; Judge J. C. Comer, Arkansas grand dragon and justice of the peace; and H. C. McCall, Texas grand dragon and policeman.

Stephenson rode to Atlanta in a private train car chartered for him by the Indiana Klan. He arrived Sunday, November 26, the day before the klonvocation was scheduled to begin. The Atlanta station was crowded with hundreds of other klansmen arriving from all over the country. Word was sent to Stephenson's car informing him of a secret meeting to be held the following evening in the Piedmont Hotel and telling him that he should make a point to be there.

Stephenson later recalled:

> I went to the hotel at their invitation and met Mr. McCall, the deputy constable; and Mr. Comer, the Justice of the Peace; and Kyle Ramsey, the Imperial Kligrapp, a bartender from New Orleans, Louisiana; and Dr. Evans, the tooth-doctor—dentist—from Dallas. . . . I don't recall the exact words of Evans, but the deputy constable from Houston (McCall), who was Evans' "heavy man" in that situation, suggested that a man by the name of Fred Savage . . . that Fred Savage and I go out and see Colonel Simmons and put him in a frame of mind so that he would not object too strenuously to Dr. Evans' election as Imperial Wizard the next day. Prior to that, Comer told me that Colonel Simmons was guilty of terrible immoralities. I told him that I knew nothing about that and I had seen no proof of it, but I had heard charges whispered and bruited about so long, I didn't believe it; that Simmons impressed me as being a cultured gentleman. He said, "What have you to suggest?" And I said, "Nothing that I know of, except to lay the facts before the organization tomorrow and let them solve it. They can solve it better than we can."

This was not the right answer as far as Evans and his friends were concerned.

It also shows how close Stephenson came to being cut out of the Klan's future. McCall told Stephenson to leave and "think it over for an hour," then come back to the hotel to continue the discussion. When Stephenson returned, he had decided to go along with the group's plans. Grand Dragon McCall told him, "You and Savage go out and see Colonel Simmons and tell him that these charges are going to be made against him on the floor tomorrow." With that, Stephenson and Savage drove out to Klankrest, the imperial wizard's home.

It was late at night when Simmons was woken from a sound sleep by a knock at his door. Donning a robe, he answered and found his security chief, Savage, and Stephenson standing on his front porch. It was sometime between 3:00 and 4:00 A.M. They told Simmons they were "out for an early morning drive and couldn't sleep with all the excitement." After chatting for a few minutes, Stephenson began to question Simmons about the election that was to take place that morning. Simmons was to be officially elected imperial wizard and governor, titles he had simply granted to himself until now. The election was to be simply a formality, something to fill up the time with a little pomp and circumstance that Simmons had tossed onto the agenda. But now Stephenson and Savage were asking Simmons what he planned to do about it.

"I told them nothing," Simmons later recalled. "I supposed the convention would confirm me in the two offices I held, without any opposition." He also planned to add a new position, top administrative officer, to manage the organization while he took care of other matters. They asked who he was considering. He replied probably Judge Grady of North Carolina. Had he considered Hiram Evans for the job? He replied that he had not and that he did not think Evans was right for it. He then made it clear that it was time for this late-night interview to end.

Then Savage spoke up, "Well, Colonel, we both just dropped around to tell you that, whatever happens on the convention floor tomorrow, there will be armed men stationed round on the floor to protect your honor."

Simmons was roused by this. "Protect my honor? What do you mean?"

Savage went on, "There is a certain crowd of men here who say if you are nominated for the office of Imperial Wizard tomorrow, they will get up on the floor and attack your character. And we've just come to tell you that the first man who insults your name will be killed by a sharpshooter right on the spot where he speaks. There'll be enough of us with firearms to take care of the whole convention, if necessary."

Simmons was thunderstruck. Sharpshooters? Firearms? Attacking his honor? What did any of this have to do with his klonvocation? But before he could reply, the plotters made their suggestion: "to preserve the harmony and peace and wonderful carrying-on of the Klonvocation as we have it, let's beat those birds, and give them a message in which you refuse to allow your name to come before them to succeed yourself."

They told him that, instead, he should name Hiram Evans—there was that name Evans again!—to be a temporary replacement for the imperial wizard until a suitable man could be picked for the job. Simmons could stay on as emperor and, thus, avoid a revolution. "They told me that we could avoid bloodshed if I would agree to have Hiram Wesley Evans elected imperial wizard," Simmons recalled. "I didn't know what kind of men these fellows were, or I wouldn't have believed them. I found out afterward that all this talk was a fine 'frame-up'—a lie to deceive me, told by men I trusted implicitly."

Stephenson told a slightly different version of the story a few years later, a version which conveniently left out any mention of guns or sharpshooters:

> When we told Colonel Simmons that Mr. McCall, the deputy constable, had informed us that a character attack would be made on Simmons from the floor next day, Mr. Simmons said, "Men, there isn't a thing in those charges, and I would like to face them." He was very definite and apparently confident in his position. Savage then asked him if he wouldn't like to be relieved of the detail work in connection with the Imperial Wizard's duties, and he said that he had always intended to do that. Then we said to him that Evans was going to be nominated for Imperial Wizard the next day, and that was entirely satisfactory with him. I told him there that night that so far as the Indiana and Ohio organizations were concerned, that any attack on the floor, we would require to be proved; that they couldn't go any further with the whispering. And Colonel Simmons said that was splendid; seemed to be very happy about it.

Simmons did not discover the trick that had been played on him until it was too late to do anything about it. Instead, he went back to his bed and spent the rest of the early morning hours tossing and turning, unable to sleep. "I saw visions of a bloody shambles among the 1,000 delegates the next day," he said. Stephenson and Savage left the imperial wizard's home that night with their mission accomplished. Simmons's fear of bloodshed would take care of the rest. "I prayed for divine guidance," said Simmons. "I didn't want any killing in the hall."

Later that morning, a very tired Simmons called some of his closest friends and advisors—several of whom were actually enemies—to a prayer meeting at Klankrest. Evans, Stephenson, and Savage were all there. So was Sheriff Lowry of Fulton County, Georgia, a klansman and close friend of Simmons. The banished Edward Y. Clarke was invited. The renowned sculptor Gutzon Borglum, who was then hard at work on the Klan-financed Stone Mountain Confederate Memorial, attended. Judge Charles J. Orbison from Indianapolis was also included, along with about another dozen more faithful klansmen.

Simmons briefly explained his predicament to this private gathering, then announced his intention to name Evans to the imperial wizard's post. Simmons would content himself with the title "emperor" until the current trouble blew over. Then he asked all the klansmen present to kneel and join him in a prayer for guidance, a prayer for the Klan.

Not everyone in the room was happy with the decision. Borglum, always something of an idealist and dreamer, felt Simmons had been unfairly judged. "Who on earth, who knows men, could accuse Simmons of anything but dreams and the fondness for the aid to dreams?" Borglum would later write in a letter to Stephenson. Others were also surprised, but they did nothing to stop Simmons from following through with his decision. After the prayer meeting, they went before the entire assembly, and Simmons announced, "Evans is to be the imperial wizard."

The double-cross had worked. Simmons was out. Evans was in, and Stephenson along with him.

"When I went out to 'The Palace,' however, within the next few days, I saw Evans sitting at my desk in my office," Simmons told a reporter a few years later. "He didn't get up to give me my place. He said to me, 'Colonel Simmons, I'm going to put you on a great white throne in this palace. I am planning to make a throne-room for you where you can meet all your visitors. You stick to me.' But he never got around to making the throne-room."

For Simmons, there would be no more throne rooms ever again.

Chapter Eight

The Start of a New Regime

1922–23

Imperial Wizard Hiram Evans rapidly set about the task of reorganizing the Klan to suit his purposes. He gave his friend and fellow Texan H. C. McCall the plum position of serving as the Klan's "envoy" to Washington, D.C. The job was primarily that of lobbyist, something that McCall's background as a deputy sheriff had hardly prepared him for. Edward Y. Clarke was given the title "imperial giant" along with a medal and a life membership in the Klan—apparent forgiveness for his earlier indiscretions. Gutzon Borglum was named to serve with Clarke on a new committee to establish a national program for the Klan. Fred Savage was kept on to serve as chief of staff and imperial klaliff. Kyle Ramsey from Louisiana was named national secretary. Judge Charles Orbison would continue to serve as a member of the Imperial Kloncilium, the Klan's board of directors.

As for Stephenson, he seemed to be doing quite well in Indiana. In only six months, he had recruited more than 25,000 new klansmen in the Hoosier state. Where his predecessors had done well to bring in a few hundred members each month in the state, Stephenson and his men were now routinely signing up more than a thousand a week. Shortly before the Atlanta klonvocation, Stephenson reported 2,264 members recruited in a single week![1]

About 250,000 men in Indiana joined the Klan in the early 1920s, or roughly 30 percent of the state's white, native-born, male population. Leonard Moore has used recently uncovered Klan membership lists to analyze the ranks of people who joined the Klan in Indiana. Moore found that in almost every Indiana city with a population greater than 25,000, the Klan managed to recruit at least a fourth of the white, native-born males.[2]

Evans gave Stephenson free rein to organize and recruit in the northern states with the possibility that he would be a grand dragon within a year. At last there would be some order given to the northern Klan, which until now had been growing with little or no direction.

From the start, though, the differences between Stephenson and Evans must have been obvious to any klansman who knew the two men. Evans's background was with the Klan in bloody Texas, where the hooded order was known for whippings, floggings, hangings, shootings, and burnings of any blacks who crossed paths with the organization. Violence did not occur in isolated incidents in Texas; instead, it seemed to be the norm.

By contrast, in Stephenson's Indiana realm, the Klan used the threat of violence more often than violence itself to enforce its will. Apart from the nighttime activities of the Horse Thief Detective Association, Indiana in the 1920s would see no spectacles of Klan lynchings, only a couple of riots and a few other incidents. Most of the Klan violence in Indiana resulted from direct encounters with rival, anti-Klan groups rather than cases like those in other states, where the Klan would seek out and attack private citizens without any apparent provocation.

Stephenson had joined the Klan primarily to organize a political power base. His first connection with the Klan stemmed from his efforts to carve himself a niche in local politics. Stephenson did not join the Klan because it was the Klan. Rather, he joined because it promised him a way to build his own power group. Had the Rotary, the Elks, the Moose, or the Odd Fellows offered him a similar chance to gain power rapidly, Stephenson probably would never have bothered to join the Klan at all. For him, the Klan was simply the right organization at the right time.

By comparison, Evans truly believed in the righteous cause of the "Invisible Empire." He followed the teachings of the Klan as a true disciple of white supremacy.

But not Stephenson. His beliefs were as changeable as a fancy suit of clothes. In Oklahoma, he had been a Socialist. In Evansville, he was a Democrat. In Indianapolis, he would be a Republican. Like a chameleon, he changed his colors to blend with his surroundings. The titles and labels did not matter to Stephenson. What mattered was power. Time and again, the people closest to Stephenson would learn that the center of his life was the pursuit of power. If being a klansman would bring him a step closer to greater power, then a klansman he would be.

Money, as Stephenson had witnessed in Benjamin Bosse, was the universal exchange for buying political power. With enough money, a man could buy almost limitless power. Coal sales were good, but the Klan was better. When it came to making money, the Klan was the best game in town.

For a man in Stephenson's position in 1923, the game was also at its best. By providing the simplest management framework and distribution system, he could make a comfortable living by recruiting other men. He needed only to make a few speeches here and there, appear once or twice, smile, wave, and talk in the mysterious Klan language, and his network of organizers would do the rest.

The only problem with being a Klan leader was that it was simply too good a deal. The business was so lucrative that others were quickly attracted to it. With only a few spaces available at the highest ranks, the competition to fill those spaces became quite deadly.

Stephenson quickly recognized that life at the top could be dangerous. After the November 28 coup in Atlanta, Stephenson usually traveled in the company of armed bodyguards. Often, Stephenson carried his own handguns for protection, as did Evans, Simmons, and other Klan leaders. For his trips through northern Indiana, Stephenson was accompanied by a chauffeur and bodyguard known only by his nickname, "Terrible Tommy." Later, Stephenson would enlist a small army of ex-policemen as bodyguards. No one in his position could be too safe.[3]

Stephenson's friend, Court Asher, was first recruited as a bodyguard, but only after nearly getting into a fight with the Klan. A very busy bootlegger, Asher had been arrested and convicted three times for dealing in illegal liquor. He was convinced that the Klan had singled him out for harassment. So one night he went to the Indiana State Fairgrounds, where a big Klan rally was to be held. As he later described it to writer John B. Martin, Asher went to the rally carrying a gun and determined that "there wouldn't be no Konkave [sic]." But before Asher had a chance to start anything, a friend stepped in and introduced him to Stephenson, who signed Asher up as an investigator, a kleagle, with the salary of a hundred dollars a week plus expenses. "Steve showed me what their principles were. And it was more than I'd ever dreamed of makin', except at bootleggin'."[4]

Stephenson recognized that guns alone would not let him hold onto his position in the Klan. He needed more than firepower. He needed mind power. One important tool was already in his hands, the weekly Klan newspaper, the *Fiery Cross*. The little paper had started in late 1921 under the name *Fact!* in Indianapolis. No copies of this predecessor survive, so it is uncertain whether *Fact!* was a Klan publication from the beginning or whether it simply evolved into one. But by July 1922, the *Fiery Cross* was being published under the editorship of Ernest W. Reichard, who had offices on the fifth floor of the Century Building, next door to Stephenson's offices in the Kresge Building. At that point—before the Atlanta coup—the Klan claimed to have about five thousand members in Indianapolis.

The hand of Stephenson—promoter and ex-newspaperman—appears to have had an immediate effect on the development of the newspaper. By January 12, 1923, the circulation of the *Fiery Cross* had climbed to 50,500 copies, circulating in Indiana, Ohio, and other northern states. A year's subscription sold for five dollars. Newspaper carriers hawked the paper on the city streets each week (dangerous work, too, since the vendors were often attacked by people who didn't agree with the paper's point of view). By mid-March, the paper would claim a sales force of nine hundred boys delivering the paper to more than one hundred thousand readers, reaching some as far away as Iowa. On April 6, the paper announced that it would expand to a twelve-page paper. And it now claimed more than three hundred thousand readers (based on an estimate of three readers per copy). There were now three editions: an Ohio edition, printed on Wednesdays; an Iowa and Illinois edition, printed on Thursdays; and the Indiana final edition, printed on Fridays.

At first, the material in the *Fiery Cross* was the sort of harmless reading that one might expect from any club or fraternal publication. It carried reports of meetings and rallies, and excerpts from speeches—most of them on the topic of "100 percent Americanism." It carried news of other Klan activities in distant states and a sampling of reprinted articles from other newspapers, some praising, others condemning the work of the Klan. The paper became a popular advertising vehicle for merchants eager to show their support for the Klan. Advertisers offered discounts to Klan members, some of whom boasted of their "TWK" window signs, which stood for "Trade with the Klan." Employment ads eagerly sought "young, white, Protestant, 100% Americans" to work as stock clerks, warehousemen, and salesmen.

As Stephenson pointed the Klan in a more political direction, the tone of the paper also began to change. Now banner headlines would support or denounce particular politicians. The paper would wage a scathing battle of words against Lawrence Lyons, the leader of the Republican party, a factor which would lead to Lyons's resignation. The paper began publishing the names of prominent Catholic businessmen, an act that implied klansmen should blacklist these firms and one that would ultimately spark an awesome retaliation.

While Stephenson used the paper to marshal his forces and unify opinions among his followers, he also kept a surprisingly low profile in the publication. On the few occasions when he is mentioned, the paper refers to him only as "Steve" or "The Old Man," never by his full name. Most klansmen had no idea who the mysterious "Old Man" was. It would be months before Stephenson would finally step out from behind this facade and reveal his identity.

Often the *Fiery Cross* gave front-page coverage to sermons delivered by ministers who favored the Klan. Stephenson was busy enrolling the Protestant clergy in the cause of the Klan. Perhaps more than any other Klan leader of his day, he realized the importance of winning the ministers to his side. With their support, his group and its actions would appear to be sanctioned by the highest authority. Stephenson realized that the support was a two-way street. To get support, he must also give it. So items began to appear in the Klan paper:

• In Franklin, Indiana, the Reverend J. L. Stout of Grace Methodist Episcopal Church preached that the nation could not survive part-Roman Catholic and part-Protestant because the Roman Catholic church owed allegiance to "a foreign dictator"—the pope.

• In New Concord, Ohio, the Reverend Frank L. Brown of the Methodist Protestant Church based a sermon on the text from John 8:32, "And ye shall know the truth and the truth shall make you free." The paper reported that Brown spoke to a standing-room-only crowd of fifteen hundred people and said, "I see no fault with [the Klan]. It is purely a Protestant organization, believing in and supporting the laws and government of our land."

• In Newport, Kentucky, the Reverend W. B. Harvey posted a notice on the bulletin board of his Baptist church encouraging the Klan or any other organization to clean up the town and rid it of "disorderly houses." Harvey said, "I am for law and order, first, last, and always."

• In Zanesville, Ohio, a crowd of about two thousand came to the Methodist Protestant Church to hear (again) the Reverend Frank L. Brown preach about the Klan. "These men have acted in the spirit of Jesus Christ," he said.

• In Urbana, Illinois, the Reverend J. F. MacMahon delivered a sermon on "the true principles of the Ku Klux Klan." During his sermon, he said he "would like to occupy the pulpit of any Negro church and explain that the principles of the Ku Klux Klan would benefit any community where law-abiding Negroes, who know the problems of their race and want to keep the race and color pure, will be aided by the Ku Klux Klan, since every Klansman is pledged to see that there is no fusion of white and negro blood."

Stories of this type became regular features in the *Fiery Cross*. The stories showed that the Klan supported the Protestant churches. They also served as publicity for the ministers who were willing to preach pro-Klan sermons—an important fact for the ministers who often faced sparsely populated pews on Sunday morning. The ministers had only to embrace the Klan, and their churches would be filled as well as their offering plates. Frequently, the reports in the *Fiery Cross* told of crowds that stood outside churches straining to hear the words of a pro-Klan sermon. Most importantly, the stories "proved" that the Klan had the support of the church and, indirectly, the blessings of God.

Stephenson made the best possible use of this support. He enlisted some ministers as regular Klan lecturers, sending them out to make a career of traveling from town to town preaching pro-Klan sermons. One of these was the Reverend V. W. Blair, who kept a very busy schedule preaching for the Klan. In a single issue, the *Fiery Cross* reported back-to-back appearances by Blair. The first one was on February 1, 1923, at Arcadia, Indiana, where a hundred klansmen attended a rally and heard him preach about the Klan. The next day, he preached a sermon in Rushville, Indiana, to "the largest crowd ever seen" at the Rushville Coliseum, an event that was thoroughly reported in the *Rush County News*. The names of other "Klan ministers" appeared with similar frequency in the pages of the *Fiery Cross*, suggesting a very large force of religious supporters.

Fear of the Catholics was a frequent drawing card for the Klan's ministers. In Muncie, Indiana, a minister delivered a sermon on "The Godliness of America" to explain the Catholic threat to his congregation: "They say the Pope isn't wanted in Italy. France has been approached and she doesn't want him. The Balkans say no. Russia—'Not on your life!' England, Germany, Switzerland, Japan—all refuse. And they say the Catholics are building a great cathedral in our national capital at Washington which is to become his home. I don't know this. It's just talk, but that's what they say."[5]

There were at least three cases in Indianapolis where ministers who opposed the Klan lost their churches. The Reverend

James M. Eakins of the Memorial Presbyterian Church resigned under pressure from his congregation after he preached a strong anti-Klan sermon. The Reverend F. E. Davison of the Englewood Christian Church was deposed by his congregation under similar circumstances. (The Reverend George Smith of Saint Philip Neri Catholic Church publicly praised Davison for his actions).

The most dramatic removal was that of the Reverend Clay Trusty, Sr., whose own church members from the Seventh Christian Church burned a cross in front of his house as a sign of their opposition to his anti-Klan position. But even these events were publicized in the *Fiery Cross*, apparently to suggest to other Protestant congregations how to handle stubborn ministers and to warn ministers who did not quickly fall in line.

Another popular Stephenson technique of solidifying control over the Klan was his use of Klan rallies. Most of these were a combination of family reunion, circus, public party, band concert, political rally, parade, and horse show. Some smaller rallies were simply evening ceremonies that usually featured a cross burning and the initiation of new members. These were often held in an open field or public park. Whatever the size or purpose, the Klan rallies were an aspect of Klan life that appealed to all people. Who could resist the temptations offered by this *Fiery Cross* ad for a Klan rally in Valparaiso, Indiana? "Gigantic—20 Brass Bands—Free Acts—Colossal—A BIG BARBEQUE—High Tight-Wire Walking 100-ft. In The Air—Wild Bronco Busting—Outlaw Horses—Imported Texas Cowboys—National Speakers—200 Horsemen—ALL DAY, ALL NIGHT!" This May 19, 1923, rally attracted a crowd of about fifty thousand people.

Stephenson did not invent the Klan rally. That credit probably should belong to Simmons. But Stephenson took a good idea and built it to its grandest potential. The 1923 Fourth of July Kokomo meeting was the largest in Klan history—before or after Stephenson—and the many smaller ones that came after it were inspired instances of propagation. In Valparaiso, Evansville, Noblesville, and all over Indiana, these rallies were anticipated as the biggest events of the year, filling the towns and their newspapers with comments—and often praise—for weeks before and months afterward.

Huge rallies were also staged in the Ohio territories that were under Stephenson's control, the most popular one being the giant summer outings that were held at Buckeye Lake, about thirty miles east of Columbus, Ohio. The weekend Klan rallies there drew thousands from all over the Midwest and north central states. Witnesses recall the mile-after-mile traffic jams with streetcars parked on rail sidings and automobiles lined up along all the roads leading down to the lake. These rallies were the great, wild orgies of patriotism that captured the imagination of his followers.

Further down the scale of public demonstration, but just as important in the minds of the participants, were the open-field ceremonies around the fiery crosses, where the Klan held secret, late-night meetings to initiate new members. These events were usually staged by the local klaverns. The ceremonies combined elements of mysticism, religion, patriotism, and white supremacy, culminating in the ritual lighting of the huge gasoline-soaked wooden cross.

The crosses burned brightly on Christmas Eve, 1922. On that night, in Indiana alone, the flames were seen in Franklin, Fort Wayne, and Edinburg. The Indianapolis suburb of Irvington was also the scene of a Christmas cross burning that year, but the fire department arrived quickly and extinguished the flames. In early January, crosses burned in Newark, Ohio, with two ceremonies held in a single week. On January 20, 1923, a group of two hundred nineteen marchers paraded through downtown Noblesville, Indiana, several miles north of Indianapolis in Hamilton County. It was the Klan's first public appearance in the town. The klansmen marched from the horse show grounds on North Ninth Street down to the courthouse square in Noblesville. There, they built a cross, eighteen feet tall and ten feet wide, on the southeast corner of the courthouse lawn and lit it.

After a similar parade in Lafayette, the city's mayor and the city council passed an ordinance prohibiting "masked parades." Other anti-Klan mayors would try this same method of quelling the Klan, to no avail. In Portland, Indiana, Captain E. A. Fulton of the Indiana National Guard led members of the Muncie Klan through the town. Fulton paraded without a mask, in defiance of the town ordinance against masked parades. Mayor Thomas Fleming and thirty of his deputies mounted a fire truck and parked it in the street in an attempt to stop the parade. Later, Fulton's participation in the march was the subject of an investigation by the Indiana National Guard, but the matter was quietly dropped after a short study.

In early February 1923, the Indiana Klan held its "first annual Klonvocation somewhere in Howard County." It was staged in an outdoor tent, but in spite of the winter weather, sixteen thousand people came. Imperial Wizard Hiram Evans and Imperial Kloncel Paul Ethridge came up from Atlanta to take part in the ceremony. In a noon speech, Evans called for "law and order" to take control of the Hoosier state and for klansmen to work at cleaning up the "vice and liquor" in the state. Speeches, however, were not the only attractions at the event. The *Fiery Cross* reported that the crowd consumed "2,000 pounds of meat, 1,500 loaves of bread, 15,000 buns, and several thousand pounds of cakes and pies." The klansmen at the meeting represented seventeen Indiana cities and towns plus smaller organizations.

One week later, on February 17, the thermometer hovered at seven degrees with a strong thirty-five-mile-per-hour wind when a thousand klansmen marched through Frankfort, Indiana, in a night parade to initiate three hundred new members. A light snow was on the ground, and more snow was falling when the parade started at 10:00 P.M., led by two klansmen mounted on white horses (one was probably Stephenson himself). Next came a car with an electrically lit fiery cross followed by the Muncie Klan band playing marching music in an open bus. Twenty klansmen marched through the snowy street carrying a huge flag. (The *Fiery Cross* later claimed this was "the same flag carried by Col. Theodore Roosevelt during his tour of the world following his presidency.") Then came several Klan floats, each featuring local people dressed up to represent themes such as "The Separation of Church and State," "Law and Order," "Protection of Pure Womanhood," and "Just Laws and Liberty."

More reports of cross burnings and celebrations came from all over the country in the weeks that followed. In Louisville, Kentucky, a cross burned within 150 yards of the mayor's residence. (Arthur Hamlet, secretary to Mayor Houston Quinn, advised local citizens to keep indoors.) Between 3,000 and 4,000 people attended a Friday night cross burning in Topeka, Kansas, in March. At about the same time, the Des Moines, Iowa, Klan was reporting 5,000 men had joined their organization. Two crosses burned in Dover, Delaware, on the night of March 23. The same evening, the klansmen in Wilmerding, Pennsylvania, delivered an American flag and a purse with money to the pastor of the English Lutheran Church, commending him for his work. In Freeport, New York, the editor of the *New Amsterdam Review* received a note from the Klan on March 23 denying that cross burnings were meant to intimidate blacks. The next night, a thousand people gathered for a fiery cross ceremony in Memphis, Tennessee.

Between 500 and 600 people attended the first meeting of the Klan in Wapato, Washington. The Klan in Owensboro, Kentucky, announced that it had brought in 475 members and expected that number to double in one month. On March 26, two crosses burned on the hills east and west of Chillicothe, Ohio, for the second time in a month. In Chicago, the Klan reported that membership had doubled since last August.

Between February and March, 51 Klan organizations had applied for charters in various cities around the country; 32 had been accepted, and 19 others were pending. The Klan was every-where during those early months of 1923. Stephenson was riding high with the organization. But with the success came the opposition.

Chapter Nine

The Rising Opposition

1923

By the spring of 1923, it was becoming clear to millions of Americans that the Ku Klux Klan was not merely a Halloween spoof. There was a sinister element to all the patriotic blather about racial purity and the separation of church and state. If these were true Americans—so the reasoning went—why did they need to hide their faces behind masks and hold secret meetings? There was talk all over the country now of the Klan-related murder of two white men in Mer Rouge, Louisiana, in August 1922. In that incident, a planter's son and a garage mechanic were brutally murdered for having openly opposed the Klan. What patriotic organization could condone such behavior? This Klan business was becoming a serious issue, one that could not go unanswered.

One former Hoosier, Elmer Davis, in the article "Have Faith in Indiana," described an expatriate's view of the situation back home:

> One finds it hard to imagine why the Klan has such a hold on Indiana. What has the nervous Protestant to be afraid of in a state which has hardly ten percent of Catholics and one percent of Jews? Well, he finds a good deal to be afraid of. One hears strange tales among Hoosiers—for instance, that the lease on the Vatican has expired, and the Pope, unable to pay the increased rent demanded by the landlord, is now living in disguise in Cincinnati, ready to cross the frontier the first dark night, seize Indiana by a *coup d'etat*, and turn it into a papal satrapy. . . . Just why, out of all the Protestant communities on this planet, the Pope should select Indiana as the object of his wicked desires is not apparent to the foreigner; but to the Hoosier it is clear enough. Indiana is the most desirable spot on earth, and any potentate might reasonably covet it. . . . This theory seems to be widely held in the rural districts, and the Protestants are all on guard."[1]

Davis could write tongue-in-cheek about the Klan hysteria—he was, after all, safely living in New York City at the time.

But other groups took the matter more seriously. The Klan was beginning to show an interest in politics, particularly on issues concerning education and public school instruction. If the group managed to emerge as a political force, what impact might it have on other parts of the community? A few mayors were trying to deal with the problem by enacting anti-mask parade ordinances, but often the klansmen got around the law by simply marching without their masks.

Some citizens enacted their own personal anti-mask ordinances. In Indianapolis, the Rabbi Morris M. Feuerlicht leaped into the street during a Klan parade and began ripping hoods off some of the participants, an act of individual courage for which he was long remembered.

In Oklahoma, Governor Jack Walton had grown tired of the Klan's reign of terror, which included brutal beatings and public whippings in the state capital. He declared a state of martial law during the summer of 1923 in an attempt to curb the Klan; this backfired, however, when voters decided they preferred the Klan's law to martial law and impeached Walton.[2]

In Indianapolis, racism was simply part of daily life. The black population grew rapidly as more blacks left the agricultural South for jobs in the industrialized North. In 1922, the whites in Indianapolis started arguing for segregated schools. Proponents usually cited a higher incidence of disease among blacks to justify the segregation. Two groups—the Indiana Federation of Community Civic Clubs and the Indianapolis Chamber of Commerce—led the campaign for a separate high school for blacks. Their effort received vigorous support from the Klan. The National Association for the Advancement of Colored People twice filed lawsuits to stop the construction of the school but lost both times. Thus was the all-black Crispus Attucks High School created.

For the most part, however, the blacks in the community did not offer much more than verbal opposition to the Klan. And who could blame them? The number of registered klansmen in the city would soon outnumber the black men in the city by almost two to one. And the newspapers were full of stories from other states where the Klan conducted murderous programs of lynchings, beatings, and shootings of blacks. Who could say that a show of force on the part of the black community might not trigger similar violence in Indiana?

Catholic groups were also becoming concerned about the growing strength of the Klan. The *Indiana Catholic* newspaper had been speaking out against the Klan since May 1921, when the Klan first became a visible force in Indianapolis. Through its editor, an Irish immigrant named Joseph Patrick O'Mahoney, the weekly paper became one of the loudest voices in opposition to the Klan. While O'Mahoney incorrectly interpreted the Klan's Anglo-Saxon Protestant views to be part of a British plot on American soil, he nevertheless was one of the leaders in speaking out against the Klan.[3]

O'Mahoney would soon urge other Catholic editors to follow his lead in condemning the Klan. As many have observed, perhaps rightly, this kind of opposition merely added fuel to the Klan's fires and helped prove its claims of Catholic hostility. But this kind of work eventually galvanized Catholic opinion against the Klan.

Another group rapidly forming an opposition front against the Klan was the American Unity League, a Chicago-based group formed in June 1922. The league was intended to be a multifaith, multiracial organization to battle the Klan. Its chairman was black, the Reverend Bishop Samuel Fallows of the Reformed Episcopal Church. The league maintained its offices in a new high-rise building in downtown Chicago—the Unity Building—on North Dearborn Street. A brash Chicago lawyer and native Hoosier, Patrick H. O'Donnell (later dubbed "Mad Pat" O'Donnell by the Klan), served as president of the league. He was a loud and very capable spokesman against the hooded order. In only a few months of campaigning, O'Donnell was able to enlist fifty thousand members of the league in Chicago, compared to the Klan's claimed membership of one hundred thousand in the city.

In March 1923, the Irishmen of the Ancient Order of Hibernians staged an elaborate St. Patrick's Day program in Indianapolis. Several hundred people crowded into Tomlinson Hall on Market Street, just across from the Indianapolis courthouse. O'Donnell had been invited to come down from Chicago and address the crowd. His appearance came at the same time that the Klan's membership was beginning to swell, the Protestant clergy was endorsing the organization, and the fiery crosses were lighting up the skies all over the state. O'Donnell built his speech on an analogy to St. Patrick's driving the snakes out of Ireland. "We are growing to drive the Klan out of Indiana!" he declared. "We are going to redeem Indiana and re-annex it to the American Union!" The crowd roared. "Mark what I tell you! If they are not exposed and driven from Indiana, they, the Ku Klux Klan, will corrupt your juries, dominate your elections, elect their puppets to power and place, undermine your laws, and violate the principles of your constitution."[4]

O'Donnell's speech was a battle cry for the people who opposed the Klan. A few weeks later, in April, an Indianapolis chapter of the league was formed. Judge James Deery, the new chapter president, called on a variety of notable Jews and blacks to help lead the organization. The *Indiana Catholic* applauded this development and declared that more chapters should be formed around the country.

Ironically, in forming the league, the Catholics were, in effect, forming their own kind of "Klan." They were fighting fire with fire. Just as the Klan's *Fiery Cross* reported on the activities of the Klan, a new league newspaper called *Tolerance* now reported the activities of the league. *Tolerance* devoted much space to publishing Klan membership lists—usually stolen from Klan offices—and the names of prominent klansmen. With headlines such as "DEATH TO THE INVISIBLE EMPIRE!" and "DRIVE OUT THE SNAKES!" *Tolerance* seemed anything but tolerant.[5]

Just as the Klan was busy forming klaverns, now the league was rapidly starting chapters. Like the violent factions inside the Klan, there was also a violent faction inside the league. These league members took the call to "destroy the Klan" literally.

In the spring and summer of 1923, the league was credited with a string of firebombings in Chicago aimed at Klan-connected businesses. In one case, the target was a building that housed the publishing offices of the Chicago Klan's newspaper, *Dawn*, but the paper, its staff, and equipment had moved out of the building only a few weeks before the bombing.

The formation of a league chapter in Indianapolis raised the ire of the Klan. But on April 1—notably April Fool's Day—the Indianapolis league members pulled off a trick that would spell war with the Klan. It was Easter Sunday and a moonlit night. In the early morning hours, someone broke into the offices of the Indianapolis Klan on the third floor of Buschmann Hall at Eleventh Street and College Avenue. The burglars must have known exactly what they wanted. They found a list of 12,208 names of local klansmen, which they raced off to Chicago for the publishers of *Tolerance*. The robbery must have been carefully planned and well timed. On the afternoon of the same day, *Tolerance* hit the streets of Indianapolis with wildly jubilant headlines: "INDIANA'S REDEMPTION IS AT HAND! KU KLUX 'JUG' SPRINGS LEAK, BOTTOM FALLS OUT, IN FACT! WHO'S WHO IN INDIANAPOLIS!" And with that fanfare, *Tolerance* published seventy-four names from the list with the promise of more to come in future installments. At the top of the list was the name "CHARLES J. ORBISON, former Judge, law partner in the firm of ORBISON, OLIVE, BRENNAN & ZECHIEL, 1506 Merchants' Bank Bldg." That was the standard form of the Klan lists published in *Tolerance*, giving not only the klansman's name, but his professional titles, business affiliations, business address, and sometimes even his home address.

The same issue of *Tolerance* featured a half-page story next to the names of the Indianapolis klansmen. Bearing the headline "INDIANA CENTRAL COMMITTEEMAN RENOUNCES KLAN," the article consisted solely of a copy of a telegram and letter, both from Lawrence A. Lyons, chairman of the Republican State Committee. The telegram, dated March 27, was addressed to "Freeman or Stewart," two of the Indianapolis Klan recruiters, and read: "Some thirty days ago, I was induced to join the Ku Klux Klan through misrepresentations. Since my action I am convinced that your organization is wrong and un-American in its principals and purposes. Accept this as resignation from this un-American organization and I demand you take my name from your Roster at once." The telegram and a letter with the same date were sent to the American Unity League with the announcement that Lyons wished to make public his renunciation of the Klan.

It may have been a political blackmail job (what did the league have on Lyons?), or it may have been simply a change of heart on Lyons's part. At first, the Klan tried to take all this bad news very lightly, bluffing along in its first statements to the effect that the *Tolerance* lists were insignificant, that the league had not stolen a Klan membership list at all, but that the league had merely acquired a list of local Protestants who might be eligible to join the Klan.

But bluffing aside, the Klan moved swiftly to seek a court injunction in the U.S. District Court in Chicago to prevent *Tolerance* from publishing any more lists. The Klan eventually won the injunction, but it was too late. Copies of the list had already been printed and were being distributed like wildfire all around the state, to the vast and lasting embarrassment of many prominent citizens who had thought they were joining a secret organization whose membership lists would never be made public.

The Klan's next response was more vengeful. On Monday, April 2, it published a front-page story in the *Fiery Cross* about the weekend burglary. Stephenson and his men had decided that the theft must have been orchestrated by an insider. The letter and telegram in *Tolerance* pointed a finger of suspicion at Lawrence Lyons. The Klan's headline screamed, "LYONS BETRAYS KLAN OATH! REPUBLICAN STATE CHAIRMAN MAKES DEAL WITH AMERICAN UNITY WHICH BARGAINS IN HUMAN CHATTELS." The story went on to call Lyons the "Benedict Arnold of Indiana . . . born in Hell, and inspired by Satan, betrayer of the

Republican party and people of Indiana . . . Lawrence Lyons is not to be even dignified as the Judas Iscariot of the Indianapolis Klan." (The hyperbolic attack sounds familiar enough to have come from Stephenson's own hand.) The article swore that Lyons would be cast into "political oblivion." On the front pages of the April 27 and May 11 issues of the paper, the Klan printed names of prominent Catholic businessmen and their companies, a reversal of *Tolerance*'s own game.

Stephenson and the Klan benefited rather than suffered from the publication of the membership lists. The organization gained stature because of the incident. Rather than reducing the Klan's numbers, which had been the goal of the league, the publication of the lists resulted in an increase in members. This fact was later documented in an audit of the Indiana Klan by the accounting firm Ernst & Ernst.[6] *Tolerance* proved what the Klan had been saying all along: the Catholics were out to get the Klan and would use any tactic available to achieve their goal. The more violent and organized the opposition to the Klan became, the more people wanted to join the organization. As would be proven time and again, the harder its opponents fought the Klan, the faster it grew.

Stephenson personally benefited from the Lyons episode. Lyons was forced to resign, clearing the way for the appointment of a new state chairman, one who might be more dependable, more willing to go along with Stephenson's plans. In a telegram from his Columbus, Ohio, offices on April 4, Stephenson contacted Ed Jackson, secretary of state; James A. Collins, Marion County Criminal Court judge; George V. "Cap" Coffin, Marion County Republican chairman; and Ora J. Davies, state treasurer—all key Republicans—with the following message:

> Permit no selection to be made and permit no one to be named to succeed Lyons until I have had an opportunity to confer with you. See that Lyons hands in his resignation at earliest possible moment so it will be unnecessary to further embarrass him by forcing same. His position is intolerable. We do not seek to hit him when he is down but if he forces us we will tell the whole truth about why he betrayed his solemn trust and why he betrayed the confidence of life long friends in gentlemens agreement of honor. Block Clyde Walb appointment.
>
> The Old Man

In the wake of the stolen lists furor, Stephenson authorized the expenditure of several thousand dollars to hire more guards and bolster security around sensitive Klan documents. In spite of these precautions, the telegram printed above was still circulated into the hands of the *Tolerance* publishers, who in turn printed copies of each of the telegrams to each of the recipients over the next four issues. In printing the telegrams, the *Tolerance* editors included a note: " 'The Old Man' is Mr. D. C. Stephenson, former King Kleagle of the Ku Klux Klan of Indiana, usually alluded to as the 'Grand Goblin.' " This is the earliest known reference—April 15, 1923—which links Stephenson to his "Old Man" identity and correctly identifies him publicly in print.

The publication of the Klan lists also provided more substantial proof of the Klan's connection with ministers and the churches. In the same April 1 issue that carried the first list of Indianapolis klansmen, *Tolerance* also published a list of Methodist Episcopal churches whose ministers were included in the Klan membership lists. It pointed out that eight of twenty-nine Methodist Episcopal churches were in the hands of Klan ministers. A few weeks later, the May 13 issue of *Tolerance* carried a lengthy list of Indianapolis Klan churches, complete with the names and addresses of the ministers. At that count, there were twelve Methodist Episcopal, six Baptist, three Presbyterian, one Society of Friends, one Free Methodist, two Disciples of Christ, two Nazarene, one United Brethren, and twenty-two various other ministers whose churches were unknown—all counted as Klan ministers.

In the weeks ahead, *Tolerance* lists would name thousands of klansmen from large cities and small towns all over the nation. Each week's issue carried a list of cities across the bottom of the front page to advertise which lists would be printed that week: "St. Louis! Chicago! Louisville! Indianapolis! Pittsburgh! Columbus! Springfield! Lafayette! Akron!"

Among the prominent names in Indianapolis:

E. Howard Cadle, businessman and founder of the Cadle Tabernacle;

Ed Jackson, Indiana secretary of state (who would soon become regular feature material for *Tolerance*);

Judge James A. Collins, Marion County Criminal Court;

Bert A. Gadd, funeral director and member of the Indianapolis school board;

Bowman "Bo" Elder, national committeeman for Indiana in the American Legion (and a Democrat—proof that there was at least some crossover Klan membership);

Dr. Paul F. Robinson, Marion County coroner;

John L. Duvall, Marion County treasurer-elect and future Indianapolis mayor;

George O. Hutsell, executive secretary, Indianapolis Board of Public Works; and

Albert H. Losche, Marion County clerk (another Democrat and future mayor of Indianapolis).

The lists included the occasional touch of irony that pointed out how deeply the Klan issue had split the community. In the May 6 list, for instance, the names included Heza Clark, police reporter for the *Indianapolis Times*, the only daily paper in the city that was actively crusading against the Klan. There was also the name of Carlin H. Shank, former Marion County commissioner and brother of Lew Shank, the Indianapolis mayor who had already sworn to fight the Klan.

Often the names of "klansmen" would appear in *Tolerance* to be answered by a chorus of denials from the alleged members. Some swore that someone else must have turned in their names. Others insisted that they had not joined but had only made a donation to the Klan and, thus, had their names been accidentally added to the list. Others claimed they had joined without knowing what the organization was all about. In several cases, the offended parties sued the paper and its publishers for libel. And how could a wrongly accused individual possibly prove that he was not a klansman? The inherent unfairness of the *Tolerance* doctrine of "publish and be damned" would be the subject of debate on both sides and would ultimately help cause the American Unity League's undoing.

In the meantime, however, the pages of *Tolerance* also served as a source of news about the Klan. When compared side by side with the *Fiery Cross*, it is obvious that *Tolerance* actually provided better coverage of Klan news than did the official Klan newspaper. And the news it printed showed that not all opposition to the Klan was coming from the outside. Some of the Klan's worst enemies were its own officials, still locked in a deadly struggle for power.

At the imperial klonvocation in November 1922, the idea of starting a women's auxiliary of the Klan was discussed. Stephenson took this idea and put it to work immediately, forming his own auxiliary in Indianapolis and letting the ladies get involved in distributing Christmas baskets the following month. He picked Daisy D. Barr to run the organization and, in February, his women's group, Queens of the Golden Mask, was formally chartered.[7]

Former Imperial Wizard Simmons also liked the idea. *Tolerance* reported a March 22 story from Atlanta, Georgia, about Simmons's plans to launch a new women's order of the Klan. Simmons planned to call his group the Kamelias, with himself as its magus, or president. Ousted from the Klan's inner circle, Simmons now appeared bent on making a return performance.

Not to be outdone by Stephenson or Simmons, Imperial Wizard Evans announced in June the formation of his own women's auxiliary, known as the Women of the Ku Klux Klan, with an "expected membership of 250,000." Evans's women, who would not be affiliated with either the Kamelias or the Queens groups, would be headquartered in Little Rock, Arkansas.

This three-way rivalry over the women's organizations would add to the friction that was developing between Stephenson and Evans.

One of the strangest stories that appeared in *Tolerance* on the inner-Klan fights was the item on sculptor Gutzon Borglum and his Stone Mountain monument. In early May, the story from Atlanta, Georgia, carried the headline "IMPUDENT KLAN WOULD DEFACE STONE MOUNTAIN." The story said, "It has just become known here that the Ku Klux Klan is the leading sponsor of the movement to carve on Stone Mountain, near Atlanta, a gigantic memorial to Confederate heroes of the war between the states. The project is already assured, but the Klan backing is a new development." The item quoted Imperial Wizard Evans saying that he would raise the $2 million for the monument, even if he had to place an arbitrary assessment on every Klan in the country. The story also reported that Edward Y. Clarke had consulted with Borglum on the design of the monument and that Clarke had suggested "the hooded figure of a Klansman would look fine on the mountain alongside the figures of Generals Robert E. Lee and Stonewall Jackson."

More scandals would be reported in August, when Klan leaders discovered (supposedly by reading a listing in *Who's Who in America*) that sculptor Borglum—designer of their sacred Stone Mountain Memorial and a member of the Imperial Kloncilium—was Catholic.

Shortly after that incident, the Stone Mountain Memorial Association failed to pay Borglum his next installment on the work in progress. After that breech of faith, Borglum took one of his assistants and climbed the mountain with a large case of explosives. He struck a match to a fuse, and a short time later an explosion rocked the mountainside and erased forever the unfinished work he had done on the monument. The Stone Mountain Memorial would be completed decades later by another sculptor. As for Borglum, he left Georgia and never came back. He did go on to achieve considerable fame as the sculptor who designed the portraits of the four presidents—George Washington, Theodore Roosevelt, Abraham Lincoln, and Thomas Jefferson—on Mount Rushmore.

Chapter Ten

"Americanism Gone a Little Sour"

Summer 1923

The battles with the American Unity League, the stolen membership lists, and the accusations of traitors in the fold were all momentarily forgotten when Stephenson went up to northern Indiana for a huge rally staged in Valparaiso. He was to provide the main address to a crowd which the official Klan papers hoped would reach fifty thousand. According to the Klan's promotional releases, the May 19 Valparaiso rally was planned to "resemble the tournaments of Old England, when Knights of another age met for sport, merrymaking, good fellowship, and an opportunity to try lances with, or to pay respects to, nobles from distant parts." If it would only turn out half that well, it would still be a success. On his arrival, however, Stephenson quickly discovered that the crowd numbered less than half the anticipated 50,000, and some said the number was more like 10,000 to 20,000. Even at that, he still had a very large crowd for such a very small town.

Robert L. Duffus, a writer for the monthly *World's Work* magazine, attended the event and filed a report on what he saw. It is noteworthy that Duffus's story is a rare instance of a non-Klan, third-party account of Stephenson's rallies by an eyewitness. Duffus immediately noticed that most of the klansmen were not wearing masks. He observed:

> This was probably the first large-scale appearance of Klansmen without masks and it was a most enlightening one for innocent bystanders interested in the personnel of the organization. Had it not been for a sprinkling of robed Klansmen (looking more or less uncomfortable and absurd in the sunlight) at the railway stations, at street corners, in automobiles, and at the guarded entrances to the fair grounds, a casual visitor might have mistaken this solemn occasion for a political rally, a county fair, a Fourth of July festival, or a circus. Except for badges and banners designating each

successive delegation as it marched up from the train, and the pennants which decorated the automobiles, there was little about the visitors which proclaimed them members of an order which has made more extravagant claims, aroused greater hysteria among its opponents, and produced more gray hairs among politicians than any similar phenomenon since the collapse of the Know-Nothing party nearly seventy years ago.[1]

It was a warm, sunny day with the temperatures staying in the eighties most of the afternoon. The rally had drawn klansmen from all over the Midwest, with a particularly heavy showing from nearby Chicago. (One enterprising jeweler had arranged for a special twenty-two-car train to provide round-trip transportation for $1.25 per person.)

Duffus recognized another point about the crowd at Valparaiso: the differences between the rural and urban klansmen.

A closer inspection afforded opportunity for making, or rather for confirming, certain generalities. The rank and file of the Klan at Valparaiso were sharply divided into city members and country members. The farmers, who arrived in automobiles, usually with their families, would have seemed perfectly at home eleven years ago in a Progressive party rally—bronzed, homely, good-natured persons who might have been selected at random from the farming populations of Indiana, Ohio, Illinois, Kansas, or Nebraska. No group of men, seemingly, could be farther from the savageries of which the Ku Klux Klan had been guilty in Louisiana, Texas, Florida, Tennessee, and Oklahoma, and it was a little difficult to believe that they were taking seriously the mummery they had come to witness. A more striking evidence of the Klan's ability to be—or seem—all things to all men could not have been found.

The delegations from Chicago, who wore badges and carried banners proclaiming their home city, were of a different, and if this writer's observation of them can be trusted, an inferior type. Certainly they were not the "average American citizens, home owners, voters, and folk relied upon in the communities from which they came" which one Klan paper described them as being. Most of them could be classified as belonging to the less successful strata of the "white collar" class. They did not represent organized labor, which except in Kansas and in parts of Texas, has fought shy of the Klan, nor did they include, apparently, many members of unorganized manual laboring groups. They might have been small store-keepers, corporation employees, clerks, and clingers to the edges of the professions, with perhaps a sprinkling of more influential personages.

This is not said by way of disparagement, but rather to throw light on the nature of the Klan's appeal. The one generalization which could be applied, as I believe, to the Valparaiso celebrators was that they had social or personal grievances. This was a parade of Americanism gone a little sour.

The impression was strengthened by conversations with a number of Klansmen and Klan sympathizers. Behind the fringe of shrewd promoters, "salesmen of hate," politicians, addicts of hocus pocus, skylarkers, and bootleggers who have earned the Klan a deserved odium, is a residue of earnest and aimless discontent.

Duffus discovered that the Klansmen at Valparaiso were unique only in their complete lack of uniqueness. These were simply average Americans who, for one reason or another—in Duffus's words—had "gone a little sour."

This was the slice of American life that Stephenson was trying to reach with his words and his leadership. And there was a good chance that he would reach them. As Duffus concluded, "What could happen here [in Valparaiso] might happen anywhere in the Middle West." Stephenson knew this, too, and was working hard to see that it would happen elsewhere.

The following week, the *Fiery Cross* would report that in Cheyenne, Wyoming, the Klan had been granted its charter and that there was now a Klan organization "in every Wyoming town of more than 1,000, and some in smaller towns." The paper also reported on growing Klan operations in Colorado and Utah. What could happen in Valparaiso could happen anywhere.

Stephenson had great plans for Valparaiso. He planned to start a Klan university. His idea was to purchase the tiny and financially troubled Valparaiso College. There, he would staff a school with teachers of his choosing to offer a "100 percent American" curriculum. He wanted to buy up land around the college and develop it as housing for students and their parents. He planned a lake with a huge park around it. When his plan was complete, no one would laugh at the uneducated Klan because klansmen would have their own national university in Indiana—only a few miles from the great Catholic university of Notre Dame.[2]

Imperial Wizard Evans had heard all about Stephenson's plans for a college, but none of it impressed him. Still, he allowed Stephenson to negotiate for the college and the land around it. But when the time came for the Atlanta office to send the necessary money north to make the purchase, Evans stepped in and stopped the deal. He couldn't justify purchasing a college in Indiana with money that had come from klansmen all over the country. Stephenson met with Evans to plead for the money, to no avail. There would be no Klan college in Indiana. Stephenson was furious, but there was nothing he could do except work with his attorneys to get out of the deal.

But the Valparaiso College deal was not the last of the problems between Stephenson and Evans. They clashed in Washington, D.C., during an early June weekend meeting to develop a national strategy and policy statement for the Klan. The entire Imperial Kloncilium met at the Willard Hotel, just a few blocks from the Capitol. But what was intended to be a unifying meeting ended by sowing the seeds for the dispute that would ultimately divide Stephenson and Evans.

Four years later, Stephenson described that meeting in Washington. The disagreement involved a special vigilante wing of the Klan, controlled by Evans, known as the Black Robes.

According to Stephenson, the interview was short:

> I said to Mr. Evans, "I have looked into the Black Robe gang at Steubenville, Ohio, and I find that it is your organization." He said, "Yes, what of it?" I said, "They are committing acts of violence and bloodshed. They fired into an Italian meeting being held on a ridge north of Steubenville, and several men were seriously wounded, and . . . were killed." He said, "Too bad it didn't kill every one of the wops." I said, "That kind of thing is going to meet with a reaction." He said, "Bah! The only reaction will be fear." I said, "I don't think so. I think it will excite public opinion against the Klan, and it will ultimately end in its destruction." He said, "There ain't nobody going to destroy anything they are afraid of."[3]

Another possible cause of the split between Stephenson and Evans, however, was the failure of the Klan to develop a national policy. The meeting in the Willard Hotel was a failure. After much discussion, Evans called the members of the Imperial Kloncilium into room 712. There, Evans announced there would be a national Klan policy of "talking with newspapers from time to time." Stephenson's reaction to this (again from his 1927 testimony) was, "They'll laugh at me in Evansville if I tell them that!" Stephenson was pushing for the organization to develop something along the lines of a national political party platform. Evans, on the other hand, wanted to leave things indefinite, more informal. The lack of a well-defined program would, no doubt, have proven a major frustration for Stephenson, who saw the Klan as a political entity rather than a fraternal club. This point, combined with the issue of violence, may have been the early signs of the split in their relationship.

By being in Washington on June 2, Stephenson missed the huge Klan parade and fireworks display in Muncie, Indiana, sponsored by the Delaware County Klavern Number 4. Even though Stephenson missed it, his friend and bodyguard, Court Asher, was there to take part in the parade. The event had been billed as a "patriotic demonstration." But before the night was over, it became a public testimony on the bully-boy nature of the Klan, complete with bloody fights and whippings that would leave the town torn by the Klan issue for months to come.

It was a warm summer evening with a cloudless sky. At the center of the events in Muncie that night was George R. Dale, editor of the *Muncie Post-Democrat*. Dale was one of several editors around the state who had dared to oppose the Klan in print. For this reason, the Klan had targeted him for special attention.

On an earlier occasion, Dale and his son were assaulted by a gang of klansmen near his home. Dale was beaten and his son was pistol-whipped, the Klan's crude way of sending a message regarding his editorial policies. Later, when Dale began to campaign in earnest against the Klan, naming local police officers and other city officials who were klansmen, he was called before Circuit Court Judge Clarence Dearth, cited for contempt, given a six-month jail sentence, and fined one thousand dollars. To be sure, Dale's reporting was hopelessly biased against the Klan, but most people at the time would have agreed he had earned a right to that bias.[4]

Dale's report of the June 2 parade through Muncie gives a first-person account of the violence that night:

> The Klan marched, two thousand strong—armed, arrogant, and overbearing. Citizens in all walks of life were insulted and assaulted. Under the hypocritical guise of requiring honor to the American flag, citizens were required to remove their hats and humble themselves before the Invisible Empire, Knights of the Ku Klux Klan.
>
> John O'Neill, a gallant captain of the A.E.F. who saw hard service overseas, was brutally assaulted by a gang of Klansmen. He went down fighting but was taken to the hospital where eleven stitches were taken in his lacerated cheeks. The blow which rendered him unconscious was struck from behind by a Klansman. He was dragged from his automobile, where he was seated with his young wife, when he refused to raise his hat to a masked horsewoman, who

was desecrating the flag by sitting on it, the flag being draped over the rear end of a horse.

Captain Guy Haggarty, of the local militia, who served as an officer on the Mexican border and in France, was treated with the utmost indignity by the parading Klansmen when he went to the rescue of one of the men who had served under him in France, but who refused to remove his hat to the Klan parade.

Ex-Congressman George Cromer, seated on the veranda of his apartments on High Street, between Main and Jackson, was ordered to remove his hat, and a mob attempted to break down the door at the foot of the stairway, when they found it locked.

In Riverside a masked horseman of Muncie Klan No. 4, ordered John Valentine, one of the most prominent citizens of Muncie, to remove his hat when the masked woman went by. Mr. Valentine refused and the Klansman drew back a riding whip and gave the harsh order: "Take off your glasses, for I am going to whip your hat off your head." Valentine saw the attack on John O'Neill and was protesting against the outrage when he was accosted.

Mr. Valentine says the masked outlaw did not carry out the threat but he saw the fellow lash out with the whip and knock another man's hat off, in describing a semi-circle the whip striking a woman in the face. . . .

Dean Hensel, well known lawyer, with his family, was sitting in his automobile watching the parade. He refused to obey a Klansman's order to remove his hat. Two masked men from the Muncie Klan in the parade ran toward the automobile, accompanied by two unmasked men. The quartet were in the act of attacking Mr. Hensel when his little daughter, fearing for her father's safety, saved him from assault by jerking off his hat herself.

Former Prosecuting Attorney Frank Mann was standing in the courthouse yard when the parade went by. He wore his hat and refused to obey the "hats off" order.

"Go get him!" was the command from the ranks of Hundred Per Cent Americanism. Six men left the Klan mob and made a rush for Mr. Mann, who stood his ground. As they approached, Mr. Mann reached in his pocket for his knife, and the cowardly Klansmen, thinking he was about to shoot, turned tail and ran.

I stood at the corner of Gilbert and Washington Street, with my daughter. As the Muncie Klan was passing, one of the Muncie masked horsemen called an unmasked stranger to the side of his horse and pointing me out said: "Go get that fellow."

"Take off your hat or I will take it off for you," was the insulting order of the big ruffian, who made a pass at his hip pocket, as if reaching for a gun, and struck with his other hand, knocking off my hat, barely missing my daughter, who was leaning on my shoulder when the unexpected assault was made.

Officer Arthur Jones, night captain of the police, was standing nearby and witnessed the entire affair. I demanded that he arrest the man who had assaulted me, to which he replied that I ought to have taken off my hat when told to do so. He also told me that I ought to have known better than to stand around and thus invite trouble when a Klan parade was going by. . . .

I repeated the demand for the arrest of the man who had assaulted me, to which Captain Jones replied that I should go to the prosecutor and file an affidavit. My rejoinder was, "Captain Jones, you ought to know what your duty is. You saw the assault and it is the duty of a policeman to arrest violators of the law when they personally witness the act of law violation, and not wait for an affidavit. That man is a stranger and you are deliberately allowing him to escape."

I might also have told him, with some propriety, that the prosecutor was probably in the parade, hidden behind a mask, and that it would take too much time to page the Klan and search the two thousand nighties.

Each case of Klan violence that Dale documented that night was connected to citizens who refused to take their hats off to the American flags being carried by the passing klansmen. But, as Dale pointed out, the only people desecrating the flag that evening were the klansmen themselves, who rode in cars and on horses decorated with flags. Some had draped the flags over the hoods of their cars, others had taken flags and wrapped them around the spokes of their car wheels, and a pair had taken a flag, draped it over the front seat of their car, and were sitting on it as they rode down the street.

"The Klan itself was desecrating the flag which it arrogantly assumed to be honoring. The real purpose was to make everyone take off their hats to the Klan, not to the flag," Dale wrote. "Patriotism and courtesy demands the removal of hats when the color bearer of some military or naval organization passes, but no other organization on earth is empowered even to request such a proceeding, much less a law-breaking, murderous outfit like the Ku Klux Klan."

The Klan's actions during the Muncie parade were picked up in stories all over the Hoosier state. Other anti-Klan newspapers, such as the Winchester, Indiana, *Democrat* ran Dale's account of the parade in its entirety.[5] The Chicago edition of *Tolerance* ran a three-page reprint of Dale's story, along with some of his other anti-Klan editorials, under the banner headline: "KLUX HAS THE WHIPHAND HERE! MUNCIE, IND., SHOWS WHAT YOU MAY EXPECT!"

Among those Dale counted as klansmen were: Muncie's chief of police, Van Benbow, and day captain, Ira Coons (both marched at the head of the parade); Frank Barclay, Republican city councilman; and Harry Hoffman, Delaware County sheriff. Dale noted that Barclay and seven other members of the council had formed an alliance to accomplish anything the Klan wanted. "They are opposed to the mayor and block every action he attempts to make. This Ku Klux Klan gang . . . gives the real orders to the board of safety and the police force."

The Klan was active in other cities and towns that month. The June 25 issue of the *Fiery Cross* carried a story about a Klan rally near London, Ohio, where one thousand klansmen had gathered on a farm for a cross-burning ceremony. But they had been followed to the farm that night by two cars filled with men. Shots were fired from one of the cars toward the gathering of klansmen, but no one was injured.

One hundred twenty-nine crosses burned throughout Randolph County in east central Indiana on Tuesday evening, June 26. A story in the pro-Klan *Winchester Journal-Herald* told how "the streets of Winchester and of the surrounding towns were lighted from one end to the other. They [the crosses] were burned, several in each direction, from the center of the towns, north, east, south and west. Throughout the rural districts and on all roads in the county, crosses were seen burning, and in some parts of the county, they were elevated to a height of one hundred feet."

The Noblesville, Indiana, klansmen held another parade through that city's downtown, similar to the earlier one when they had burned a cross on the courthouse lawn. This one, on June 30, featured a hundred klansmen on horseback, the Muncie Klan marching band, and an initiation ceremony for more new members.

Preparations were being made for the great July 4 meeting in Kokomo, where Stephenson would formally receive his grand dragon title from Imperial Wizard Evans. But a preliminary rally on July 2 in Sebring, Ohio, drew in a crowd of 25,000. All roads near the town were marked with KKK signs and posters advertising the meeting. By 9:00 P.M., all the streets leading into the town were described as impassable. A parade of 2,000 klansmen marched through Sebring that night, with the Klan officers mounted on horseback at the head of the procession followed by a troupe of men carrying a huge American flag.

To attend rallies held in other states, some klansmen would go by car or train, traveling from one rally to another, making family vacations out of these extravaganzas of parades, fireworks, initiations, picnics, and cross burnings.

The great Kokomo rally represented the ultimate gathering, billed as a tri-state rally. It was the culmination of these many smaller rallies, one that would be remembered for years.[6]

Chapter Eleven

Kokomo, Indiana

July 4, 1923

The droning of the airplane's engine had been in Stephenson's ears for nearly an hour. The wind was whipping around his face, stinging the parts not protected by the thick aviator's goggles. Fumes from the engine were blown back in his face and a residue of engine oil and exhaust was settling on him. From time to time, the pilot would hurl an unintelligible comment over his shoulder, then the plane would dip crazily, as if it were being jerked on the end of an invisible string.

The pilot was a cocky young man up from the hills of Morgan County in southern Indiana, a fellow named Court Asher—ex-mechanic, ex-soldier, ex-bootlegger. He had recently been hired to serve as pilot and driver for the man who rode in the passenger seat. The plane was of the same vintage as those that had flown over the battlefields of Europe a few years earlier. It was an open-cockpit biplane with canvas wings and a fuselage covered with a golden-orange foil. It was a sparkling contraption. Asher assured his passenger that the plane was airworthy. But this came from a man who thought nothing of racing a motorcycle over dirt roads by night with a load of bootleg whiskey. In any case, this trip would not last much longer.[1]

Looking down from the cockpit, they could see the flat Indiana midlands stretched out to touch the horizon in all directions. There had been rain early in the morning, and now the day was somewhat overcast but pleasantly warm. The sun was shining through the hazy clouds, and a light breeze was blowing. It was a nearly perfect Fourth of July.

The land below them was a patchwork of cornfields and pasture land laced together with narrow country roads. As they flew low over the farms, they could see farmhands stop their work to stare up at the airplane, waving their arms at the sight.

As the small plane brought Stephenson and Asher closer to their destination, they could see that the roads below them were choked with cars and farm trucks traveling bumper-to-bumper. Dust clouds boiled up into the air along the county roads in all directions. Nearer the town, the airplane passed over railroad tracks and interurban lines. It was obvious that the trains were handling more than their usual holiday traffic. They could see long passenger trains with extra cars waiting to move into the station. This was going to be the biggest traffic jam in the history of Kokomo, Indiana.[2]

They were headed for a place called Melfalfa Park, three miles west of the city. It was easy to see the park from the air. Three large kites were flying in the breeze with an American flag suspended between them, high above the treetops. Nearer the park, the roads and even the fields were jammed with automobiles where people had simply left their machines and set out to walk the last mile or so to the park. It was only midmorning, but the park was already crowded. As the airplane made several passes over the park, the people looked up, shielding their eyes against the bright hazy sunlight to catch a glimpse of the plane. Some of them cheered when they saw the inscription on the lower set of wings: "Evansville K.K.K. No. 1."

On his final pass over the park, the pilot indicated with a hand signal that he was ready to make his descent. The nose of the plane tipped downward, and they came in very low over the trees. The plane jerked as some branches snagged the delicate fabric underside, tearing away some canvas and foil with a horrible rending sound. The pilot gripped his controls and steadied the plane, bringing it down safely on the grassy landing area that had been cleared away for them. Stephenson hauled himself out of the plane, a bit shaken but unharmed, trying quickly to erase any signs of nervousness.[3]

On this particular Fourth of July, Stephenson was near the peak of his power. He had flown to this gathering in Kokomo to be inaugurated grand dragon of the realm of Indiana, which would make him the official head of the Ku Klux Klan in the Hoosier state. Imperial Wizard Hiram Evans had come up from Atlanta to present Stephenson with his new title at what was planned as a three-state meeting of the Klan. At the same event, Stephenson would also be placed in charge of the Klan operations in twenty-two other northern states, a reward for his services and his organizational ability. It had been less than a year since Stephenson had helped Evans seize control of the national Klan. Now it was time for Stephenson to collect his laurels.

Many of the people gathered at this huge outdoor celebration were wearing the traditional Klan uniform with the white robes and tall pointed hoods. But many had taken off their masks because of the heat and humidity. It was like a gigantic county fair, attended only by members of the Klan. It was a family celebration that had been advertised for weeks in the Klan newspaper, the *Fiery Cross*, and thousands of klansmen had brought their wives and children to join in the fun. It had been billed as a meeting of klansmen from Indiana, Ohio, and Kentucky, but thousands had been pouring into the city since last evening, arriving by car and train from cities and towns all over the country.

Kokomo was a small town about sixty miles north of Indianapolis. Kokomo had been selected as the site of the rally because of its central location and because the first two syllables of its Indian name made Kokomo a perfect town for the Ku Klux Klan. On a normal day, Kokomo could boast about 30,000 residents. But this was not a normal day at all. Estimates of the crowd size varied wildly, but reporters for the state's leading newspapers put the figure as high as 200,000. Others said that it looked more like 10,000, certainly no more than 50,000. Others made guesses that fell between the extremes. In any case, it was the largest crowd at a single gathering in the town's history. Ultimately, this would be remembered as the largest meeting in the history of the Ku Klux Klan.

By the time he arrived, Stephenson had already missed the official opening of the day's events, which began with a nine o'clock welcoming invocation and sermon by the Reverend Kearns from Covington, Indiana. Kearns had talked to the crowd about how most of the disorder in America during the last forty years had been caused by people who had "entered the country without any thought of contributing anything to the building and betterment of the nation." Giving the audience time to consider this wisdom, a fifty-member boys' band from Alliance, Ohio, struck up "America," and their director led the crowd in patriotic singing. This was followed by the Ku Klux Klan band from New Castle, Indiana, which performed "The Star-Spangled Banner" and other patriotic pieces. Then came yet another preacher, the Reverend Everett Nixon from Kokomo, who led the klansmen and their families in prayer. Shortly after this, Stephenson made his dramatic entrance from the sky.[4]

What happened next would become part of the folklore that surrounds Stephenson. For half a century, most popular accounts of the Kokomo meeting have described Stephenson arriving at the park and climbing out of his plane fully clad in a purple Klan robe and hood. According to the story, he spoke to the throng, saying:

> My worthy subjects, citizens of the Invisible Empire, Klansmen all, greetings! It grieves me to be late. The President of the United States kept me unduly long counseling upon vital matters of state. Only my plea that this is the time and place of my coronation obtained for me surcease from his prayers for guidance. . . . Here in this uplifted hand, where all can see, I bear an official document addressed to the Grand Dragon, Hydras, Great Titans, Furies, Giants, Kleagles, King Kleagles, Exalted Cyclops, Terrors, and All Citizens of the Invisible Empire of the Realm of Indiana. . . . It is signed by Hiram Wesley Evans, Imperial Wizard, and duly attested. It continues me officially in my exalted capacity as Grand Dragon of the Invisible Empire for the Realm of Indiana. It so proclaims me by Virtue of God's Unchanging Grace. So be it.

He then launched into a long speech about the Constitution and "100 percent Americanism," after which the crowd went wild, showering him with money, jewelry, watches, and bracelets.

This little anecdote has made itself a permanent part of the Stephenson story. Unfortunately, there does not seem to be much truth to it. The story originally appeared in a 1928 article in the *Atlantic Monthly*, "Gentlemen from Indiana," by Morton Harrison. It was later picked up and repeated in Robert Coughlan's article "Konklave [sic] in Kokomo." Since then, the story has been repeated—and will probably continue to be repeated—by writers who focus their work on Stephenson and the Klan. But while the episode may have happened at some particular time, it almost certainly did *not* happen at Kokomo.

Even back in 1928, the editors of the *Atlantic Monthly* had the good sense to question the accuracy of the story. They added a footnote to the story, which dozens of journalists and scholars have apparently decided to ignore: "The testimony of eyewitnesses as to certain details of this assemblage is conflicting. Historians take note that the purple robe and the proclamation may have figured in later ceremonies, but in substance the report is accurate." In other words, Stephenson probably made a speech to some group similar to the one reported by Harrison, but it probably happened later.

This "historical myth" has at least one very obvious flaw. In it, Stephenson gets out of the plane and reads from a document that Evans did not present to him *until at least two or three hours later!*

But the myth is still important. That it has survived so many retellings is a strong statement about its value to the Stephenson story. It is, after all, a very good story—the idea of Stephenson telling a crowd of people that he had just rushed out of a meeting with President Warren Harding in order to attend their rally! The story illustrates the bravado and bluff, the incredible audacity that formed the heart of Stephenson's life. It is the type of story that, if it isn't true, then it should have been true. The idea that at least it might have happened later has always been a strong enough thread to keep it attached to Stephenson's story.

The best account of what really happened in Kokomo is that of John L. Niblack, who covered Stephenson's speech as a reporter for the *Indianapolis Times*. He insists that Stephenson wore a regular business suit instead of Klan robes, that there was no throwing of jewels and money, and that the size of the crowd was probably about ten thousand—a huge gathering, still, but smaller than some of the higher estimates.[5]

The Klan newspaper also carried a full account of the meeting, including the text of Stephenson's speech, but no mention is made of his invoking the president's name upon his arrival at the park.

The truth about what happened that day is, in some ways, more remarkable than the myth. It shows just how powerful the Klan was in Indiana in 1923. And it shows the scope of Stephenson's ambitions, hinting at the destiny he imagined for himself.

After a few brief remarks by other Klan organizers, the stage was turned over to Evans, who told the crowd that he had not come to announce any major programs, but simply to see for himself the amazing growth of the Klan in Indiana. He had also come to award official charters to ninety-two Klan organizations in the state. After delivering a brief speech, Evans called "The Old Man" up to the stage (note that even before this audience, Stephenson's real name was not to be spoken). Only a handful of those present knew "The Old Man's" real identity. Reporters from the major papers had been allowed to attend the meeting, but even they had been sworn to secrecy, agreeing not to reveal Stephenson's name in print.

Standing next to the most powerful klansman in the nation, Stephenson listened as Evans read the proclamation that made Stephenson grand dragon of Indiana. At the end of the announcement, Evans turned and presented Stephenson with the golden-orange robe and hood of the grand dragon's office. The crowd cheered. Court Asher had taken the plane back up into the sky and was now making low passes over the stage, displaying the "Evansville K.K.K. No. 1" slogan again and again. Thundering applause came up from the white-robed audience. Two representatives of the Indiana Klan stepped forward to present

Stephenson with gifts from the klansmen of Indiana: a gold medallion and a jeweled cross. Stephenson accepted these with a reasonable show of gratitude, then launched into a long speech, "Back to the Constitution."[6]

Stephenson often boasted that he was a "master of mass psychology," able to evaluate his audience and deliver his speech directly to them. He knew that his audience in Kokomo was a complex blend of small-town people, rural people, and some modern city types. He would try to give the Klan an air of respectability. He would let the wild-eyed amateurs sell the racial and ethnic hatred, allowing himself to reflect on the more refined aspects of the order.

So if anyone came to Kokomo expecting to hear "The Old Man's" tirade against the weaker races and inferior religions, they would have been disappointed. Stephenson did not even mention the Klan by name. Instead, he decided to talk about how American government had strayed from the intentions of the founding fathers. It was a bookish speech, more history lecture than crowd rouser. If any in the crowd were familiar with political philosophy and theory, they might have detected a curious, almost Socialist line of reasoning in some of Stephenson's suggestions for reforming government.

He began by talking in eloquent tones about the history of the Declaration of Independence, the Continental Congress, and the Constitution. In a fine, resonant voice that rang with emotion, he quoted at length the words of Franklin, Jefferson, Adams, and Paine, wrapping himself and his cause in their thoughts and ideas. It might have been a high school oratorical contest instead of a Klan meeting. He chose the most fiery passages from Paine's "Common Sense" and Patrick Henry's "Give me liberty or give me death" speech to the Virginia Assembly, delivering both a history lesson and a showman's version of the struggle for independence.

"I have studied the mind and motive of these constitutional builders," said Stephenson. "I want to bring them here and let them talk to you, through my humble interpretation, about their creation in its relations to our government and our public problems as they exist today." He then went on to enumerate the changes he claimed the founding fathers would support in calling for a new constitutional convention.

If it were up to him, Stephenson told the crowd, he would remove the spoils system from politics and eliminate corruption from government. He called for a homebound isolationist policy that would prevent what he called American imperialism abroad.

The electoral college would have to be eliminated, too, since its only purpose was "to nullify the sacred principle of the consent of the governed." Governmental units would be compelled, under his plan, to give a full disclosure of their operations, concealing nothing from the people. The national budget would have to be balanced each year, and deficit spending would be made illegal. Congress and the Supreme Court would have to be reorganized. He argued that something must be done to control inflation, "otherwise, in another fifty years, this nation will be experiencing all the agonies of a class conflict that can end only in economic chaos and political revolution. More and more will the great middle class be wiped out."

Stephenson was dealing with complex issues, things that most of his listeners probably didn't understand. But Stephenson was exercising his one great talent: convincing others of his own authority. He would stand before them and explain the need for change and the ways to go about it. If he could make these ordinary people understand the problems, why couldn't the politicians make the same sense of it and begin to solve these problems? Stephenson's philosophy may have been well over the heads of his audience, but his technique and delivery were not.

He went on to speak out against the "extreme militarists, headed by martial leaders whose self-interest lies in the parasitic growth of the army establishment." He called for a peacetime military that would work on public projects, such as engineering, construction, and water power developments. If the founders of the Constitution were here today, he said, they would outlaw war except in the cases of direct attack by hostile nations. "The solvency of the world, the sanctity and security, nay, the very existence of civilization, are involved in this problem!" he shouted.

He pointed to the recent rumors of what would become known as the Teapot Dome Scandal in the Warren Harding presidential administration as evidence of the need to clean up government corruption. In his plan, he felt that publication of all government activities was the key. He imagined a post for an official public printer. "The public printer would be a distinguished statesman, elevated to the cabinet, with importance second to none." Under this public printer, there would be a great federal organization with the "purpose and equipment necessary to prepare, print and publish . . . the complete unbiased truth with respect to all that government is and does." Probably fewer than a half dozen in the crowd knew that Stephenson had once made his living as a printer.

The present system of campaign contributions was at the root of all political corruption, he continued: "No individual or interest, directly or indirectly, should find it possible lawfully to contribute to any campaign fund. Easily workable instrumentalities and adequate finances should both be provided by the government. . . . Then a candidate would be responsible only to the public. No selfish interest, either political or predatory, could buy or pay for the representative of the people." He called for extreme punishments for public officials who violated the rules: "He should be publicly execrated, outlawed, and exiled, with his property confiscated to pay the public loss." [In just a few months, the irony of this speech would be apparent.]

Even if the crowd couldn't follow his complicated arguments, they were at least entertained by his stylish delivery. When they agreed on a point, they broke into wild applause. It was an enthusiastic reception for his first major speech as head of the state organization. It was also an impressive show of political talent, the speech that one might expect from a future governor or senator.

After more than an hour on the platform, Stephenson drew his speech to a close: "Individual billions cannot compare with a single citizen's share in a nation where the common welfare has been established and forever safeguarded by the intelligent, unselfish consent of the governed. 'Where there is no vision, the people perish.' Let that not be the epitaph of the American Republic!" The crowd roared, Stephenson bowed, and Indiana had its new grand dragon.

Now it was past noon and time to eat. Tables were lined up along the stream called Wildcat Creek that ran through the park. The long wooden tables were heaped high with mountains of meat, salads, and desserts, which the people waded through until they could eat no more. The Klan's publicity writers counted 6 tons of beef, 55,000 buns, and 2,500 pies, plus 5,000 cases of soda pop and near beer to wash it all down.

When the feeding was over, there were games for the younger klansfolk and sporting events for the adults. The sun and humidity drove many of the overstuffed klansmen back under the tall shade trees, where they fanned themselves with their programs and Klan brochures.

After this short break, the speeches resumed with an address from the head of the Queens of the Golden Mask, the women's auxiliary Stephenson began. She talked about the need for women to support the great work of the Klan. Following her speech, the crowd heard an Indianapolis attorney, billed as "the best lawyer in Indiana," speak about the legal justification of the

Klan. The lawyer defended the Klan, pointing to several Supreme Court decisions which supported discrimination between people of different races and colors.

While all this was going on, Stephenson left with some of his bodyguards, who had followed him to Kokomo by car. They drove to the Klan's headquarters in downtown Kokomo—private offices in the town's best hotel. There, Stephenson arranged to meet with some reporters for interviews. One of these, John Niblack of the *Indianapolis Times,* was only a year out of Indiana University. The *Times* was the only daily paper in Indianapolis in 1923 with a firmly anti-Klan editorial position. Niblack began questioning Stephenson with a rapid battery of questions, none designed to earn the new grand dragon's favor: What did he intend to do with the Catholics, blacks, and Jews? Did he intend to kill them, run them out, or live with them? What was the Klan's final objective? How much money did he expect to make out of it?

This was not the newspaper treatment that Stephenson wanted. He glared at Niblack and said, "Just a minute, young man. Just stop right there. You are a part of the national conspiracy to upset this Klan. I have been propounded this very same set of questions at least thirty different times in thirty different states. . . . I can see you are just a bigot. You are not for us, you are against us. So just get out of here." He motioned for his guards to escort Niblack out of the room. With that, Stephenson decided that the interviews were over for the day.[7]

At Melfalfa Park, the day-long festival was also coming to a close. A couple of ministers who preached the Klan's gospel of "100 percent Americanism" were still lecturing to whoever would stay to listen, but the crowd was thinning out after a day of so many long speeches. Besides, there was still the great parade to get ready for and the gigantic fireworks display after that.

That night, the streets of Kokomo were filled with thousands of white-robed klansmen and their families. These numbers were swelled by the many curious onlookers who had come downtown to see the strange spectacle for themselves. What they saw was a pageant most would remember the rest of their lives.

The parade began with the high Klan officials, mounted on horseback, riding down the street. Their horses pranced to the blaring music of a forty-piece band. The tune was the Klan's unofficial anthem, "Onward, Christian Soldiers." Behind them came the first of a dozen floats. Wives and daughters of the klansmen were riding on the floats, each of which presented people in costume to illustrate the values of the Klan: a hooded klansman protecting a virtuous maiden from an attacking black man; warding off the evil Catholic "papists"; and defending the flag against foreigners. Interspersed throughout the parade column were more Klan bands from cities and towns all over the Midwest—nine bands in all. One klansman marched the length of the parade route high above the crowd on a pair of stilts. A group from Tipton, Indiana, drove an open car with a large bell and chimes playing music. There were more klansmen riding on horseback, and still others marched carrying a huge American flag that stretched across the street from curb to curb. The parade extended for two miles and took more than half an hour to pass.

The purpose of the parade, besides publicizing the Klan's strength, was to raise money for a so-called "Klan hospital." At that time, the only hospital in Kokomo was operated by Catholics. This meant that "100 percent American" Protestants had to go for treatment to a hospital that owed its allegiance to a "foreign pope." So the klansmen marched through the streets with the cry "Give to the hospital! Give to the hospital!" And bystanders tossed contributions into the outstretched American flags that the klansmen carried. By the end of the parade, more than fifty thousand dollars was collected. (But only two weeks later, the people of Kokomo would learn that none of this money was ever turned over to the hospital committee.)

The parade stopped at Foster Park, where the klansmen lit one of their ceremonial fiery crosses, a large wooden cross wrapped with kerosene-soaked burlap. They sang hymns around the burning cross, including the Klan standard, "The Old Rugged Cross," then listened to a few more speeches. As the flames began to die down, some of the crowd began to head home. But most got in their cars and drove back out to Melfalfa Park for the giant fireworks display.

Torches lit the way through the park to a clearing, where two giant wood-and-paper horses stood rearing up on their back legs. The horses were painted to match the Klan's official emblem: a night-riding klansman carrying a torch astride a white stallion. Between the two horses was a fiery cross standing sixty feet in the air, the biggest cross anyone had ever seen in this part of the country. The Klan put on a spectacular fireworks show, with exploding rockets and flares lighting the sky above the park. The pointed hoods of the klansmen were silhouetted against the bright bursts of light and color. The blasts of the loudest rockets reminded many of the nighttime shellings they had endured in the French countryside during World War I. A rapid-fire chain of explosions came near the end of the show. Then a ring of klansmen picked up their torches and marched to where the unlit cross stood. At a signal, they touched their flames to the cross, and with a roar, the fire swept up the cross, leaping up into the night. The burning cross could be seen for miles around the park, proof of the Klan's new power in the North.

The fireworks brought the great Klan celebration to a close. As the tired klansmen guided their wives and children back to their cars or trains for the long journey home, they could look back on a day that promised to be only the beginning for a new and powerful voice in the land. Stephenson could bask in the warm glow of success, having finally made a positive step toward the political power he felt he deserved. The new grand dragon could now begin to plan the strategies that would make his name known throughout the nation.

It is easy to imagine these rallies as all serious business, bogged down in ritual and mystic mumbo jumbo. But they apparently were more like family reunions or festivals with more time devoted to the fireworks and parades than the actual business of the Klan. One ninety-one-year-old Howard County farmer who attended the 1923 Kokomo rally remembered it more than a half century later as "a real nice day . . . a real good party . . . we had a good time." [Of Stephenson's dramatic appearance by airplane and the ringing "Back to the Constitution" speech, he remembered nothing.][8]

At the Kokomo rally, many people gathered at the park in the morning for the opening festivities, listened to the speeches, then went downtown—about three miles away—for the parade through the city, back out to the park that evening, then back home. For some it was obviously several miles of marching, all in the name of the "Invisible Empire."

Robert Coughlan, in his account "Konklave in Kokomo," vividly recalled one image that stuck in his eight-year-old mind the night of the rally:

> As we sat on our front porch after watching the parade, we could still see klansmen of our neighborhood trickling home. Some still wore their regalia, too tired to bother taking it off before they came into sight. Others carried little bundles of white: they were the ones who still made some pretense of secrecy about being members. One of the last to come down the street was old Mrs. Crousore, who lived a few doors away. Her white robe hung damply, and her hood was pushed back. As she climbed her steps and sank solidly into a rocking chair on her porch, we could hear her groan, "Oh, my God, my feet hurt!"[9]

Chapter Twelve

The Ladies' Man

1923

After his July 4 installation as grand dragon of the northern realm, Stephenson began to display his power. Two days later, he asked his attorney, Robert Marsh, to draw up a contract to purchase a home. He had his eye set on a respectable piece of property, one of the large old houses in Irvington. Built in 1889 on one of the winding streets just east of Butler College—later Butler University—the house at 5432 University Avenue had been the home of Col. William Henry Harrison Graham and was later rented as Butler's Kappa Kappa Gamma sorority house. But now Stephenson extended a generous offer to purchase the home outright, and Ellen Graham, Colonel Graham's widow, could not afford to refuse. On July 6, 1923, she signed the contract, and the house changed hands.

The home was a good one but unremarkable compared to other homes in the well-to-do Irvington community. Stephenson would soon change that. He quickly set about transforming this rather ordinary house into a near-copy of the Klan's Imperial Palace in Atlanta. He hired a contractor to remodel the house into a classic southern mansion.

As the neighborhood watched in amazement, the one-story porch was stripped away. Four huge columns were added, giving the house a two-story portico. Inside, the walls in the front room were removed, doubling the size of the living room. A pair of columns that matched the ones on the front porch were brought inside to form a massive entryway. Behind the property was a three-car garage with a servants' quarters above the garage. Stephenson also added a kennel for his German shepherd dogs. It was a large house, but Stephenson needed such a home to fit in with his political plans. The $22,000 remodeling job would make the house into an eye-catching mansion, changing the face of both the property and the neighborhood.[1]

Stephenson's choice of Irvington as a place to make his home may have been his attempt to place himself among the "better people." Scattered around the campus of Butler College were the homes of men such as Hilton U. Brown, editor of the *Indianapolis News,* and "Kin" Hubbard, the nationally known cartoonist and humorist, as well as a host of prominent doctors, lawyers, politicians, architects, artists, and university scholars. It was a quiet town that had gradually become a suburb of Indianapolis as the city grew east and encircled it.

The locals had always fought the good fight against "demon liquor," so there were no taverns in their town. There simply wasn't much of a market for liquor, scandal, or violence in the town. There was, on the other hand, plenty of room for religion, with Methodists, Presbyterians, Disciples of Christ, and Catholics all represented by churches within the neighborhood. It was not without certain ironies that Stephenson settled among such upright and God-fearing neighbors.

Stephenson was fabulously wealthy now, and he wanted everyone to know it. A report of Klan membership in Indiana alone showed that between June 25, 1922, and July 21, 1923, Stephenson managed to bring in 117,969 new Klan members plus 724 members counted as "honorary petitioners." (The 724 figure may be the number of Klan ministers, since many reports mention that Stephenson allowed free membership for ministers.) As grand dragon, Stephenson would have pocketed commissions amounting to several thousand dollars for these new members, along with his share of the profits from the sales of robes, handbooks, and paraphernalia. He would soon be a millionaire on his grand dragon's income alone.[2]

In his garage, Stephenson parked his sleek Packard sedan, presented as a gift from the Muncie Klan (and paid for from the members' dues). He also owned a Cadillac and a large Lexington touring car, ideal for taking long trips through the countryside with room for several guests.

Stephenson was also enlarging his staff again. His personal secretary and valet, Fred Butler, lived in the new home in Irvington with Stephenson. In addition to the chauffeur known as Terrible Tommy, Stephenson also hired a former deputy sheriff from Evansville, Earl Klinck, to serve as a bodyguard and brought on another tough-looking man, Earl Gentry, to help with guard duty. Howard Bennett, another ex-policeman, served as both a chauffeur and bodyguard. Bennett's wife, Blanche, worked as a housekeeper and cook. A young man in his twenties,

Ernest W. "Shorty" DeFriese, worked part-time as chauffeur and messenger. Other men who served as bodyguards, such as Foster Strader and Court Asher, did not live in the house but were frequent guests of Stephenson. The rest of the staff worked on a live-in basis, assuring Stephenson of their round-the-clock availability. An army of other guests, stenographers, and assistants drifted in and out of the big house—all part of the framework of Stephenson's operation.[3]

The display of wealth did not end here. He furnished his house with expensive Oriental carpets and purchased a concert grand piano for entertaining guests at the huge parties he hosted. His ultimate extravagance, however, was a $55,000, 98-foot yacht, the Reomar II, which he anchored at Toledo, Ohio, on Lake Erie. He used the boat for private parties, wining and dining various politicians and government officials. Built in 1911, the boat had been made for a famous car builder, R. E. Olds (the name Reomar comes from "R. E. Olds Marine"). A slightly larger sister ship, the Reomar III, would later be owned by the Chicago gang boss, Al Capone.[4]

Stephenson had arrived in society. He had all the trappings of the rich. He also had the women.

Always the ladies' man, Stephenson's wealth made him doubly attractive to the opposite sex. Stephenson ran through a wild array of young women, seducing them in a moment, and making and breaking wedding engagement promises the way other men handled luncheon appointments. If things had not worked out as they eventually did for Stephenson, he might have ended his days on a slab in a morgue, the victim of an angry husband or an outraged father. He saved all the letters that women wrote to him and kept them in the same black, metal lockboxes where he collected the telltale receipts and signed pledges of politicians.[5]

Shortly after he left Violet, he hired a twenty-year-old woman to be his secretary in December 1922. Two months later, he took her to work for him in Columbus, Ohio, where he was setting up new offices for the Klan in Ohio. They began dating, going to movies and dinner parties together. Once he invited her to accompany him on a yachting party with his guests: Indiana Secretary of State Ed Jackson, attorney Robert Marsh, Imperial Wizard Hiram Evans, and their wives. Stephenson made love to her, presented her with a diamond ring, and promised to marry her.

They were together at the time of the Kokomo klonvocation. As the woman later told police investigators, "About July

4th, 1923, he did try to have sexual intercourse with me, once in his machine, out along the road, not very late at night. I never had to fight him off with my hands—I could talk him out of it every time. Stephenson is a beast when he is drunk. He is always accusing someone of stealing something when he is under the influence of liquor."

A month earlier, she had been in a similar situation with him in Franklin County, Ohio, on the outskirts of Columbus. On that occasion, however, deputy sheriff Charles M. Hoff and special deputy Ernest White were patrolling the area in response to complaints from residents about "immoral parties" that were being held late at night. Driving along the county road, Hoff noticed a Cadillac coupe parked with its lights off. He stopped to investigate and later described what he saw: "I saw a man and a lady in the car. . . . They were both in the back part of the car. The young lady had her clothes up above where you could see part of her body was exposed. The man had his clothes unbuttoned, his trousers unbuttoned, his coat off, and in his shirt sleeves. . . . I asked them what was going on, and he says, 'Why there is nothing going on.' I says, 'By the looks of things, it look like there has something been going on. . . . I told him they were under arrest for parking their car on the highway without displaying the proper lights."

At this point, White takes up the story: "Mr. Hoff asked him what he was doing, and he said he was just sitting here in the car. And Mr. Hoff says, 'What are you doing there with your pants unbuttoned?' and he [Stephenson] reaches around and grabbed that girl's hand and says, 'My God, would you insult this girl?' He said, 'Do you see that ring, diamond ring?' He says, 'I am going to marry this girl; we are engaged.' Hoff says, 'I don't care if you are married now.' He said, 'You have violated the law; you don't have no headlights or taillight."

Hoff continues, "He walked around back of the car and asked me if there couldn't be anything done, because he had a respectable lady with him. He said he was an official and couldn't afford to have all this notoriety and publicity." Hoff demanded to know the official's name. "At first he refused to give it. I says, 'If you don't want to give me your name, I will drive you down to jail and I know I will find out what your name is then. . . . He studied for a little bit, and finally pulled out a card bearing his name."

Stephenson pleaded guilty to the parking citation and a charge of indecent exposure on the highway. A justice of the peace, J. J. Glen, charged him $17.50 in fines plus costs.

The woman was not charged but was given a scolding and sent home.

Her life with Stephenson quickly became unbearable. "All the time I was engaged to him, I knew I would never marry him," she said. "The engagement was broken while I was in California because I heard he had been running around with women."

Less than a year after their engagement was broken, she saw Stephenson once more, sometime in May or June of 1924:

> I called him up as there were business difficulties. I told him to come around and take me out. He said he wouldn't. He said it was some plan of Evans and Bossett [sic] trying to frame him. [By that time, Stephenson had made his break with the imperial wizard, and the Indiana Klan was under the control of a new grand dragon, Walter Bossert.]
>
> He asked me who I had in the house. He came around finally. He didn't come in the house. We took a ride in his machine. I had been sick. We got in a quarrel over the Klan because he said I was working with the Klan. I was nervous and sick and crying and he wouldn't take me back home. Mr. and Mrs. Danner, Margaret Reynolds, were staying at Stephenson's home. He took me to his home and they put me to bed and gave me some kind of tablets. The tablets put me to sleep. The next day I made them call Mother and she came at once and stayed with me. My condition was that I would sleep awhile and come to again. They didn't call a Doctor until after my mother came and took me home. I don't know whether or not he had intercourse while I was unconscious. . . . He got in bed with me when I was more or less conscious, after taking the tablets. I said to him, "If you do anything to me, I will kill you, Stephenson." If he had done anything to me I would kill him. This was while in bed at Stephenson's house and before Mother came.

The incident with the woman in the back of the Cadillac was not the only time that Stephenson had trouble with the law in Columbus, Ohio. He usually stayed at the Deschler Hotel on the northwest corner of the city square in Columbus whenever he was visiting the Klan offices there. On January 5, 1924, the Deschler's house detective, Joseph A. Cleary, was eating lunch just after noon when he was called by the hotel manager to investigate a room disturbance on one of the upper floors. Cleary and the manager went upstairs to investigate. Later, Cleary described what he saw:

> I went up with him to this room and found three men. One of them, whom I afterward learned to be D. C. Stephenson, was intoxicated as drunk as any man I ever saw, and was

standing by the bed with a death-grip on the foot of the bed. The other two men were intoxicated. Their names were later given as Danner and Tatum. I think Danner was a former officer on the Columbus police force. A large mirror in the room was broken, some chairs smashed, and the room presented evidences of a wild party.

I was informed that they had sent for a manicurist and a barber to come to the room; that they had given the barber enough liquor to intoxicate him; and that a little later, when the other men were out of the room, Stephenson attempted to have intercourse with the manicurist, and that upon her refusal to permit it, he had thrown her from the room, and when a bell-boy, at her request, had gone back into the room to get her tray, Stephenson had struck him several times. I myself saw the bell-boy, and he had two large knots, one on the temple, and the other on the other side of the face back of the ear, and was at that time irrational.

Cleary arrested the trio, after a struggle with Stephenson. "One of the men kept insisting that he would not be taken down to the city prison by any other than a uniformed man. After the struggle, the police were called, and Officers Eden and Gillian took the men to headquarters."

Later, the manicurist told her version of what had happened in the room:

I went up with my tray to give him [Stephenson] a manicure. There were two other men in the room, one of them in pajamas, and Stephenson was in his pajamas, too. . . . Stephenson had put in a long distance call to Indianapolis, and he talked but he could not hear very good, and the other man went out of the room. They had all been drinking, and were talking very loud and made a lot of noise. So they went out and shut the door. After he talked on the phone, I proceeded to get ready to manicure him. All the time, he was talking and carrying on in a rather undesirable way, but I didn't pay any attention to that, because I was there on business, and tried to go ahead with it. There were three full quarts of whiskey on the dresser that I saw in his room. . . . He offered me a drink, and I told him that I didn't use it and that I didn't want any. . . . I had finished manicuring one hand, and then he got up to get a drink of whiskey and when I told him that I didn't want any, he came over and grabbed me. He said that he would give me a hundred dollars if I would allow him to have intercourse with me. Of course, he was more rude than I care to be in expressing it. . . . I told him that I was not in the habit of being insulted by anyone like that, and he said, "You little ___ __ __ _____, you will or I'll kill you." And then he went over to his grip, I thought to get a gun. Then, while he was doing that, I went out the door

that led to the hall outside. . . . The other two men who were
in the other room came out; and I was crying and they said,
"Don't pay any attention to him; he is a good fellow; he is
drunk; he is all right when he is sober." They said, "You go
downstairs and don't bother about it."

But the manicurist went down and got the bellboy, the
manager, and the house detective to straighten things out. It
took Stephenson's attorney one day to get him out of the Columbus jail. To avoid publicity, the hotel and the manicurist refused
to press charges against him, but the story still managed to
make the Sunday editions of the *Ohio State Journal* and the *Columbus Dispatch*, where the incident was carried to shocked
klansmen all over the state. Could this really be the man who
was in charge of the Klan?

Stephenson simply shrugged off the entire episode. A
few weeks later, in mid-January 1924, he was introduced to a
young intern at Methodist Hospital in Indianapolis. A small-town
woman, her father ran a small business in Anderson, Indiana,
and Stephenson's fast life-style impressed her. On her first visit
to his home, she noticed that several other party guests had
brought their own illegal liquor. Stephenson invited her to accompany him to the January 26 official opening party of the new
Indianapolis Athletic Club, one of the top society events of the
year. He had already been accepted as a member of the private,
downtown men's club. Attorney Robert Marsh and his wife made
the outing to the new club gala a foursome. The well-dressed
couples, the long lines of expensive cars parked outside, the glit-
tering ballroom filled with music and dancing—all must have
made a tremendous impression on Stephenson's latest conquest.

"I became engaged to Stephenson after that, and he asked
me to marry him. We were engaged for some time, but broke it
off in April, early in the month," she later recalled when questioned by investigators.

This relationship was not marked with threats or violence
as were the earlier affairs. But Stephenson was at his pompous
worst with the young intern. "He has told me about his power in
Indiana," she said. "He said once that he could elect anyone he
pleased for governor. I have heard him say that he had great political power and that the courts always favored a man who had
political power. He told me that he had had affairs with many
women, and that he had been married. He always carried a gun
when I knew him."

Their relationship was, however, marked with correspondence, mostly letters she wrote to him after the engagement was

broken. Again, he saved the pathetic collection of love letters as he had all the others.

On May 9, 1924, she wrote, telling him that she had "a good chance for three years at the University of Minnesota—if you have had a change of heart I think I shall take the offer." Two days later, she wrote that "I don't want to get married and don't believe you do either. Want to go somewhere else and let loose. If you won't join me someone else will." But two days after that, she was having second thoughts, admitting that her last letter was rather foolish and stating, "I am not going to weep my heart out because you care nothing for me. Have known all along you saw a great deal of Miss Andrews." With that outpouring complete, the young intern apparently passed entirely out of his life.

The last of these brief affairs occurred later in the fall of 1924. It was October, and Stephenson was hosting a huge party at his Irvington home. The incident involved a young woman who was employed to act in a motion picture about the Klan (no record of any finished film was ever found). The actress attended the party as a guest of an attorney friend of Stephenson's. She later described the scene with about forty or fifty couples who kept coming and going from the house throughout the evening. Drinks were served, and Stephenson hired a three-piece band from the Hotel Washington to provide dance music for the evening. Of the people from Stephenson's staff, she remembered meeting Fred Butler, the valet, and the two bodyguards, Earl Gentry and Earl Klinck. "I think everyone who worked in Stevenson's [sic] office carried a gun. I don't recall seeing him personally with a gun, but all his men did."

Her attorney friend had too much to drink and was taken to one of the guest rooms to sleep it off. Another friend of the attorney's volunteered to take the woman home whenever she was ready to leave. By half past midnight, she decided that she was ready to go.

> I went up to get my wraps and after I had started down I remembered I had forgotten a shorthand book and went back to get it and just as I got down the steps Mr. Stevenson was coming in the front door and I thought I would go up and tell him what a very enjoyable evening I had had. As I was standing there he took me by the arm and pushed me to the back door and told me that Margaret Reynolds was out in the rear of the house crying. I asked him what she was crying for and he said he didn't know. He shoved me out the door by that time and onto the driveway. . . .
> I began to grow alarmed by that time and called to [a friend] to follow me. She got as far as the back door and

someone stopped her. . . . I was pushed out into his garage and up in a room and locked the door. . . . I was knocked down several times, bitten and I would say had general cruel treatment. . . . He first tried to force himself on me and then tried to be nice. When he saw he couldn't get what he wanted, he said that he should kill me. I told him to go ahead and do it, that I would get the gun for him. After he got tired and in a stupor, he said, "Now you get out of here." And he pushed me out the door and half way down the steps.

Klinsch [Klinck] and a youngster whom they called Shorty [DeFriese]. These two and Mr. Johnson [the attorney's friend] were waiting for me and Klinsch seemed very concerned and he and Shorty asked me how badly I was hurt. Mr. Klinsch had come to the door and Stevenson had told him to go away. I called to him, but he evidently did not hear me because he didn't come in. I asked him why he didn't come when I called and he said he didn't hear me and if he had he would have come in.

Again, there is a pattern of guns, intoxication, biting, and attempted rape, all things that would soon mark Stephenson's record in a far more serious case.

Stephenson always claimed that his imprisonment had resulted from the efforts of Imperial Wizard Evans and other enemies inside the Klan to frame him. Many people believed him and held to his claims of innocence for many years. Certainly it is worth noting that the first of these episodes—the arrest in the car near Columbus on June 10, 1923—came less than two weeks after Stephenson had locked horns with Evans at the Willard Hotel meeting in Washington, D.C. Had Evans simply decided to "hang a woman on Stephenson" as many later claimed? It seems doubtful that anyone could have put him in such perilous situations not once but a half dozen times with so many women and in so many different circumstances and locations—all with the same repeated patterns of seduction and assault. It is difficult to believe, after studying so many of these cases, that Stephenson was not to blame for the events that later took him to prison.

Chapter Thirteen

Brief Glory

Summer 1923

Stephenson's first month as grand dragon in July 1923 was a whirlwind of activity. Besides the grand dragon's post, Imperial Wizard Evans appointed Stephenson king kleagle of Kentucky, Maine, Michigan, Minnesota, New Jersey, Ohio, and Wisconsin.

The day after Evans sent these orders to Stephenson, Indianapolis was rocked by its first incident of Klan-related violence. It was Tuesday, July 10, and the Klan had planned to hold a cross-burning ceremony at the Westview Baptist Church's carnival and social. Mayor Lew Shank was under pressure from both sides. The American Unity League's *Tolerance* was suggesting complicity between city hall and the Klan, although the Klan's *Fiery Cross* expressed hope that Shank would ease back on issues like the anti-mask parade ordinance. Shank knew he had to make a stand one way or the other on the Klan issue. He chose to fight.

The temperature had hovered around ninety degrees all that day, and by early evening it was still hot. But a crowd of seven thousand people still gathered at the Westview Baptist Church to hear Klan lecturer Fred B. Griffiths. His topic was the usual material on "100 percent Americanism" with a cross lighting scheduled immediately after the talk. Instead, several city policemen arrived and began giving orders for the klansmen not to light the cross. The crowd became angry at this. The Reverend Luther B. Jones urged the people to keep calm and "remember our pledge to uphold the laws." At that, the klansmen picked up their cross and marched along Morris Street about a mile from the church to what was then the city limits. There, they placed the cross on soil a few steps beyond the jurisdiction of the Indianapolis Police Department and held their ceremony.

But the west side Indianapolis klansmen were still not happy with the interruption of their meeting. One week later, on July 18, they lit a large electric cross, which did not violate the city's cross *burning* ordinance, close to the site of the Westview

Church incident. Shortly after the cross was lit, a crowd of five thousand people gathered about a block away and set fire to a traditional wood-and-gasoline cross. City officials decided to meet the Klan's challenge by dispatching fire trucks to the scene to extinguish the burning cross. Here, the firemen—most of whom were Catholic—encountered a barrage of rocks and sticks thrown at them by the angry crowd. One fireman was injured. The department called for support from the police, who arrived with revolvers drawn. Two klansmen—a truck repairman and a Republican committeeman—were arrested and taken away.

Unrelenting, the Klan fired up yet another cross the following evening in a nearby schoolyard. Again, the fire department was dispatched to put out the flames. Mayor Shank angrily demanded the loyalty of every man in his cabinet "regardless of their membership in secret organizations" and swore to continue fighting the Klan.[1]

This controversy allowed the Klan recruiters to paint the city administration as "pro-Catholic" and "anti-Klan." The headlines that these incidents produced in the local press made the Klan seem more attractive to people who were its most likely members.

Stephenson left Indianapolis during this cross-burning controversy on Thursday, July 12, and headed for the Ohio klonvocation at Buckeye Lake, several miles east of Columbus. This meeting was to be similar in style to the July 4 celebration in Kokomo, but this time it was sponsored by the Klans of Columbus, Lancaster, Newark, Springfield, and Zanesville, Ohio. Both Stephenson and Evans were scheduled to appear as speakers.[2]

The village of Buckeye Lake was a quiet summer resort in 1923. Situated on the north shore of a 3,300-acre lake, the village had a year-round population of about two hundred. In the summer months, though, the village swelled with the arrival of vacationing boaters and fishers. A yacht club was located near the middle of the lakeshore. Stephenson rented a large boat there for his summer outings (the Reomar II was too large to carry overland to the lake). There was also a dance hall, known as the Pier Ballroom, and a large amusement park.

When the *Fiery Cross* announced that Buckeye Lake would be the site of the three-state Klan klonkave, the residents of the tiny town were both shocked and excited at the prospects. How could they possibly serve so many klansmen from all over Indiana, Ohio, and Kentucky? Even in peak season, they never had as many people as the Klan was now predicting would attend the July meeting. On the other hand, even if it was crowded, it would be more business than they had ever seen before and the biggest thing that was ever likely to happen in the village.

When the klansmen began to arrive, they came by car, truck, and train. The interurban lines brought klansmen in from cities and towns all over Ohio. Full trainloads came from places like Columbus, Canton, and Akron. Private rail cars carried klansmen from more distant points all over the Midwest. The fancy train cars were parked on sidings along the main road leading north out of the town, forming a gaudy line of luxury almost a mile long, all decorated with banners to declare their various points of origin. Automobiles were parked in every vacant lot and yard in town. The sight of thousands of white-sheeted klansmen and their families cavorting around the lakeside would be remembered generations later by the people who were there.

Russ Walters, twenty-four that summer, was working in his father's local icehouse. The arrival of fifteen thousand klansmen in mid-July meant that the demand for ice would go right through the roof. Walters had worked in his father's business since he was old enough to carry a pair of the heavy ice tongs. He helped harvest the ice in the winter, cutting three-hundred-pound blocks out of the lake, then storing the ice in large warehouses, packing it in sawdust to keep it from melting.

But the Klan arrived with only a few weeks' warning. The village didn't have much chance to prepare for such a sudden arrival. The Walters' ice supply was quickly exhausted by the hot, sweltering klansmen and their families. Walters drove his father's truck all over Licking County trying to find more ice. After each trip back, there were still more cries for the huge chunks of ice. Back out he would go, driving farther and farther each time to find warehouses that could spare some ice. Years later, sitting on his front porch on a crisp October morning, Walters recalled that weekend in 1923 as the busiest time he ever spent in the ice business.[3]

Charlie Essex was nineteen when the Klan came to Buckeye Lake. He remembers the incredible crowd: "You could put your finger in any spot," he said, "and there was a klansman."

The klansmen who came to Buckeye Lake were, according to Essex, "the most orderly bunch of people I've ever seen. They didn't get into fights and they didn't go around tearing up property." During the four-day meeting, he recalls that "they burned crosses north of the lake on the Neel Farm and east of the park on the Bounds Farm." The cross burnings were impressive nighttime ceremonies calculated to awe both klansmen and townsfolk.

Like Walters, Charlie Essex said he joined the Klan because "it was easier to join the Klan than it was to *not* join them."[4]

As Walters recalled, "I paid my dues to join 'em, but I never went to more than one of their meetings. It just wasn't smart to not join 'em—so many other people belonged to the Klan then. I never even put on my robe. There was a boy over here a-ways who really liked it all, so I gave him my robe for him to wear. That was the last I ever saw of it."

The town had prepared for meetings, cross burnings, bands, and festivities. But they hadn't planned for the trash and litter that came with fifteen thousand vacationing klansmen. "They were real orderly," said Essex, "but when they left, all the fence rows around here for miles were white with trash, piled up with trash that had blown up against the fences. It took a long time to clean it all up."

Stephenson did not spend much time preparing for the Buckeye Lake meeting. For his speech, he simply reread the "Back to the Constitution" address he had given at Kokomo. After the speech, the Ohio klansmen presented their new king kleagle with a large diamond ring and an inscribed gold watch. During the evening klavern meeting, fifteen hundred new candidates were brought forward to become members under the flame of the burning cross. The only mishap of the evening was the death of a sixty-three-year-old klansman from a combination of heat and rheumatism.[5]

Early on Sunday morning, at about 3:30 A.M., Stephenson was seized by one of his typical urges. On this trip, he had brought along four secretaries. One was an eighteen-year-old stenographer who later told what happened in the private cottage Stephenson had rented for them by the lake.

"He came into my room about 3:30 o'clock, a.m. He was clothed in his underwear. He was intoxicated. When I heard him coming into the room, I thought it was one of the other girls, but when I realized it was he, I jumped from the bed. He tried to kiss me, put his arms around me and told me it seemed every one in the office had gone back on him but myself. He tried to force me on the bed. He then released me and left the room." No charges were filed, Stephenson never mentioned the incident to anyone, and the case was forgotten—or nearly so.[6]

Imperial Wizard Evans left the Buckeye Lake meeting a day early, since he was scheduled to lead a meeting of all the Klan's grand dragons—billed as the first annual meeting—in Asheville, North Carolina. The first day of Evans's meeting, July 15, overlapped with the last day of the Buckeye Lake klonvocation, and Evans knew that his presence was required in Asheville, where there was much tension between the different Klan factions.

The newest grand dragon, however, did not go to Asheville. Stephenson may have begged off the trip citing the pressures of local Klan business. After two full weeks of "klonvocating"—and chasing his young secretaries—he was probably ready for a rest. Instead, he sent Judge Charles Orbison to represent him.

There is no complete record of Stephenson's activities during the next month. It is, of course, a matter of historical record that President Warren G. Harding died in San Francisco on August 2. And it is known that a large group of klansmen went to Washington to attend the funeral. As a national officer, Stephenson was probably among them. While Harding had never publicly given his active support of the Klan, he had certainly never spoken out sharply against it. Once, in the summer just before his death, Harding made a veiled reference at a Shriners' convention about how fraternal organizations should operate within the framework of the law. This was viewed by some as a mild slap by the president against the Klan. For the most part, however, Harding had tried to stay out of the Klan's way, providing nearly the best kind of presidential relationship the Klan could have wanted.

Stephenson spent the rest of late July and early August playing with his newest toy—the yacht Reomar II—on Lake Erie. Court Asher later recalled that it was during August that Stephenson threw a huge yachting party, inviting several politicians and their wives aboard the boat. Among those on the guest list were Ed Jackson, Indiana secretary of state; James "Sunny Jim" Watson, the U.S. senator from Indiana; Victor Donahey, governor of Ohio; John Duvall, the Marion County treasurer from Indianapolis; Imperial Wizard Evans; and some U.S. congressmen, along with several judges and some state legislators from Indiana and Ohio.

A Klan parade in the steel town of Carnegie, Pennsylvania, which ended in violence and death, interrupted the idyllic life of cruising the lake. On August 25, word came to Stephenson that Evans had gone to the suburban town outside Pittsburgh to participate in the town's parade and initiation ceremony. A Klan turnout of ten thousand had been expected, and there had been rumors all week of possible violence because the town was evenly divided between Catholics and Protestants. Just before the marchers were ready to step off at the start of the parade, word came that the mayor of Carnegie had refused to grant the Klan a parade permit. Pennsylvania Grand Dragon Sam Rich huddled with Evans and other Klan organizers. They decided to go ahead with the parade without a permit.

An angry crowd gathered on a bridge that led into the town to block the path of the Klan parade. The klansmen simply marched past and down toward another bridge, but they found that one was also barricaded. The klansmen pushed their way through the barricades and marched into the town of Carnegie. They were met by a hail of rocks and sticks hurled by an angry mob of several hundred who had vowed to stop the Klan parade in its tracks. Police tried to step in, but the situation exploded into a full-scale riot.

The angry klansmen fought back the assaults of the rock throwers and pushed their way into Carnegie, down one block, then halfway down another. Suddenly, there was gunfire. One klansman fell down in the street. His fellow marchers carried him to a nearby doctor's office, but Thomas Abbott, shot through the temple, was already dead.

The marchers regrouped. Some wanted to get guns of their own and go back to settle the score. Evans and the others convinced them it would be wisest to leave quietly and quickly. Within a few minutes, the mobs on both sides dispersed, and the Carnegie riot was over. The toll: one dead and several others injured on both sides by rocks and debris. The anti-Klan forces declared it a victory, having stopped the Klan's celebration.[7]

Stephenson was not in Carnegie the day of the riot, but he got in his car and drove over to survey the situation as soon as he heard of it. In the time it took him to get there, the situation took care of itself, except for several cases of rattled nerves and the bereaved mourners of the young klansman. Stephenson's presence there was simply an appearance, nothing more.

Stephenson was not well loved by the klansmen in Pennsylvania. He had come into their state and tried to change the focus of the Klan from a fraternal order into a political order. As one klansman, A. L. Cotton, told historian Emerson H. Loucks in 1930, Stephenson tried to change too much too quickly:

> When D. C. Stephenson came in we were ordered to call in our rituals, altar equipment, and paraphernalia. Meetings were to be held monthly instead of weekly. Stephenson told us that the oath could be administered anywhere. The Klan was supposed to be "a movement" not "an Order." Now, everybody was supposed to buy robes. So the five dollars was

just added to the initiation fee and the robe was sent auto-
matically. The price of the robe was even raised to $6.50 for a
short time. Incidentally, we found out afterwards that the extra $1.50 was to be divided equally between the Kleagle who
got the member and the King Kleagle, [Sam] Rich, but Rich
kept it all.

We did call in the rituals for about six weeks. During
that time, progress virtually ceased in Pennsylvania. The few
members that did come in were not reported and the money
was kept under another name. I, myself, went down to Evans
to protest against Steve's methods but found that Evans was
supporting him. Evans merely repeated the talk about how
we wanted to make this into a great movement, not just a
lodge. Rich, for his part, straddled. He tried to keep in the good
graces of Evans and still keep his field force satisfied. All of
us in the field at that time seriously objected to the abandon-
ment of ritualistic work and the mere collection of money.

We redistributed the rituals and kept on; but the same
care was no longer given to the selection of members. Of
course the membership grew. They came in by the hundreds;
but the old spirit wasn't there.[8]

Cotton's complaints against Stephenson can also be read
as an accurate description of how Stephenson was trying to
change the Klan in the other states that now fell under his control. He wanted the Klan to become a movement, not just an order. He had always wanted to build the Klan into a political force,
transforming it from a fraternal lodge into a political party organization. At least in late August 1923, Evans was still supporting
Stephenson's vision of the Klan as a "great movement."

Cotton's assessment of Stephenson's effect on the Pennsylvania Klan also contains the roots of the Klan's first serious
complaint against Stephenson: "The few members that did come
in were not reported and the *money was kept under a different name.*" Cotton also criticized Stephenson for the abandon-
ment of ritualistic work and *the mere collection of money*"
[emphasis added].

It is difficult to say when the differences between Stephenson and Evans began to widen the gap between them. But the
June meeting at the Willard Hotel in Washington, D.C., when
they disagreed over the national policy, may have been where the
problems began. Edgar Allen Booth, the author of *Mad Mullah
of America*, claimed that the quarrel between Evans and
Stephenson involved the following issues:

• Stephenson's demand that more men from the North be
placed on the Imperial Kloncilium.

• Evans's anger over Stephenson making too much on the
sale of Klan robes.

• Stephenson's claim that too much money was being spent to get a Klan-backed candidate elected to the U.S. Senate from Texas.

• Evans's demand that Stephenson present a financial accounting of his operation and Stephenson's counterdemand that an audit of the national organization be conducted.

• Both men fighting for control of the *Fiery Cross*.

• Stephenson's total control of the northern Klan and his disregard for Evans's orders.

As Booth wrote:

> Each was seeking political control through the Klan, but each wanted the personal advantage of this control. The Klan sought control of America by "peaceful methods." Evans would gain the control of political America through placing klansmen in Congress. Constitutional amendments were to follow as different states lined up with men favorable to the Klan program. . . . To Stephenson this procedure was far too slow. He had by this time had his first taste of political power. . . . Already, in Indiana, Ohio, Illinois and Michigan, politicians were beginning to cast about for favor in the eyes of Stephenson. This was especially so in Indiana.[9]

As recently as August 2, Evans had written a glowing letter to Stephenson about his recruiting work:

> I have been going over your record while handling the field work of the Extension Department of the Knights of the Ku Klux Klan. I find that during the period of time from February 17th., to July 14th., 1923, you have remitted to the Imperial Treasury of the Knights of the Ku Klux Klan $641,475.00. You have rendered service through the Columbus, Ohio, office at a total cost of $159,786.00, thus serving the Klans to their satisfaction at a cost from your office of perhaps $1.25 per man. . . . And when we add to this magnificent record your refusing all remuneration and turning salary earned by you in to be used for the general good of the Order, I feel the Order owes you, and I hereby express to you sincere appreciation of your work.[10]

But Evans was also beginning to have doubts about Stephenson. Was Stephenson shortchanging the order to line his own pockets? Surely, this young coal salesman was working some clever, hidden angle. Even as he was writing glowing letters to Stephenson, Evans was also hiring the Atlanta office of a national accounting firm, Ernst & Ernst, to send a team of auditors north to go through Stephenson's books. This was highly unusual—the Klan auditing the books of one of its own trusted grand dragons.

Whatever Evans suspected, the auditors turned up nothing negative. As they wrote in their final report on August 27, "In our examination we found very few differences between the number of men received into the organization and the number remitted for to National Headquarters. The difference in most cases were overpayments, some of the petitioners having been reported twice. These differences, however, were adjusted by refunds from National Headquarters. . . . The system of handling the reports was changed during the year and particular care appears to have been used since January 1923, to maintain proper records and filing of reports."[11]

But what did that line mean in Evans's letter to Stephenson, the part about "refusing all remuneration" and turning in salary for the good of the order? He was doing no such thing. Or if he was, it was some sleight-of-hand bookkeeping too sly for even an army of auditors to catch. After all, this was the same period of time when Stephenson was buying his house, his yacht, several cars, and more than one diamond engagement ring. He was not paying for all that on a coal salesman's salary.

Was there something strange going on inside Stephenson's operation? Or was Evans merely beginning to suspect every shadow that moved as someone intent on deposing him just as he had done to Simmons? Still, there were the complaints from the Pennsylvania Klan to consider. And there were stories circulating about Stephenson and his women. There was just enough "wrong-ness" in the air to make the imperial wizard uneasy on his throne.

The final break between Stephenson and Evans came in mid-October. There is no exact record of what happened. There is one surviving note which suggests the tone of their final exchanges. In it, Stephenson wrote to Evans:

> I have just been informed by telephone that rumors are being circulated in Atlanta, Georgia, to the effect that I have threatened to cause the great states of Indiana and Ohio to withdraw from the National Organization unless you resign your position. No honest man who knows me would make such a statement. It is with the greatest concern and deepest grief that I receive this fanciful dream of some distorted mind. I have never in my life made a threat against any man nor have I ever betrayed a trust and as God is my guidance and sustaining power I shall never divert from this purpose to do right. This is not to be in any way construed to mean that I approve all the members of the Kloncilium because I could not honestly do that but it does mean a faithful reply to my own conscience and emphatic disavowal of any

thought of treason on the part of either myself or the thousands of other honorable men in the northern states.[12]

Two weeks later, the *Fiery Cross* carried a short item reporting that "The Old Man" was planning to retire after only three and a half months as grand dragon.

If the split between Evans and Stephenson was not friendly, it was at least accomplished in virtual silence. In a letter dated September 27, Stephenson, with his approaching "retirement" in mind, gave his instructions to the top-ranking Klan officers in Indiana and the management of the *Fiery Cross*. Stephenson's letter gives the closest thing to an official explanation of the feud between Atlanta and Indianapolis:

> Because of recent misunderstandings, and apparent conflicts of jurisdiction having arisen in Indiana, possibly thru the lack of written definition of the relationship of each of the responsible parties, who have been so kind as to help us thru many Indiana battles, I am herewith taking action to remedy this matter. . . .
>
> The Grand Dragon's office [in] Indiana has placed the responsibility for all policies and operations in Marion County in the hands of George V. Coffin. All individuals connected with the official personnel in Marion County will be governed accordingly, and no action of any kind shall be taken contrary to policies laid down by Captain Coffin. Captain Coffin, in the discharge of his responsibilities in Marion County, shall be responsible to W. F. Bossert, and to no one else.[13]

The letter placed all authority for all Marion County legal matters in the hands of Stephenson's attorney, Robert I. Marsh. It also outlined the business operations of the *Fiery Cross*. Milton Elrod was to continue as editor of the paper but was given instructions not to print anything without first having it approved by Coffin and Bossert. Harry Bloom was given the job of business manager for the paper with responsibility for handling all the paper's funds. Ernest W. Reichard, the founder of the paper and still on the masthead as publisher, was now given the additional titles of assistant editor and assistant business manager. Marsh, Elrod, Bloom, and Reichard were all given orders to report to Grand Klaliff Walter F. Bossert, an attorney from Liberty, Indiana. How closely the letter's instructions were followed is unknown. But within a month, Evans conferred the grand dragon's title on Bossert.

There may have been an uneasy truce arranged between Stephenson and Evans, an agreement to keep their personal differences quiet to avoid creating more problems within the Klan. Stephenson may have been concerned about presenting a unified front for the Klan in the political arena as they approached the Indiana gubernatorial primary races in the spring of the following year. A truce of some kind had been made, since Evans and Stephenson shared a platform at a Veterans Day Klan rally in Fort Wayne, Indiana, on November 11, less than a month after the split had occurred. At the rally, Stephenson surprised the audience with a short speech on America's dwindling coal resources. It was the last speech he would give to a nationally affiliated Klan gathering.

Booth hints in *Mad Mullah* that part of the reason for the split may have been an attempt by Stephenson to resolve the fight between Simmons and Evans. Stephenson's plan, according to Booth, was to get the two wizards back together and then take them on a whistle-stop train tour of the country delivering speeches for the Klan.[14]

Stephenson arranged a meeting with Evans to discuss the possibility of reconciliation. Evans came to Indianapolis and stayed at the Lincoln Hotel. Correspondence between the two men was conducted by couriers, who carried messages back and forth between Evans's rooms in the Lincoln Hotel and Stephenson's suite of rooms in the Hotel Washington. Simmons was supposed to have attended the meeting as well but never arrived. After a string of courier-carried messages, Evans finally conceded to meet with Stephenson face-to-face at the Hotel Washington.

"The men had hardly met when Simmons was forgotten and Senator Mayfield of Texas became the topic. This was always a sore spot with Stephenson," Booth writes. "In the heat of the argument, Stephenson cried out that 'too damn much money was spent to elect Mayfield,' and that Evans knew it. The conference broke up with a more muddied complexion, if possible, than when it started."[15]

In spite of these squabbles, the split continued to be kept quiet. The rank-and-file members of the Klan were probably unaware that a split had taken place. Not until the following spring, in May 1924, did Stephenson decide to make the split public and escalate the feud into an open war.

Chapter Fourteen

"The Law in Indiana"

1922–23

"Indiana has a political world. One D. C. Stephenson was the self-appointed monarch of this world for some time. . . . He boasted that his word was 'law in Indiana.' " That is how one political observer, in a 1925 newspaper article, summed up the brief reign of Stephenson in Indiana.[1] The word "monarch" was a good one to describe Stephenson. It was a title that he would have been only too glad to accept. The slogan "the law in Indiana" would become the label that most people would later associate with him.

Stephenson, the Klan, and politics had been intermingled ever since his unsuccessful bid for Congress in the spring of 1922. It was his plan to make the Klan into a powerful political force—and perhaps a party of its own—that would be able to make or break political careers. He saw the Klan as an enormous lobbying group, one that would soon be able to cut its own political deals.

While Stephenson was starting to develop the Indianapolis Klan during the summer of 1922, he was also beginning to shape its political identity. The big contest in Indiana's November 1922 general election was the senatorial race between the incumbent Republican, Senator Albert J. Beveridge, and Democratic ex-Governor Samuel M. Ralston. Beveridge, acknowledged as a powerhouse within the national Republican party, was easily considered the favorite over Ralston. Two events developed, however, which changed the course of the election and proved the emerging power of the Klan.

The first event was the appearance of the governor of Kansas, Henry Allen, who came to Indiana campaigning for Beveridge. A former Wichita newspaper editor, Allen had developed a national reputation for his outspoken resistance to the Klan. In Kansas, Allen stopped Klan demonstrations, encouraged his attorney general to start legal actions to drive the Klan out of the state, and delivered several strong speeches opposing the Klan. On his swing through Indiana, Allen was scheduled to speak in favor of Beveridge to audiences in Greencastle, Indianapolis, and Richmond—three cities where the Klan had significant followings.

The results were disastrous. Allen delivered attacks on the Klan, thus eroding whatever support Beveridge might have had among Republican klansmen. The results showed up in the election results from those three cities—usually solidly Republican—which all swung over to the Democrat, Ralston. Later one politician—not a klansman—answered a reporter's questions about why Beveridge lost, saying, "Blame it on Henry Allen."[2]

But there was more than just Allen to blame. The second episode that showed the Klan's strength in an early political test came during the heat of the senatorial campaign. Ralston was scheduled to deliver a speech in Terre Haute on the campus of Saint Mary-of-the-Woods, a Catholic women's college. Given that there were so many Catholics in the crowd, no one was quite ready for the comments that Ralston delivered. In his speech, he advocated the complete separation of church and state. This remark was heard by klansmen and Catholics alike as a heavy jab at the Roman Catholic church.

The Klan saw Ralston as a brave politician who dared to face the Catholics on their own ground. The organization published Ralston's speech on a sheet titled "Where Courage Counts" and papered the state with copies of it. Come November, the results were obvious when Ralston triumphed over the favored Beveridge by more than thirty-three thousand votes. On all sides, it was clear the Klan had played an important role in Ralston's win.[3]

The hand of the Ku Klux Klan was also seen in other Indiana races that fall. At the top of the 1922 Republican state ticket were Ora J. Davies for state treasurer, William G. Oliver for state auditor, Ed Jackson for secretary of state, David Meyers for judge of the Indiana Supreme Court, and Patrick Lynch for clerk of the Indiana Supreme Court. On election day, all of them won except two: Oliver and Lynch. Oliver was a Presbyterian, but he had angered the Klan by refusing to support an attempt by the Klan to oust a Catholic schoolteacher. He had also refused to fill out one of the Klan's political questionnaires. Lynch, who was Catholic, finished fifty-two thousand votes behind the rest of the ticket.[4]

Religion became an election issue in the race between Judge Joseph Shea and Judge David Meyers for the Indiana Supreme Court. Shea was Catholic, a fact widely publicized by the Klan, and he was crushed by his Protestant Republican opponent.

In Marion County, the Klan recorded a stunning victory in the county clerk's race. Normally, the office would have gone to the Republican contender by about 10,000 votes. But Democrat Albert H. Losche went into the election with the support of the Klan. He upset his Republican opponent by 12,000 votes—2,000 votes ahead of the winning Republican side of the ticket.

Three Republican candidates for the state legislature were defeated, while eight other Republicans from Marion County were elected. Of the three who lost, one was black, one was a Jew, and one was Catholic.

In the race for the U.S. Congress, Republican Merrill Moores squared off against Democrat Joseph Turk. Being the Catholic in that match, Turk lost by more than nine thousand votes, and Moores won the Indianapolis district seat in the U.S. House of Representatives.

Many other Indiana races were also decided by the Klan vote. In Grant County, a local candidate, who happened to be Protestant, was revealed as being romantically involved with a Catholic woman. The Klan opposed his candidacy, since the young lady might eventually persuade him to become Catholic.

In Delaware County, the traditional party affiliations were destroyed by the Klan-influenced elections. The Klan threw its support to the Republican ticket. This caused many black voters who had always voted with "Mr. Lincoln's party" to switch and vote Democrat for the first time. A Democratic candidate for judge who was cited by the Klan as being Jewish was soundly defeated.

In Blackford and Wells counties, a Catholic candidate for prosecutor was beaten by the Klan-backed Republican candidate, even though the Protestant Democrats carried the other key races in that area.

How did Stephenson and the Klan manage to pull off this highly theatrical political coup? Most fledgling special-interest groups would have counted themselves lucky to influence a handful of candidates in their first attempt at power brokering. Not Stephenson! His Klan organization went leapfrogging back and forth between Republicans and Democrats, carefully picking individual candidates and working to defeat the ones who did not measure up to the "100 percent American" criteria of the Klan. At least in 1922, the Klan was a force that straddled political lines, ignored traditional rivalries, and settled scores according to its private agenda. But how did the Klan do it?

Organization was the key to Stephenson's success. By mid-1922, he had assembled the support arm of the Klan that he called his "military machine." Writer Max Bentley managed to capture a description of this machine in his May 1924 article, "The Ku Klux Klan in Indiana," for *McClure's Magazine*. Some of the article suggests that Stephenson himself was probably the primary source for the story. As Bentley wrote:

> Stephenson organized it [the Indiana Klan] along combined political and military lines. There was one klanton for each county, one province for each of Indiana's thirteen Congressional districts and one realm for the state as a whole.
>
> From a political point of view, the exalted cyclops of a klanton had a status similar to that of a county chairman, the titan of a province would be the Congressman and the district chairman in politics, and the Grand Dragon was governor. Along military lines each county was in charge of a colonel, each realm had a brigadier general, while over all sat G-1, "The Old Man" himself.[5]

When signing correspondence to klansmen in the field, Stephenson often signed himself as "G-1," corresponding to the military designation of the commander in chief. The military machine was only a fledgling operation in the elections of 1922. There were no state-office elections in 1923, the year Stephenson rose to the grand dragon's post. Stephenson used that year wisely, working to develop the machine and fine-tune it in time for the important gubernatorial race of 1924. In 1922, the Klan had managed to assert its power in several areas around the state where it had built up large memberships. But by 1924, Stephenson hoped to have his political system developed into a statewide organization that would blanket Indiana.

A rare glimpse of what the military machine was to become is found in the testimony taken by Indiana Attorney General Arthur Gilliom in 1928 during his investigation of the Klan's corrupting influence on state politics. One of the many people who testified was Samuel H. Bemenderfer, a textbook salesman and former officer of the Muncie Klan. Bemenderfer had joined the organization in June 1922. He served as klaliff, or vice president, of Delaware County Klan Number Four from 1923 to 1924.[6]

Bemenderfer recalled, "We had in our military organization in Muncie a little over a hundred men that were active as officers in it." He estimated there were between 200 and 250 men active in the Muncie military machine. "Officers were called precinct captains. [Above them] we had the lieutenants and captains, and my office was as President or, as general would be in a military staff."

Bemenderfer told how he had been called down to Stephenson's Indianapolis offices in late 1923 or early 1924 to discuss with other Indiana Klan leaders the strategy of the military machine for the 1924 elections. Stephenson furnished them each with organizational charts on how to construct a military organization.

> He showed us the blue-prints of the different counties and townships, brought down in blocks . . . showing us how to control county and township and precinct blocks. . . . He said that this was their way of operating, particularly in the south part of the state, and the blue-print—and, in fact, the only blue-print I ever saw, was one covering Evansville, which he held at that time.
>
> He said that it was to be used in all the different counties in the state, and he wanted us to make others up in the same kind of blocks. . . . He did not state exactly why he wanted it, but he said we could not work efficiently without it in the counties. . . .
>
> He said that there was to be established a telephone system which would go directly from his office over this private wire to every county in the state, and in turn, from the military directory in each county, they would go direct to the other officers, and it would pyramid—each man would be responsible to get that message to his officers, and in that way, carry the instructions of the state office into every precinct, and in fact, to every block in the county inside of thirty minutes . . . for the purpose of controlling the election.

Bemenderfer told how the military machine members discussed political candidates at regular Klan meetings, explaining to the rest of the klansmen which candidates were "friendly"—supportive or at least tolerant of the Klan—and which were "unfriendly." Candidates in the latter group included those Protestants who openly opposed the Klan, as well as any office seekers who happened to be Catholic, Jewish, black, or foreign-born.

Slates of candidates acceptable to the Klan were distributed, according to Bemenderfer, to "every home in the county." As he recalled, "One circular was printed for each party, prior to the primary, and that was placed in the homes . . . and, after the nominations, the entire ticket again was printed and X's were placed in front of those men that we should give political preference to."

The Klan slates were distributed in what became known as the clothespin campaign. Thousands of printed slates were folded, and a small wooden clothespin was attached to each. On the night before an election, hundreds of klansmen and young boys would swarm through the streets of every city and town tossing the clothespinned slates onto the front porch or step of every house. In the morning, the voters would open their doors to find the message from the Klan waiting for them. This process was repeated all over the state, from the largest cities down to the smallest towns, wherever the Klan could make its presence felt. Compared with the Klan's organization, the Republicans and Democrats were running rather lackluster campaigns.

Part of Stephenson's political plan was a massive poll that would record the voting preference of all the voters in Indiana. In this respect, he was years ahead of his time. The art of comprehensive polltaking would not become a standard feature of American party politics until at least three decades later. But by early 1923, Stephenson could see the value of knowing what the voters were thinking and being able to predict how they would vote. His poll was designed to pinpoint the strongholds of the Klan and the weak spots, where more Klan pressure was needed.

According to Bemenderfer, Stephenson had poll books made up with the names of every registered voter in each county. These were given to the head of each military machine group with instructions that klansmen canvass their areas and return the completed books to the state headquarters in time to prepare for the 1924 primary elections. Armed with this information and his telephone network, Stephenson would run the entire state from his Indianapolis office during the political campaign.

Bemenderfer told how the Muncie Klan had polled every registered voter in Delaware County. In his words, the pollsters "covered the county like a blanket." After asking each voter a list of questions, the klansman would indicate which voters were friendly or unfriendly to the Klan-approved slate.

The plan seemed perfect, or nearly so, but Stephenson soon ran into a snag. Thanks to the split between his organization and the Evans-Bossert side of the Klan, Stephenson was beginning to lose the confidence of the Muncie klansmen. The first poll completed, Bemenderfer and the others decided to not turn the poll books back over to the state office. Sometime, probably in the fall of 1923 but before the split between Evans and Stephenson, Bemenderfer was called to Indianapolis for another meeting with Stephenson to discuss the Delaware County poll. "Stephenson inquired, in his office, from me if we were ready to turn over to the state office the complete records of our military organization, showing the telephone number and address of all precinct captains. And I told him no," said Bemenderfer. "So he turned me over to a man by the name of Bob Lyons . . . one of the state officers under Stephenson." Robert W. Lyons was the son of a Richmond, Indiana, minister. His father was a personal friend of U.S. Senator James E. Watson. The younger Lyons, an attorney, was a close associate of Stephenson in state political matters but was soon to join the Evans-Bossert group.

Bemenderfer further recalled:

> Mr. Lyons said, "Bemenderfer, you haven't turned over to the state office the complete records of the military organization in Muncie and Delaware County." I said, "Just what is the purpose of these records—that you want all these records from Delaware County—that you want the telephone numbers and the addresses of all these captains of the different precincts?"
>
> "Well," he said, "strictly speaking, it is none of your business." I said, "Now, Mr. Lyons, we are making it our business, and we are not going to turn that information over to you, because we are going to have something to say about the control of our military organization in Delaware County ourselves, and if we have such a vote and turn this information over to you, you will use it to switch our support at the last moment, and we refuse to permit anything like that to go on." He said, "You refuse to take instructions from the state office?" I said, "Yes," and then he called in Walter Bossert.

Walter F. Bossert was a thirty-eight-year-old attorney from Liberty, Indiana, a small community in the east central part of the state. He had attended Indiana University, where he lettered in basketball and baseball and earned a law degree in 1907. He had served as deputy prosecuting attorney for the old Thirty-seventh Judicial District. From 1916 to 1922, he was Sixth District chairman of the Indiana Republican party. In 1923, the same year he was to become grand dragon of the Ku Klux Klan, Bossert was named to the Republican State Committee. He was tall and broad-shouldered with dark hair and a prominent forehead. A relative once described him as "distinguished looking . . . he looked like a Senator ought to look." [Bossert ran unsuccessfully for the U.S. Senate in 1938.][7]

As Bossert arrived at the meeting to face Bemenderfer, he said, "Bemenderfer, you will turn over this list to us, will you not?" And Bemenderfer again said that he would not. Bossert said, "You know if you don't turn this list over to us that there are ways and means to get this information." Bemenderfer replied, "That is probably true, but our Board of Directors refuse to do it, and I am obligated to carry out their instructions."

Bossert told him, "We are going to send a man down to get that list." Bemenderfer again asked why the list was so important. "That is none of your business," said Bossert.

That was the end of the Delaware County Klan's face-off with Stephenson and Bossert. It was also very nearly the end of its association with the national Klan. In March 1924, less than two months before the primary elections, the members of the Delaware County Klan seceded from both the state and national Klan organizations. The Muncie klansmen formed their own splinter group, first becoming the "Klan of the North" and then the "Independent Klan of America." Threatened with lawsuits from the imperial wizard in Atlanta, they finally dropped the word "klan" from their name altogether and became the "Knights of American Protestantism" with Sam Bemenderfer as their first president. After that, the Klan was essentially dead in Muncie. When sociologists Robert and Helen Lynd arrived there to conduct the first of their famous Middletown studies of life in a typical small Midwestern town from 1924 to 1925, they concluded that "by 1925 the energy was mainly spent and the Klan disappeared as a local power, leaving in its wake wide areas of local bitterness."[8]

Few klansmen were willing to oppose the trio of Stephenson, Bossert, and Evans as Sam Bemenderfer had done. Fewer still were willing to take the drastic step of breaking away from the main organization. Most were content to join in a lockstep march with the other Klans, following orders from whoever seemed to be giving them. In this way, Stephenson's military machine continued to work smoothly throughout the rest of 1923 and 1924.

But why did it work? Why did the political parties allow it to work? These are the most tantalizing questions of all when looking over the brief reign of D. C. Stephenson. Perhaps the answer lies in the fact that Stephenson was a political carnivore, the type who fed on the insecurities of nervous candidates and office holders. Their fear was his meal ticket. Best of all were the "almost successful" politicians, the ones who refused to believe they could carry an election on their own, the ones who felt sure the voters would turn against them at the last possible moment. If only they could nail down one more fragment of the electorate, buy the support of just one more splinter group, get one more block of voters to say yes—then they could rest more easily. This was the kind of politician—and there must have been many of them—before whom Stephenson would dangle his tempting catch of patriotic klansmen, all ready to vote his will at a single word. The voters he controlled were his bait. Ed Jackson was just the kind of politician who found that sort of bait irresistible.

Chapter Fifteen

The Man Who Would Be Governor

1923–24

Ed Jackson was a popular politician in 1923, not the sort of man who most people would have thought needed the support of the Klan. He had a reputation as a tireless campaigner and an affable pipe smoker who usually got along well with reporters. As secretary of state and an obvious candidate for the governor's office, Jackson was known to walk from his home in Irvington on East Washington Street five miles to his office in the statehouse. His home, a modest two-story affair, was only about a mile from Stephenson's mansion. In good weather, Jackson could be seen waving and smiling at the passing streetcars filled with commuters as he walked to work.

The forty-nine-year-old Jackson was a rags-to-riches story of success. Born on a farm in Howard County, near Kokomo, Indiana, his father was a millworker who wandered from job to job all over the state. Poverty forced the younger Jackson to find work in a stave factory at an early age. As he grew older, though, he began to study law at night. In 1893, he opened his own law practice, sharing an office with a doctor in the small town of Kennard, Indiana. Even then, the income from his law work was so small that he continued to work as a day laborer in a brickyard. Within a few years, however, he had developed a reputation as a good lawyer, and he ran successfully for the office of prosecuting attorney in Henry County. Jackson's initiation into politics had a lasting effect on him. After a term as prosecutor, he went on to be elected circuit court judge of the county.[1]

Then in 1916, Jackson announced that he was a candidate for secretary of state on the Republican ticket with gubernatorial candidate James P. Goodrich. Jackson campaigned hard for office in the 1916 primary and won his spot on the Republican team that was swept into office that fall, ending an eight-year rule by the Democrats. He took office in 1917, but he only held the position a year before resigning his office to enlist in the army. He was given the rank of major and served in Europe with troops from Indiana.

He returned victoriously from the war a year later as a genuine war hero, then opened a law office in Lafayette, Indiana. Shortly after his return, the man who had succeeded him as secretary of state, W. A. Roach, died in office. Governor Goodrich picked Jackson to return to the statehouse and finish the rest of the term.

In 1920, Jackson ran again for secretary of state, this time as an incumbent sharing the ticket with gubernatorial candidate Warren T. McCray, a cattleman from Kentland, Indiana. Jackson won, then went on to earn a third term in the office in the 1922 elections. By this time, though, he was getting anxious to run for the governor's seat. It was generally acknowledged by 1923 that Jackson would be the front-runner for governor in 1924.

Jackson must have met Stephenson sometime in 1921 during his second term as secretary of state. It was Jackson, after all, who signed the incorporation charter for the Ku Klux Klan on August 13, 1921. In fact, it was the issue of the Klan that first began to drive a wedge of mistrust between newly elected Governor McCray and Secretary of State Jackson. Since the Klan was a secret society, the applicants for the charter (Stephenson would have been one of them, along with Joe Huffington and other state officers) refused to sign their names to the document. McCray, who had no doubt heard of the trouble the Klan was causing in other states, decided that a charter with no names was not legal. Jackson, though, ruled against McCray and said that in this instance the charter was perfectly all right. To settle the dispute, the matter was turned over to the state's attorney general, who finally decided that since the Klan was a fraternal order, no signatures on the charter would be necessary.

While pursuing this argument, however, McCray galvanized his position. He announced that klansmen could not parade in public streets while wearing disguises. A few of Indiana's mayors agreed with McCray, but most ignored the governor's advice. Soon the Klan was parading through cities and towns all over Indiana, with thanks to "friendly" Ed Jackson.[2]

The incorporation papers that Jackson signed described the purpose of the Klan as being "a patriotic fraternal order with no insurance or beneficiary features, designed to teach and inculcate amongst its membership greater respect for the stars and stripes and constitution and to strengthen the majesty and supremacy of the regular organized forces of law and to increase patriotism of the purest kind among its membership." Who, after all, could disagree with any of that? Jackson was not going to be seen taking issue with law and patriotism!

The battle over the charter for the Klan instantly cast Jackson and McCray into the roles they would play throughout the days of the Klan. McCray was the Klan's steadfast enemy, and Jackson was its benevolent supporter and ally. This relationship was to have a lasting effect on the political careers of both men.

For some time, the issues surrounding Jackson and the Klan subsided. But in the spring of 1923, the whole business came roaring back to life. The event that revived it was the theft of the Klan membership lists from Buschmann Hall. In its third installment of names from the Indianapolis Klan roster, *Tolerance* ran a banner headline on page 1: "SECRETARY OF STATE ON ROLL! INTERESTING KLUX NEWS FOR INDIANA!" On page 2, another banner headline read "INDIANA SECRETARY OF STATE!" with the subhead "WE HAVE WITH US TODAY EXALTED POLITICIAN ON ROLL OF THE KU KLUX KLAN!" A two-column photograph of Jackson ran underneath the headline "WELCOME, KLANSMAN!" The caption read:

> We would rather say, "Good Bye, Klansman!" Mr. Lawrence E. Lyons has set Ed Jackson a very good example [Lyons had just resigned from Klan]—an example to be followed by every man whom the people have honored with their confidence and have entrusted with office, when he is caught in company with "reformers" whose uniform is the eye-hole mask of the highwayman. Will Ed Jackson likewise get out? If not, the honest people of Indiana—WHO ARE IN THE MAJORITY—know exactly what to do with Ku Klux Klansmen in public office. If Lawrence E. Lyons is compelled to resign, WHY NOT ED JACKSON?

Inside the paper, *Tolerance* published an editorial that contained a barely veiled death threat: "A dead Klansman may not be a good Klansman. Who can penetrate the hereafter? But it's a cinch he's out of politics." The editorial went on to say:

> Mr. Klansman, so long as you continue a Klansman, enrolled in a band of "reformers" whose chosen regalia is the shroud of the terrorist and the mask of the highwayman, you are either a dupe and a fool, or a knave. Take your choice. . . .
> Mr. Ed Jackson, Indiana's secretary of state, holding an elective office, was the choice of 540,260 voters, of whom not more than 316,000 could have been Klansmen. That means that he has betrayed all but 316,000 voters of Indiana—betrayed 755,680 of the voters to be exact. . . . The decision

which Mr. Jackson now faces is momentous—for him. We doubt if he will have the courage to make it. In that case, the people of Indiana will make his decision for him. He is done.[3]

But Jackson was far from done. Against this withering attack of public criticism, he had nothing to say. Other prominent citizens who were named as klansmen in *Tolerance* wrote letters to the paper publicly denying any connection with the Ku Klux Klan and demanding retractions. A few even filed lawsuits charging the anti-Klan newspaper with libel. But Jackson did nothing. When a reporter from the *Indianapolis Times* tried to reach Jackson for a reaction to the *Tolerance* story, he found that the secretary of state was "unavailable for comment."[4] There was nothing Jackson could say in response to the articles. If he admitted that he was a member of the Klan, he would only cement the charges *Tolerance* was making. If he denied his Klan connections, he would be ostracized by the Klan and, even worse, he would lose Klan members' votes in the gubernatorial elections that were barely one year away. There were many more klansmen in Indiana than there were readers of *Tolerance*, so Jackson kept his silence. Week after week *Tolerance* used every opportunity it had to link his name to the Ku Klux Klan.

Judging by the results of the 1924 elections, Jackson's scrape with *Tolerance* did nothing to hurt his voter appeal. If anything, it may have helped him with the Klan and its sympathizers. He was a candidate the Catholics could not stand, a man who had earned the wrath of the "papists." The *Tolerance* scheme to expose Jackson backfired. Instead of embarrassing him, the stories served only to give him free publicity.

Throughout the *Tolerance* episode and the election that came later, Stephenson stuck by his friend and neighbor, Ed Jackson, inviting him to parties on the Reomar II, where they hobnobbed with other key political figures. They went on hunting and fishing trips together. Stephenson presented Jackson with several thousand dollars to fund his gubernatorial campaign. During the campaign itself, Stephenson gave Jackson a Lexington touring car to use on stumping trips around the state and lent him the services of one of several chauffeurs. After Jackson's victory, the two men exchanged gifts at Christmas. Stephenson gave Jackson an expensive repeating shotgun, and Jackson gave him a sorrel saddle horse named Senator. Their friendship seemed to be the kind that might last forever.[5]

So Jackson quietly weathered the publicity *Tolerance* gave him during the summer and fall of 1923. Jackson knew he could count on his friends in the Klan. Nor was he alone in the pages of *Tolerance* because many prestigious attorneys, judges, policemen, and a host of other top political office holders were rapidly joining him there.

If any of the *Tolerance* furor caused Jackson to worry, at least he was not the only Republican with a summer full of bad news. McCray was also having his share of problems. The governor owned a two-thousand-acre farm in Newton County, where he raised some of the finest cattle in Indiana. He routinely came away from the Indiana State Fair with an impressive pile of trophies and ribbons. On his inauguration day, McCray was said to be worth $3 million, one of Indiana's wealthiest farmers.

But McCray's fortunes soon reversed. Before taking office, he bought cattle and property aggressively, expanding his operations rapidly. As a result, he was seriously overextended when prices fell out of the cattle market in the farm depression of 1921. Like many other farmers, McCray was caught in a tight money squeeze. He had plenty of cattle, but no one could afford to buy them. After a time, prices began to plummet, and with them went McCray's fortune.[6]

The governor began to borrow money in a wild gamble to save his farm. He borrowed from banks until they refused to lend him any more money. Then he began to borrow against cattle sales that had never happened (he forged the promissory notes that he used as collateral). In a last desperate move, he borrowed $155,000 from the state's agricultural board and put the money in his own personal account.

By the summer of 1923, McCray had a debt of more than $2 million hanging over him. And then it happened: someone started stories flying about how the governor was in serious financial trouble, with rumors of embezzlement and bankruptcy. Who started the rumors? Was it Jackson? Was it Stephenson? No one knows.

McCray called a meeting of his creditors in Indianapolis on August 31 to announce that he would be willing to turn over everything he owned to them except his home to satisfy his debts. Three weeks later, a group of Republican leaders met to discuss McCray's fate. The new head of the Republican State Committee, Clyde Walb, pushed to have McCray resign immediately. The others decided it was too soon for that. They decided to wait.

But they did not wait long. In early October, a Marion County grand jury began to investigate some of the charges that were being made about McCray's unusual methods of obtaining money from the state. On October 6, the federal bankruptcy court became involved when three Fort Wayne banks asked to have the governor declared bankrupt. The walls began to crumble around McCray.

Ironically, McCray's son-in-law, William P. Evans, was also the Marion County prosecutor. In that role, he was responsible for the grand jury that was now investigating his wife's father. Evans had a reputation as a flawlessly honest man, so he requested the courts to appoint a special prosecutor on the case. The judge who named the special prosecutor was Judge James A. Collins, whose name and photograph had recently been featured in the April 23, 1923, issue of *Tolerance* as a member of the Klan. Judge Collins appointed two special prosecuting attorneys, Clarence W. Nichols and Eph Inman, the latter of whom became Stephenson's own attorney two years later.

Less than two months after Collins picked the special prosecutors, the grand jury returned an indictment against McCray for embezzling $155,000 from the state. The indictment was handed down November 30. A week later, Evans gave his letter of resignation to his father-in-law.

In McCray's darkest hour, D. C. Stephenson arrived to tempt him with an offer of money and a miracle: immunity from prosecution. It sounded too good to be true—and of course, it was. The offer came with a price tag and a question: could the governor of Indiana be bought for a mere ten thousand dollars in cash?

The scheme had been hatched between Jackson, Stephenson, and some of the other top Klan officials. With Evans resigning as prosecutor, the Klan wanted to fill the vacant spot with its own handpicked attorney. Since the prosecutor had some discretionary powers in choosing which crimes to prosecute, it would be helpful if the post was occupied by someone considered friendly to the Klan.

The offer to McCray was this: accept a briefcase containing ten thousand dollars to help ease his financial problems, then name Klan-supported attorney James E. McDonald to the prosecutor's job. The new prosecutor would take over the grand jury investigation in the embezzlement charge, the prosecution would slowly grind to a halt with delaying motions, and McCray would eventually be given immunity from prosecution or conviction.

Stephenson and Jackson picked Fred B. Robinson, a state purchasing agent, to serve as their messenger to McCray. It was about 10:00 A.M. on Saturday, December 8, a springlike day with temperatures in the mid-sixties. Robinson was called by Jackson to meet with him immediately about an important matter.

Robinson went to the secretary of state's office, where he found Jackson waiting with three other men: George Coffin, the Marion County Republican leader; attorney Robert W. Lyons; and Stephenson. They briefly explained their plan to Robinson, handed him a satchel with ten thousand dollars in cash, and told him to deliver it with their message to McCray in the governor's office next door.

Robinson did exactly as he was told. He presented the briefcase to McCray along with the offer of immunity in exchange for McCray's agreement to name MacDonald prosecutor. Then, as Robinson later recalled, "Governor McCray turned in his chair to face me and said, 'Under no circumstance will I entertain such a proposition, Fred. I have already decided to appoint William H. Remy, the Chief Deputy.' " This was particularly bad news for the Klan, since Remy had a reputation as a tough, young, and scrupulous lawyer with absolutely no soft spot in his heart for the Klan.

Robinson carried McCray's refusal back to the secretary of state's office and the waiting party. Jackson was furious. Robinson later claimed that Jackson said, "You didn't put it to him like you should, or like I would. I will take it myself." Then Jackson picked up the satchel and went to see McCray himself.[7]

Face-to-face with the man who had the greatest motive to put him in prison, McCray turned on Jackson and his pile of money in a rage: "You can take your money back to your office, Ed. I am astounded! My fortune I struggled so hard to accumulate and to preserve, and my good name may be in ruins, but I will never surrender my integrity. Take your money and get out!"

Had McCray acted differently, the rest of the Stephenson story might have had an altogether different outcome. Remy might not have been appointed prosecutor; it was Remy who later served as prosecutor in the Stephenson trial. If McCray had taken the money and given the job to MacDonald, it is possible that the case against Stephenson might have never been pressed. Instead of murder, he might have been tried for a lesser crime, or he might have simply been released. The importance of McCray's decision to refuse Stephenson and Jackson's offer was to have delayed but far-reaching results.

The case proceeded against McCray. On February 25, 1924, a federal grand jury in the U.S. District Court in Indianapolis returned an indictment against McCray on charges of using the mails for fraud—since he had mailed the forged promissory notes to his bankers—and for violations of federal banking laws. He was tried not once but twice in 1924. First came the trial in

Marion County Criminal Court. After three weeks, that trial ended in a hung jury, and the charges were dismissed on April 11. Next came the federal court trial, where a long parade of witnesses took the stand to show how McCray's inept financial transactions had resulted in his multimillion-dollar debt. Bankers came to testify how the governor had duped them with his phony promissory notes. Finally, on April 28, the case was turned over to the jury, which took only fifteen minutes to find McCray guilty. Two days later, on April 30, Judge Albert B. Anderson sentenced McCray to ten years in the federal prison in Atlanta and a ten-thousand-dollar fine.

The day before his sentencing, McCray made his last trip to the governor's office under the guard of a U.S. marshal. There, he sent his written resignation from the governorship to secretary of state Ed Jackson. The next day, while McCray was being sentenced by Judge Anderson, Emmet F. Branch, the lieutenant governor, was sworn in to finish the rest of McCray's term as governor.

Throughout his trial, McCray steadfastly declared his innocence. He was a farmer, not a lawyer, and he had not realized that his financial dealings had been in violation of the law. Most of McCray's political friends agreed; the governor may have broken the law, but he was not a crook. Just the same, McCray got on the afternoon train the very day he was sentenced and left Indianapolis to begin serving his term in Atlanta. McCray's departure from the statehouse cleared the way for Jackson and the real crooks, who would come later.

Chapter Sixteen

The Feuding Klans

1923–24

There was very little peace and goodwill left in the Klan by Christmas, 1923. The split between Stephenson and Hiram Evans had reached a momentary lull, as if it only existed on paper in the heated notes that had passed between the two men. Walter Bossert had taken the grand dragon's title, but Stephenson still had a loyal core of followers who would answer only to him. If this arrangement seems confusing now, imagine how difficult it must have been for the klansmen of 1923 who were still trying to decide whose orders they should follow!

For a brief moment during the December holidays, Klan leaders tried to give the organization a more agreeable look. This year as in the past, the Klan staged an odd spectacle for the press. Klansmen drove around the city in all their hooded finery on Christmas Eve, dropping off baskets of Christmas food and presents at more than a hundred homes in Indianapolis, including those of blacks and Catholics. It was their way of proving that the Klan did not mean any harm to honest, law-abiding citizens, and it gave them a chance to get favorable Klan publicity to offset the stories in *Tolerance*.[1]

Imperial Wizard Evans did not have much time for holiday frivolities. He started out the new year with an order from the Imperial Palace banishing Emperor William Simmons from the Ku Klux Klan for "high crimes and misdemeanors."[2] Evans was tired of dealing with Simmons and his pathetic attempts to win back his place in the hooded order. The banishment order only made official the policy that Evans had been using to deal with Simmons since 1923.[3]

By coincidence, January 5, 1924, the day Evans banished Simmons, was also the day Stephenson was jailed in Columbus, Ohio, for the attempted rape of the manicurist at the Deschler Hotel.[4] It was not a good day for Evans's opponents.

In fact, it seemed that 1924 would not be a promising year for Stephenson. Later in January, the Klan offices in Fort Wayne, Indiana, were burglarized, then set on fire by anti-Klan activists (the American Unity League was suspected but not implicated).[5] At the end of February, a court in Akron, Ohio, granted Stephenson's second wife, Violet, a divorce from him citing cruelty as the grounds for the decree.[6] Then in mid-March, the Delaware County Klan announced that it was officially severing ties with the Indiana and national Klans.[7] To top off events for Stephenson, an announcement came on April 7 from the imperial wizard's office that made public Stephenson's banishment from the "Invisible Empire."[8]

But once again Stephenson seemed to benefit from what looked like a bad situation. The banishment did nothing to hurt him. He had already been out of command since his resignation the previous October. In fact, the move to make the split both final and public was taken by Evans, not Stephenson. This gave Stephenson the weapon he needed to retaliate. He took his time and planned his next moves carefully. Stephenson decided that the fight with Evans could wait until after the May primaries.

In the primary race for governor, Ed Jackson was running well ahead of his Republican challenger, Lew Shank, the mayor of Indianapolis. There was much interest in the election, since Shank represented the anti-Klan forces within the Republican party while Jackson was drawing Klan support from all over the state. "If I belonged to the Ku Klux Klan, I wouldn't deny it, as Ed Jackson does!" said Shank in a front-page article in the *Indianapolis Star*.[9] Jackson didn't bother to deny Shank's charges. There was no need to.

The Klan sponsored a huge rally for Jackson at the Cadle Tabernacle in Indianapolis on Friday night, May 2, the week before the primary.[10] There were few worries in Jackson's camp about having him too closely associated with the Klan.

In fact, it may have been the Klan's support that accounted for the huge voter turnout that year. The Tuesday primary election was considered the largest showing of voters in Indianapolis history. It was a landslide victory for Jackson. He drew 224,973 votes statewide, compared with Shank's 94,534. Ora D. Davies, the other anti-Klan Republican candidate for governor, drew a mere 9,000 votes. Most voters knew Jackson had been working in league with the Klan and did not care.[11]

For the Democrats, Dr. Carleton B. McCullough won with a plurality of 93,802 votes over a field of no less than eight gubernatorial candidates. His closest competitor was Lafayette's mayor, George Durgan, with 50,033 votes. Durgan, who earlier tried to stop Klan parades in Lafayette with an anti-mask ordinance, was the only Democratic candidate who had openly campaigned on an anti-Klan platform. McCullough eventually came out in favor of an anti-Klan plank in the party platform, but he waited until the week after the primary to do so. The fall election would be not so much a race between two candidates as it would be a public referendum on the Klan.[12]

In other Indiana political races, Klan-supported Ralph Updike upset the incumbent Merrill Moores in the Seventh Congressional District race (Moores was the man who had received unsolicited Klan support in the 1922 election when his opponent was Catholic). Down in Evansville, Congressman William E. Wilson, the man who had kept Stephenson out of the First Congressional District race in that city, was upset by Klan-supported Harry Rowbottom. Three days after the election, George V. "Cap" Coffin, the klansman who worked so hard to get out the vote for the Klan slate in Indianapolis, was rewarded by being named Marion County Republican chairman.[13]

Stephenson's response to Evans had waited long enough. With the primary behind him and his power demonstrated by amazing wins for the candidates backed by his military machine, Stephenson now called for a statewide meeting of Klan leaders to be held in Indianapolis at Cadle Tabernacle on Monday, May 12.[14]

This time, the hood was off. There would be no "Old Man" or "G-1" or mysterious "Steve." This time the meeting was called by Stephenson in an open press conference. Stephenson had finally decided to go public and take the offensive against Evans's and Bossert's control of the Indiana Klan.

The *Indianapolis News* carried the announcement of Stephenson's meeting on the front page under the headline "SOUNDS WAR CRY IN KLAN DISPUTE; D. C. STEPHENSON, EX-DRAGON OUTLINES OBJECTS OF MEETING SCHEDULED FOR TODAY."[15] Stephenson told the reporters of a plot by Bossert and former governor James P. Goodrich to take control of the Klan for political purposes. Stephenson claimed he was prepared to do battle with the southern-controlled faction of the Klan. Stephenson portrayed Evans as the wicked overlord who was trying to control a Hoosier organization from his office in Atlanta.

Stephenson told the reporters:

> The Marion County situation is deplorable. Only heroic and immediate action can save it with a solid and unbroken

front. The trouble arose as the result of overdone, arbitrary dictation from individuals who do not live in the county and have no interest in our welfare except as they are able to use the organization for selfish political purposes.

There can be no "czarism" in America, and it will cease in the Indianapolis organization tonight, when its members assemble at Cadle Tabernacle and formulate plans to perfect an organization of Marion county men and vest the whole authority and control of the organization in the membership, instead of allowing some hand-picked stranger to sacrifice our man-power and voting strength like a chess player sacrifices his pawns.

He went on to describe Evans and Bossert in such complimentary terms as "money-mad" people who were "dreaming of power and a fancy salary." He likened them to Judas and Benedict Arnold, and this was only the announcement for the meeting![16]

Cadle Tabernacle, the site of the meeting, was known as the unofficial home of the Klan. It was a huge, interdenominational house of worship built in 1921 by E. Howard Cadle, a reformed alcoholic who wanted to show his thanks to God. The tabernacle was built of stucco and brick in a Spanish style. The front resembled the Alamo mission in San Antonio, Texas, making the building a true oddity for many years in Indianapolis. Inside, there was regular seating for crowds of 10,000 with temporary seating for an extra 2,000.[17]

Cadle had embraced the Klan and welcomed them into his church. In 1923, he invited a traveling evangelist, the Reverend Dr. E. J. Bulgin from Portland, Oregon, to preach at the tabernacle for an extended engagement. Bulgin was a Klan organizer and recruiter whose sermons included lengthy pro-Klan orations. On April 2, 1923, before a capacity audience of 12,000, Bulgin's sermon was interrupted by the appearance of 18 robed klansmen. The leader carried an American flag as the group marched to the stage and formed a semicircle behind Bulgin. They presented him with a letter commending his work on behalf of the Klan and two checks. One check for $300 was payable to Bulgin; the other check, for the same amount, was to the tabernacle.[18]

Tolerance was making life difficult for Cadle. In one issue, it showed a picture of smiling Ed Jackson shaking hands with Bulgin, part of the paper's drive to link the gubernatorial candidate with the Klan. On another occasion, it ran a story telling how Cadle had discovered that the director of his three-thousand-member choir was Catholic. Being a good klansman,

Cadle demanded the director's resignation.[19] The tabernacle's directors suggested that the action might be too drastic, but Cadle insisted that either the Catholic choir director left or else he would close the tabernacle. Cadle won.

With its solid reputation as a Klan stronghold, Cadle Tabernacle seemed the perfect place for Stephenson to strike back against Evans and Bossert. It was a cloudy afternoon as somewhere between seven hundred and eight hundred Klan leaders from around the state came to hear Stephenson's address at 2:00 P.M.[20]

The speech they heard was unlike any other Stephenson had delivered in the past. He never spoke directly about the Klan. He usually delivered lengthy speeches with political and historical overtones, such as "Back to the Constitution" or "Roosevelt's Unfinished Program." But the speech he gave that afternoon was different.

He began by explaining the differences that had arisen between himself and the Atlanta organization. He claimed Evans and Bossert had "prostituted the Klan for political purposes and were seeking to govern the organization by the imperialistic methods of defeated Germany." He told how, in backing Jackson for governor, the Klan was supporting the "highest type of Christian gentleman who ever served a public office in Indiana," adding that "we must, without compromise, elect this man in November whom we nominated on May 6."[21]

The rest of Stephenson's afternoon speech has been lost, but newspaper summaries suggest it was the same speech that Stephenson published and distributed to Indiana klansmen. Titled "The Old Man's Answer to the Hate Vendors," it had apparently been written before the primary election in reply to Evans's order banishing Stephenson from the Klan.[22]

"The Old Man's Answer" was self-consciously patterned after the Declaration of Independence. Stephenson hoped to accomplish similar results with it. The letter began, "To the Faithful Sons of Hoosierdom: The hour of fate has struck. The venality and jealousy of the men who carried the rebel flag in '61 is now invading Indiana. . . . It is a cowardly attempt on the part of a few 'yellow-livered' Southerners who hate everything that is pure throughout the State of Indiana. Their plan is to double-cross and sell out our organization to the common enemy and defeat all our men in November."[23]

The letter went on with a long list of evils committed by the Atlanta officers against the Indiana Klan, mimicking Jefferson's charges against the British. A short portion of the list gives an idea of the rest of the document:

- "They have prostituted justice by mishandling funds which should be used for a Holy purpose. . . .
- "They have lied repeatedly and attempted to cover it with additional falsehood.
- "They have never done anything for any local organization in Indiana and they have stood in the pathway and progress of the state office.
- "They have accepted bribes from bootleggers on promises of immunity from prosecution.
- "They have abused women and have hired delinquent girls to indulge in evil things."[24]

One might well have asked how Stephenson came to have such knowledge of Klan crimes and why he had not spoken up sooner—but, of course, no one did.

The most unflattering section of the letter was Stephenson's description of Evans: "The present national head is an ignorant, uneducated, uncouth individual who picks his nose at the table and eats peas with his knife. He has neither courage nor culture. He cannot talk intelligently, and he cannot keep a coherent conversation going on any subject for five minutes. His speeches are written by hired intelligence. The only thing he has ever been known to do was to launch an attack upon the character and integrity of men eminent in talent and virtue."[25]

Again, one might ask if all that were true of Evans, then why had Stephenson consented to work with Evans in the first place, and why had Stephenson not spoken up sooner against the man?

The letter concluded with Stephenson invoking "the divine providence that guides us" and the "unborn babies of the coming generation" who were relying on the Klan to be steadfast. Finally, he gave the Klan leaders specific instructions: "Hold all funds in your local treasury until the millions they have already taken from Hoosiers are accounted for."[26]

One klansman in the audience at Cadle Tabernacle later recalled that Stephenson had used such phrases as, "We don't need the Georgia Crackers to come up to Indiana and tell us how to do. . . . Let them stay below the Mason-Dixon Line. We can take care of ourselves."[27]

When he finished his first speech, Stephenson announced that he was appointing a special committee to draw up a constitution and bylaws for a new, independent Indiana Klan and that the job would be done that same afternoon. They would all meet back at the tabernacle at eight o'clock to hear the committee's report.[28] He knew he was proposing a radical move: to break away from the national Klan, form a new Klan, and retain control of it with a new constitution—all in a single day! But it was something that had to be done quickly. If any of these state Klan leaders were given time to think things over, they might lose heart and abandon him, staying with Bossert and the southern leadership. There could be no hesitation and no time for discussion or debate. To succeed, everything must happen on the same day.

A few hours later, everyone returned to hear the committee's report. The speed with which Stephenson's committee managed to come up with a complete program makes it clear that the real work had been completed long before the meeting and that the committee, if it did anything at all, simply rubber-stamped the plan. Besides a new constitution and bylaws, there was also a long list of resolutions to consider. All were placed before the membership to be voted on. The resolution included points which called for:

• the vesting of control of the Indiana Klan in the hands of Klan leaders elected by the state's membership;

• keeping funds raised by the Klan inside Indiana;

• election of Klan officers in Indiana instead of the old appointment system;

• proper representation of the Indiana Klan on the Imperial Kloncilium; and

• a national and state program for the rejuvenation of the Klan.[29]

After the resolutions had been read to the assembly, Stephenson called for a motion to have the report of the committee accepted. Receiving the motion and a second, he asked all who favored the acceptance of the report to stand. Nearly all the klansmen present stood up in an instant. Then he asked all those who did not favor acceptance of the report to also stand. No one in the hall moved to rise. The constitution, bylaws, and resolutions had all passed unanimously.

Next he called for election of officers. Stephenson himself was listed for the title "grand dragon." For grand klaliff, he chose Earl Sigmon, owner of the Sigmon Coal Company. For the post of nighthawk, or messenger, he named Dr. M. L. White, a local dentist. There were supposedly representatives from ninety-one of the ninety-two counties in Indiana present for the voting, yet the three known appointees in Stephenson's inner circle were all from Indianapolis. The voting was again unanimous.[30]

Stephenson was once again grand dragon of Indiana, but this time by his own hand. He had crowned himself grand dragon by the same manner in which his idol, Napoleon Bonaparte, had crowned himself emperor.

"God help the man who issues a proclamation of war against the Klan in Indiana now!" he roared to the crowd immediately after his election. "We are going to Klux Indiana as she has never been Kluxed before!"[31]

Then he launched into another speech, his second of the day. This time it was a political speech calling for straight salaries for all public officials, major revisions in the state laws regarding primary elections, and the defeat of radical and Bolshevistic segments of the national government. He identified Wisconsin Senator Robert LaFollette, who was then being discussed as a possible presidential candidate by the rural Progressives, as an "arch red of America who is trying to drive a wedge into the federal government."[32]

On Klan issues, Stephenson said that besides the regular local dues, every klansman in the state should contribute an extra twenty-five cents, of which twenty cents should go to the state headquarters and a nickel should be sent to Atlanta. (This last point was a joke, meant only for effect; nothing suggests that it was ever carried out.) The grand dragon, he said, ought to serve the state without a salary, and the books of the Klan should be open to all members for their inspection. (Again, this was mostly for effect. Stephenson did not need a salary from the Klan; he was getting rich enough solely on commissions.) He called on klansmen to help drive bootleggers out of the state and urged them all to work hard to "put the militant spirit back in the Klan."[33]

His fury that night was at its best. "Either the Klan is a damnable mockery and ought to be disbanded, or it represents the militant will of the Master!" he bellowed. "I'll appeal to the ministers of Indiana to do the praying for the Ku Klux Klan and I'll do the scrapping for it!

"There's been a lot of talk going around and there's going to be a lot more!" he said. "And the fiery cross is going to burn at every crossroads in Indiana, as long as there is a white man left in the state!"[34]

Some said that Stephenson's greatest moment had been the meeting at Kokomo, where Evans conferred the grand dragon title on him. But surely this one was greater. In Kokomo, power had been given to Stephenson. At Cadle Tabernacle, he was seizing the power.

There was only one problem with Stephenson's plan. Now Indiana had two grand dragons: Bossert by decree of the Imperial Palace, and Stephenson by vote of the Indiana Klan leaders.

This new dilemma was confusing for klansmen anxious to stay on the good side of the organization. It was even worse for the politicians who were eagerly courting the Klan vote. Even the simple matter of collecting dues for the organization became impossible. If a klavern treasurer sent the dues to Atlanta as he had always done, he would be in trouble with Stephenson. But if he kept the money in his local treasury, he would risk the wrath of the imperial wizard. A head-to-head confrontation was in the making.

The clash was only one day in coming. Stephenson and Bossert both showed up at a Republican organizational meeting the day after the Cadle Tabernacle meeting.[35] The event was the Sixth District Republican meeting in New Castle, Indiana—Bossert's home district. When the two men finally met face-to-face, they got into a loud argument over Klan business and Stephenson's revolt. The incident was picked up by reporters and carried all over the state: "Witnesses said hot words passed between the two and each took a couple of swings at the other before friends intervened. No damage resulted, but the near fight was the sensation of the meeting."[36]

Hearing the news from Indiana, Evans decided it was time to step in and settle the matter. Bossert would not be able to fend off his former boss on his own. So Evans called a special meeting to discuss the problem with all heads of the klaverns in Indiana. They were to meet in Indianapolis at the Lincoln Hotel, Sunday, May 18, where they would receive special instructions from Evans.[37]

The local papers announced the meeting. Stephenson helped publicize it by sending a telegram of his own to each Klan leader—with copies for reporters—urging the leaders to send "every officer of your organization" to the meeting. Evans and Bossert were playing right into Stephenson's hands. Hadn't he just told the Klan leaders how the Atlanta organization was trying to run the show in Indiana? Now, as if to prove Stephenson right, the imperial wizard was coming up from Atlanta, angry and ready for a fight.

The story in the *Indianapolis News* announced the meeting with the headline "OBEY EVANS'S CALL, STEPHENSON

ORDERS; INSURGENTS TOLD TO ATTEND RIVALS' MEETING
HERE ON SUNDAY." Stephenson was quoted saying that Klan
leaders should be "instructed to enter that meeting prepared to
make a demand that no action of any nature be taken there except and only after both sides have been presented. Truth seeks
no defense, it only demands an opportunity to be heard."

The Sunday meeting ended by raising more questions
than it answered. The Evans-Bossert faction tried but simply
could not pull the group together. Their disarray was complete.
They could not even agree on a place to hold the meeting. It was
moved from the Lincoln Hotel to Cadle Tabernacle until someone
pointed out that Howard Cadle seemed to be too friendly with the
Stephenson camp. So it was moved to the Indianapolis Klan's
regular local meeting site, the third floor of Buschmann Hall.
Throughout the day, other klansmen were stationed at the other
two locations to give stray Klan leaders the directions to
Buschmann Hall.

Between eight hundred and one thousand klansmen
turned out to hear what the imperial wizard had to say. But
Evans suspected that Stephenson had more tricks up his sleeve,
so Evans issued an order banning reporters from the meeting
followed by another order that the credentials of all klansmen be
checked and all Stephenson loyalists be turned away. Of course,
the problem then became one of determining who was loyal and
who was not. As a result, many klansmen were turned away at
the door and never even got inside the hall.[38]

The klansmen who did get inside were still not guaranteed
a place to sit. Buschmann Hall was much smaller than Cadle
Tabernacle. As the newspapers later reported, "a number of recognized klansmen were unable to find seats in the hall and they
gathered in a lower corridor to discuss Klan topics and review
happenings of the recent primary election."

Inside the hall, Evans skirted the issues. He did not discuss the matter of whether Klan political problems would be controlled by Atlanta or by the individual Klans. When it was all
over, he left it to Evansville's Joe Huffington—Stephenson's
former mentor was still an Evans man—to give a statement to
the waiting reporters.

"There is no more dissension among Indiana klansmen
who are in good standing," Huffington said. "The Klan officials
today by unanimous vote upheld the present administration of the
organization and pledged their loyalty to constituted authority
of the Klan in the future." If this was a victory, it had a hollow
sound to it.[39]

Stephenson was also claiming victory. His supporters told the press that nearly half the Indiana counties had failed to attend Evans's meeting. The northern Indiana klaverns had stayed away. Most of the ones who had come were from southern Indiana. Considering Huffington's appearance as Evans's spokesman, this point may have been true. The seats at the meeting might well have been stuffed with rank-and-file Evansville klansmen to give the appearance that Evans had just as much support as Stephenson.

On paper, both men were claiming the upper hand. Both were still locked in a stalemate over Indiana.

But Stephenson's power had been seriously cut back. As grand dragon under Evans, Stephenson had claimed control of twenty-three northern states. In reality, he may have visited less than a dozen of the states he supposedly controlled and exercised power in fewer states than that. His work had been concentrated in Indiana and Ohio. Now his power was limited to Indiana alone. There was no talk in any of his "breaking away from Atlanta" speeches about taking any other northern states with him. There were no references to Ohio, Pennsylvania, Michigan, or any of the other states he had once held title over. After Stephenson's public attack on the Atlanta leadership, there were no further mentions of his office in Ohio or trips to visit his other realms. From this point on, Indiana would be his home and his battleground.

The last time that Evans and Stephenson met face-to-face was probably the day of the Notre Dame riot in South Bend, Indiana. If Stephenson's version of the story is true, that final meeting lasted only a few minutes on the highway south of the city.

The Klan in St. Joseph County had always been outnumbered. South Bend was the only major city in the state with a Catholic population large enough to stand up against the Klan. The city was growing fast, with a manufacturing economy centered on the Studebaker automobile company. South Bend had more than 70,000 citizens, with large blocks of Polish (4,200) and Hungarian (3,200) immigrants.[40] Both ethnic groups included many of the city's Catholics. The city was also home to Notre Dame, the prestigious Catholic university. Located on the north side of town, the university had a beautiful parklike campus dominated by church spires and a huge golden dome. A statue of the Virgin Mary stood atop the dome overlooking the entire city. Ever since the appearance of the Klan in South Bend, trouble had been brewing between the town's militant Protestant and Catholic factions.

The Klan began publicizing regular Monday meetings in South Bend in mid-January 1923. The first outdoor Klan meeting was held in the neighboring community of Mishawaka, Indiana. Not long afterward, the opposition forces began to organize, and a South Bend chapter of the American Unity League was formed. The *South Bend Tribune* began an editorial campaign denouncing the Klan. The *South Bend News-Times* wavered at first but eventually climbed on the bandwagon to campaign against the Klan. Faced with such opposition, the Klan limited itself to an occasional cross burning and small rallies.

One student of the Klan has analyzed the characteristics of the South Bend klansmen based on a sample of fifty-four known klansmen. In her 1977 study, Jill Nevel noted, "On the whole, the Klansmen were solidly lower-middle to middle class. The average Klan member, then, tended to hold a white collar job, to be married and have a family, to own his home, and to consider South Bend as a relatively permanent home."[41]

The stage was set for a confrontation between the Protestants and Catholics when the Klan announced it would hold a tristate meeting in South Bend for klansmen from Indiana, Illinois, and Michigan. The meeting would be complete with a parade and a picnic on Saturday, May 17, 1924. This was supposed to be a typical Klan get-together, with speeches by prominent klansmen, flag-waving parades, marching bands, and a cross-burning ceremony. Unable to sort out the problems caused by the split in the Klan leadership, the St. Joseph County klansmen took no chances; they invited both Stephenson and Evans to speak.

The meeting was well publicized with advertisements in the *Fiery Cross* and posters tacked up on telephone poles for miles around. It was the type of event that certain people—both Catholics and Protestants—had been waiting for. The meeting was to be held the day before Imperial Wizard Evans denounced Stephenson's rebellion at the Buschmann Hall meeting.

Stephenson drove his car up from Indianapolis to attend the South Bend meeting. Five years later, when questioned by the Indiana attorney general, Stephenson gave a mild version of what happened that day.[42] He said he had driven to the Klan's headquarters, three blocks south of the St. Joseph County courthouse in South Bend. When he got to the building, he found a milling crowd of "perhaps three hundred curiosity seekers" and "eight or ten mischievous kids" who wore the Notre Dame school colors. As he watched, the students went to a nearby grocery and bought a basket of potatoes. The students then took aim with their potatoes and threw them through the glass windows of the Klan offices, which were on the top floor of the building and marked by an electrically lit fiery cross in the window. In his account, Stephenson maintained that, aside from the potato-throwing incident, "there was no violence. No blows were passed. There was no rioting. There was no impassioned shouting or crying out. There was no demonstration of violence whatever."

Afterward, Stephenson talked with the Klan leaders: "I took the Klansmen assembled in the hall about a mile and a half east of town, and there talked to them about an hour, admonishing them not to make any public demonstration."

Then he said he headed back to Indianapolis. "About a mile and a half from South Bend, where the filling station is on one side and the drugstore on the other, I met Imperial Wizard Evans and three automobile-loads of men whom I knew to be gunmen, deployed on each side of the street, waiting for the Pope and the Knights of Columbus to come marching out with a cannon, they said was assembled in South Bend. I told Mr. Evans they could put their popguns away and go right on down town. They were in America, not in Georgia."[43]

That such a conversation took place seems highly improbable. The idea of Evans lying in wait in South Bend for the pope seems ludicrous enough, but the notion of Evans and a gang of gunmen allowing Stephenson to escape makes the whole episode even more unlikely. It may be only one more grand Stephenson lie, or it may be that Stephenson passed Evans and his procession on their way up to South Bend to ride in the parade. The conversation is a typical piece of Stephenson folklore.

What is certain, however, is that the South Bend rally proved to be quite literally one of the worst beatings that the Klan ever received in Indiana. The confrontation there between the Klan and Catholics left several people injured and many hospitalized on both sides. One report claimed that the problems had started a few weeks earlier when several klansmen invaded the Notre Dame campus and wrecked one of the study halls. Now the students were out for vengeance.

The Klan blew the incident out of proportion to suit its purposes. Stephenson deliberately understated the problem. The newspapers covered the story with an anti-Klan, pro-student bias. No one could possibly have seen everything that happened that Saturday, since the "riot" was scattered over various parts of the city and fought in a series of skirmishes rather than a single confrontation.

Despite Stephenson's claim that he saw no violence, many other people did.[44] Both Klan and anti-Klan positions agree that a group of Notre Dame students gathered down by the train station to greet the klansmen who were coming to attend the rally. The students roughed up some of the klansmen, stole their robes and regalia, yanked American flag pins off their robes, and got into fights at the train station. The South Bend police, with many Catholics in its ranks, threw up its hands and said that nothing could be done to stop the fighting. Eventually, some of the policemen even joined the action and were pulled into the fray on one side or the other. One motorcycle patrolman later told how he was attacked by students who saw that he was wearing a Masonic pin (Masons were suspected—often correctly—of holding joint membership in the Klan). Another policeman was seen supplying potatoes to the anti-Klan protesters, who quickly turned them into missiles.

It must have been a bewildering day for the klansmen, most of whom had expected a friendly Klan meeting like all the others they had attended. The klansmen were not prepared for fights. Many had decorated their cars for the evening parade with American flags draped over car hoods and wrapped around wheel spokes. Students stopped the cars at intersections and stripped the flags off. The Klan reporters picked up stories— and, no doubt, invented others—about Catholic students beating up young mothers carrying babies, and striking young children and old people. The anti-Klan papers carried stories about students who bravely stood their ground against klansmen carrying loaded guns. The truth, as usual, was probably somewhere between the two extremes. In any case, May 17, 1924, was not a peaceful day in South Bend.

A spring thunderstorm ended the worst of the day's activities. No one felt like fighting in the rain. Klansmen waited to find out if the parade would be held in spite of the weather. Finally, the word was passed down that the parade and evening's ceremonies were cancelled "due to weather." Hundreds of bruised, wet, and angry klansmen dragged themselves back home to end what must have been one of their worst days.

The violence ended with nightfall. The police began making arrests on the streets again. (Only eight arrests for the entire day were reported in the papers!) By day's end, it seemed that the Catholic students had scored the victory, but such victories were fleeting. By engaging the Klan in street fights, the students only supplied the Klan with fresh evidence of the violent nature of the Catholics. The riot soon became a recruiting piece for the Klan. In a matter of days, the Klan presses were rolling out thousands of pamphlets, "The Truth about the Notre Dame Riot on Saturday, May 17, 1924." The pamphlets, which gave the Klan's side of the story in all its lurid detail, were distributed widely. Soon the recruiters in northern Indiana were reporting a record surge of new members rushing to join the Ku Klux Klan.

Chapter Seventeen

On the Campaign Trail

Summer 1924

After the fiasco in May at Buschmann Hall, Hiram Evans decided it was time to deal with Stephenson. Evans wanted his former ally to be tried by a Klan tribunal on "certain charges" and a "major offense," as the published report later described it. Working with Evansville Exalted Cyclops Joe Huffington, Evans began to execute a plan to remove Stephenson from the Klan forever.

The tribunal began by assembling six charges against Stephenson: violating the Klan oath of allegiance, disrespect of virtuous womanhood, conspiring against the order, habitual drunkenness, commission of an act unworthy of a klansman, and violation of the constitution and bylaws of the Klan.[1]

On June 4, the tribunal sent Stephenson a set of three letters informing him of the charges against him. This was followed the next day by a letter from Huffington telling Stephenson that he would be tried before the tribunal in Evansville on June 23 at the Klan's headquarters at Number One Edgar Street. Then the Klan began to send investigators—most likely some Klan attorneys—to travel around Indianapolis and Columbus gathering testimony from witnesses to support the six charges. The investigators spent a hot, dusty June driving all over Indiana and Ohio to collect statements. They went to Columbus, Ohio, on June 9 to take the statements of the deputies who arrested Stephenson making love in his parked car in Franklin County, Ohio. The next day they questioned the Deschler Hotel house detective, a policeman, and an attorney about Stephenson's arrest for the attempted rape of the hotel manicurist. They also conducted an anonymous interview with the manicurist.

Next, they raced back to Indianapolis, where, on June 12, they took testimony from two klansmen about Stephenson's split with the national Klan. They also collected some of his pamphlets to use as exhibits at the tribunal. A few days later, still in

Indianapolis, they took two more statements from klansmen about how Stephenson had "demoralized" the Klan.

The last piece of evidence was taken in Evansville on the day of the tribunal, June 23, when the investigators questioned the secretary who told how Stephenson had attempted to make love to her in the cottage at Buckeye Lake.

The tribunal did not take long to reach a decision. Even though Stephenson was not present, the tribunal found him guilty on all six charges and called for his "banishment forever and ostracism in any and all things by each and every member of this order." To make sure the banishment would be publicized, the tribunal authorized publication of all the materials used in the case against Stephenson. The letters, testimony, and decrees made up a thick booklet of more than fifty pages, which was distributed throughout Stephenson's former territory in hopes that he would be permanently scandalized and abandon his hopes of heading a splinter group.

But Stephenson was never one to give up so easily. He simply dismissed the report as another shameful plot of the southern Klan. As he later said, "Evans started a campaign of slander against me and every conceivable form of vulgar and libelous statement was circulated through the state of Indiana in whispering campaigns and through the employment of anonymous literature."[2] Stephenson waved it all away as if it were not worthy of an answer. The Indiana klansmen and politicians were left to make up their minds and choose which side of the Klan they wanted to be on.

For most politicians, the choice was easy. Bossert was backing ex–Governor James Goodrich, while Stephenson was backing Ed Jackson, who was ahead of the field for the fall election. Most of the Republican forces lined up behind Stephenson and Jackson.

There was more than the governor's race to consider in 1924. There was also a presidential election to think about. So while the Klan was investigating him, Stephenson packed his gear aboard the Reomar II and left to attend the Republican National Convention June 10 to 12 in Cleveland, Ohio.[3] It was generally acknowledged that President Calvin Coolidge would win the nomination to seek a term of his own (Coolidge had been in the White House less than a year following the death of President Warren G. Harding). But the race for vice president was considered open. The name of Stephenson's close friend, U.S. Senator James E. Watson from Indiana regularly came up as one of the top contenders for vice president. Stephenson went to the convention to help Watson in any way while keeping a low profile.

Evans was also at the Cleveland convention, but he made no attempt to keep a low profile. The imperial wizard arrived with a throng of sixty klansmen, including Indiana Grand Dragon Walter Bossert and *Fiery Cross* editor Milton Elrod, who had jumped over to the Bossert camp. Evans intended to publicize the Klan's growing role in national politics and to make a splash in the press.[4]

The splash was not long in coming. Writing a story about the vice presidential race, a reporter asked Elrod which candidate the Klan would support. "All our boys throughout the nation will understand only one thing, and that is Senator James E. Watson for Vice President—flat," said Elrod.[5]

This blunt announcement of Klan support came as a shock to Watson, who had tried to delicately tiptoe around the edge of his association with the Klan. (Once when he was questioned in Indianapolis about the Klan, Watson replied, "I am not a member of the KKK or of the Catholic Church, but I haven't anything against anyone for belonging to either."[6]) Now, however, with the Klan openly embracing him during a party convention, Watson cried, "Are they trying to kill me politically? I don't belong to the KKK. If they have issued a statement naming me, they have done it for the express purpose of injuring me."[7]

Watson was right. By siding with Bossert, Elrod was aligned with the Goodrich faction of the Indiana Republican party, the segment usually considered "anti-Watson." No doubt, Elrod's quote was a deliberate effort to torpedo Watson's political hopes by giving him an unsolicited Klan endorsement.

Evans immediately withdrew the Klan's endorsement, saying that only he could give an endorsement and that he had not done so. But the withdrawal was ignored. The damage was done. The Republicans abandoned Watson and decided to go with a dark-horse candidate, retired General Charles G. Dawes, for vice president. "My God, they have ruined me!" Watson moaned to reporters.

Stephenson saw all this happen but was powerless to save his friend. After the convention, he received a letter from Watson complaining about the treatment he had received from Elrod at the Cleveland convention. Watson said he would be glad to continue to help Stephenson and the Klan, but Watson must be able to keep his support under wraps. The episode is included in *The*

Mad Mullah of America, where the author, Edgar Allen Booth, reports walking into Stephenson's office to find him reading a letter from Watson:

> I had just seated myself near his desk after exchanging greetings. He sat before the desk nervously puffing a big cigar. "My God, Booth, look at that! Look at that!" he cried most dramatically. "Where are the men of Washington's day! Are we to be placed in the category of ingrates!" He tossed me the letter as he talked.
>
> I had the letter in my hand and now glanced at it and saw that it bore Senator Watson's name at the bottom.
>
> "Read it," he cried, "are the thirty pieces of silver still changing hand? Have we no longer men with us? God give us men!"
>
> "Well, keep still, Steve," I replied, "and I will read it."
>
> He now stopped talking and began furiously to puff on his cigar as I read the letter. It began "Dear Steve," and deplored Elrod's action at Cleveland. It stated that the writer was not only willing but glad to do all he could for Stephenson and the Klan, but that he wished to remain under cover. [Apparently even Senator Watson did not understand the split that had taken place in the Klan and assumed that Stephenson was somehow still in charge of Milton Elrod!]
>
> When I handed back the missive, Stephenson again cried: "God give us men! Men who will not stoop to the acts of a mongrel! And, Booth, just as sure as you are sitting in this office, Doc Evans had a hand in that. I know his rotten tactics. He is trying to force Watson out into the open. He is trying to force the Senator's hand with me! He's trying to make Watson be good. He had Milt do that just as sure as the sun will set tonight. Evans and his clique will stop at nothing. They already have half of Congress scared to death. But I'll whip the dirty dollar-grabbers and profaners of womanhood."
>
> He bewailed the fact that he had resigned and declared "Evans was profaning that which he [Stephenson] had built."[8]

The trip to the Cleveland convention was probably Stephenson's last excursion on his yacht. Shortly after 3:30 A.M. on June 27, the quiet lagoon of the Toledo Yacht Club in Bayview Park was rocked by a tremendous explosion. A ball of fire went up into the air, and flames were soon licking at what was left of the Reomar II. Three Toledo residents, guests of Stephenson's, had been aboard the boat when the explosion occurred along with Stephenson's bodyguard, Earl Klinck. The force of the blast knocked Klinck unconscious; he was carried off the burning yacht by an unidentified boy. The others managed to escape, but Stephenson's beautiful yacht was a total loss.

Arson was suspected immediately, but the case was never solved. Six months later, on December 15, John H. Bundy from Muncie, Indiana, would confess to setting the fire on the yacht. But he retracted his confession two days later, insisting that he had been coaxed by Fred Butler, Stephenson's secretary, and Klinck to confess. No other arrests were ever made.[9]

Was this a warning from Evans? Was it a sign that Evans was prepared to play rough if Stephenson didn't quiet down? It may be significant that the bombing took place only three days after the Evansville tribunal voted to banish Stephenson. Look at the record: Simmons had been banished and discredited before the entire Klan, and Edward Clarke had been pursued by lawsuits from Atlanta to Houston. Bad things were bound to happen to people who dared to cross Evans's path.

Evans was never implicated in the bombing, but if he had ordered it, then it had its desired impact. After the incident, Stephenson was seriously frightened for his life. More bodyguards were added. They all carried loaded guns at all times. Wherever Stephenson went, these men would accompany him.

On one occasion, two reporters, Walter Shead and John Niblack from the *Indianapolis Times,* dropped by Stephenson's offices on the third floor of the Kresge Building. "We went into his room and he was sitting at a big desk facing the old Indiana Trust Building," Niblack recalled. "All of a sudden, he jumped up and came around the desk and said, 'Get to one side! Don't stand there in front of that big window. There are people lying over there in the point of the Indiana Trust Building with highpowered rifles just trying to shoot me and they might hit you by mistake.'" After the interview, Shead and Niblack walked over to the Indiana Trust Building and went up to the roof. They found no guns or would-be assassins. Had the gunmen gotten scared and left? Niblack concluded that Stephenson must have been suffering from hallucinations.[10]

After these incidents, Stephenson kept a lower profile in Klan affairs. He continued to be quite active in politics, but he stayed away from the big Klan activities. A large, statewide Klan meeting was held at Cadle Tabernacle in September by the Bossert side of the Klan, but Stephenson did not interfere. There was a national klonvocation in Kansas City, Missouri, that same month, but Stephenson did not go. It might not have been safe for him to go; with the business of getting Ed Jackson into the governor's office, Stephenson had enough work to keep himself occupied. He was beginning to plan his strategy for the organization to pursue after the elections.

———————————

Ed Jackson was having a better summer than his friend Stephenson. Jackson's campaign for governor was going smoothly. His opponent, Dr. Carleton McCullough, had publicly announced the Democratic party's tough anti-Klan policy.

"The Republican party has been captured by the Ku Klux Klan, and has as a political party for the present, ceased to exist in Indiana," said McCullough. "The Democrats must accept the challenge and fight for the principle of religious liberty and the constitutional guarantee of the state and of the nation."[11] Nice words, but with a view like that, McCullough and the Democrats were well on their way to an honorable defeat. This left Jackson free to indulge in the usual political traditions of kissing babies and eating fried chicken.

Jackson's talents in the campaigning department astounded even the seasoned political reporters who followed his campaign trail. He visited most of Indiana's ninety-two counties during the campaign, often with several speaking engagements in each one. "On one occasion," noted Horace M. Coats of the *Indianapolis Star*, "he made twenty-one speeches in a single day, a record for political candidates in Indiana, and wound up his campaign the night before the election at Evansville with his one hundred and seventh speech. Mr. Jackson mixed work with pleasure and eating of fried chicken during his campaign, and was the butt of many a joke and prank during the tour. He established a reputation as a chicken eater which none of his companions was able to equal."[12]

Jackson's running mate was an equally popular former state senator, F. Harold Van Orman, a hotel owner from Evansville. Apart from serving two sessions in the Indiana General Assembly, Van Orman's only other claim to fame was his term as president of the Hotel Men's Benefit Association of the United States and Canada. He made a good candidate for lieutenant governor—completely unthreatening to Jackson.

Jackson toured the state in comfort, riding in the back of Stephenson's luxurious Lexington car, which had been lent to him for the duration of the campaign. He sat in the back seat as Stephenson's chauffeur drove from one campaign stop to the next. He invited reporters to ride along with him and told jokes along the way, puffing on his pipe.[13]

It was this down-home style of campaigning that charmed the voters. Even the knowledge that the Klan firmly backed Jackson did not bother most people. McCullough fought the Klan issue as hard as he could, but in November on election day, he was still 82,481 votes short of a win. Jackson and the Klan-supported ticket won the day with 654,784 votes to McCullough's 527,303. Jackson had won and so, in a sense, had Stephenson.[14]

Stephenson had big plans for himself and Jackson. In conversation with friends, Stephenson talked about the possibilities of backing Jackson for president in 1928. The power of Jackson as governor would be nothing compared to the power of Jackson as president.

There was also the matter of old Sam Ralston, whose health was rapidly failing and who might not make it through his term of office as U.S. senator. Ralston was the senator who had earned the Klan's respect by insulting the Catholic audience at Terre Haute, Indiana, with his speech on the separation of church and state. Though Ralston was a Democrat, he was still counted as a Klan-supported politician. If Ralston died soon, Stephenson told others, he felt he had a chance to be named by Governor Jackson to replace Ralston. Imagine Senator David Curtis Stephenson from Indiana! It was the very thing he had sought all his life. It was his destiny to lead the people, and filling Ralston's shoes was a quick road to the political success Stephenson had always longed for.

But Ralston was still clinging to life. And Jackson had not yet moved into the governor's mansion. The inauguration was scheduled for January 12, 1925, and there was plenty of work to do to prepare for that great occasion.

Chapter Eighteen

A Plan for the Statehouse

January 1925

The Klan victory at the polls in November 1924 initiated planning for the 1925 meeting of the Indiana state legislature, where the Klan would attempt for the first time to make its mark on the state's law books. But the Klan was divided, each half with its own agenda of favored legislation. The two Klans, one led by Walter Bossert and one by Stephenson, would work in entirely different ways.

Whatever else he may have been, Bossert was a true believer among klansmen. Unlike others, he did not join the Klan to make money; he joined because he believed in the Klan's patriotic theme. In addition to the Klan, Bossert also belonged to the Masons, where he was a member of the Scottish Rite, a thirty-second-degree Mason, and a member of the Eastern Star Order. He was also a member of the Knights of Pythias. Like Simmons, Bossert was a compulsive joiner. He was equally devoted to the Republican party, which he served in several leadership roles. Like Stephenson, Bossert saw the political potential for an organization like the Klan. But unlike Stephenson, Bossert felt the Klan's focus should be only on the issues of religion, patriotism, and morality.

"Bossert stood out alone," wrote one klansman who knew him well. "Good looking, clean cut and sincere; highly educated and cultured, it is even now hard to reconcile him with the Imperial Kloncilium. Bossert had a code of honor. Double-crossing, double-dealing or the betrayal of friends was not found in his idea of things. . . . Highly intelligent, he talked of the needs of America, and all through his talk never once did he exhibit the extreme prejudice which filled the talk of so many other members of the Imperial Kloncilium."[1]

It is not surprising that Bossert developed a unique political agenda for the Klan. Thanks partly to his efforts, the 1925 Indiana legislative session would forever be remembered as the

"Klan legislature" because of the obvious presence of the Klan within the statehouse. Bossert's Klan supported legislation to drive Catholics out of the education field, to tighten the state's responsibilities over moral questions, and to increase patriotic education in the public schools. Most Klan bills never became law, but a brief look at some of the Klan-supported bills in the 1925 General Assembly gives a good idea of Bossert's chief concerns[2]:

• *Prohibition of religious garb in public schools.* This bill was aimed at Catholic nuns who taught in public schools. In some parts of Indiana, the scarcity of teachers made it necessary to hire qualified nuns to teach in the public schools. By prohibiting the wearing of religious habits, it was thought that the nuns would be forced out of the school system.

• *Bible reading.* This bill would have made it mandatory for public school teachers to read portions of the Bible to their classes. Another section of the bill called for teaching students about the federal and state constitutions.

• *Teacher qualification.* This bill would have required teachers in public schools to have been educated in Indiana public schools. The theory was that this would eliminate Catholic-educated teachers from the public school system.

• *Religious education.* Presented in the senate, this bill would have called for two hours of religious instruction each week besides the regular school curriculum.

• *American flag display.* One of the few successful Klan bills, this one required public schools to display the American flag, which practically all schools did anyway.

• *Abolition of parochial schools.* The most brazen of the Klan-sponsored bills, this one would have abolished all parochial and nonmilitary private schools. It also called for fines or jail sentences for parents who sent their children to such schools.

• *Textbook requirements.* This bill called for Catholic schools to be required to teach from the same textbooks used in public schools.

• *Movie censorship.* This bill called for the establishment of a state commission to censor "immoral motion pictures."

The Klan relied on a small group of "Klan legislators" to introduce the bills that made up its legislative package. This group—mostly Republican—was led by George W. Sims of Terre Haute, who followed Bossert's orders with unswerving devotion.[3]

The Klan had one powerful opponent, Senator James J. Nedjl of Lake County, who was chairman of the Senate education committee. Since many of the Bossert Klan's bills pertained to educational issues, most had to pass through Nedjl's committee. The opposition to the Klan that Nedjl led was strong enough to stop most of the bills in committee or to kill them with votes on the floor.[4]

But opposing the Klan was not without its price. Nedjl sponsored a bill that would establish an old age pension for people over age sixty-five (in the days before federal Social Security). The bill was defeated by opponents who descended on the bill and its sponsor, calling the idea "socialistic" and comparing it to the works of Marx and Lenin.[5]

Of the few Klan bills that did become law, most were harmless, such as the bill requiring public schools to display the flag, which passed easily. The big Klan bills made plenty of fodder for newspaper reporters and were given strong headline treatment in the papers. These bills were good for making news, but when it came to garnering votes, nearly all of them failed.

It may be that the Klan's failure to deliver on its promises in the legislature led people to become disenchanted with the organization. What was the use of paying ten dollars to the Klan if the Klan couldn't do any of the things it said it was going to do? While other events added to the Klan's demise, this often-overlooked failure of the Klan in the political arena should not be discounted.

Stephenson, of course, had a different idea about what to do with his newfound political power. While Bossert's legislation may have been bigoted, it was an accurate interpretation of what his klansmen wanted. By comparison, Stephenson's legislation was blatantly designed to accomplish one thing: to win Stephenson more political power and line his pockets with money. Questioned by prosecutor Will Remy before a Marion County grand jury in 1926, Stephenson's friend and confidant, Court Asher, recounted Stephenson's political plans for the 1925 legislature.[6] There were probably more, but Asher specifically named the following bills that Stephenson supported:

• *Highway commission reform bill.* By far, this was the most important bill on Stephenson's agenda. It is also the most difficult to decipher. The bill would have stripped the existing highway commission of power and made the commissioners directly responsible to the governor. According to Stephenson's plan, Jackson would then name Stephenson's friends to the commission, and they would divide the state's lucrative road construction contracts. It became popularly known as the "road ripper" bill. The contracts connected to it would have been worth millions of dollars.

• *Nutrition bill.* This bill would have required nutrition education in public schools. Why would Stephenson have an interest in this issue? He had just commissioned the writing of a book, *One Hundred Years of Health,* which was to have been sold statewide for use in the schools as the only textbook for the classes that would have been created by this bill.

• *Fire insurance bill.* Stephenson did not support this bill. Instead he offered to have the bill killed if interested lobbyists would pay him enough to guarantee its defeat.

• *Utility reform bill.* Using the opposite tactic that he employed in the insurance bill, Stephenson supposedly had a bill introduced that would bring about stricter regulation of utilities. Then he approached the utilities for "donations" to assure that the bill would be killed. According to Asher, one utility official, Samuel Insull, paid Stephenson $200,000 to eliminate the bill.

• *Oleomargarine bill.* This bill would have called for more descriptive labeling on packages of oleomargarine. Asher is not clear on this one, but presumably Stephenson tried to collect money from the dairy industry to make sure that the bill passed.

• *Stream pollution bill.* This bill would have prohibited manufacturers from dumping trash into streams. According to Asher, Stephenson planned to ask companies for $75,000 in the interest of stopping the bill.

At just a glance, it is easy to see Stephenson's motives were self-serving and devious. After all, who would suspect a Klan leader of attempting to influence bills on oleomargarine or stream pollution? Who would have thought that a man who supported "100 percent Americanism" would have also been so deeply involved in plots to extort thousands of dollars from lobbyists all over the state?

Apparently few people knew about Stephenson's agenda. Even today, some modern writers have confused Stephenson's legislative plans with those of the Bossert Klan, assuming—incorrectly—that Stephenson also supported the doomed attempts to restrict parochial education. Like most of the legislators, Stephenson simply did not take Bossert's program seriously. He was too busy with his schemes to make a fortune inside the cool, marbled hallways of the statehouse.

Stephenson made it easy for lawmakers to support his legislation. All his bills had at least the outward appearance of creating some sort of public service. Who could argue with bills to clean up Indiana's rivers and streams? Wasn't an educational program on nutrition a good idea? Even the "road ripper" bill could be considered a way of improving the state's highway system.

On the other hand, a legislator had to go out on a political limb to support any of the Bossert Klan's bills. Even if legislators happened to agree with one of Bossert's bills, simply voting in favor of it would label them as klansmen whether or not they actually were members. Legislators had to weigh each bill carefully and decide whether they could afford to upset all the Catholics in their districts by voting for a bill that might hurt their parochial schools. It was much easier simply to ride along with Stephenson—and perhaps find a juicy campaign contribution in return.

In spite of their differences, Stephenson and Bossert probably shared one trait as they prepared for the 1925 General Assembly. Both men had elaborate programs planned, so they must have spent most of their time between the November elections and the start of the General Assembly in January looking for sponsors to present their pet legislative programs.

January came in mildly that year and brought with it the inauguration of Governor Ed Jackson.

The political world still served as both entertainment and government. Next to murder, politics held the attention of newspaper readers better than anything. Campaigns, elections, investigations, speeches, hearings, and an occasional scandal-of-the-week helped take the average citizen's mind off more pressing problems. In a country that had rejected kings and coronations, the inauguration of a governor provided an American replacement at the local level for the older, European, storybook ceremonies.

Jackson was inaugurated in high style. Usually the Republicans held the gala inauguration party for a Republican governor in their own private club, the Columbia Club on Monument Circle. But in 1925, the Columbia Club was not available. The Republicans were in the process of building a newer, bigger, better club building, and it was not ready in time for the inauguration. So the Republicans planned to take their party up the street to the newly completed Democrats' clubhouse, the Indianapolis Athletic Club. This would be a gala to remember.

The inauguration was scheduled for noon on January 12, 1925, in the main corridor of the statehouse. A light snow was falling outside as more than five thousand people crowded into the Capitol, jamming stairways, halls, and corridors to catch a glimpse of the new governor as he took his oath.[7]

Jackson's inaugural speech was memorable only for its brevity, taking less than three minutes to recite. It was a bland address that dealt with the duty of office holders to honor the will of the people. It included a section which noted that courage was needed in public service. "There will be those who will offer counsel from a class viewpoint; also those whose counsel will be prompted by selfish motives; there will be others who will attempt to dictate and failing in that, will try to harm by criticism. Against all these one must be fortified by manly courage sufficient to do right uninfluenced and undeterred. A public servant owes all to those he serves."[8] The speech was an eerie prediction of the very problems that would plague Jackson's administration.

Stephenson had an indirect hand in planning the inaugural festivities. Stephenson's personal secretary, Fred Butler, represented his boss on the committee. Stephenson, of course, was also included among the guests of honor at both the inauguration and the dinner.[9]

As soon as Jackson took his oath, the members of the decoration committee—mostly Republican volunteers from the statehouse staff—quickly began to put the fourth-floor ballroom of the Athletic Club in order for the evening dinner. Soon one hundred fifty of the state's top Republicans and their wives or guests would fill the ballroom, a magnificent room with a high vaulted ceiling, golden scalloped moldings over the tall windows, and a gleaming dance floor. Tonight, tables were arranged around the dance floor with a bandstand for the Athletic Club Orchestra on the east wall, opposite the entrance.

Stanley C. Hill was in charge of getting all the place cards in position according to the seating chart worked out by the inaugural committee.[10] He had recruited a friend, Madge Oberholtzer, to help with the name tags. Dark-haired Oberholtzer was manager of the Indiana Young People's Reading Circle, a special section of the Indiana Department of Public Instruction. The twenty-eight-year-old statehouse worker had a knack for planning parties, and since Hill had dated her many times, he did not feel that he was imposing by asking her to help with the governor's dinner. Just for working on the committee, she would be included as a guest at what had to be one of the top political parties of the year—the very top in Republican circles.

So Hill and Oberholtzer worked that afternoon, filling out name tags, checking them against the lists on the seating charts, and putting them in the proper places. Here were Senator Watson and his wife . . . over there was the new state attorney general, Arthur Gilliom from South Bend . . . here was the poet William Herschell, who had been asked to read some of his sentimental verses that evening . . . here were Mr. and Mrs. George

Ball, part of the wealthy Ball family from Muncie . . . there was former Governor Emmet F. Branch with his wife . . . Mr. and Mrs. Frederick Schortemeier, the new secretary of state . . . here was the new lieutenant governor, Harold Van Orman, and his wife. And so it went.

Hill had put his name right next to Oberholtzer's on the invitation list, and they were to be seated at the same table as Fred Butler, Margaret Reynolds, and Stephenson. It was difficult work getting all the names in all the right places, but at last they were finished. The name tags were in place next to each gleaming plate and shining silver place setting. The couple left to get dressed for the party.

Hill, a young widower with three children, had been dating Oberholtzer since October 1923, often dining with her and accompanying her to parties. Hill had met Stephenson during the past election and was now working with him on a real estate deal in Florida.

That evening, Stephenson attended the dinner and sat across the table from Hill and Oberholtzer. Stephenson came with an attractive young secretary on his arm, whom he introduced to Hill. In turn, Hill introduced Oberholtzer to Stephenson.

The entertainment for the event was not too captivating.[11] There were short speeches from the new governor and lieutenant governor. Willis Dye, chairman of the inaugural committee, introduced honored guests, and Roltaire Eggleston, an entertainer, offered toasts. Robert E. Heun, head of the local Rotary Club, pledged the support of all the area's Rotarians to Jackson's administration. Poet Herschell stood up to recite his rustic favorite, "Ain't God Good to Indiana." Then Eggleston amused the crowd with some magic tricks.

During all this gaiety, there was time for the guests at Stephenson's table to become better acquainted. Stephenson began to talk freely with Oberholtzer. He would have noticed, no doubt, that she was single and not wearing any engagement ring. In polite dinner conversation, he probably learned that she worked in the statehouse and lived in Irvington, just a few blocks down the street from his house. For her part, Oberholtzer probably already knew a great deal about Stephenson from her talks with Hill, from the inside news that was carried on the statehouse grapevine, and from whatever stories were circulating through Irvington about the wealthy new owner of the old Graham house.

Finally, at some point during that long evening, the orchestra began to play, and Stephenson invited Madge Oberholtzer to dance.

Chapter Nineteen

The Law Makers

January 1925

Madge Oberholtzer was an attractive and ambitious young woman, though not, as some reporters would later portray her, either particularly striking or beautiful. She was quick-witted and intelligent, according to her friends, and she knew how to hold up her end of a conversation. In a word, she was interesting.

She had been the second and last child born to George and Matilda Oberholtzer. Her brother, Marshall, was not quite two on the day his sister was born, November 10, 1896. The family lived in Clay City, Indiana, in the west central part of the state, where their relatives worked in the neighboring coal mines. Madge's father, a postal clerk for the railroad, was a slight man with a large moustache and bright, twinkling eyes. Her mother was heavyset with broad shoulders and a wide frame. Both of Madge's parents had been born in Indiana—Matilda in Clay County and George nearby in Owen County.[1]

When Madge was seven, the family moved from Clay City to Indianapolis when her father took a postal clerk job at Union Station. They rented a home on the east side at 27 Dillon Street, then later moved to another house on South Hawthorne in Irvington. On October 4, 1903, Matilda Oberholtzer asked that her membership be transferred from the Clay City Methodist Church to the Irvington Methodist Church, and the family began to put down new roots.[2]

Madge's childhood in Irvington was unremarkable. Jean Brown Wagoner, the daughter of *Indianapolis News* editor Hilton U. Brown, was a childhood friend of Madge's. The Browns lived in a large house atop a hill at the west edge of Irvington.

"Everybody loved Marsh and Madge," Wagoner recalled many years later. "She was a free, easy-going, rough-and-tumble kind of girl. She was happy-go-lucky, but always feminine . . . except when we all wore overalls in the summer. I never thought of her as being intellectual, but she was intelligent, a very frank, honest kind of girl."[3]

Madge attended grade school in Irvington, then attended Emmerich Manual High School in downtown Indianapolis, where she graduated in 1914. Marshall had also attended Manual, graduating in 1912. Then he went on to Purdue University to study engineering. Madge decided to go to Butler College in Irvington, just a few blocks from the big white house her parents had recently purchased on University Avenue. Going to Butler, she would be able to save money by living at home and by walking down the winding avenue to her classes.

At Butler, she signed up for classes in English, mathematics, zoology, and logic. A classmate remembered her: "Madge wasn't much good at math or logic. I seem to remember that English was her major. I tried to help her with logic, but I just couldn't get it through her head at all. In fact, we used to say back then that her heart ruled her head, rather than her mind." The classmate, Lena Pavey Morrow, in a 1979 interview, recalled, "She was an independent soul, yet timid. I don't think anybody disliked Madge. But she didn't make a great effort to make people like her, either."[4]

In her first year at Butler, Madge pledged the Pi Beta Phi sorority to which Lena, one year older, also belonged. It was about this time that Madge probably entered the big house at 5432 University Avenue for the first time. Ellen Graham, who would later sell the house to Stephenson, always invited the Pi Phi's to hold their rush parties in her home, since the sorority did not have a house of its own.

Madge did not date very often in college. Morrow recalled that there had been a group of local Irvington girls who often dated some of the young dental students at Butler. "But she never really ran around with the group of us in Irvington." Wagoner remembered that, when it came to dating, "the boys always had to do the asking, but even so, Madge always managed to find enough partners at dances whenever she felt like it."

Marshall once invited her to come up to West Lafayette, Indiana, for a visit on Purdue's campus. Perhaps trying to play matchmaker for his younger sister, he arranged a date for her with one of his friends. Madge dated Marshall's friend briefly, but she soon broke off the relationship, later explaining to her friends that it was "impossible": the young man was Catholic. After that, no one could recall Madge having any one particular beau or any long-lasting love interest.[5]

Madge studied at Butler for three years, then left at the end of her junior year. No one knows why she did not go back to finish her degree. The 1917 issue of Butler's yearbook, *The Drift*, provides a photograph of Madge on the verge of womanhood: a strong chin, a long but attractive nose coming down to a broad, firm mouth, and a head covered with ringlets of closely bound dark hair. The entry in the yearbook beneath her name reads, "Madge is a timid little creature with a baby voice, who allows professional gruffness to frighten her into speechlessness, but once outside of the depressing influence of class-room walls she waxes adjectivorous and verbiforous and is able to hold at bay the most fluent masculine word-artist on the campus."[6]

Instead of returning to school that fall, Madge decided to look for work. She became a grade-school teacher, taking a position with a school in the small east central Indiana community of Hagerstown in Wayne County, about sixty-five miles from home.[7] One year of that, however, was enough for Madge, and she returned home at the end of the term. Her next job was a clerk's position for the American Central Life Insurance Company from 1919 to 1920. She got her first job with the state in 1921 as a clerk in the statehouse. In 1923, she took a job as an office manager with the Acme Motion Picture Projector Company.[8]

Then Madge suddenly decided to take time off from her career and do something different. She had purchased her own Ford coupe and had learned to drive it. So in 1924, she quit her job with a finance company. Accompanied by Ermina Moore, a good friend whom she had met at the statehouse, she headed west for a bit of traveling, touring, and sight-seeing.

Ermina Moore was about four years older than Madge and a graduate of Indiana University. At thirty-one, she was much like the sort of person that Madge wanted to be: a strong-willed, independent woman. She was not rich, but at least she had a place of her own, a rented half of a wood-frame double on the east side. Madge had met her at the statehouse in the office of the state superintendent of public instruction, where Moore worked as a secretary. The two soon became friends.

They returned from their western vacation in October, and Madge went back to the statehouse, this time as manager of the Indiana Teachers and Young People's Reading Circle, a lending library program for teachers that was organized under the Department of Public Instruction.

Madge's job entailed filling book orders received from teachers all around the state. Most of the time, she worked in the book management office in the Lemcke Building on Pennsylvania Street, a few blocks from the statehouse. Her other office was in room 227 of the statehouse, and she reported directly to

Superintendent Henry N. Sherwood. The job paid between $3,000 and $4,000 annually, which was considered a good wage. The job was considered management and, thus, was better than a clerical spot and more to her liking.[9]

When Madge met Stephenson in early 1925, rumors were flying around the statehouse that the Reading Circle program—and, consequently, Madge's job—was about to be budgeted out of existence by the legislature. Madge was twenty-eight years old, unmarried and without prospects, and she was still living at home with her parents. She needed her job.

The times had not been easy for Madge's parents, either. Ever since they bought the big white house in Irvington, it was obvious that they had taken on more property than they could manage.[10] To supplement her husband's postal clerk income, Matilda Oberholtzer decided they should begin taking in boarders. An older woman, Eunice Schultz, and her son, who was a teacher at Butler, were among the Oberholtzers' tenants. A retired fireman, Charles Householder, who apparently was having trouble with his marriage, was also staying in the house. With her parents struggling to make ends meet, Madge's paycheck from the Reading Circle was a source of much-needed income.

If marriage was a possibility for Madge, Stanley Hill with his three small children apparently did not meet her expectations. Or perhaps she was simply not interested in matrimony as a way to get out of her parents' house. In any case, the two were friends but definitely not engaged. Then Hill introduced her to Stephenson, a man who must have seemed mysterious, rich, and important, a man who might even be able to use his political clout to save her job.[11]

After meeting Stephenson at the inaugural dinner, Madge began seeing him on a regular basis. "After the banquet, he asked me for a date several times, but I gave him no definite answer," she told her friends later. "He later insisted that I take dinner with him at the Washington hotel and I consented and he came for me at my home in his Cadillac car, and on this occasion we dined together."[12] The restaurant was the Hotel Washington's Café George, a small, intimate restaurant in the hotel basement that was decorated in a Pennsylvania Dutch style.[13] It was a place where Stephenson often entertained his guests. "After that, he called me several times on the phone, and once again I had dinner with him at the Washington hotel with another party," Madge recalled. "Subsequent to this I was once at Stephenson's home at a party with several prominent people when both gentlemen and their ladies were present."[14]

Madge claimed she only went out with Stephenson a few times. But Stephenson's friend, Court Asher, reported that the two were often seen together throughout the 1925 session of the General Assembly. Asher said Madge was one of Stephenson's regular messengers that he used to carry his instructions back and forth from his office down to his friends at the legislature. Asher also said that Stephenson had hired Madge to help write his nutrition book, *One Hundred Years of Health*, and that Madge was planning to help sell the books to the schools once Stephenson's nutrition education bill made it through the session. In her position at the Department of Public Instruction, Madge would have had the right connections to help Stephenson with his scheme. The nutrition education bill was one of Stephenson's that eventually made its way through the legislature.[15]

Asher's version of the relationship between his former boss and Madge was also supported somewhat by attorney Will Remy, who said that Stephenson "told her that he was writing a book, and wanted to employ a stenographer to do some private work for him on certain evenings."[16] As the session of the General Assembly continued, Madge would be seeing more and more of Stephenson.

Stephenson's mind was occupied by more than Madge Oberholtzer. He was working on two major projects in those early months of 1925. First was his political agenda for the state legislature. If his bold scheme worked, millionaire Stephenson would soon be able to multiply his wealth and consolidate his political power. Second was the Indianapolis city election of 1925 in which a new mayor would be chosen. Using the same strategy he had employed in Governor Jackson's campaign, Stephenson was preparing to finally seize the city offices from Mayor Lew Shank's control. By successfully completing these two projects, Stephenson would be the undisputed behind-the-scenes boss of politics in both the city and the state. That could not hurt his chances of eventually being named to the U.S. Senate, whenever Sam Ralston's illness finally overtook him.

In the state legislature, Stephenson made his presence felt early and quite publicly. A hot topic of debate was whether Indiana should continue to hold direct primary elections or return to a system of picking candidates through party delegates. Former U.S. Vice President Thomas R. Marshall sided with former Governor James P. Goodrich in favoring the repeal of the direct primary system. But Jackson thought the current primary system was just fine and should not be changed. An *Indianapolis Times* article January 7 identified "Albert J. Beveridge, former United States Senator [from Indiana], and D. C. Stephenson, political advisor to Governor-Elect Ed Jackson" as being in defense of the existing system. At a meeting in the Claypool Hotel where the issue was debated, both men had spoken against repealing the primary system. Stephenson had spoken in support of the current law and told the audience of about a hundred listeners that the repeal movement would fail in the legislature. (He was right; it did.)[17]

The daily newspapers all seemed well informed of Stephenson's positions, not only in the primary system debate but on all the major issues. He was a regular source of news for the statehouse press corps, and all the dailies seemed to reflect this by exhibiting a clear understanding of the split in the Klan. The reporters understood the difference between a "Stephenson bill" and a "Bossert Klan bill"; they also understood the impact of the split in the Klan. A short article in the *Indianapolis Times* January 8 was headlined "DEMOCRAT POWER IN HOUSE GROWS" and speculated that the factionalism in the Republican party might give more power to the minority Democrats during the legislative session. "The Republican majority, admitted to be 'a little unwieldy,' is split into Klan and non-Klan groups," the article pointed out. "The Klan members are divided into adherents of D. C. Stephenson, political advisor of Governor-Elect Ed Jackson, and Walter Bossert, head of the 'regular' Klansmen. Stephenson claims a working majority over all other combined."[18]

Just like Stephenson, the Evans-Bossert faction was trying to be quite visible during the 1925 legislative session. The Klan called a meeting at the Indianapolis Athletic Club on January 6. The *Indianapolis Times* published a front-page story reporting a call for "Ku Klux Klan members of the Indiana General Assembly" to attend the strategy planning session. Imperial Wizard Evans was supposed to attend, but the article noted that he had just undergone an appendectomy and was still recovering from the operation.[19] Out of this meeting came the shape of the "regular Klan" program for the session with its long string of anti-Catholic educational reform measures. The Klan chose to put its strength behind the religious garb bill, the antiparochial education bill, and all the rest.

The Klan's decision to push for its education package made it necessary to control the House committee on education.

Bossert wanted James M. Knapp, a Republican representative from Hagerstown, to become the head of the education committee. Knapp would be willing to go along with the Klan's program and ease the bills through the legislature.

But Bossert's scheme hit a major stumbling block. Bossert's Klan had fought the nomination of one representative, Harry G. Leslie, for Speaker of the House. Instead, the Klan backed the Kokomo representative, George W. Freeman, but Leslie had won anyway. At one point, it was reported that the Klan offered to pull Freeman out of the Speaker's race if Leslie would agree to support the Klan's educational package. Leslie turned down the offer. He did not need Bossert's support, since he already had Stephenson's and Jackson's support. Knapp was named head of the House education committee, but now the Bossert Klan would have to face a victorious enemy in the form of Speaker Leslie, a man who would now use his enormous power to fight their program.[20]

Bossert might have rested easier after getting Knapp into the right position on the House education committee. But then Bossert found he was completely blocked in the Senate by the appointment of anti-Klan Senator James J. Nedjl, head of the Senate education committee. In a bicameral, or two-house, state legislature, it is necessary for supporters of a bill to move their legislation through similar committees in both the House and the Senate before a bill can become law. With Nedjl controlling the Senate's education committee, the stalemate between Klan and anti-Klan forces would obviously cancel each other out.

Nedjl was also involved in another Klan-centered dispute. Bossert was pushing for Senator Thomas A. Daily of Indianapolis to be named president pro tem of the Senate. Senator Daily was identified in the papers as pro-Jackson, pro-administration, and pro-Klan. An "anti-administration" wing was quickly organized among the senators, and Nedjl was selected as this group's choice for president pro tem. Immediately, the Senate Republicans were split into two camps over Nedjl and Daily.

When the senators voted, Nedjl won. Daily went howling to the newspapers, telling reporters that his defeat had been engineered through Stephenson's crooked dealings. "I consider Stephenson a political mountebank," said Daily. "He organized the Ku Klux Klan in Indiana, got their money, and got out and now is attempting to break it up." Daily said he had split with Stephenson over the automobile racing issue, a bill that had been introduced in the Senate which would have prohibited the running of the Indianapolis 500-Mile Race on Memorial Day. Stephenson, George Coffin, and the Marion County Republicans wanted Daily to oppose the bill. But Daily refused, saying that the race was a "desecration of Memorial Day." Daily assumed that his refusal on this bill had triggered Stephenson to withdraw his support for Daily as president pro tem, which allowed Nedjl to win. Daily called the incident an example of Stephenson's "political chicanery."[21] (The opponents of the Indianapolis 500-Mile Race bill lost their case, as they had in previous years, and the race continued for years as a Memorial Day event.)

There were other signs, too, that things were not going the way that Bossert hoped they would. As January wore on, each of the Klan's education bills was introduced in the legislature. In the Senate, the bills were usually sponsored by Republican George W. Sims from Terre Haute. The Klan bills were typically supported by a faction considered by the press to be the hard-core Klan: Republicans John S. Alldredge of Anderson, C. Leroy Leonard of Silver Lake, Roscoe Martin of Logansport, C. Herman Pell of Carbon; and Democrat Earl W. Payne of Bloomington.[22] Repeatedly on the Klan issues, these six senators voted as a block to support the legislation. One by one, the rest of the legislature voted the Klan bills down. The bill to ban religious garb in public schools was defeated in the Senate, 40–6. The bill to require Bible reading in the schools failed, 26–20. The bill requiring teachers to have a public school education was postponed indefinitely, 41–5.[23]

In the House, the Klan's support was stronger. The religious garb bill in its House version passed by a 67–22 vote. A bill requiring parochial schools to use the same texts as public schools passed, 64–20. The Bible reading in schools bill passed, 75–11.[24] But most of these were empty victories, since the Senate effectively killed the bills. Only the least controversial Klan bills managed to make it into the law books. In the end, the most notorious Klan bills all died either quietly on the floor in roll call votes or silently in committees.

The Klan, as always, proved it could generate publicity, but it was poorly equipped to deliver on any of its promises. This fact, perhaps more than others, may have been the real reason people lost interest in the Klan so quickly. They had been drawn in by the Klan's promise to "set things right" in the country, but the public soon realized that Klan politicians had no better luck than any other politicians. Like most political promises, the Klan's naive promises ran headlong into reality, and the people who had once supported the Klan soon became disenchanted.

Stephenson probably sensed the doomed nature of Bossert's efforts. After all, hadn't he experienced the same thing himself during his idealistic days as a Socialist reformer in Oklahoma? Stephenson must have enjoyed watching his opponents blunder and trip over their own rhetoric, crashing in dark failure over each broken promise.

Chapter Twenty

Stephenson's Triumph

February 1925

By February, the Klan was beginning to wear out its welcome in the Indiana General Assembly. Two people who were not amused by the Klan's antics were Lieutenant Governor Van Orman and House Speaker Leslie. Lobbyists for the Klan and other groups were besieging both the House and the Senate. Not that lobbying was anything new in Indiana politics, but this year the whole business had simply gotten out of hand. Lobbying was governed by a code of honor, conducted in offices, private clubs, and the better restaurants. It might even be conducted in the hallways of the statehouse. But now the lobbyists, like an infestation of rats, seemed to be everywhere.

The lieutenant governor delivered a blistering attack on the lobbyists February 5. He noted that lobbyists from various groups had been brazenly summoning senators out of the chambers to give them their voting instructions. "Lobbyists are absolutely making senators do their bidding. They are coercing them, hauling them about and sitting at their very desks," said Van Orman. "Lobbyists must be driven from this chamber if they do not have enough conscience in their own hearts to allow the senators to do what they believe is right."[1]

This led to Van Orman's order to the General Assembly doorkeepers to allow no lobbyists into chambers. "The time has come when these lobbyists must be driven from the chamber!" Van Orman shouted, adding that this would be his final warning. The senators applauded Van Orman—and the one lobbyist who was still lingering in the chamber during the lieutenant governor's tirade decided that perhaps it was time to leave.[2]

As the session moved into February, Stephenson gained visibility in a different way. He was involved in the unusual incident of the bolting Democratic senators. The so-called "bolt" occurred over a bill which would have gerrymandered Lawrence

County from the Second to the Third Congressional District. Sponsored by Republican Senator Will K. Penrod of Loogootee, the bill had more than enough votes to pass in the Republican-controlled Senate. By its passage, however, the Democrats were sure to lose a congressional seat. So rather than sit idly by while the bill was passed in their presence, the Democrats decided to "bolt" and leave the state. They reasoned that their absence would prevent a quorum in the Senate, creating a legislative stalemate and bringing the General Assembly to a grinding halt. Without the Democrats for a quorum, the Republicans would not be able to vote for their reapportionment plan.[3]

On Thursday afternoon, February 26, the Democratic floor leader, Senator Joseph M. Cravens, rented a motor bus, and at 2:00 P.M., fifteen rebellious Democratic senators boarded the bus and fled to Dayton, Ohio. They sent word back to the legislature that they would return whenever the Republicans promised that the Penrod bill would either be defeated or withdrawn.

The entire episode has the ring of a college fraternity prank, but it made front-page news. House Speaker Leslie denounced the Democrats' move as "exceedingly humiliating to the state." A Marion County grand jury threatened to investigate the case, and the Republican prosecutor, Will Remy, said he would consider bringing a case against the Democrats.

But the bolt only lasted one day. The next day's *Indianapolis Times* carried the banner headline on its front page: "D. C. STEPHENSON BEHIND MOVE WHICH BROUGHT 15 ABSENT SENATORS BACK: REPUBLICAN POLITICAL BOSS ASSURES DEMOCRATIC FUGITIVES MEASURE THEY ARE OPPOSED TO WILL BE DROPPED." The article went on to say that the senators came back "because D. C. Stephenson, Republican political boss, promised them: immunity from arrest; that the Penrod gerrymander bill, which would make the Second Congressional District safely Republican, would either be withdrawn or killed; that indictments against the seceding Democrats, if returned, would be quashed."[4]

Indianapolis Times reporter Walter A. Shead had followed the senators' bus to Ohio. He told how Stephenson had left Indianapolis shortly after the bolt and had met the senators that evening in Dayton. (Bossert had sent Joe Huffington and Robert McNay, a Klan grand titan, as his representatives to talk with the Democrats.) Accounts of what happened in Dayton vary, but it seems that Stephenson met with senators Joe Cravens and Harvey Harmon—both of whom later denied meeting with

Stephenson—to negotiate a settlement of the dispute. Stephenson supposedly promised to use his political influence with the governor to stop the Penrod bill if the senators would agree to return.

Shead met Stephenson in the lobby of the Gibbons Hotel and asked him what was going on. "Oh, I'm just visiting friends here in Dayton," Stephenson grinned, "and attending to a few little business matters."[5]

After a series of telephone calls to Indiana and negotiations with representatives of the lieutenant governor, the rebellious senators announced that they would return. Stephenson, accompanied by Omer Hawkins, the Marion County sheriff, and H. Walker DeHaven, a state representative from Indianapolis, followed the Democrats back to the Indiana state line. Stephenson was driving his limousine. As the bus crossed the state line, he roared by them on his way back to Indianapolis.

Both Cravens and Hawkins vigorously denied that Stephenson had any part in cutting a deal with the Democrats. The two gave the credit to Van Orman. But the *Indianapolis Times* loudly acclaimed Stephenson's role in negotiating the return, and the paper's version of the incident was the one most widely accepted. Everything the paper claimed Stephenson had negotiated actually happened: the senators were never prosecuted, the grand jury investigation was dropped, and the Penrod bill died. Perhaps Stephenson was instrumental in settling the matter, or maybe he was only showing his uncanny ability to steal the limelight from almost anyone.

Democratic Senator Charles S. Batt of Terre Haute, one of the bolters, later insisted, "I didn't even know he [Stephenson] was in Dayton, but of course I don't know everyone in that town. This Stephenson is a sort of P. T. Barnum person. When there is anything going on, he rushes on the scene and gives out an interview to get the resultant publicity. I suppose if we had stayed in Dayton, Stephenson would have said he ordered us to stay!"[6]

Stephenson, meanwhile, was moving along briskly with his own plans. He was trying to get the legislature to move on his schemes for nutrition, stream pollution, fire insurance, highways, and oleomargarine.

The fire insurance bill was introduced by Democratic Senator W. S. Chambers of New Castle, to abolish a 1919 law that had established a state insurance rate-making bureau. The 1919 law had included a rule barring out-of-state companies from entering Indiana to sell insurance at a rate below that which was set by the rate-making bureau. Chambers hoped that by eliminating the law, he could improve competition among insurance companies and get lower rates for consumers. The insurance lobby opposed this. Stephenson stepped in to strike a deal where, for a price, he would use his influence among the legislators to stop the bill. The bill seemed certain to pass in the Senate (where Stephenson held little power), so most of his efforts were concentrated in the House. After enough contacts with the right people, the bill was killed. It came up for a vote on February 12, and the representatives voted to indefinitely postpone the bill. Stephenson had won.[7]

Compared with the regular Klan, Stephenson managed to make an impressive showing in the General Assembly. Many of the legislative questions that concerned him were decided in his favor. Compared with Bossert's dismal record of legislative failures, Stephenson usually managed to make good on his promises.

Stephenson had a more personal interest in his bill on nutrition. House Bill 287, passed March 9, was probably the most innocent-looking piece of legislation to come out of the General Assembly that year. The bill specified that the state superintendent of public instruction—Madge Oberholtzer's boss—"is hereby authorized and directed to provide by proper rules and regulations for the teaching of a course in diet and nutrition in all elementary and high schools in the state." The bill carefully went on to define exactly what information was to be taught in these classes: "knowledge of nutrition, diet instructions, how to combine and balance food, the food needs of the body, knowledge of food equivalents."[8] While the bill did not mention a specific textbook by name, Stephenson was making sure that only a single book—the one he was hiring Madge Oberholtzer to help write—would meet the requirements of the course description.

Working quietly, Stephenson hatched a scheme that would make him a steady income for years if all went right. He had purchased a small publishing house, McClure Publishing.[9] He hired Madge to help write *One Hundred Years of Health* and made sure her Reading Circle connections would help get the book placed in elementary and high schools all over the state. By controlling the entire process, Stephenson would rake in a small fortune. The plan was shrewd, calculating, and virtually undetectable.

Stephenson directed his legislative strategy from his eight-room office in the Kresge Building, which now resembled a general's war room. Phones jangled constantly, and the clatter of typewriters filled the air as his secretaries typed mountains of correspondence. Representatives and senators sat in his outer office waiting for their chance to confer with Stephenson. Unlike

the tactless hordes of lobbyists who plagued Van Orman and Leslie in their legislative chambers, Stephenson did his lobbying
from his own office, letting the law makers come to him and using messengers to carry his instructions back and forth to the
statehouse. Court Asher later recalled that Democratic representatives Russell Duncan, Joseph C. Buchanan, and H. Walker De-
Haven of Indianapolis were among the regular visitors to
Stephenson's offices. Republican Senator Delbert Blackburn
from Evansville also visited frequently. Asher described Madge as
one of Stephenson's messengers, along with five or six others,
including Earl Klinck, Fred Butler, and Howard Bennett.[10]

And there were the political parties at his home in Irvington that greased the way for his legislation. It seems that there
were two kinds of parties held at Stephenson's house. Some were
quite respectable affairs—black-tie events attended by some of
the city's leading political figures, with a small orchestra playing
dance music in the front room and fine foods and drinks served
by attendants. At other times, however, the parties were more
like Roman orgies. Asher once recounted how Stephenson enjoyed dressing up in a costume like a mythological satyr, with
several women acting the part of naked wood nymphs. The
women would dance and strip off their clothes while Stephenson
would take a whip and lash them as they danced around the room.
The one who could stand the pain longest would win the privi-
lege of being his sexual partner for the evening. Stephenson's
parties—both kinds—soon became legendary, and politicians
could measure their importance to Stephenson's organization by
the number of times they were invited back. Court Asher remembered one judge being led away from one of the parties quite
drunk and weeping that someday he would be "too old to come
to Steve's wonderful parties."[11]

Stephenson's most elaborate scheme involved the state's
highway commission. The plan required the cooperation of the
governor, and the records show that Jackson played his part
willingly. The story began with rumors surrounding the disposal
of $8 million worth of surplus war materiel by the members of
the highway commission. Following World War I, the federal government had gotten rid of most of the surplus war materiel by
distributing it to the states to use or dispose of in any way the
states saw fit. In Indiana, the materiel—mostly trucks, wagons,
and machinery—had been turned over to the highway commission. Most of the seven-year-old supplies were in bad repair,
rusted and ruined from lack of care. The commission members
decided to sell most of the materiel for scrap metal. But during

David Curtis Stephenson, August 21, 1891–June 28, 1966
(*Indianapolis Star* photo, Robert Van Buskirk Collection)

In 1923, Stephenson spent $22,000 to remodel this Irvington home as a nearly perfect replica of Klankrest, the Klan's national headquarters in Atlanta, Georgia. (*Indianapolis Star* photo, Robert Van Buskirk Collection)

Members of the Klan display their regalia at a meeting of the Women of the Ku Klux Klan at Hartford City, Indiana, circa 1925. (Indiana Division, Indiana State Library)

Ku Klux Klan members are seen leaving a church at Knox,
Indiana, presumably after making a public appearance to present a
donation to the church during its Sunday morning services. Such
church visits were typical displays for the Klan in the early 1920s.
(Indiana Division, Indiana State Library)

The South Bend, Indiana, drill team poses for a group portrait at Knox, Indiana,
May 30, 1924. (Indiana Division, Indiana State Library)

Stephenson's nemesis, Imperial Wizard Hiram Wesley Evans (center), led the Klan in a march on Washington, D.C., in August 1925 while Stephenson awaited trial in his Noblesville, Indiana, jail cell. Walter Bossert, who replaced Stephenson as Indiana's grand dragon, marches in a business suit next to Evans. (Collection of Kenton H. and Audrey D. Broyles)

John I. Duvall, Mayor of Indianapolis, 1926–28 (*Indianapolis Star* photo, Robert Van Buskirk Collection)

Ed Jackson, Governor, Indiana, 1925–29 (*Indianapolis Star* photo, Robert Van Buskirk Collection)

Asa J. Smith, Indianapolis attorney (*Indianapolis Star* photo, James E. Farmer Collection)

Sporting straw boaters, Stephenson (far left) and Earl Gentry (front, right) stroll from the Noblesville, Indiana, jail to the June 17, 1925, bail bond hearing. Earl Klinck (back, center) is escorted between Hamilton County Sheriff Charles A. Gooding (far right) and one of his deputies. (*Indianapolis Star* photo, Robert Van Buskirk Collection)

A page from the Indiana Hotel register shows the false name "Mr. & Mrs. W. B. Morgan, Franklin," which Stephenson used to register himself and Madge Oberholtzer in room 416. Stephenson's bodyguard, Earl Gentry, is registered on the next line in room 417. (*Indianapolis Star* photo, Robert Van Buskirk Collection)

Madge Oberholtzer (*Indianapolis Star* photo, Robert Van Buskirk Collection)

William H. Remy, Prosecutor, Marion County, 1924–29 (*Indianapolis Star* photo, Robert Van Buskirk Collection)

Warren T. McCray, Governor, Indiana, 1921–24 (*Indianapolis Star* photo, Robert Van Buskirk Collection)

Indianapolis, Indiana.
Feb. 12th 1925

In return for the political support of D.C.Stephenson, in the event
that I am elected Mayor of Indianapolis, Ind. I promise not to appoint
any person as a member of the Board of Public Works with out they first
have the endorsement of D.C.Stephenson.

I also aggree and promise to appoint Claude Worley as Chief of Police
and Earl Klenck as a Captain.

Signed by me this 12th, Day of Feb.1925.

A copy of the letter (above) in which Indianapolis Mayor John Duvall pledged to make appointments that would be agreeable to Stephenson, in return for his support, helped convict Duvall and send him to jail. Stephenson kept this letter, along with many other incriminating documents, in his legendary black boxes (left). (*Indianapolis Star* photos, Robert Van Buskirk Collection)

Cutting a very stern-looking figure as she appeared at the trial, Madge's mother, Matilda Oberholtzer (left), posed for the photographers outside the courthouse with her husband, George (second from right); their son, Marshall; and his wife, Renua. (*Indianapolis Star* photo, Robert Van Buskirk Collection)

Stephenson's attorney, Ephraim "Eph" Inman (left), is shown on the steps of the Noblesville, Indiana, courthouse with Will Remy, Marion County prosecutor. This picture shows why the newspaper reporters dubbed Remy the "boy prosecutor." (*Indianapolis Star* photo, Robert Van Buskirk Collection)

The only existing photo of the jury that convicted Stephenson in 1925 (*Indianapolis Star* photo, Robert Van Buskirk Collection)

During the 1939 appeal, an *Indianapolis Star* photographer snapped this unusual shot of Stephenson shaking hands with Will Remy, the prosecutor who put him behind bars in 1925. The *Star's* photo editor knew news when he saw it; a handwritten instruction to the camera room on the back of the photo warns: "Do not touch their hands. They are to show by all means." (*Indianapolis Star* photo, Robert Van Buskirk Collection)

Stephenson types in his jail cell at Noblesville, Indiana, during the 1945 appeal, using his cot as a seat and a folding chair as a table for his typewriter. (*Indianapolis Star* photo, Robert Van Buskirk Collection)

the 1925 General Assembly, it was rumored that graft and corruption had influenced the way the commission disposed of the materiel. Charges accused the members of the commission, through crooked management, of lining their own pockets and shortchanging the state by several million dollars. On February 19, the newspapers revealed that secret sessions were being held by the House Ways and Means Committee, which was investigating three state agencies and paying particular attention to the highway commission.[12]

In two weeks, a Marion County grand jury became involved in the legislature's investigation, and indictments were returned against several people involved in the highway commission scandal. On March 4, arrest warrants were issued charging the commissioners with grand larceny and embezzlement. Sheriff Omer Hawkins arrested the director of the Indiana Highway Department, John D. Williams, and Earl Crawford, a member of the highway commission. Also arrested were Moses Goldberg and Victor Goldberg, two Indianapolis junk dealers who had purchased the surplus war materiel. An indictment was also returned against George Bartley, a former Highway Department employee who had once been in charge of the department's garage and storehouse and who had since moved to Florida.

Members of the highway lobby—mostly from construction and paving companies—protested that the charges were trumped up and that the whole investigation was politically motivated. The $8 million in war surplus supplies, they claimed, had only been worth a fraction of what the federal government claimed it was worth. There had been no short selling of goods, and therefore, no larceny. The lobbyists eventually proved to be correct, and the charges were dropped.

But while it lasted, the politicians and the newspapers made the most of the highway scandal. The story was front-page news for all three Indianapolis dailies. Editorials called for immediate reform of the highway system. It was time for a complete housecleaning, they said. Indiana needed a new highway organization, one less prone to corruption. The governor himself joined the chorus and urged a new highway control system that would be more responsible to the people. William H. Kissinger, a Republican representative from Columbia City, quickly penned a bill that would unseat the current highway commission and create a new board to be appointed by the governor. Kissinger's bill—opposed by the highway lobbyists—quickly became known as the "road ripper" bill, and the issue heated up, dominating the last days of the session.

What only a few legislators knew was that Stephenson planned to help Jackson name the new members and the new director of the highway commission. Stephenson had instigated the scandal, the investigation, and the legislation. But what did he stand to gain from it?

Stephenson's primary business was still coal sales. The highway issue provided him with an excellent opportunity to pay off some of his political allies and to corner some lucrative coal contracts. Stephenson and his friends had already started to form a new company, the Hammond Construction Company. With a new highway commission—*their* highway commission—in place, he and his partners would be guaranteed some of the juiciest public contracts in the state. Lawrence F. Orr, state examiner and head of the State Board of Accounts, would get a piece of the state's auto parts purchases for his Columbus, Indiana, firm. George V. "Cap" Coffin, head of the Marion County Republican party, would get a percentage of the cement contracts. Lawrence Cartwright, Republican chairman for the Eighth Congressional District, would get contracts for crushed stone. State Republican chairman Clyde Walb, who helped Kissinger write the road ripper bill, and Johnnie Owens would get state contracts for their companies. Stephenson, of course, would get the coal contracts. The millions to be doled out under these new contracts would make the question of whatever happened to the war surplus materiel seem insignificant by comparison.[13]

But the road ripper bill was not only Stephenson's greatest plot, it was also his greatest failure. Kissinger's bill successfully made it through all three readings in the House, despite a loud barrage of opposition from people who suspected that the bill must be hiding some other scheme. Passed to the Senate, the bill came down for a final vote on March 9, the last day of the 1925 General Assembly. It was not, however, brought up for a vote. The Senate could have chosen to suspend the rules and vote on the bill anyway, but there was not enough support to draw the needed number of votes for a suspension of rules. As a result, the road ripper bill died for lack of a final vote. Stephenson's great contract scheme was unwittingly thwarted by the legislators.

———————————

Stephenson did not have time to mourn the death of his carefully planned highway scheme. He knew politics was always a win-lose proposition. This had been his first year as a power within the legislature, and he had not done badly. While the road ripper bill had lost, he had won several others. In a year or two, he would wield even more power. There were also other matters to attend to, particularly the coming primary elections, which were less than two months away.

Stephenson was supporting Republican John L. Duvall, the Marion County treasurer, for mayor. Duvall was a fifty-year-old lawyer and banker who had been elected treasurer in 1922. More important in Stephenson's mind, however, was not Duvall but Ralph Lemcke, Duvall's only serious Republican opponent. Lemcke had held the treasurer's post before Duvall and was now being supported by Republican party boss William A. Armitage, who had been a kingpin during Mayor Lew Shank's administration. Armitage was said to be the person who controlled the city's gambling ring and one who did not gladly tolerate newcomers like Stephenson. Duvall was not the issue of the election; defeating the Armitage side of the Republican machine was. If Duvall was running against Lemcke, then Duvall would be the man Stephenson would support. As Duvall recalled years later, "A committee of fourteen representatives of the Klan called on me at the Treasurer's office . . . and wanted me to be the candidate for Mayor, assuring me that I would be elected. After considering the matter two weeks, I decided to run."[14]

Duvall soon learned that there were certain strings attached to any offer of support from Stephenson. Just before Christmas, 1924, he was summoned to Stephenson's offices in the Kresge Building. On the evening of December 22, the two men met alone to talk about Duvall's candidacy. Stephenson carefully explained the condition of his support and had Duvall sign a contract, which Stephenson typed and presented to him. The short contract simply stated that Duvall would make no appointments as mayor without first consulting Stephenson. For the mere price of his signature on the paper, Duvall would have the full force of Stephenson's organization behind him in the 1925 primary.[15]

But there were more considerations. A week or so after the end of the 1925 General Assembly, Stephenson called a meeting of about thirty members of his organization. They met at the Hotel Washington to talk about Duvall's campaign and how the organization could best be used to Duvall's advantage. After the meeting, Stephenson called Duvall aside to talk with Claude Worley, a former sheriff from Franklin, Indiana, and one of Stephenson's close friends. Stephenson wanted to make sure that Worley would be taken care of in the election. Already Stephenson had gotten his bodyguard, Earl Klinck, a job as a

Marion County deputy sheriff under Sheriff Omer Hawkins. This time Stephenson extracted a promise from Duvall that Worley would be named chief of police after the fall election. Duvall agreed to this arrangement.

Stephenson also wanted an understanding with Duvall that a city highway commissioner position would be added to the city's board of public works and that Stephenson would be allowed to name that commissioner. Through this channel, Stephenson would have an open line to the city's paving contracts. Under the terms of the contract, Duvall agreed to these points as well.[16]

"I had the support of the Ku Klux Klan at that time at the height of its power in Indiana politics," said Duvall. "I was nominated in that primary and immediately began an active campaign, and was elected in the fall elections, taking office the following January. They never gave me a chance to be Mayor and did everything they possibly could to ruin my administration."[17]

Stephenson was an extremely powerful man in the state by March 15, 1925. He had successfully controlled the governor's election and the movements of several key legislators during the General Assembly, and he was now pulling the strings on a puppet mayoral candidate. Sunday, March 15, was a cool but pleasant spring day. Stephenson rang up Worley and asked him to bring his wife over. Stephenson took one of his many girlfriends, and the four of them went for a leisurely afternoon drive.[18]

A few blocks down the street, Madge Oberholtzer's parents were both feeling ill, suffering from late winter colds or flu. Matilda Oberholtzer had recovered sufficiently from her illness to go to church that Sunday morning, but her husband was still quite ill. Madge drove her mother to church, dropped her off, then returned to take her home when the service was over. It was a cold morning, with the temperature in the mid-twenties. The weather warmed a bit in the afternoon, and Madge picked up her friend, Ermina Moore, and the two went for a Sunday drive. They returned later that afternoon—Madge had a date with a gentleman at five o'clock and did not want to be late.[19]

It was nearly 10:00 P.M. when Madge returned home from her evening out. Her mother had already gone to bed, but she was still awake when she heard Madge come in the house. Matilda told her daughter that Stephenson's secretary, Fred Butler, had called for her sometime that afternoon with an important message from Stephenson. It was apparently something to do with the nutrition book that Madge had been working on for him. Madge had already started to get ready for bed, but she went back downstairs and dialed Irvington 0492. Stephenson answered the phone. Madge told her mother that Stephenson had asked her to "come down if I could to his home, that he wished to see me about something very important to me; that he was leaving for Chicago and had to see me before he left."[20]

Madge went back upstairs to tell her mother that she was going up the street to see Stephenson. Her mother knew that it concerned the book her daughter was working on and that Stephenson was sending one of his men down the street to escort Madge. Everything seemed quite proper.

Madge was wearing a black velvet dress and was in a great hurry. She went downstairs and put on her dark winter coat, but she did not take time to pick out a hat. Then Earl Gentry, one of Stephenson's bodyguards, came to the door to walk Madge up to his boss's house. Matilda Oberholtzer could hear Gentry's voice in the entryway, then she heard the front door close. She went to her upstairs bedroom window and looked down the street just in time to see Madge and a very tall man crossing University Avenue to the other side of the street. It was a clear night, and the moon was shining. She watched the pair walking between the pools of light from the streetlamps, walking west down the street.[21]

Madge Oberholtzer Comes Home

March 1925

The sun had just come up on Monday, March 16. It was shortly after six o'clock, and attorney Asa J. Smith was still upstairs getting dressed.[1] Downstairs his wife, Lena Tweedy Smith, whom he always addressed simply as "Tweedy," was busy fixing breakfast for Asa and his nephew, Albert Sigmend, who was living with the Smiths while he attended Butler College. Sigmend had an 8:00 A.M. class that required rising early to get from the Smith's house on the north side down to the Butler campus on the east side. Asa had nearly finished dressing when he heard the telephone ring downstairs. Tweedy answered it, then called up to her husband that the call was for him. He asked who it was, and she replied that it was one of his clients, a Mrs. Oberholtzer. Asa came downstairs to take the call.

The thirty-one-year-old lawyer knew Matilda Oberholtzer only slightly. He had met her through a friend of Tweedy's, Ermina Moore, who happened to be a friend of Madge Oberholtzer's. Through this connection, Matilda had once called on Smith to handle a small legal matter for her. He had visited the house once or twice, but did not know the family very well beyond that.

Now he found himself talking to a frantic-sounding woman on the telephone. Madge's mother was pouring out her story about her daughter's disappearance. Smith recalled:

> She told me that her daughter, Madge, had left home the previous evening in answer to a telephone call from D. C. Stephenson; that she had left about 10 o'clock the evening before and had not returned. That Sunday afternoon several calls had come to the Oberholtzer home for her daughter and that she, Mrs. Oberholtzer, had answered the phone in her daughter's absence; that they had given the number for her daughter to call . . . and had said that it was Stephenson's secretary talking and that it was very important for Stephenson to get in touch with Miss Oberholtzer.

Matilda said that Madge had come home a little before ten o'clock, returned the phone call to Stephenson's house, and left a short time later with one of Stephenson's men. "Mrs. Oberholtzer watched them leave and that," said Smith, "was the last she had seen of her daughter."

As Smith listened to the story, he was jolted completely awake by the distraught mother's tale. Stephenson, the Klan leader, the governor's political advisor, involved in what was beginning to sound like a possible abduction? Could that be possible? It might be nothing. Madge was, after all, a grown woman, and if she had decided to stay out all night, then that was her business. But something in Matilda Oberholtzer's voice suggested that this was not ordinary behavior for Madge.

In his calmest voice, Smith told Madge's mother that everything would probably turn out all right. "I told her not to worry and that I would investigate and call her back," he said. As soon as he hung up the receiver, he thumbed through his directory for the number of Bert C. Morgan.

A federal prohibition enforcement officer, Morgan was a close friend of Harry G. Leslie, Speaker of the House in the Indiana General Assembly. As a prohibition officer, Morgan would also be allowed to carry a gun, which might prove helpful if Madge's disappearance turned out to be anything other than routine. Morgan lived in Irvington, near the Oberholtzers, and might be able to pick up some news around the neighborhood.

Morgan had not yet left for his downtown office when Asa Smith called. Morgan listened as Smith repeated the story as he had heard it from Matilda Oberholtzer. Smith was ready to jump in with everything, suggesting that they go over to Stephenson's house and demand to see the Oberholtzer girl. Morgan suggested a slower approach to see what else was going on. "No, it is probably not as serious as it looks," said Morgan. "Meet me at my office and we'll talk about the matter."

Heading downtown to Morgan's office in the Federal Building, Smith tossed the sketchy details of the story around in his head. Of course, he already knew something about Stephenson; everyone in the Republican party did, and Smith was a good Republican. He was not, however, a Klan Republican. Smith's house on North Winthrop Avenue backed up to the Indiana State Fairgrounds, where Stephenson had held several of his Klan rallies. Smith with quite familiar with the Klan and what it stood for, but he did not agree with its philosophy or its practices.

Smith was a veteran of World War I, an ex-Marine who had fought the Germans outside Paris, was wounded in the battle of

Belleau Wood, and returned home a decorated war hero. His eyes had been injured by mustard gas in France. He had recovered his vision, but even now he looked at the world through squinting eyes behind a pair of wire-rimmed glasses. He had seen the Klan parades in Indianapolis and viewed with intense dislike what he considered the Klan's desecration of the American flag. He considered their "100 percent Americanism" doctrine a fraud. He was also not pleased to see the leader of his political party, Governor Jackson, so eager to welcome the Klan's support. It was not good either for government or for the party, in Smith's mind. But he also realized that Stephenson was powerful in politics, a man who would have to be dealt with very carefully.

Smith arrived at Morgan's office at 8:30 A.M. He asked to use Morgan's phone and called the Oberholtzer house to see if Matilda had heard anything from her daughter and to get Ermina Moore's office telephone number. Since Moore also worked in the statehouse as a clerk for the State Board of Education, she might have an idea of what had happened to Madge. As Morgan listened, Smith outlined the story over the telephone to Moore. He asked if she could come over to the Federal Building right away to discuss the problem.

Smith considered Moore to be quite levelheaded. As the three talked in Morgan's office, the telephone rang. It was Tweedy Smith with the news that Matilda Oberholtzer had just called and asked that Asa call her immediately. The attorney hung up and dialed the Oberholtzer's number. Matilda, quite excited, told him that she had just received a telegram from her daughter. It simply said, "We are driving through to Chicago. Will be home on night train. Madge."

Perhaps things would be all right after all. There was nothing to do now until the evening trains from Chicago rolled into the station. Smith asked Morgan and Moore to join him that evening to meet the trains.

That night, the three waited on the platform at Union Station, watching as each of the Chicago-to-Indianapolis trains arrived and unloaded its passengers. Each time they searched the platform for Madge or Stephenson, but neither of them got off any of the trains. The trio waited until the last train pulled away from the station around 10:00 P.M., then discussed what they should do next. They decided to go out to Irvington and tell the Oberholtzers the news that their daughter still was not home.

They explained the difficulty to Madge's mother, who was now more worried than before. Smith said he would call Stephenson's house. He dialed and got a wrong number. He checked the number again and redialed but got no answer. He suggested that perhaps they should get in his car and drive down the street to have a look around Stephenson's house.

By now it was after 11:00 P.M. A crescent moon could be seen at times through the clouds. Smith drove his car up the winding, narrow University Avenue, around the fountain at Irving Circle, across Ritter Avenue, and down past Stephenson's house. The lights were off, and the huge white house was dark. Smith let Ermina Moore and Matilda Oberholtzer out of his car, and they went up to Stephenson's front door. Smith drove his car down the block, turned around, and parked the car on the south side of the street, where he could see the house clearly.

"They kept knocking for about 15 minutes. After that, then a light appeared and someone, a man, came to the door. He was clad in a dressing gown," said Smith. The man was probably Stephenson's secretary, Fred Butler. "The three stood at the door and talked for some minutes. I could not distinguish what they said." As he watched the house, Smith saw a couple of cars come down the street, from the direction of the Butler College campus, and they passed his car.

"The light of another car appeared behind me, but I observed presently, it did not pass me. I turned to look and saw a big closed car, a sedan, drive into the Stephenson yard. It was some distance from me," he said. "The Stephenson lawn is very spacious, and on one corner the drive begins and winds back to the garage in the rear. This car drove back to the garage. From its headlights, I could see the reflection of a large garage with room for several cars, apparently. As the sedan reached the door, I could hear the loud barking of dogs coming from the direction of the garage. When the car reached the garage, the lights of the car were snapped out. Then the door opened and a light shone from within. The car drove in and the lights all went out."

The two women were still standing on the front porch of the house. Smith stayed in his car and watched. A few minutes later, he heard the sound of footsteps coming from the direction of the garage, and he saw a short, young man—Stephenson's driver, Ernest W. "Shorty" DeFriese—come up on the front porch and talk with the two women and the man in the robe. Soon the women came back to Smith's car and told him that the two men claimed they did not know where Stephenson was. Again there seemed to be nothing more to do, so Smith took the two women back to their homes, then he drove back to his house on North Winthrop.

He had been home only a few minutes when Matilda Oberholtzer called again. She had just received a call from someone who said he was a friend of Madge's. The caller said that he had a date with Madge for that evening but that he had received a telegram from Madge from South Bend, Indiana, saying she had been delayed and would not be back until morning. He said Madge had also asked him to call her mother and tell her not to worry.

"I told Mrs. Oberholtzer that, of course, that was a fake message to alleviate her distress, but that it probably indicated they had been in touch with someone who knew where Madge was," Smith recalled. It was well after midnight when he finally got to bed that night.

Early next morning, he got another call from Matilda, worried because she had still not heard from Madge. Smith thought about the situation and decided perhaps it was time to bring in more outside help. He knew that George Oberholtzer had been ill, but he asked Matilda to bring her husband with her to meet him at the Harry C. Webster Detective Agency in the Hume-Mansur Building, across the street from the Federal Building.

It was Tuesday, March 17, and Madge's father had been sick in bed since Saturday. He had been so ill, in fact, that his wife had not yet told him about Madge. Even now, as George remembered, "She merely mentioned the fact that Madge was in trouble and wanted me to come downtown with her. During the trip downtown she told me piecemeal that we were going to the detective's office, that Madge had been gone since Sunday night and that she just couldn't stand it any longer and that we just had to do something."[2]

The temperature was hovering just above freezing, and there was a trace of snow on the ground. As he had promised, Smith met the Oberholtzers at Webster's office. There, with Matilda Oberholtzer supplying the emotions and Asa Smith supplying the facts, Madge's story began to unfold for both the detective and the girl's father. The meeting lasted almost until noon. At one point, Webster asked Matilda if she still had a copy of the telegram she had received from Madge. No, she did not. He then asked her to go down to the telegraph office and get a copy for him to study.

After hearing their story, Webster advised the Oberholtzers to call him immediately if there were any new developments, and the Oberholtzers returned home. Smith walked back down Pennsylvania Street to his office in the Fletcher Trust Building.

"A little later," Smith recalled, "Mrs. Oberholtzer called me to say that Miss Madge was home and asked me to come out. I called Miss Ermina Moore and met her and drove her out in my car."

Madge had been brought back home while her parents were downtown in the detective's office. The only one home at the time was Eunice Schultz, the Oberholtzer's boarder, who later recalled, "I was in the kitchen. I heard groaning and I went to the dining room and saw Madge being carried upstairs by a man, a large man. . . . I stayed downstairs till the man came down. . . . He said she was hurt in an automobile accident and I asked him if she was badly hurt. He said he thought no bones were broken. I asked him who he was. He said his name was Johnson and he was from Kokomo."[3] Then he hurried down the stairs, keeping his face hidden as he neared the door and saying he must be hurrying on. She later identified the man as Earl Klinck, one of Stephenson's bodyguards.

Schultz looked out the window as the man left and noticed a big car parked at the edge of the driveway; the car was gone when she came back downstairs. Next she went into Madge's room. What she saw was horrifying.

Madge was in very bad condition. "She was groaning every breath," said Schultz. "I saw her bruises. On the right cheek was a circular wound. It was dark in color. There was a bruise on her left chest of the same shape, only deeper. The wound on her chest was open. . . . She just groaned, 'Oh,' and said, 'Dear Mother.' "[4] Madge told Schultz that she thought she was dying and asked her to call the family doctor, John K. Kingsbury.

Dr. Kingsbury's office was in Irvington, just a few blocks from the Oberholtzers' home. He wasted no time getting to their house after receiving the call from Schultz. He later described what he saw when he arrived:[5]

> I went upstairs and saw Madge Oberholtzer lying on a bed in the northwest bedroom. She was in a state of shock. Her clothing was disheveled and her hair disordered. Her body was cold. Her dress lay open at the breast exposing bruised areas with two or three lacerations or cuts on the left chest. The right cheek was bruised. I made a superficial examination through her clothes to determine whether there were any broken bones—I had been informed she was in an auto accident. . . . She said she did not expect, or want, to get well—that she wanted to die.

Kingsbury asked Madge what she meant. At first she was hesitant, refusing to talk about what had happened to her. She said she would explain everything to him when she had recovered. "I didn't know whether she was going to get better or not," said Kingsbury, "so I pressed her for an answer to my question." Madge thought a moment, then began to tell Kingsbury an incredible story.

She told him about the message from Stephenson's house on Sunday and how she had been escorted to his house late that evening. Once inside Stephenson's house, she saw that he was very drunk and she felt that she was trapped. "He came forward and caught both of her hands in his and she said she wanted to go home. . . . He told her she was going to stay there," Kingsbury said as he reconstructed Madge's story. "She went to the telephone to call her home, but the receiver was taken from her hand by someone and replaced on its hook. . . . Later she tried it again with the same result."

Madge told Kingsbury how she was taken into the kitchen, where Stephenson and some other men were mixing drinks, and how they forced her to take two or three drinks. She was soon overcome by a wave of nausea and sunk into a chair. Then she was told that Stephenson was going to Chicago and he planned to take her with him. Madge started to cry and told the men she wanted to go home, but instead she was forced outside into a car and driven downtown to Union Station. There, they boarded a train. Madge, still feeling the effects of the drinks, was pushed into a lower berth in a private compartment with Stephenson. A companion of Stephenson's climbed into the upper berth of the same compartment, and the train rolled out of Union Station, bound for Chicago.

Stephenson reached down and took hold of her black velvet dress, pulling it off over her head. He ripped the rest of her clothes off and began to mistreat her. "She said she didn't recall all that happened to her on that ride," said Kingsbury. "But she said she was bitten, chewed, and pommeled."

In a few days, Madge would recall more graphically, "After the train had started, Stephenson got in with me and attacked me. He held me so I could not move. I did not know and do not remember all that happened. He chewed me all over my body, bit my neck and face, chewing my tongue, chewing my breasts until they bled, my back, my legs, my ankles, and mutilated me all over my body."

Instead of riding through to Chicago, Madge told Kingsbury that they had stopped just short of the Indiana state line, getting off the train in Hammond, Indiana. They went to a hotel, and she was put in a room with Stephenson. They laid down on the bed, and Stephenson soon fell asleep.

As Kingsbury recalled:

She found Mr. Stephenson asleep, took his revolver from his pocket, or grip, wherever it was, intent on killing him as he slept. Then she thought it would reflect on the disgrace that would bring on her family, and decided to kill herself; that she stepped into an adjoining room where there was a mirror; that she put the revolver to her temple, looking in the mirror to be sure she shot where she intended, when she heard a step outside the door and the door knob turned, slipped the revolver into the fold of her dress and in came one of the other men. . . . She slipped this revolver back to the place where she got it and decided to seek some other means of ending her life.[6]

Later that morning, she asked Stephenson for money to buy a hat and some cosmetics. Stephenson ordered one of his men to give her fifteen dollars and take her out to get what she wanted. First they went to a milliner's shop, where she bought a small black silk hat. Then they went to a nearby drugstore, but instead of buying cosmetics, Madge went to the back of the store, out of hearing range of her guard, and asked the clerk for a box of mercury bichloride tablets. She slipped the pillbox into her coat pocket, and she and the guard went back to the hotel.

Once in her room, Kingsbury said, she told him that "the other two men left and she set out on the table or washstand 18 tablets, intending to take them all—started taking them by threes—that she got down the first three and second, and then could not get down any more because of the intense distress in her stomach."

At last, the story began to fall together for Kingsbury. There had been no automobile accident; the girl on the bed was the victim of an unsuccessful suicide attempt using mercury bichloride tablets. Kingsbury said she told him about her guard's reaction to the discovery of her poisoning:

> She started vomiting, and she must have fainted, she re-membered little, but sometime in the afternoon, the door opened and in came someone whom she called, "Shorty." She said Shorty asked her what was the matter. She didn't want to tell. He urged that she tell and she pointed to the cuspidor which was pretty well filled with blood . . . and she said, "I have taken poison." He said, "What kind?" She said, "Bichloride." She said he said, "My God" and left the room.[7]

Stephenson immediately stormed into the room and de-manded to know why she had taken poison. She told him that she wanted to kill herself, and Stephenson called her a fool. He sent out for a bottle of milk and forced her to drink it. Then he ordered Shorty to go get the car so they could return to India-napolis. On the way back, Shorty drove, and Stephenson sat in the back with Madge wedged between himself and Earl Gentry.

Then, according to Madge's story, Stephenson began to lose his nerve and panicked. First he wanted to take her to a hospital in Hammond and have her stomach pumped. But that was too risky. He ordered them to stop and buy more milk and a bottle of ginger ale. Madge could not choke the fluid down her throat. Instead she became violently ill, vomiting all over the inside of the car. They threw the milk into a stream as they drove over a culvert. Stephenson began to worry. She might die in the car. "This takes guts to do this, Gentry, she is dying," he said at one point. He pulled out a bottle, and he and Gentry began to drink as the car sped through the twilight countryside. Madge began to cry and scream. At one point, she begged to be thrown out of the car and left by the side of the road, where someone might find her and take her for help. But Stephenson told Shorty to drive on.

They arrived at Stephenson's house in Irvington on Monday night, March 16, sometime between 11:00 P.M. and midnight. (It was Stephenson's car that Asa Smith had watched pull into the garage that night.) Madge told Kingsbury she had begged Stephenson to call her doctor and get her medical aid but that Stephenson refused. (By this point, Stephenson had seen the car parked in front of his house and the women talking to Fred Butler on his front porch. He knew he was in danger of being found out.)

Stephenson raged around in the sleeping quarters above the garage, where he had taken Madge. "I remember Stephenson said to me, 'You will stay right here until you marry me.' . . . and he said, 'You must forget this, what is done has been done, I am the law and the power.' "

By morning, however, Madge had drifted off into a fitful sleep, and Stephenson's temper had subsided. Earl Klinck woke her and said he was going to take her home.

"She had no medical help," said Kingsbury, "was brought home by some man who carried her upstairs and put her in the room where I saw her upon my first visit."

This was the story that Madge told Dr. Kingsbury and would soon tell others. But at that moment, the doctor was anxious about what he could do for his patient. He had already called the nurses' exchange and asked them to send over a full-time nurse to be with Madge. The service had assigned Beatrice Spratley, a British nurse who had only been in the city about a year, visiting her brother. The nurse had arrived at the house moments before Kingsbury.

Now they began to work on Madge. It was shortly after noon when they inserted a tube down her throat to flush out her stomach. They tried to raise her dangerously low body temperature by covering her with blankets. By half past noon, Kingsbury decided he had done everything that could be done for the moment. He left Madge in the nurse's care and said he would drop back by later that afternoon to check Madge's progress.

George and Matilda Oberholtzer returned home shortly after Kingsbury's departure. They called Asa Smith, who dashed out to their house with Ermina Moore. Smith later recalled, "When we reached the house, a nurse was in charge under a doctor's order. Miss Ermina Moore went up to see Miss Madge alone. Mrs. Oberholtzer then told me that she had bichloride of mercury in her system.

"Miss Moore came down in a few minutes and I went up to see Miss Oberholtzer with her mother. Miss Oberholtzer was in bed moaning, and her face was bloated with marks on it. She said to me, 'I'm done for.' Her mother showed me her chest. It was a solid mass of black, blue, and purple.

"I said to Miss Madge: 'Who made these marks on you?'

"She said: 'Stephenson.'

"I said: 'How did he make those marks on you?'

"And she said: 'With his teeth.' "

A Dying Woman's Statement

March–April 1925

Madge Oberholtzer's case must have looked, at first glance, like an open-and-shut case of assault and battery, rape, and a possible kidnapping charge. All Asa Smith needed was the consent of the young woman's parents to allow him to file their case against Stephenson. But there were other considerations. What if she recovered from the poison? Would they drop the charges to avoid having her story spread all across the papers? Or what if she eventually became well enough to take the stand and testify against Stephenson? There was no need to move with unnecessary speed until they had a better idea of Madge's physical condition.

Several times during that first week, Smith dropped by the Oberholtzer house to check on Madge's progress. During his visits, she told him the same story she had told Dr. Kingsbury. She told it to him piecemeal, but by the end of the week he was able to sit down with her and hear the entire tale from start to finish. He was also able to ask her questions about some of the details and clarify points that had been unclear at first.

"She told me several times that she did not expect to get well," said Smith. "And one night when I left she was in great agony and said, 'Goodbye,' in a voice portraying much suffering. When I saw her next, she said: 'When I said 'Goodbye' to you, I thought it *was* 'Goodbye.' "[1]

Smith talked about her condition with Kingsbury, who told him that she might die within the month. Kingsbury was a man whose opinion and judgment Smith respected. At thirty-nine, Kingsbury carried himself with an athletic stride that reminded others of his days at Butler College, where he had been a star in football, basketball, and tennis (he had played every minute of every football game during his four years as Butler's fullback).[2]

Both men realized how difficult it would be to build a case against Stephenson. An accurate account of Madge's story was essential. They would have to work together to make sure it was all done properly. If Madge were to die—as Kingsbury had said she might—it would be even more difficult to bring Stephenson to justice.

These same thoughts must have been going through George Oberholtzer's mind as he watched his only daughter slowly dying. At the end of the first week, he went down to Smith's office and said, "I want you to take my place in this matter and represent me and do whatever should be done in this affair. Bring legal action, sue if you think best. I place it all in your hands."[3]

Smith began by talking with Griffith D. Dean, the attorney with whom he shared offices on the sixth floor of the Fletcher Trust Building. Dean was much older than Smith and had more than twenty years of legal experience, seventeen of those years in Indianapolis.[4] Dean subleased one of his three offices to Smith, and the two shared a stenographer, Helen D. Clermont. Dean was one of the few lawyers in the city that Smith trusted enough to bring in on the case. Smith sat down with Dean and explained the Oberholtzer case to him, asking if he would be willing to help handle the matter. Dean agreed.

It was probably Dean who suggested that they should go talk with Stephenson about the matter. After all, if the young woman recovered, the family would probably want the whole business hushed up. No publicity, no lawsuits, and the best out-of-court settlement that could be arranged. Dragging the episode into court would not be in Madge's best interests, so why not go to Stephenson now, confront him with what they already knew, and lay the groundwork for a favorable settlement?

Smith and Dean went to the offices of Stephenson's attorney, Robert I. Marsh. They had heard Stephenson was out of town, but Marsh suggested that the two go to Stephenson's office and talk with his secretary, Fred Butler, to arrange an appointment.

The two attorneys left Marsh's office, walked across the street to the Kresge Building, and went up to the third floor to Stephenson's suite of offices. They introduced themselves to the receptionist and asked to see Butler. After sitting awhile in the outer office, they were finally shown into Butler's office. As they walked in, Dean came straight to the point and asked where they could find Stephenson. To their surprise, Butler told them Stephenson was in the office next to his. "Well then, we prefer to consult with him," said Smith. Butler asked what they wanted to talk with Stephenson about. "A personal matter," Smith replied.[5]

Butler left the room, then came back shortly to announce, "Mr. Stephenson is very busy this morning and will give you three minutes." Dean snorted, "Stephenson must be a very busy man." Butler calmly replied, "He is."

But before they could walk into Stephenson's office, Stephenson was up and met them at the door, saying, "Gentlemen, I know what you wish to see me about. I just got in from New York this morning and have a copy of your detective's report on my desk. The whole thing has struck me like a thunderbolt. Mr. George Cowan [another of Stephenson's attorneys] advised me that you would call upon me. Mr. Cowan will call at your office at two o'clock this afternoon with power of attorney to represent me. I am very busy this morning."

Dean and Smith turned as if to leave, but then Smith turned back and told Stephenson that they would like to speak with him privately for a moment. Stephenson snapped his fingers and motioned for Butler to leave the room. The two lawyers sat down, and Dean said, "The matter we wish to talk to you about, Mr. Stephenson, was concerning Miss Madge Oberholtzer. We have been employed to bring suit against you for responsibility for her condition."

Stephenson's face flushed slightly. He thought a moment, then said, " 'To bring suit.' . . . Well, I'll tell you, I've stood an awful lot of persecution. I am not looking for trouble, and would prefer to avoid it, but I am a scrapper. I've stood already more than any other human being, I suspect, but I can stand more."

"You may have stood more than any other human being, save one, who has suffered more than you have ever suffered," said Smith.

"And who might that be?" Stephenson asked.

"Miss Madge Oberholtzer," Smith replied.

At this, Stephenson began to look impatient, drumming his fingers on the desk. He turned to Smith and asked, "Is this conversation personal or professional?" Smith did not reply. After a moment, Stephenson asked again, "Are we talking professionally?" Smith replied, "Perhaps." Stephenson then indicated that the interview was over. "Well, as I have said, George Cowan will be at your office at two o'clock."

Smith and Dean went back to their offices to wait for Cowan. Two o'clock arrived, but Cowan did not. Shortly after two, they received a call from Robert Marsh, who said that Cowan would not be coming and that Stephenson had asked Marsh to represent him in the matter. Marsh said he would see them in their offices later that afternoon.

Marsh arrived at 4:00 P.M. He said that Stephenson denied any connection to the business with Madge Oberholtzer. Marsh said Stephenson knew the man who had committed the act and that it had happened in Stephenson's house. For this, Stephenson was willing to admit some possible financial responsibility. He would be willing to pay a reasonable settlement to keep his friend out of the picture.

Smith and Dean told Marsh they did not believe a word of Stephenson's story and that they would stick by what Madge Oberholtzer had told them. Marsh asked what they wanted to see done about the business. "We told him that if the girl lived, she should be taken care of and provided for financially as long as she lived; that the opportunity should be afforded to her to go away—far away—from the scene of her disgrace, humiliation and mutilation, and that all the money in the world would not suffice to compensate her," said Smith.

Marsh asked how much they wanted.

"I have heard that Stephenson was worth $100,000," said Smith. Marsh insisted that his client wasn't worth more than $25,000. He told them that he would recommend that Stephenson make a payment of $5,000 to the girl.

In the week that followed, Marsh and Cowan met with Smith and Dean several times to discuss a possible out-of-court settlement. The four lawyers haggled over the amount, with Marsh holding to his figure of $5,000, and Smith and Dean demanding more. The meetings were first held in Dean's office, then in Marsh's office. Finally they reached a point where Dean and Smith said they would recommend that Madge accept $10,000 if it could be shown that Stephenson could not afford more. Marsh still felt this was too much to ask.

But suddenly on March 26, nine days after Madge had been brought home, the case took a new turn. Smith heard from George Oberholtzer about his daughter's condition. Dr. Kingsbury had told Oberholtzer that his daughter was dying and that the lawyers should try to get a formal statement from her as soon as possible, or it might be too late.

On the morning of March 26, after talking with Oberholtzer, Smith called Ermina Moore and asked her to come over to his office. On each of her daily visits to see Madge, Moore had been taking careful notes of everything Madge had said about her abduction. Smith had suggested that Moore take the notes as a way of preparing a formal statement for Madge to sign. Smith had been taking similar notes of his own. Now, on Kingsbury's advice, he began the difficult task of assembling the two sets of notes into a single statement. Smith later described the process of how they prepared the statement[6]:

> Taking Miss Ermina Moore's notes and my own outline, I took yellow paper and wrote down from them, reading out loud as I wrote, in the presence of Miss Moore and Mr. Dean, the statement that Miss Oberholtzer had made to me and to Miss Moore. As I wrote and read, if I got anything wrong, Miss Moore would correct me, and I continued so doing until I finished the statement.
>
> I then called in our stenographer, Mrs. Clermont, and dictated from the pages on which I had written, word for word, as nearly as we all could remember, the statement Miss Oberholtzer had made. This took, as I remember, until nearly one o'clock.
>
> In the afternoon, Mrs. Clermont typed the statement. When she had finished it, I locked it in my safe, and the next morning went over it and corrected typographical errors.

On Saturday morning, March 28, George Oberholtzer called again. Madge was still declining, and Kingsbury again warned them that there might not be much time left. He had started to give her morphine injections to block the pain.

Smith asked Moore to come by his office early that morning, and with Griffith Dean helping, the three went over the statement again. They filled in some blanks they had left in the first draft and found a few more typographical errors. Smith still wasn't satisfied with the ending. He rewrote the last two pages of the statement in longhand and had this part added. With all the changes and corrections in place, they had the secretary type a second draft of the statement. It was 4:00 P.M. before the revision was complete.

Dean and Smith took this draft and went through it all again to proof the copy for mistakes. This time, they found only a couple of errors, and they had the secretary retype those pages. Smith bound the pages in the proper order. Accompanied by Moore, the two attorneys left to go out to the Oberholtzers' house. Dean had decided to go on his own and take the streetcar to Irvington. While Smith went to get his car, he sent Moore over to the English Hotel to find a notary public who would go with them. When he arrived at the hotel, he went inside and found Moore talking with another woman, the notary. They left and drove straight to the Oberholtzers' house. Smith carried the statement.

The sun was down by the time they reached Irvington. Madge's parents were waiting for them. Smith called Kingsbury, telling him that the statement was ready and that he should come over as soon as he could. When Kingsbury arrived, the two men talked for a moment, then Smith told him, "I did not wish to take a statement of this kind from the girl because it was a rather brutal thing to do, unless there was absolutely no hope of her recovery." Smith knew that the deathbed statement would not hold up in court unless he could prove by the testimony of the other witnesses that Madge believed she was dying at the time she signed the statement; a deathbed statement signed by someone who did not believe death was near would not be accepted by the court.

The doctor went upstairs to talk with Madge. Shortly afterward, he came back downstairs and said, "I have told Miss Oberholtzer that she cannot possibly get well and she understands it and is willing to make her statement. Then Smith, Dean, Moore, and Kingsbury went upstairs. The Oberholtzers waited downstairs with the notary public.

In the bedroom, Dr. Kingsbury took his position near the head of Madge's bed. Asa Smith knelt at one side of the bed, beside the dying woman. Griffith Dean sat on the left side of the bed, near the foot. Ermina Moore sat on the opposite side of the bed.

Madge was pale and weak but still conscious. Kingsbury said, "I have explained to Miss Oberholtzer that she cannot get well and she understands and is reconciled."

Smith asked her if this was true. Madge nodded and said, "It is. I understand."

Smith told her, "Madge, it is necessary to feel in making a statement of this kind, that you cannot get well and that you are going to die." Again she indicated that she understood. Then Smith read the opening section of the dying declaration, the part that stated she knew she was near death. He asked her if this was accurate, and she said that it was.

"Madge, I have had typewritten very carefully what you have told us about your condition, and it is necessary for me to read it to you very slowly and very carefully," said Smith. "I will not be tiresome any more than is necessary, but you must say whether or not what I read to you is true."

Smith slowly began to read the dying declaration.

The declaration was the same story Madge first told Kingsbury and Smith on the day she was brought back home. It told how she had met Stephenson at the governor's inaugural dinner; how they had dated a couple of times; how she had gone to his house the night of March 15 in answer to his telephone call; and how she had been carried aboard the train, kidnapped, and raped.

She recalled in the statement one point which she had not told the doctor: that before they boarded the train to leave Indianapolis, Stephenson had stopped by the Hotel Washington. " 'Shorty' got out and went in the hotel and came back. They would not let me out. I was dazed and terrified that my life would be taken and did not know what to do. Stephenson would not let me get out of the car and I was afraid he would kill me. He said he was the law in Indiana."

As Smith continued to read, Madge added missing details to the statement. She remembered that the hotel they had gone to in Hammond was the Indiana Hotel and that there were two black bellboys and two black girls in the lobby when they first entered. Stephenson, she said, had forced her to send the telegram to her mother and dictated what she was to say. She also noted that Earl Gentry had tried to ease her pain from Stephenson's brutal attack on the train by putting hot towels and witch hazel on her head and bathing her body. She recalled that their hotel rooms were 416 and 417, and that Gentry stayed in 417 while she stayed with Stephenson in 416. After Stephenson had slept, she said, he became apologetic. "Stephenson said he was sorry, and that he was three degrees less than a brute. I said to him, 'you are worse than that.' "

The statement went on with her account of how she obtained the mercury bichloride tablets and took them in the hotel room, as well as with the rest of the story of her return to Indianapolis and, finally, to her home.

Smith stopped at the end of each sentence and asked her if it was the truth. Each time, she indicated that it was, except for three or four points where she made minor corrections in the statement. The last part of the statement read, "I, Madge Oberholtzer, am in full possession of all my mental faculties and understand what I am saying. The foregoing statements have been read to me and I have made them as my statements and they are all true. I am sure that I will not recover from this illness, and I believe that death is very near to me, and I have made all of the foregoing statements as my dying declaration and they are true." When Smith finished reading this part, he asked her, "Do you feel that you are going to die or live?"[7]

"To die," she said.

"Do you affirm what I have just read?" he asked.

"I do," she replied.

Then Smith gave her a pen. He took a magazine and used it to support the statement, propping it in front of her with a pillow. Kingsbury and Moore helped raise Madge up in bed.

Smith held the pen in her hand, guiding it toward the page. "Madge, the pen is now at the end of the statement that I have read to you, and if it is true you may sign it," said Smith. As they all watched, Madge slowly signed her name.

Smith took a second copy of the statement, written in the form of an affidavit, and called in the notary to witness Madge's signature on the document. The notary came upstairs and entered the bedroom. She asked Madge if the statements in the affidavit were true. Madge swore that it was all true. The notary watched as Madge signed the second statement. The notary put her seal on the document and wrote down her notary commission expiration date. The group then said good night to Madge and went downstairs.

It had taken nearly an hour and a half to complete the task. It was now about 7:30 P.M. Kingsbury and Moore stayed to comfort Madge's parents. Smith, Dean, and the notary got into Smith's car and headed back downtown. Along the way, the attorneys dropped the notary off on the east side at a grocery near her home and proceeded to their offices in the Fletcher Trust Building. It was a cool evening, and a new moon was shining—a thin sliver of light in the sky. First, they stopped by the safety deposit department of the trust company and asked the clerk there to keep at his office a few minutes longer. They went up to their offices on the sixth floor and placed two unsigned copies of the declaration in Smith's office safe. They went back downstairs and put the two signed copies of the statement in Smith's safety deposit box. Afterward, they went to a nearby restaurant and had dinner. Eventually Dean went home to his apartment in the Morton Hotel on Monument Circle, and Smith got back in his car and drove home.

Shortly after Smith arrived at his house, the telephone rang. It was the Marion County prosecutor, Will Remy, who had already gotten wind of the Oberholtzer case and knew that Smith was working with the family.

"Is there not something I had better see you about soon?" Remy asked Smith.

"I think right away," said Smith.[8]

The following morning was Sunday, March 29. Smith called Remy at home and made an appointment to meet him later in the morning at Remy's father's house. Then Smith drove to his office, picked up a copy of the unsigned statement from his office safe, and invited Dean to go with him to visit the prosecutor.

That Sunday afternoon, the three men discussed the developments in the case, and Remy listened as Smith read

Madge's statement aloud. Remy asked questions about the exact procedure with which the dying declaration had been taken. He knew that the entire case would hinge on the statement. Without the statement to use in court, the case would probably be lost. As he listened, Remy knew that Smith was about to hand over to the prosecutor's office the only material that would most likely bring a prison sentence for Stephenson. But a prison sentence would not be easily won in any local court. It would require a legal fight. Will Remy, the man Stephenson had tried to block as Governor McCray's last official appointee, was the man who would have to lead the fight.

A Death in Irvington

April 1925

After hearing Asa Smith's account of Madge Oberholtzer's abduction, Will Remy quickly began to gather information that would be needed to bring charges against Stephenson. On Remy's orders, Smith delivered the signed originals of the dying declaration and affidavit to the prosecutor's office on Tuesday. Next, a statement was taken from the woman's father, and a formal complaint was filed. By Thursday, April 2, Remy had the warrant for Stephenson's arrest prepared, and the matter was turned over to the Indianapolis Police Department.[1]

The job of bringing in Stephenson went to Lt. Jesse L. McMurtry, a detective with the department. Expecting trouble, McMurtry took three other detectives with him and went to look for Stephenson at the Hotel Washington.[2] When they arrived, they found Stephenson was not in his own suite on the thirteenth floor. They went up two more floors, and, stepping off the elevators and across the hall, they knocked on the door of room 1532. A man came to the door. The detectives told him they were looking for D. C. Stephenson. The man identified himself as Fred Butler, then told them that Stephenson was not there. The detectives asked to come in and have a look for themselves. Once inside the small single-bed sleeping room, one of the detectives recognized the man who had opened the door as Stephenson himself. Attorney George Cowan was also in the room. McMurtry informed Stephenson that he was under arrest on charges of assault and battery with the intent to commit murder, kidnapping, and conspiring to commit a felony.

As the detectives watched, Stephenson slowly removed a Horse Thief Detective Association badge from inside his coat, then reached into a pocket and pulled out an automatic pistol. He put the pistol, the badge, and some papers into a suitcase. As he did so, he explained that he had to carry weapons at all times because of his connections with the Ku Klux Klan and that he never knew when there might be an attack on him. When he had done this, he said that he was ready to go with them.

A police car was waiting outside the hotel to drive them to the police headquarters. As Stephenson was about to enter the car, he balked. Headquarters was only a block away, he asked, couldn't they simply walk? The detectives consulted. Then McMurtry told the driver to take the car back while he and the other two officers strolled down the street with their prisoner.

Stephenson was taken first to the detective department for a brief questioning by Jerry E. Kinney, supervisor of detectives. Then Stephenson was taken down to the lockup for booking. Attorney George Cowan had a little trouble coming up with the ten-thousand-dollar bond for Stephenson's release, but eventually he found two bondsmen, Louis Brown and Thomas Whitlock, who posted the bond. Stephenson was back on the street just a few hours after his arrest. The morning edition of the *Indianapolis Star* carried the complete story of his arrest and release on the front page. The story, headlined "STEPHENSON HELD ON ACCUSATION OF GIRL NEAR DEATH," gave the first public details of the Oberholtzer kidnapping.[3] Wasting no time, Will Remy announced that a Marion County grand jury would begin investigating the case the following morning.

Stephenson faced Remy in police court during the formal arraignment. At thirty-four, Remy was a year older than Stephenson, but he looked considerably younger. He was slightly taller than Stephenson, and his face was thin and angular with a prominent nose and very large ears. He had a schoolboy look about him, accented by his closely cropped, dark brown hair, which he always wore neatly parted down the middle. Reporters had dubbed him "the boy prosecutor."[4] At first glance in the courtroom, he hardly seemed a proper match for the smug, self-confident Stephenson. But Remy had already faced Stephenson before and had won.

Remy came to the prosecutor's office in 1921 as deputy to prosecutor William Evans. At that time, Remy already had a good reputation for himself, after a year's work in the city prosecutor's office. When Evans resigned in 1923 during the scandals surrounding his father-in-law, Governor Warren McCray, he recommended Remy as his replacement. Remy had served out the remaining year of Evans's term, then decided to run for the office on his own in 1924.

Remy was a devout Republican who had kept the faith with his party throughout the Klan years. But unlike most of his colleagues, he chose to campaign hard in the primary of 1924 on an anti-Klan platform. When he deliberately threw himself in the path of the Klan, most political observers wrote off his chances of winning. Yet to everyone's surprise, Remy not only won the primary, but he led the Republican ticket, getting fifteen hundred votes more from the Marion County voters than Calvin Coolidge did in the presidential race. His victory was regarded as a serious upset for the otherwise Klan-dominated Republican ticket.[5]

Shortly after the general election in November, Remy received a call from newly elected Congressman Ralph Updike, who invited him to attend a special formal dinner at the Severin Hotel for all winners of the Marion County elections. Remy accepted.

The night of the dinner, Remy arrived at the hotel and was directed to a private dining room.[6] There, he found the rest of the county's elected officials, all dressed in formal evening attire and seated around a U-shaped table. Stephenson was seated at the center of the head table. Remy was seated at the end of one side. A lavish meal was served to the officials, then Stephenson gave a short address, congratulating them all on their victories. After Stephenson sat down, the new Marion County sheriff, Omer Hawkins, rose and said, "Well, I guess we all know why we are here, and I'll start off. I realize that I owe my nomination and election to the Old Man. I now pledge that I will make no official appointment, nor do any official act, which does not meet with the approval of D. C. Stephenson."

Remy watched in surprise and anger as each of the officials seated around the table rose and gave the same pledge. He quickly realized this was Stephenson's way of putting pressure on him to fall in line with the rest of the Republican organization. When Remy's turn finally came, he stood at his seat and said, "I have had a good dinner and have enjoyed meeting you chaps. I hope that we can give Marion County a good administration." The room fell quiet as he sat down. No one applauded. Remy had won his election on an anti-Klan platform; he was not about to give his pledge to Stephenson, now or ever.

A few days after the dinner at the Severin Hotel, Stephenson dropped by Remy's office for a personal visit. Accompanied by two of his armed bodyguards, Stephenson said that he felt he needed personal protection from the police and that his life was being threatened by a gunman with a contract to kill him. Could Remy offer any legal protection?

Remy's only advice was that Stephenson and his bodyguards should leave their guns on his desk and rely on the law for protection. Remy told them that as prosecutor he was often threatened himself but that he did not carry a gun or hire bodyguards and he saw no reason Stephenson should either. Stephenson left in a huff. Shortly after that, Remy discovered that the county commissioners, apparently acting on Stephenson's orders, had cut off appropriations for most of the funding for the prosecutor's office. As a result, Remy had to start paying for law books and office supplies out of his own pocket.[7]

Remy had good reason to welcome the opportunity to pursue Stephenson with the full force of the law. This was Remy's one chance to put Stephenson away. If he missed it, there was no telling what revenge Stephenson might take on him or his family.

Ironically, the Oberholtzer case would become a matter of professional rivalry between Remy and Asa Smith, according to friends who knew both men. Having gone to the trouble of carefully securing the dying declaration from Madge Oberholtzer, Smith felt he had done the spadework on "his" case. Now Remy was coming in as prosecutor and taking it out of the hands of the family's lawyer. There was also the possibility that the Klan would infiltrate the prosecutor's team and valuable information would leak out and find its way to Stephenson. Smith could not bring himself to trust anyone else.

Leroy New, a lawyer who later worked with Smith and often heard him talk about the Stephenson case, recalled, "Asa never trusted even the other members of the prosecuting team. . . . He never knew whether the Klan would be able to infiltrate the prosecutor's team. He didn't trust anybody, including his own people—even Remy. He simply did not have any way of knowing who were secret members of the Klan, and they very well could be able to disclose evidence to Stephenson. He said he felt that if he could get the dying declaration into evidence that would be the whole ball game. He knew that Stephenson's men would do everything they could to keep the declaration out of the trial."[8]

Smith's attitude must have deeply rankled Remy. But this was more than a pair of lawyers suffering from bad nerves and paranoia. Their fears were justified. In the coming months, both men would receive many death threats, and Remy would have at least one narrow brush with attempted murder.

The arraignment had been scheduled for the day after Stephenson's arrest, Friday, April 3, but Klinck and Gentry could not be found. Stephenson promised the police that the two would return to Indianapolis and surrender to the police, but that had not happened. On April 4, Sheriff Hawkins told reporters there was still no trace of Stephenson's men.[9] Stephenson said the two had left town on business and would soon return.

Someone asked Hawkins if it were true that Klinck was on the sheriff's payroll as a deputy. Hawkins said Klinck had been discharged, but it was true Klinck had been appointed to the department just two months earlier.

Finally, on April 6, the arraignment took place with Stephenson alone in Marion County Criminal Court before Judge James A. Collins, one of the many local politicians who had been identified earlier as a klansman in *Tolerance*. Stephenson explained to the judge that Klinck and Gentry were still out of town "on a business trip." John Niblack covered the arraignment for the *Indianapolis Times*. He found Stephenson in the county commissioner's office at the courthouse waiting for his attorney to arrive. Niblack asked Stephenson if he had any comments about the case. "I refuse to discuss such trivial matters," said Stephenson. Then with a smile, he added, "How would you boys like to be fishing right now and watch a red darter spinning in front of a bass?" Niblack pressed him again about the charges. "Nothing to it! Nothing to it!" Stephenson bellowed. "I'll never be indicted!"[10]

Earlier Stephenson had told a reporter from the *Indianapolis Star* that the charges were all the result of political chicanery. "They are aiming at me for 1926," he said, implying that the Klan was trying to keep him from running for political office. He added that since he had been connected with the Klan, there had been more than fifty attempts to shake him down, but not one had been successful. He strongly hinted that the Oberholtzer case was simply one more problem caused by the rift between him and the Evans-Bossert Klan.[11]

But in spite of Stephenson's confident bluster, he had secured the services of Ephraim "Eph" Inman to serve as his counsel at the arraignment. Inman was one of the city's most colorful and most persuasive lawyers, the best-known criminal lawyer in Indianapolis. His towering presence and resonant voice had a captivating power in the courtroom. At the arraignment, Inman entered a plea of not guilty for Stephenson, then requested that Judge Collins quash the indictment.[12] The judge said he would consider Inman's request and would hear arguments on the pleas on Saturday, April 11. After the brief morning session in court, Stephenson walked out jauntily, in good spirits, still a free man.

Later on April 6, Klinck and Gentry reappeared in the city, just as Stephenson promised they would. Stephenson himself drove the two down to Sheriff Hawkins's office to surrender. A klansman in his own right and quite sympathetic to Stephenson,

Hawkins made the arrests as simple as possible. A bond of five thousand dollars for each man was quickly arranged, and the two were immediately released from custody.[13]

All three defendants stood before Judge Collins on Saturday morning as the judge listened to arguments to quash the indictments. Stephenson, Gentry, and Klinck sat at a table on one side of the courtroom with Inman representing all of them. On the opposite side sat Remy along with his deputy, Judson Starke, and Charles E. Cox, a former Indiana Supreme Court judge and a noted attorney whom Remy had brought in to help with the case. After hearing the arguments to dismiss the indictments, Judge Collins announced that he would study the case and rule on the request the following Thursday.

Meanwhile, Madge Oberholtzer was sinking fast.[14] On April 2, the same night Stephenson was arrested, she slipped into a coma. Dr. Kingsbury told reporters he did not expect her to live long. He called her brother, Marshall, to come from Linton, Indiana, to give his sister a transfusion of blood. The transfusion was performed April 3, and, for a few days, her condition improved slightly. On April 7, Kingsbury called in three specialists—Dr. John Warvel, Dr. J. A. MacDonald, and Dr. Henry O. Mertz—to conduct more blood tests and make recommendations on whether a kidney operation might be required. By April 12, the doctors were telling the newspapers that they had given up all hope of saving her life. She had been unconscious for more than a week now, and death could occur at any time. On the morning of April 13, the *Indianapolis Star* carried the headline "MISS OBERHOLTZER REPORTED BETTER" over a story that announced that her temperature had dropped several degrees and the doctors had decided to postpone the kidney operation.

On the morning of April 14, Kingsbury visited the Oberholtzers. He left their house shortly after 10:00 A.M. and stopped to talk briefly with the waiting reporters who were gathered outside the house. Madge seemed to be resting easier now, he told them, but this was probably the result of the regular morphine injections she was now receiving.

Madge Oberholtzer died half an hour later with her parents and nurse at her bedside.[15]

Kingsbury quickly returned to the house. He called Paul F. Robinson, the Marion County coroner, to arrange for an immediate autopsy. Shortly afterward, just as a heavy downpour began, an ambulance arrived at the house to take Madge's body down-town to the Shirley Brothers undertaking parlor. Dr. Robinson had arranged for Dr. Virgil H. Moon, a pathologist from Indiana University's School of Medicine, to conduct the autopsy. Kingsbury attended along with Drs. Mertz and Warvel.

As coroner, Robinson decided to let several local reporters into the morgue to watch as the autopsy was performed. Next morning, the papers carried the coroner's verdict that Madge's death had been caused by mercurial poisoning, apparently as a result of the mercury bichloride tablets she had taken. The coroner, whose name had also once been featured on the *Tolerance* list of Indianapolis klansmen, announced that a full inquest into Madge's death would be held.[16]

By now, the public was well aware of everything that had happened so far in the case. The story of Madge's abduction and rape had been dramatically played on the front pages of all three dailies. Kingsbury had given complete accounts of her story about Stephenson, virtually the same as the story that was contained in the dying declaration. Public sentiment and indignation was beginning to rise against Stephenson. The papers were referring to him as the ex–grand dragon and the banished Klan leader. Then, as if the Oberholtzer matter was not enough, the papers were also running stories about how a woman named Nettie Hamilton, who claimed she was Stephenson's first wife from Oklahoma, had just arrived in town with a young daughter in tow, ready to sue her famous ex-husband for support payments![17] (Stephenson, who said that he did not know the woman, claimed that she had been brought in from somewhere by Evans as part of the plot to ruin Stephenson. However, Hamilton continued to write to Stephenson for more than a year, begging him to at least admit that the young girl was his daughter. He never did.) The public image of the once mysterious "Old Man" was dissolving as each new revelation of his private affairs marched out into the daylight and found its way into the newspapers.

Madge was buried on Wednesday morning, April 16. As the local papers noted, the sun was shining brightly and the birds were singing outside the Oberholtzer home, where the funeral services were held. Her well-publicized death turned the funeral into a public display. Hundreds of people milled around outside the home waiting for a glimpse of the casket. Throughout the morning and early afternoon, florists' vans arrived, bringing a virtual garden of floral arrangements. Flowers were crowded all over the dining room, where Madge's casket was laid. The overflow of flowers spilled out onto the porch, then along the walkway in front of the house. More people in the crowd outside arrived carrying even more flowers.

All three dailies sent reporters and photographers to cover the funeral. Mary E. Bostwick, a reporter from the *Indianapolis Star* who usually covered society and entertainment news, turned in the most vivid account, complete with a description of Madge in her coffin: "The girl wore a simple gown of black chiffon, made over a slip of warm red, and lay in a casket of tufted violet velvet. . . . On the silver plate on the inner edge of the casket was engraved the single word, 'Madge.' The girl's face was peaceful. Whatever horrors she had undergone—whatever secrets were locked away forever when death closed her lips . . . had left no trace on her face. Her expression was serene and peaceful."[18]

After the service, Madge's casket was carried out to the hearse for the procession to nearby Memorial Park Cemetery. Down the front steps of the house came both ministers, followed by Matilda Oberholtzer, who walked with support from her husband, George, on one side and Madge's nurse, Beatrice Spratley, on the other. Marshall Oberholtzer walked behind his parents, followed by the honorary pallbearers, the women who had been Madge's sorority sisters in the Pi Phi chapter at Butler College. Then came the casket, now closed with the top covered with flowers. The casket was carried by six young men, most of whom had known Madge since college. A photographer leaped in front of the pallbearers to snap a picture of the somber-faced procession with the casket for the *Indianapolis Star*.

The funeral procession drove slowly up Arlington Avenue, then turned east on Washington Street for the short drive to the cemetery. At the graveside, the Reverend C. H. Winders delivered a prayer for the family. By this time, both the mother and father were weeping and near collapse. More flowers were heaped upon the casket, and it was slowly lowered into the ground. So it was that Madge had passed into martyrdom.

Late that same night, sometime after midnight, several cars pulled into the long driveway of Stephenson's mansion. Several men got out of the cars and went into the house. Stephenson's German shepherd dogs were barking loudly in their kennels at the rear of the house. Stephenson was no longer living there. Since the reappearance of his former wife, he had moved all his things out of the house and had been staying in his rooms at the Hotel Washington. At 1:30 A.M., the neighbors were roused by an explosion that rattled the windows of the surrounding houses. Running outside, the neighbors could see flames inside Stephenson's house. All the cars were gone. The fire department arrived quickly and had the flames extinguished in an hour. There was extensive damage to the house, including several windows that had been blown out by the explosion. Inside, investigators found cans of gasoline and coal oil. All the gas jets in the house had been turned on.

Stephenson had probably been counting on his friend, Judge James Collins, to go along with the request to quash the indictments against him. But now the heat of public resentment toward Stephenson was too hot for Collins to ignore. On April 16, the same day Madge was buried, Collins announced that he had rejected Eph Inman's request to quash the indictments. Two days later, the charges against Stephenson were raised to second-degree murder, and a new warrant was issued for his arrest.

Collins received the murder indictment just before noon on Saturday morning, April 18, and he promptly passed the order along to the Marion County sheriff's department to have Stephenson, Gentry, and Klinck arrested. But something went wrong. Sheriff Hawkins happened to be eating his lunch when the indictments reached his office. He made no move to hurry along with his food. Nor did any of his men. Instead, they waited until nearly 3:00 P.M. to send someone out to look for Stephenson. The police made their rounds to the fire-damaged Irvington house and the rooms at the Hotel Washington, but there was no sign of Stephenson.

The next morning the papers were speculating that someone had tipped off Stephenson, giving him time to slip out of town. Prosecutor Remy was indignant that Hawkins had so leisurely allowed three hours to pass before even attempting to find Stephenson. Inman assured reporters that his client would turn himself in on Monday morning.[19]

Monday dawned cloudy and cool. Three men walked into the delicatessen of a hotel on the corner of Pennsylvania and St. Clair streets, just after 8:00 A.M. and ordered breakfast. The counterman must have recognized at least one of his customers, since Stephenson's face had appeared several times in all the daily papers. The three ate slowly, as if they were waiting for someone else to arrive, but when no one did, they paid their bills and walked nine blocks down the street to the Consolidated Building.

Shortly after they left, Hawkins and his deputies pulled up in front of the deli in their police patrol car. They went inside, looked around for Stephenson, asked which way he had gone, then drove on down Pennsylvania Street. Hawkins went straight to the Consolidated Building and up to Inman's law offices, where he found Stephenson, Gentry, and Klinck chatting with their attorney. As with most of Stephenson's dealings with Hawkins—the man who had pledged at the Severin Hotel that he would not "do any official act which does not meet with the approval of D. C. Stephenson"—the arrest was a simple, friendly affair. A photo in the papers showed the three arrested men, all in business suits, walking to the Marion County jail; Klinck was smiling and laughing, and Hawkins was in the lead.[20] By noon, the three men were comfortably situated in the elite "federal row" section of the jail, normally reserved for federal prisoners. For the first time in his life, D. C. Stephenson was behind bars in the state of Indiana.

An Investigation Begins

April–May 1925

The period between Stephenson's first arrest on April 2 and his second arrest April 20 on the murder charge was a hectic time for the prosecutor and the police. For two and a half weeks, after official actions against him were made public, Stephenson was still a free man. The case against him, resting as it did on a dying woman's testimony, was a fragile one. With all his powerful connections, would Stephenson be able to build an alibi? Would he buy witnesses to testify for him? Would he persuade the judge—a known klansman—to dismiss the case on some vague technical grounds? There were no answers. The best thing Will Remy could do was to start building his best, airtight case against Stephenson.

For the moment, the Indianapolis Police Department (as opposed to the Marion County sheriff) was still quite cooperative. These were the last days of Mayor Lew Shank's administration. Shank was now a lame-duck mayor and not at all hesitant to use the city offices to help put Stephenson away. Everyone knew that the political climate would change dramatically in a few months if John Duvall won the mayor's race with the Klan's support. In the meantime, the anti-Klan police department would move to suit the will of the prosecutor.

Jerry E. Kinney, supervisor of detectives, was handed the job of investigating the case and searching for witnesses who might support the statements made in Madge Oberholtzer's dying declaration. Kinney was a good cop, a veteran of the police department with thirty-eight years of service and absolutely no love of the Klan.[1] Back in 1919, when George V. "Cap" Coffin resigned as chief of police, Kinney was picked for the job by then-Mayor Charles W. Jewett. But Kinney was a Democrat when Republican Lew Shank took over city hall in 1922. Consequently, the first thing Shank did was to break Chief Kinney back down to captain. The matter wasn't personal; it was simply politics.

Two years later, Shank raised Kinney up to supervisor of the detective division. With Duvall riding his way to city hall on the back of the Klan, Kinney could surely tell that his own position in the department would once again be in doubt: Kinney was Catholic. (And, in fact, when Duvall eventually became mayor the following January, *his* first move was to break Kinney back down to captain.)

The sixty-year-old Kinney was used to the ups and downs of politics, and he apparently did not let it affect his work. He had handled strikes, riots, and tough criminals.[2] The son of an Irish railroadman, Kinney was known as a devout Catholic who was active in the Irish Ancient Order of Hibernians and the Knights of Columbus. As such, he knew most of the active members of the anti-Klan American Unity League, and he would have been aware of Stephenson's movements.

On April 3, the day after Stephenson's first arrest on kidnapping and assault charges, Kinney took the train up to Hammond, Indiana, to look for witnesses who could support any part of Madge Oberholtzer's story.[3] The most important witnesses, he knew, would be the ones who could testify that they had seen a man and a woman answering the descriptions of Stephenson and Oberholtzer entering the hotel. Kinney went straight to the Indiana Hotel in Hammond, armed with a couple of photographs, a list of questions, a small ring-bound notebook, and a pencil for taking notes.

Kinney talked with Pericle Primes, the owner and manager of the hotel, and explained that he wanted to question some of the hotel employees, especially anyone who had been working there in the early hours of Monday, March 16.[4] Primes checked the work schedules and came up with the names of the night clerk, the bellboys, two elevator operators, a housekeeper, a maid, and the Western Union telegraph manager. The ones who were already in the hotel were summoned to the office one by one to be interviewed. Calls went out to find the others and bring them to the hotel for police questioning.

Kinney started with the night clerk, Ted Wilson, a young man in his early thirties who had been on duty at the time when Stephenson, Gentry, and Oberholtzer were supposed to have arrived at the hotel.[5] Kinney showed Wilson the photographs and asked if he had ever seen any people who looked like that sign into the hotel within the last couple of weeks. Wilson puzzled briefly over the pictures, then went to the hotel's register. Two signatures—a Mac Kennedy and an L. S. Sebree—were at the top of the page for Monday, March 16. Directly below those two names was the signature registering Mr. and Mrs. W. B. Morgan from Franklin, Indiana, and immediately below that, Earl Gentry from Indianapolis. Wilson identified the photograph of Stephenson as Mr. Morgan and Oberholtzer as Mrs. Morgan. They had stayed in room 416, and Gentry had been assigned to the adjoining room, 417. Wilson's identification was positive, and it matched the story that Madge had told Asa Smith and John Kingsbury in her deathbed statement.

Kinney spent the rest of the day interviewing the other hotel workers.[6] Lillian Reed, a maid, recalled that she had been asked to bring several towels up to the room to be used as hot compresses and how, in cleaning the rooms, she had discovered blood-covered sheets, a handful of bullets in a dresser drawer, some oranges and witch hazel, an empty milk bottle, and an empty whiskey bottle—all things that Madge had mentioned in her story. It was not very likely that a maid would soon forget a set of customers like that!

So it went through the day. A bellhop remembered the trio, and an elevator operator remembered how she had taken the three up to the fourth floor. Lee Ayres, the hotel's day clerk, recalled the three checking out of the hotel on Monday afternoon and leaving in an automobile. At every turn of his questioning, Kinney found that Oberholtzer's story held up nicely. Only one minor discrepancy appeared: in her statement to Kingsbury, she said she had disposed of the mercury bichloride bottle by throwing it out the bathroom window. As clerk Ted Wilson pointed out, room 416 had no window in the bathroom. This was a minor point, one that the attorneys could worry about later.

After finishing with the hotel's staff, Kinney walked around for several blocks near the hotel looking for a shop that sold women's hats and was located near a drugstore.[7] In this pursuit, he had less luck. After pounding the pavement for a long time, he only managed to find one shop clerk who vaguely recalled selling a black hat to a woman who matched Madge's description, but she had no records, and her memory seemed a bit hazy—not the sort of person the lawyers would risk on the witness stand.

With the drugstores, Kinney struck out completely. No pharmacist at any drugstore near the hotel could recall selling a bottle of mercury bichloride to a young woman of Madge's description. This point had been a long shot. Mercury bichloride was a common antiseptic in 1925, and the likelihood of someone remembering a single purchase—no prescription was needed— was roughly the same as the odds of someone remembering the sale of a particular bottle of aspirin. Other attempts were made later to locate the drugstore where Madge bought her poison, but no one ever succeeded in positively identifying it.

Despite these two failures, Kinney's trip was a success. In just a few hours, he had substantiated most of Madge's story and had located the key witnesses who would be used in court to provide support for the prosecution. Kinney returned to Indianapolis that night and filed his reports the next morning.

The attorneys soon found more people to build their case against Stephenson. On Monday, April 6, they questioned the young actress who told them how Stephenson attacked her in his home after one of his parties in 1924. The next day, Remy took a statement from Levi Thomas, the porter on the train that Stephenson and the others had taken to Hammond. Thomas recalled the trio boarding the train and was willing to testify to that fact.[8]

On April 15, the day after Madge died, Remy collected statements from Dr. Kingsbury and Dr. Henry O. Mertz, getting them to describe the treatment they gave Madge for her injuries and to talk about her physical condition before her death. Dr. John H. Warvel gave a supporting statement to the prosecutor on April 16, the day of the funeral. The next day, Remy took statements from Madge's father and her nurse, Beatrice Spratley. The following week, the coroner's office released a report on the autopsy along with a chemical analysis of Madge's organs. Coroner Paul Robinson's findings were not exactly what the prosecutor wanted to hear, since Robinson reported that "Madge Oberholtzer's death was due to Mercurial Poisoning, self administered."[9] This was a medical fact, but one which carefully ignored that the self-administration was done under duress. Remy had to show that her death was the direct result of Stephenson's attack and that this was not a case of suicide but a case of murder.

On May 1, Remy took a statement from James H. Wricks, a porter on the train who remembered seeing bloodstains on the sheets of the beds in Stephenson's train compartment. Remy also interviewed another porter, Preston Brown, who recalled talking with Levi Thomas about the three passengers who boarded their car that night. A neighbor of Stephenson, Josephine Lowe, came down to Remy's office to tell how she had been awakened during the night of March 16 by the barking of Stephenson's dogs and shouts, which came from the direction of his garage.

By this time, Stephenson had been behind bars for nearly two weeks. Reports in the papers indicated that all evidence pointed against Stephenson and that the prosecutor firmly intended to pursue the case. Now people were beginning to come forward with their stories about Stephenson—people who might otherwise have been afraid to talk while the former grand dragon was still free. Two more women came forward—a young secretary and a hospital intern—who told the prosecutor about their grim love affairs with Stephenson. Jack Culbertson, the night clerk from the Hotel Washington recalled that he had placed the train reservations for Stephenson on the night the trio left for Hammond.[10] Slowly, piece by piece, story by story, the case against Stephenson began to take shape.

All three of the city's dailies began, first cautiously and then more boldly, to report on the Stephenson case. The stories unfolded in piecemeal fashion, from the first report of Stephenson's arrest on April 2 to the death and funeral of Madge Oberholtzer and Stephenson's second arrest on April 20. Each paper ran the story—with emphasis on Madge's abduction—on the front page in those early weeks.

Some writers have claimed that the *Indianapolis Times* was the only one of the three dailies that was truly anti-Klan. It would be more accurate to say that the *Times* was the only paper to carry on an anti-Klan crusade. For at least two years before the Oberholtzer case, the *Times* had generated many stories that ridiculed the Klan. "Klan-baiting" stories, which mocked the seriousness of the Klan, became stock items in the *Times*, which thrived on a muckraking style of journalism.

But in fairness to them, the *Indianapolis Star* and the *Indianapolis News* were not pro-Klan. Those papers simply had not given the Klan much in-depth coverage before the Oberholtzer case. Only after the split between Stephenson and Bossert became public in May 1924 did *Star* and *News* reporters bother to write much about the Klan. Had the *Star* and *News* been the pro-Klan papers that some observers later claimed, it would have been more logical for them to fold the Stephenson story quietly into the back pages with the rest of the police blotter stories and court reports. The fact that they did not bury the stories gives a more balanced view of how matters stood with the press and Stephenson.

The prominence of the story in the papers led to a great shift in public opinion. Until the Oberholtzer story broke in the papers, the public was divided into roughly three large groups over the Klan issue. Some people either belonged to or supported the Klan; this was a sizeable group of respectable, mostly middle-class citizens. A second, smaller group openly opposed the Klan;

for the most part, these were the religious and ethnic groups that the Klan had attacked. The third group, perhaps as large as the first, included people who did not think much about the Klan one way or the other—people who had remained silent on the issue. As many who lived in that time have said, the Klan was easier to ignore than to fight. Until this point, these people had simply avoided making enemies among their neighbors and had done their best to ignore the Klan's presence.

But now, with daily newspaper stories about Stephenson and his outrages against the martyred Madge Oberholtzer, it was impossible to ignore the Klan. Wasn't Stephenson the former grand dragon of the Klan in Indiana? Hadn't he led rallies where the Klan talked about the need to protect "virtuous American womanhood"? Was this an example of how he intended to protect women?

After Stephenson's arrest, Walter Bossert's office quickly issued a statement from the current grand dragon, urging that justice be meted out to Stephenson for his criminal deeds. But Bossert's message was largely ignored. Stephenson had been a klansman, and now his crime was tainting the entire order. In a matter of days, the silent public found its voice and rose up in an angry denunciation of Stephenson and the Klan.

Five hundred of the Oberholtzers' Irvington neighbors turned out for a meeting Sunday, April 26, at the Irvington Methodist Church to voice their opposition to an attempt to re- lease Stephenson, Gentry, and Klinck on bail.[11] The three were being held without bail, and the community wanted to let the courts know it would be angered by any effort to free Stephenson.

Thomas Carr Howe, the former president of Butler College and a leading figure in the community, spoke to the angry group. Howe was a quiet man with round-rimmed glasses that gave his angular features an owlish look. His voice rang with emotion when he spoke of the need to see justice carried out. For Howe, the death of Madge Oberholtzer may have been doubly sig- nificant, and everyone knew it. His eldest daughter, Mary Eliza- beth, had died in a strikingly similar tragedy only eleven years earlier. Caught in a hopeless love affair with one of the university professors, Mary had gone quietly to her room and taken poison to avoid causing any shame for herself or her family. Now Thomas Howe told the crowd that he "looked upon the case just as if the victim had been shot down in the street," and he said that public sentiment would not be satisfied until justice was obtained. He told them this was no mere suicide, as the defense lawyers would claim, but an outright case of murder. Howe also announced that a special fund had been created to raise money for the legal assistance that might be required to prosecute the case.[12]

In the ensuing weeks, other groups around the city held similar meetings, demanding that justice be done—with the implication that justice could only mean the conviction of Stephenson. Women's sewing groups and church organizations issued their statements.

Public resentment was felt in other ways, too. The primary elections were held May 5, and the police were operating under orders from the police chief, Herman Rikhoff, to keep members of the Horse Thief Detective Association far away from all public polling places. The association, of course, had once been an integral part of Stephenson's organization—the "enforcement" arm of the Klan. On voting days in the past, members had turned out in large numbers to intimidate anti-Klan voters, driving through black neighborhoods and displaying their guns as a warning for the blacks to stay home. But this time the police were making it clear that the "detectives" were not welcome anymore in Indianapolis. Early on election morning, the police began to sweep through the city, singling out known members of the Horse Thief Detective Association and arresting them for carrying concealed weapons. The city issued an order that revoked the police powers of the "detectives," and the real policemen went gleefully about the task of rounding up association members. As the election day wore on, the police arrested fifty-four members in a single day![13]

By mid-May, Judge James Collins had good reason to wish that he had never heard of Stephenson or the Ku Klux Klan. Collins was caught in the middle by the pressure from the public and press, his responsibilities as a judge, and his commitments to his former friend and political ally. On the one hand, Collins owed Stephenson for past political support. On the other hand, it might cost him his own political future if he tried to save Stephenson. The papers and the public were watching carefully to make sure the case would not quietly fade away. So what could he do?

Collins refused to grant Eph Inman's request that Stephenson be freed on bond. He also sidestepped Inman's other motions. Inman had a reputation as a wizard in the art of legal maneuvering, and now he was putting on a display of that talent. Failing in the request for bond release, Inman filed a motion to quash the murder indictments. Failing that, he filed a motion to strike one of the four counts of the indictment—a move that would have nullified the effect of the other three counts. At each turn of the defense attorney's strategy, Remy was ready with objections, and in each case, Collins declined to rule in favor of Stephenson.

It was a clear, warm morning on May 15 when the defendants came before the bench to enter their pleas to the charges against them. Stephenson, Gentry, and Klinck were led into the courtroom, handcuffed and linked together on a chain. As the charges of the indictment were read, Stephenson stood with hands in pockets, leaning against the brass railing in front of the judge's bench. Klinck, the tallest of the three, stood gazing out the window while Gentry kept his eyes fixed on the floor. The reporter from the *Indianapolis Star* noted all were clean shaven, neatly dressed, and visibly nervous. Stephenson seemed plainly nervous and slightly pale. At various points during the reading of the indictment, Stephenson would whisper to his two companions and they would nod. Finally, Judge Collins asked Stephenson how he wished to plead. Stephenson leaned over to Inman, whispered for a moment, then replied in a very low voice, "Not guilty." Klinck and Gentry entered the same plea, and the three were taken back to jail.[14]

Eight days later, on May 23, Inman filed a motion with Judge Collins, requesting a change of venue to another county. Following the usual procedure, Remy was allowed to name three adjoining counties to which the case might be transferred. Then Inman was allowed to choose from these three counties the one to which the case would be transferred. Remy named Shelby, Boone, and Hamilton counties. Then Inman deliberated over which would be most acceptable for the defense. Finally, he picked Hamilton County, and the case was delivered to the Circuit Court of Judge Fred E. Hines. Judge Collins was rid of the case; and Stephenson, Gentry, and Klinck were headed for Noblesville, the seat of Hamilton County.[15]

The Trial Before the Trial

May–August 1925

Judge Fred Hines was as unhappy to see Stephenson transferred to Hamilton County as Judge Collins was happy to see him leave Marion County. For one thing, this was a hot case that would attract unruly crowds and a flood of reporters to the courtroom. A very quiet man, Hines did not enjoy such spectacles even though he had long since gotten used to them.[1]

What bothered Hines more than the sensationalism of the case was that his court once again was being used to handle spill-over cases from Marion County. When he was told that the Stephenson case was coming to his court, Hines replied that he did not see how he could possibly hear the trial before the start of the October term. (In the heat of an Indiana summer, a trial in August would comprise its own form of cruel and unusual punishment.) Besides, didn't he already have one Marion County murder case waiting to be heard? Young Edward Prater was already sitting in a cell at the Hamilton County jail waiting to be tried by Hines for the murder of an Indianapolis streetcar conductor. Like Stephenson's, Prater's case had been transferred from Marion to Hamilton County. The result was an unfair burden of cases on the smaller county court, making it a hostage of the larger Indianapolis courts.[2]

By now, Stephenson had added Ira Holmes to his defense team to assist chief counsel Eph Inman. By having the case moved to Hamilton County, a third lawyer, Floyd Christian of Noblesville, was also added to serve as local counsel. Judge Hines probably was not looking forward to this theatrical array of defense attorneys.

The judge did not enjoy turning his court into a stage for "showstopper" lawyers, and Inman fit that description. His presentations before juries were so dramatic and forceful that it was not uncommon for opposing counsel to openly warn the jurors not to allow themselves to be swayed by the eloquence of his appeals. Inman had made a name for himself in a Bloomfield, Indiana, murder trial where two sons were accused of killing their father. It was the first case in Indiana where a dictagraph, an early recording machine, was used to record the confessions of the sons and admitted as evidence to the trial. Undaunted by his clients' recorded confessions, Inman successfully argued that, in spite of the confessions, the boys were not guilty. An angry spectator later mailed an anonymous letter to one of the boys after their acquittal: "Your next trial will be before the Great Jehovah and Inman cannot do you any good there." Inman relished the story and often repeated it, pointing out the letter's double meaning as one of the finest compliments he ever received.[3]

Holmes was also an attorney with a flamboyant reputation. The forty-nine-year-old Indianapolis attorney was a distant cousin of U.S. Supreme Court justice Oliver Wendell Holmes. Active in Republican politics, Ira Holmes served as one of Marion County's election commissioners. But he allowed neither his position nor his lineage to interfere with his business. He was most widely known for his defense work for bootleggers. Since Prohibition, Holmes had been handling a steady stream of bathtubgin cases, usually with successful results. It was widely known that his fees were among the highest anywhere. In the Stephenson case, Holmes lived up to his reputation. A newspaper story told how Stephenson had "sold" his Irvington home to Holmes in exchange for Holmes's legal service in the upcoming trial.[4]

The most unassuming of Stephenson's lawyers was Floyd Christian, who was apparently hired simply to provide assistance during the jury selection process and to give opinions during the trial on technical legal matters. Christian's appearance on Stephenson's side of the bench also lent some respectability to the affair. Christian was a member of the oldest law firm in Hamilton County and was quite skilled in handling murder cases. He was a member of the Murat Shrine, the Masonic Lodge, the Scottish Rite, and the Presbyterian church—all proper credentials for a leading member of the bar in Hamilton County. Unlike the other two attorneys on Stephenson's side, Christian was a quiet, patient man whose one great passion besides the law was stamp collecting.[5]

These were the men who would use every imaginable legal maneuver to persuade Hines to release Stephenson, Klinck, and Gentry and dismiss the charges against them. It would be at least a couple of months of legal cat-and-mouse games with motions and rulings and more motions and more rulings. It was not the sort of thing that a quiet man of Hines's disposition would enjoy. It would not be a good summer.

———————

Sheriff Omer Hawkins lost no time removing Stephenson, Klinck, and Gentry from Marion County to their new quarters in the Hamilton County jail. Two days after Judge Collins granted the change of venue, Hawkins bundled the three prisoners in his car and quickly drove them out of the county.

It all happened with very short notice on Monday morning, May 25. Just before 10:00 A.M., Hawkins announced that they were leaving immediately for Hamilton County. Hawkins had been heavily criticized for the way he handled Stephenson's arrest. The prosecutor hadn't liked it and neither had the public. Now Hawkins simply wanted to get Stephenson out of his way.[6]

It was a cold, clear morning. The three prisoners were brought to Hawkins's office in their shirtsleeves and unshaven. Stephenson had sent Fred Butler to get them each a fresh change of clothes. But Hawkins bluntly announced that he wasn't waiting; they would leave immediately. A hard frost had left a chill in the air, and a sharp wind was blowing outside. "My God! I'm not going this way!" Stephenson protested. "I'll freeze!" After more than a month in jail, he was still not used to taking orders instead of giving them. Someone lent Stephenson an overcoat to wear during the trip to Noblesville. He gratefully wrapped the coat around himself. Smoking a pipe and looking rather meek, he was led out to the waiting sheriff's car along with his two former bodyguards.

The sheriff's car was an open touring model, and the wind chilled the prisoners as they sped through the city. Hawkins order his deputy to drive fast and ignore the traffic signals. A car loaded with reporters followed them, but it was soon lost by the speeding patrol car. The sheriff's group arrived in Noblesville in record time—about forty-five minutes—with the reporters pulling up in front of the jail several minutes later.

Hawkins turned his prisoners over to the custody of the Hamilton County sheriff. He briefly introduced Stephenson to Sheriff Charles Gooding. The reporters noticed that Stephenson seemed visibly embarrassed by the stiff formality of the introduction. He took off the borrowed coat, gave it to Hawkins, and asked him to return it, saying, "I want you to thank the gentleman who loaned me this for his courtesy." Gooding seemed to think that he was also expected to say something, so he struck a pose and tried to sound fierce for the Indianapolis reporters, announcing, "These men will be given the same privileges as the other prisoners, and no more!" Then he led them upstairs to their cells.[7]

The Noblesville jail—a red brick, two-story structure—was about forty years old. The cells were small—four feet by fifteen feet—built with the idea that jails were intended to serve as punishment for the prisoners they contained. The jail had a reputation for being an extremely insecure building; one prisoner had once escaped by simply walking out of his unlocked cell and out the door. Gooding was known to be a pussycat with his prisoners. As long as a prisoner did not go out of his way to earn Gooding's wrath, he could expect "hotel service" from the sheriff and his wife. Because the sheriff's wife was such a good and generous cook, it was said that most prisoners left the jail weighing more, not less, than they did when they arrived (Stephenson was no exception to the rule).

As the trio was led up the narrow flight of stairs to their cells, they passed the cell where Edward Prater stood watching the three older men being locked up. As they filed past Prater's cell, Earl Gentry stopped to shake hands with the teenager who was accused of murder. "Hello, kid," said Gentry. "You here too?"[8]

Noblesville was a typical small-town county seat in 1925. The town of less than five thousand people centered on the courthouse square with its shops and drugstores. The courthouse itself was a three-story Gothic structure with a clock tower that had a clock face on each side. The town, which had just passed its hundredth anniversary, had flourished during the 1880s, when natural gas deposits were discovered nearby and speculators pumped money into the community. It was a Republican town, and during the recent popularity of the Klan, it had been one of the Klan's strongholds in the state. The torchlit parades had been held often in Noblesville, and fiery crosses had burned several times in official Klan ceremonies only a few yards from the jail where the former grand dragon was being held. Noblesville had been a "100 percent American" town long before the Klan appeared, and it would continue as such long after the Klan's departure.

The Hamilton County Circuit Court, where Stephenson's trial would be held, was on the second floor of the courthouse. A long flight of marble stairs led up to a dark wood-paneled room.

The entrance to the courtroom was a pair of double doors at the back of the room that opened with a full view of the judge's bench. There were wooden folding seats, theater-style, with room to handle a crowd of four hundred spectators. Built in an era before courts were accustomed to having swarms of reporters descend on them, there were no facilities to handle the telephones and typewriters of the reporters. Eventually, one of the public restrooms on the second floor was taken over to serve as a temporary pressroom during the trial. The judge could enter the courtroom from a door behind the bench. Plaintiffs and defendants sat at two large tables directly in front of the bench. The jury was seated in a wooden box to the right of the bench. All were separated from the audience by a heavy, carved wooden railing.

Inman, of course, wanted to make sure his client would not become part of any drama in this courtroom, so he quickly launched a motion with Judge Hines to quash the indictments. It was the same strategy he had tried unsuccessfully with Judge Collins. Hines also rejected the motion.[9]

Inman then requested another bail bond hearing as an attempt to get his clients out of jail. Hines agreed to hear this argument and set a date of June 16. Then Inman filed a motion that would require the prosecution to turn over to the defense copies of the dying declaration and the register page of the Indiana Hotel. Prosecutor Remy filed a countermotion to strike Inman's motion from the court records. On June 12, Hines ruled on both motions, saying that no alleged dying declaration had been submitted to him as evidence by the prosecution, but that if the prosecution planned to use such a statement, the court would require that copies be furnished to the defense before the start of the June 16 bail bond hearing.

Stephenson's attorneys had laid out a simple but ambitious plan of attack. They would strike hard at the dying declaration and get it thrown out of court during the bail bond hearing. The hearing, after all, was essentially a trial without a jury, since it would simply be a hearing before the judge with attorneys from both sides present. If the defense lawyers could defeat the dying declaration at this stage, their chances of winning a case before a jury would be greatly improved. Without the dying declaration, the prosecution's case would be weakened and perhaps destroyed.

By the morning of June 16, however, the defense attorneys still had not received a copy of the dying declaration. At the start of the hearing, Inman made a surprise move; he called Remy to the witness stand for the defense. Remy was shaken by this. He told the judge that he was not prepared to be a witness, and that he had no firsthand knowledge of the case. Nevertheless, Hines ordered Remy to take the witness stand.

Inman asked Remy whether he had in his possession a sheet from the register book of the Indiana Hotel. Remy replied that he did. Inman asked if Remy would produce that sheet for the court. Remy said he would turn it over to the court as evidence but not to the defense for inspection. Inman asked again if he would turn it over to the defense attorneys for their examination and then to the court. Remy said no, that he would only turn it over to the court itself.

"Do you have in your possession a paper signed by Madge Oberholtzer which you expect to introduce, claiming it to be a dying declaration?" Inman asked.

"I have the dying declaration of Madge Oberholtzer," said Remy.[10]

The hearing dissolved into an argument over whether Remy should be forced to let the defense examine the two crucial documents in the prosecution's case. Remy argued that the only way he would allow the defense attorneys to examine the documents would be if the defense would first agree to have the documents entered as evidence in the hearing.

This was the very thing Inman wanted to avoid. Inman hoped the dying declaration could be dissected before it was entered as evidence and that "disagreeable" portions could be removed as "incompetent for introduction." By gradually slicing the most incriminating parts out, the defense might weaken the force the document would have as evidence.

Judge Hines called for a compromise. The documents would not be turned over to the defense. Instead, court stenographers would type copies of the nine-page dying declaration and provide these copies to the defense. Then the defense would be allowed to call witnesses to prove its case using any or all of the statement, or the defense could object to the entire dying declaration.

Remy turned over the declaration and the hotel register page but only after winning partial protection for the documents. The court adjourned for an hour, resuming at 1:30 P.M.

In the afternoon, Inman began by calling medical experts to the witness stand. He wanted to prove three things: that Madge Oberholtzer's death was the result of self-administered mercurial poisoning; that her mind was "cloudy" when she gave her dying declaration; and that the poison, though self-administered, might not have been swallowed and might not have been taken with suicidal intent.

To build the groundwork for his case, Inman called the attending physicians who had worked with Madge—Dr. John MacDonald, Dr. Virgil Moon, Dr. John Warvel, and Dr. Henry O. Mertz. One by one, the doctors each gave virtually the same testimony. Each said he felt the cause of Madge's death was mercurial poisoning and that the poison had been self-administered. Inman asked each one if he had noticed any bruises or lacerations on her body. Each time Inman asked, "In your opinion, did they cause Madge Oberholtzer's death?" Each time, the doctors indicated that her death was caused by the poison, not by the bruises and cuts.

After repeating this scene with each of the four doctors, Inman suddenly changed his tactics and called Asa Smith to the stand. He wanted to grill Smith on how the dying declaration had been obtained. Inman hoped to uncover technical weaknesses in the document and, perhaps, lead the judge to declare it inadmissible as evidence.

Inman began by establishing that Madge had not written the dying declaration herself, but that Smith had pieced together the story himself over a period of time. What followed was a tense, grueling session as Inman verbally battered Smith and the declaration on the witness stand.

"Who wrote these words, 'dated March 28—1925'?" Inman asked.

"I did," Smith replied.

"You wrote it. Did you write it at that time and in her presence?"

"Well, I am not sure. I had a fountain pen and I dated it, but I don't know whether in the adjoining room, but it was right at the time."

"Did she write her name with the fountain pen you had?"

"I don't know about that. I think possibly Mr. Dean furnished the pen."

"Did he have a fountain pen?"

"As I remember."

"And was it his pen, as you recall, she wrote her name with?"

"I could not swear. He had a fountain pen."

"You had one of your own?"

"Yes."

"And it is your judgement, Mr. Smith, that Miss Oberholtzer wrote her name with the fountain pen of Mr. Dean?"

"This is my memory. I wrote that [the date] with mine. I remember I had a fountain pen and we furnished her with a pen and she signed her name, and that I wrote that in right away at the time, I don't remember whether in or out of the room or whether I used my pen or the same pen, I don't remember."[11]

So it went for nearly an hour as Smith gave a point-by-point description of how he wrote the dying declaration, based on Madge's testimony, of how it was typed and corrected, and of how she eventually signed it.

As Inman proceeded with the questioning, Smith quoted parts of the statement from memory to illustrate how he had written the document. Each time, the defense attorneys were on their feet objecting that the statement could not be read into the court record until the court ruled on its admissibility. Finally, the court erupted once more in arguments between the attorneys on both sides. Hines ended the dispute by temporarily adjourning the court and continuing the hearing until the following morning.

The next day's testimony still left the issue unresolved but tilting somewhat in favor of the prosecution. Hines began by ruling that the dying declaration could not be introduced by the state as evidence at that time. But he left the door open, pointing out that it might be introduced later in the trial. This seemed a temporary victory for the defense.

The defense continued to call witnesses to the stand: attorney Griffith Dean; Dr. John Kingsbury; and Madge's brother, Marshall Oberholtzer. During their testimony, both Kingsbury and Madge's brother told their versions of Madge's story—the same information that was contained in the dying declaration. Twice Inman attempted to strike from the record sections of testimony that dealt with the material in the dying declaration. Both times Judge Hines overruled the defense objections, allowing the stories to stand.

Far worse for the defense was Kingsbury's testimony that Madge had been in full possession of her mental faculties when she signed the dying declaration—a point that damaged the defense's claim that she had signed the document in a "cloudy" state of mind. None of this was new information. Kingsbury had told virtually the same story to the newspapers in April. But this time, the story was now part of the official court record and an integral part of the case against Stephenson. Even though Hines had not yet admitted the dying declaration as evidence, copies of the declaration had been released to the newspapers. All the dailies ran the full text of the declaration, a point that further galvanized public sentiment against Stephenson.

The third day of the bail hearing went even worse for Stephenson. The defense called witnesses nurse Beatrice Spratley, Matilda Oberholtzer, George Oberholtzer, and coroner Paul Robinson. Matilda Oberholtzer wept loudly at several points during the day's testimony—a fact noted by all the newspapers. During his time in the witness box, Madge's father sat with his eyes fixed on Stephenson, who sat between attorneys Inman and Holmes at the defense table a few feet away. "When he left the stand, Mr. Oberholtzer, in a slow pace, almost paused at the table where Stephenson sat and glared directly at him," wrote the reporter for the *Indianapolis Star.*

Once again, the defense tried to convince Hines to strike portions of the testimony from the records, asking that he remove all portions of the previous day's testimony that dealt with material found in the dying declaration. By now, however, Hines was adamant. He refused to grant the requests and ruled that all testimony would stand as it was recorded.

As the tide turned against them, the defense attorneys decided there was nothing more they could do to keep the declaration out of court. They filed a motion to have the declaration introduced as evidence. But they did so with a statement claiming that the declaration did not relate to the material facts of the case or to the Oberholtzer homicide. No matter what the defense said, the dying declaration was now an official part of the record. For Stephenson, this was the worst thing that could have happened.

Hines heard closing arguments on Friday, June 19, then announced that he would rule on the request for bail the following Thursday. During his closing argument for the prosecution, attorney Charles Cox said, "I am going to make a statement that perhaps should not be made, but if this man had harmed a daughter of mine, no man-made law would prevent me from taking his life."

After a week of long and argumentative proceedings, on June 25 Hines announced that he would not grant bail for any of the defendants. The defense immediately requested that the case go to trial at the earliest possible opportunity—as early, perhaps, as Monday, June 29.

Hines and the prosecution seemed visibly shocked by this unexpected move. Suddenly Inman seemed to be trying to speed up, rather than slow down, the court process. Hines studied his court calendar and said he could not possibly hear the case sooner than Monday, July 6.

But Inman had more tricks up his sleeve. On June 30, he filed a request asking that Earl Klinck be tried separately from Stephenson and Gentry, and that Klinck be tried first. But on July 2, Hines ruled all three men would be tried together beginning July 6 as scheduled.

The morning of the trial date arrived, and the defense was still trying to employ its tactics to throw the prosecution off guard. After an entire morning of waiting for the defense attorneys to appear and begin their presentation, Hines finally threw up his hands and declared the court adjourned, saying that the case would not be heard until the start of the October session. Minutes after Hines said this, Inman strolled into the courtroom. Inman said he was prepared to file three motions, and requested that the judge reopen his court. Hines refused to call the court in session and, glaring at Inman from the bench, said that any further motions could be filed privately during the court's recess.

What followed was more of the same. On July 26, Inman filed another petition requesting another bail bond hearing. Hines refused.[12]

Knowing that Judge Hines was losing his patience, Inman played his last card. On August 10, the defense filed a request for a change of judge. The motion claimed that Hines was biased in his rulings and prejudiced against the defendants.

Hines apparently took the charges of bias to heart: "They rushed into court with an affidavit charging bias and prejudice. That is nothing but plain perjury! Attorneys at this bar know that I am not biased or prejudiced and know that I am able to give these men a fair trial. I have no reason to be biased for I do not know these men—never saw them before in my life. But now I am out of it. . . . This court is not interested further in this case. I am only sorry that the case cannot be taken out of this county."[13] After more than two months of grappling with the case, Hines sounded relieved to be rid of Stephenson and his high-priced lawyers. Who could blame him?

But now the search for a new judge had to begin.

A New Judge Arrives

August–October 1925

Judge Hines still had to find someone to take his place on the bench. The law called for Hines to choose the names of three judges who could possibly hear the case and place their names before the attorneys for both sides. The prosecution could strike one name from the list, the defense could strike another, and the remaining name would be the judge who would hear the case. Before any of this could happen, however, Hines had to find a list of judges who would be willing to put their names in for what promised to be a difficult case. He began to assemble a list of names on Monday afternoon, August 11, immediately after Stephenson's attorneys requested a change of judge. After pulling together a list of nine names, he began to call each of the judges on the telephone to see who would serve.[1]

Of course, all the judges had good excuses for turning down the case. Most pleaded with Hines that they already had too many cases on the dockets of their own courts. Some said they couldn't stand traveling across the state to hear a case in Noblesville. Others told Hines that they had "family reasons" for staying home. Of course, none cited the simple reason that the case was political dynamite that might spell the end of the political future for any judge who heard the case.

Hines quickly ran through the list of nine names with no acceptances. Then he went back to his legal directory and searched out several more names to call. This work continued into the early evening. At last, he got two judges to agree to have their names submitted—Judge C. W. Mount of Tipton County Circuit Court and Judge Herbert A. Rundell of Owen County Circuit Court. Now he had only to find a third.

Twilight was fading, and Judge Will Sparks was sitting down to dinner with his family at their home in Rushville, Indiana, when the telephone rang. The judge left the table, answered the call, and talked for several minutes. He eventually came back into the dining room, and his wife asked him who had called. Sparks did not give her a direct answer; he said only that it was a call from a judge. Della Sparks was not used to being put off this way. She pressed him for more—a judge, then which judge? He seemed reluctant to reply, then said, "a judge in Noblesville." Well then, she asked, what did this judge in Noblesville want? Sparks explained that the judge needed him to be one of a three-judge selection panel, for an upcoming trial. Now his wife was on the scent—a trial, which trial? "A murder trial," he answered. But which murder trial? Finally, he told her it was the Stephenson trial. Next she wanted to know what his answer had been. Sparks told her that he did not feel that he should be serving on a selection panel, since everyone knew that he had always been an outspoken opponent of the Ku Klux Klan. Besides, he figured he would be the first name struck from the list anyway, so what was the use of saying yes?

Now dinner could wait all night. Sparks's wife would hear nothing of this sort from her husband. She told him to get right back up from his chair, go back to the telephone, and let Hines know that Sparks would be willing to serve on a panel of judges, and would hear the case if he were chosen. "You have an obligation to serve, whether you think you ought to or not, Will Sparks!" she told him.[2] So he rang up the operator and waited for his connection with Judge Hines in Noblesville. Thus, Sparks reluctantly became the third of the judges whose names would be put before the attorneys. Even so, he did not believe for a moment that he would be chosen.

At age fifty-three, Sparks was not eager for the publicity that would be associated with the Stephenson murder trial.[3] He had already served seventeen years on the bench of the Rush County Circuit Court and was content with his position there. He was a Republican and a Mason, but the Klan held no attraction for him. He had heard all the anti-Catholic talk, and he knew that most of it was rooted in uneducated paranoia. Sparks was Methodist, but he and his family lived just up the street from the Catholic church in Rushville, and he knew many of its parishioners. None were burying guns in their basements for the day of the pope's revolution. Nor was there evidence of any of the other pathetic lies that the Klan was circulating.

Sparks had watched the Klan transform his town from a friendly, open community into one where neighbors no longer trusted neighbors. The Klan had managed to whip up fear and hatred where none had been before. Sparks's own secretary, a

Catholic woman, realized her religion might reflect badly on her boss in his last election. She had volunteered to quit her job to avoid causing him any embarrassment. Sparks would not hear of her quitting, saying that if he lost the election because of his secretary's religion, then the election probably wasn't worth winning in the first place. (In fact, the question never came up during the campaign, and Sparks was reelected without incident.)[4] This affair had confirmed many of Sparks's negative impressions of the Klan. Now he stood in a position where he might be called to judge one of the Klan's former top officials. The irony of that could not have escaped him.

The following morning, Hines brought his list of three names into the Noblesville courtroom and placed them before the attorneys from both sides. The judge explained how difficult it had been to come up with three names, and that of the three, one had been quite reluctant to serve and the other two had not been formally confirmed. Then the lawyers deliberated for a few minutes, deciding whom to cut from the list. The prosecution had the first chance, so Remy struck Judge Mount's name from the list. Inman conferred with the other defense attorneys, then rose and announced that they would strike Judge Rundell's name. So Judge Will Sparks became the replacement for Judge Hines. With noticeable relief, Hines said, "I believe the proper thing now would be to call Judge Sparks and see about a trial date."[5]

The Klan was not about to remain quiet through all this. Only days before, on August 8, members of the Indiana Klan had traveled to Washington, D.C., to participate in one of the Klan's most incredible gatherings—a march down Pennsylvania Avenue in the heart of the nation's capital. The sight of 125,000 klansmen parading through the city on that hot August day made front-page news in papers all over the country. The event had an eerie quality, with hundreds of men in white robes marching with the Capitol dome and the Washington Monument as backdrops. Imperial Wizard Hiram Evans boldly marched through the city in his hood and robes but without a mask covering his face. Indiana Grand Dragon Walter Bossert marched along with his fellow klansmen, wearing a conservative business suit and no robe at all—a statement that, even without his robes, a klansman was still a klansman.[6]

Evans caught a train bound for Indiana that same afternoon. He was scheduled to appear in Noblesville at a chautauqua, an outdoor series of lectures, plays, and concerts.[7] Sunday, August 9, was billed as "Klan day" at the chautauqua, and Evans led a parade down through Noblesville to the courthouse square. The day was hot but overcast with clouds that threatened rain. But that did not keep away the crowds who came to hear Evans.

It was crucial, of course, that Evans put as much distance between the Klan and Stephenson as he possibly could. It was up to Evans to keep reminding people that Stephenson had been drummed out of the organization months ago, even before the Oberholtzer murder. He could not allow the impression to linger that the Klan was somehow responsible for the young woman's death. Whatever Evans told the crowd in Noblesville, it was not kind to Stephenson.

Evans delivered his speech on the courthouse square, within earshot of Stephenson's second-floor jail cell. One account of what happened that day was told by Stephenson himself, who recalled the episode fourteen years later:

> On August 9, 1925, the streets and sidewalks of the city of Noblesville were filled with masked and robed figures. The street intersections were under the control of masked and robed men, and some of these were in plain view of the jail windows where I was confined.
>
> A few minutes before noon on "Klan Day" . . . a number of robed and masked figures assembled at the west side of the Hamilton county jail, immediately beneath the window opening upon my place of confinement, and in angry and profane words, these robed and masked men shouted threats at me, asserting they would kill me if I attempted to reveal klan interest in my conviction. This demonstration continued for several minutes and was discontinued only when [Sheriff] Charles W. Gooding . . . went among the robed and masked men and ordered them to leave the vicinity of the jail. For some time, the robed figures refused to leave, and arrogantly defied the sheriff, but they finally went away after repeatedly shouting threats. . . . Later in the afternoon of the same day, the robed and masked men returned and repeated the same threats. The sheriff again ordered them away, and they departed, but remained in the vicinity of the jail and court house until some time after dark. . . .
>
> Thereafter, on several nights each week, during the remainder of the month of August, through the month of September, and during the first two weeks of October, 1925, [local klan officials] held numerous secret meetings in Noblesville and Hamilton county for the purpose of stirring up public sentiment in the county against me, to aid in bringing about my conviction.[8]

Even if Stephenson exaggerated, at least part of what he said was true: public sentiment was most certainly stirred up against him. It was in this setting that Judge Sparks would have to find enough impartial men to form a jury and then conduct a trial.

In October, Judge Sparks began commuting more than sixty miles from his home in Rushville—driving his car to Noblesville each Sunday, staying in a hotel in Noblesville through the week, then returning home for a brief visit with his family on Sundays. At times during the fall of 1925, it must have seemed that the trips to and from Noblesville would last forever.

The task of selecting twelve jurors to serve in the Stephenson trial proved to be nearly impossible. Jury selection began on Monday, October 12, as the first of a constant stream of men from Hamilton County came through the courtroom. Most were farmers, with an occasional businessman, truck driver, salesman, or office worker. As always in Hamilton County, there were no women considered for jury duty because, as the papers laconically noted, there was a "lack of accommodations in the Hamilton County Courthouse juryroom." One by one, the men took the stand and submitted themselves to a barrage of questions by both the defense and the prosecution.[9]

There was no chance of finding anyone who, by now, had not already heard about the spectacular murder case, so the questions were limited to asking the prospective jurors if they "had an opinion" about the case. Most did. They were dismissed.

More questions: "What do you think about capital punishment?" "What do you think of the Ku Klux Klan?" "Are you married?" "Do you have any daughters?" More dismissals.

When the defense asked a fifty-six-year-old farmer from near Fishers Station if he had any opinions about the case, he replied, "It's a poor man that hasn't formed an opinion one way or another." The defense rejected him immediately.

The process dragged on for days as more prospective jurors were called and more were rejected. A few were excused by Judge Sparks for illness or business reasons. The reporters from the dailies sent their papers stories about each day's interviews—and rejections—of jurymen.

All but one of the first hundred men who had been called were rejected. The lone survivor of the first hundred was farmer

W. O. Inman (no relation to attorney Eph Inman). A call for a second hundred prospects went out, and more men came to face the lawyers' questions. Nearly all of this group were rejected as well. The number of acceptable candidates was still not enough to fill the jury, so a third call for another hundred men was made. It was without precedent in Hamilton County that three hundred venires, or calls for jurymen, would be made in order to seat a jury.

Throughout the process, Stephenson's friends and enemies were hovering around the courthouse in Noblesville. Both the defense and the prosecution were concerned about rumors that some state politicians had been talking to prospective jurymen about the case. The *New York World* ran a story about how the jurymen were being questioned about their biases. Inman was asking potential jurymen if they had talked with Will H. Adams, the former reporter of the Indiana Supreme Court and one of Madge's former employers. Adams, according to the story, was considered a bitter political enemy of Stephenson's, as was Newman T. Miller, the former state fire marshal. Miller had recently presented evidence to a Marion County grand jury that resulted in Stephenson's indictment for the arson fire that had burned his Irvington house. Both Adams and Miller were rumored to have been talking to potential jurors about Stephenson.[10]

Hamilton County assistant prosecutor Ralph K. Kane was helping the state's side of the case in the jury selection process. He also questioned potential jurymen about their contacts with state political figures—Henry Roberts, a statehouse custodian; Milo Hershey, a state policeman; and Robert Humes, superintendent of the state police—all political appointees of Governor Ed Jackson, who had been circulating around Noblesville while the Stephenson case was underway.[11]

And another lawyer—John Kiplinger, from Rushville, Indiana—was added to the defense side of the case. Kiplinger, a personal friend of Ed Jackson's, lived in the same town as Judge Sparks. It seemed obvious that Jackson was trying to exert what influence he could on behalf of Stephenson.[12]

By Wednesday, October 28, Judge Sparks's patience with the attorneys on both sides was beginning to wear thin as they continued to reject candidates who did not display any unreasonable bias.

That morning, Inman had rejected one potential juryman because he had read some of the testimony that had appeared in the June bail bond hearing. He also rejected one of the "veteran" jurymen who had survived longer on the acceptable list than most of the others.

Five more men were questioned, until they found Harley Huffman, a thirty-nine-year-old truck driver from Clarksville who passed the examination by both sides. Now there was only one position remaining to be filled. Three men were questioned, and the lawyers agreed on the last one, Clyde Clark, a forty-five-year-old farmer from near Westfield.

Under questioning by Inman, Clark said he would not be influenced by the fact that the case involved the death of a woman. Inman asked if the fact that the father of Justin Roberts, the Hamilton County prosecutor, had once served as Clark's attorney would in any way influence his thinking. Clark replied that it would not. The prosecution briefly questioned Clark, then handed the jury panel back to the defense. Inman and the other defense attorneys conferred for a few minutes, then returned the panel to the state. Finally, the jury was filled. Then Kane, the assistant prosecutor, rose and said, "Let the jury be sworn."[13]

The announcement that the jury had been accepted came as a shock to the reporters, some of whom were apparently preparing to leave the courthouse. "Acceptance of the jury came like a bolt from a clear sky," wrote Horace Coats of the *Indianapolis Star*. They scurried back into their places, and people who had been milling around in the hallway outside hurried back into the crowded courtroom.

The jury selection process had required the interviewing of 260 men. No one could remember a more lengthy jury selection in the history of the state.

Shortly after 3:30 P.M., Judge Sparks swore in the jury. Then he delivered a short lecture to the twelve who had been accepted: "I know there are men on this jury who are hardly in a position to serve. I know some of you would like to be relieved of the duty, but it just can't be done. I don't want to be here any more than you do. But it is a sense of duty. I have sickness at home and am in as bad condition as you are. But the courts have to go on. I am not asking you to do a thing that I am not doing myself."

The trial could now begin in earnest.

―――――――――――――――

In the midst of the jury selection process, the Stephenson trial had to share the headlines with another major event for the Hoosier state. On October 14, after more than a year of ill health, United States Senator Samuel M. Ralston finally died.

Stephenson, no doubt, read the news in his jail cell. If things had worked out differently, he would have been the one that Ed Jackson would have named to fill out the senator's term. Instead, that honor would now go to Stephenson's friend, attorney Arthur Robinson, who would go to Washington, D.C., to take his seat in the U.S. Senate while Stephenson sat in a jail cell in Noblesville awaiting his trial for murder.

The Opening Gambit

October 29–31, 1925

The first day of the trial, October 29, dawned cold and cloudy. A light snow covered the ground, and the pavement was icy as Sheriff Gooding led Stephenson, Klinck, and Gentry from their jail cells to the courthouse shortly before 9:00 A.M.

The twelve jurors were seated in the jury box looking somber and official, all wearing dark suits and ties. Judge Sparks entered from his chambers behind the bench, took his seat, and the court convened promptly at nine o'clock.

The judge invited the state to make its opening statement to the jury. Attorney and former judge Charles Cox stood to make the presentation for the prosecution. Cox was an accomplished orator—probably the most eloquent on the prosecution's side—who loved purple prose and dramatic words.[1]

"This is not an ordinary murder case," Cox told the jurors. "Usually murder is a deed of hate, of revenge, a deed committed with a gun, a knife, or a bludgeon. This was murder committed by a man, aided by his two satellites, a man who, the evidence will show, said, 'I am the law in Indiana.' This case is to determine whether we are to protect the sanctity of the honor and chastity of womanhood."

The state's main witness, Cox said, would be none other than "Madge Oberholtzer, clean of soul, but with her bruised, mangled, poisoned and ravished body, standing by her grave's edge, with the shadowy wings of the dark angel of death over her, will tell you, so far as possible in the circumstance, the story of her entrapment, of her being drugged, kidnapped, assaulted, beaten, lacerated with beastly fangs, and finally, as the culmination of indignities and brutalities unheard of in a civilized community before, how she was forced by the loss of all a good woman holds most dear, to take the deadly poison which contributed to her untimely death."

After briefly describing Madge Oberholtzer's abduction, Cox then launched into a profile of Stephenson. "The evidence will show that he had a double personality," said Cox. "That on one side of him was the sympathetic, cultured, attractive man of the world; that he was an impassioned orator; that something about him enabled him to attract and dominate better men and women.

"The evidence will show that there is another side of him and that side showed him a violator of the law; to be a drunkard and a persistent destroyer of women's chastity. A typical Dr. Jekyll and Mr. Hyde."

Ira Holmes leaped up from the defense's table, objecting to Cox's depiction of Stephenson as a dual personality. Judge Sparks overruled the objection and told Cox to proceed with an explanation of the prosecution's case, though it might not be possible to bring out in evidence all the assertions in the opening statement.[2]

Cox spoke an hour. "I said to you that Madge Oberholtzer would be the principal witness for the state and her story—assail her memory how they may—is of itself sufficient warrant to brand the black word 'Guilty' on the brazen foreheads of the defendants," he said. "But the state will give you more, far more, than her story. She will be supported, corroborated by credible witnesses, by unassailable facts and by inescapable inferences until there can rest in no man's mind a reasonable doubt of the guilt of these men."[3]

Stephenson sat calmly through all this, occasionally commenting to his attorneys in a whisper but displaying no emotion. Gentry and Klinck sat behind him at the defense table, both resting their cheeks on their hands, attentive but quiet.

After Cox finished, the prosecution called its first witness: Madge's mother, Matilda Oberholtzer. Dressed in black, she was visibly nervous, and her hands were quivering. Her voice shook as she answered the questions put to her by Will Remy. When he began to question her about Madge's departure from their home on March 15, Matilda's voice became firm and strong. But her voice cracked again as she told about how Madge looked upon her return.

Remy asked her to tell the court how Madge looked after she was brought back home. Matilda began to sob and uttered a low moan: "Oh . . . she was torn and bruised."

"Any wound upon her body of any sort?" Remy asked.

"Yes, her breasts had open wounds all over."

"Just describe the wounds to the jury as you saw them."

"On both sides they were bruised. On this side [she indicated one side] was a round bruise, a kind of jagged place all around on the side. On the right side of her face, both sides were bruised."

"Now Mrs. Oberholtzer, state whether the bruise—describe how the bruise appeared, as to whether there were any prints of any sorts in the bruise."

"Yes there was. It was a large round—rather round imprint all around."

"The bruise had an imprint around it?"

"Yes."

"And where else did you notice, if any place?"

"Bruises all the way down to her ankles and on her hips."[4]

The next witness for the prosecution was the elderly Eunice H. Schultz, who boarded at the Oberholtzers' house and who had seen Madge first when she was brought back from Stephenson's house. Schultz was a small woman with large eyes behind a sturdy pair of round, dark-rimmed glasses. She wore a large black hat with ribbons on it for a most funereal effect.

Remy questioned her about what happened when Madge was brought back home. "I was in the kitchen," she said. "I heard groaning and I went to the dining room and saw Madge being carried upstairs by a man, a large man. . . . I stayed downstairs till the man came down. . . . He said she was hurt in an automobile accident and I asked him if she was badly hurt. He said he thought no bones were broken. I asked him who he was. He said his name was Johnson and he was from Kokomo." She told how the man had then hurried downstairs, attempting to hide his face from her view as he neared the door.

"Did you get a good look at his face?" Remy asked.

"Yes, as he came down the steps."

"Do you see that man in the courtroom now?"

"Yes, sir," she replied. "Right there, dressed in dark clothes with dark hair." And she pointed to Earl Klinck.

She told how she then hurried upstairs to find Madge on the bed. "She was groaning with every breath. I saw her bruises. On the right cheek was a circular wound. It was dark in color. There was a bruise on her left chest of the same shape, only deeper. The wound on her breast was open." Remy asked if Madge said anything to her. "She just groaned, 'Oh,' and said, 'Dear Mother.' "

Under cross-examination, Inman asked Schultz when she had identified the mysterious man as Klinck. She said she recognized him in the criminal courtroom in Indianapolis. Inman asked her, wasn't it true that attorney Cox had pointed Klinck out to her during the June bail bond hearing and told her who he was? She denied it. Inman ended his questions and dismissed her.

Next, Remy called Dr. John Kingsbury to the witness stand. Kingsbury told how Schultz had called him to the Oberholtzer home, and he told how he found Madge lying on her bed: "Her dress lay open at the breast exposing bruised areas with two or three lacerations or cuts on the left chest. The right cheek was bruised. I made a superficial examination through her clothes to determine whether there were any broken bones—I had been informed she was in an auto accident. I made no further examination then."

Remy asked if Madge had said anything.

The doctor replied, "She said she did not expect, or want, to get well—that she wanted to die." Kingsbury told how she first refused to tell him what had happened to her, then when he asked her again, she began to tell her story. He then repeated for the jury Madge's account of her abduction.

Stephenson's defense attorneys argued hotly with the judge to have the entire story stricken from the record. Judge Sparks overruled the objections each time and instructed Kingsbury to continue with his testimony.

"From the appearance of the lacerations," Remy asked, "would you say they were such as might have been the result of bites by human teeth?"

"In my opinion, they were," said the doctor.

He described his treatment of Madge and told how he had eventually informed her that he did not think she would recover. "She said, 'All right, I'm ready to die.' " He added that the lack of early treatment was probably responsible for her failure to recover.

"In your opinion, what would have been the prospects for recovery if she had had medical aid four or five hours after she took the poison?" Remy asked. The defense attorneys again leaped to object, but the judge overruled them. Kingsbury said that her chances "would have been better." Remy asked if the delay in getting medical attention for Madge had lessened the chances of prolonging or saving her life. Again the defense objected and again was overruled. "Most certainly, in my opinion, it did," said Kingsbury.[5]

During cross-examination, Inman tried to discredit Kingsbury's testimony by pointing out discrepancies in what he had just told the jury compared to what he had said during the June bail bond hearing.

Inman hoped to build a defense by showing that Madge had not died of staphylococcal infection—the fault of the bite wounds which Stephenson had inflicted on her—but that her death was caused by the mercury bichloride, which was self-administered. This would make the difference, Inman believed, between a murder and a suicide. If he could prove her death was suicide, then Stephenson could not be held guilty of murder.

Inman also hoped to blunt the dying declaration by proving that Kingsbury believed his patient might recover. In order for a dying declaration to be admissible as evidence in a trial, the patient must be dying, must be aware that death is about to occur, and must have no hope of recovery. But Kingsbury held firmly to his claim that Madge died because of the poison.

George Oberholtzer was the prosecution's first witness after the court's lunch recess. Cox led the questioning. Madge's father answered in a soft, low voice, and several times the judge had to remind him to speak louder so that his answers could be heard.

"When did you first see your daughter after you went back to your home that afternoon?" Cox asked.

"I judge it was about an hour before I could control myself," said Oberholtzer, explaining that she was already in bed and that he talked with her only a few minutes.

"What did she say to you, if anything?"

"That she was going to die."[6]

George said it was a week before he could talk with Madge about what had happened to her. He told the court how he had tried to encourage her to get well. "She said, 'No use, Daddy. I am not going to get well.' "

Cox asked George to tell the court what Madge had told him about her abduction. Once again, the defense attorneys were on their feet objecting that this was an attempt to repeat the dying declaration, a statement that should be ruled inadmissible. Judge Sparks delivered a short speech to the courtroom, explaining that he felt the dying declaration ought to be considered admissible because it had so far met all the rules for the admissibility of such statements. Once again, Sparks overruled the defense, and George repeated the story—the fourth time in a single day that the story had been told.

George Oberholtzer said Madge had told him, " 'Daddy, that was the longest trip from Hammond. I was so sick, I thought I would die every minute. And I begged and begged them to get me a doctor. And when they refused that, I asked them to put me out to the side of the road that somebody might pick me up.' "

He had asked his daughter why hadn't she cried out for help? "She said that they stopped at the Washington Hotel, while Stephenson had Shorty, the chauffeur, call Claude Worley [the former sheriff of Franklin, Indiana] to look after protecting them on their trip. I says, why didn't you make an outcry? She says, 'Why, Daddy, I had no show. Stephenson was on one side and Gentry was on the other, both of them with a gun in my side, telling me if I made a noise, they would shoot me through.' She says, 'He told me his word was law.' "[7]

October 31, 1925

More snow fell that night, and the temperature barely crept above freezing. Next morning, everyone was talking about winter's early arrival in the state. Outside the courthouse, cars and trucks moved at a slow crawl, trying to avoid sliding on the icy streets.

Inside the courthouse, a full audience packed Judge Spark's courtroom to the doors, all eager for the start of the day's testimony. Spectators lined the walls and filled the aisles in the courtroom, almost down to the rail that separated the jury from the spectators.

Defense lawyer Floyd Christian entered a motion to stop the submission of evidence and discharge the jury. Christian claimed that Judge Sparks's remarks to the jury the day before had prejudiced the jurors. The motion would have had the effect of beginning the case again, starting with the selection of a new jury.

"If this was suicide, then it can't be homicide, for the two are diametrically opposed," said Christian. He insisted that Madge had taken the poison on her own. He pointed out that suicide had been considered a complete defense against homicide in several Indiana cases. But Judge Sparks overruled the motion.[8]

Attorney Asa Smith was the first witness Friday for what would be the roughest interrogation so far in the trial. Remy began the questioning for the prosecution by asking the usual introductory questions. But when he asked questions about Smith's war record, Inman objected that the information was not material to the case. "I have a son who was a soldier, too," Inman remarked.[9]

Under Remy's questioning, Smith told how he met the Oberholtzers and became their attorney, and how Madge's mother first notified him of her daughter's disappearance. He described the Monday night visit to Stephenson's house with Ermina Moore and Matilda Oberholtzer, and he told how he saw a car pull into the driveway and enter the garage. He told how he went out to the Oberholtzers' house the following morning after Madge's return. As he entered the room, Madge looked up at him and repeatedly moaned, "I'm done for." The defense successfully objected to Smith detailing any of their conversation.

Next, Remy questioned Smith about how he had prepared the dying declaration for Madge to sign. Smith acknowledged that he had written the declaration in his own office two days before Madge signed it. He said that he had written it based on his conversations with Madge and on notes that Madge's friend, Ermina Moore, had taken down at Madge's bedside. Smith said that he had reduced into writing "what she said to me in the words she used as I remembered them."[10]

Smith told how he had gone back over his notes with Moore and with his partner Griffith Dean, then had his secretary type a draft.

On Saturday morning, Smith said, he had word purported to come from Dr. Kingsbury. At this the defense objected but was overruled. Smith explained how he, Dean, Moore, and a notary public went over to the Oberholtzer house at about 5:00 P.M. Kingsbury was there and told them that he had just had a conversation with Madge. She had told the doctor that she felt she was about to die. Kingsbury had told her that there was a strong possibility that she would not recover.

Smith, Dean, and Moore had been admitted to Madge's room and, while Kingsbury listened, they went through the draft of the dying declaration with Madge line by line, making corrections and additions as she noted them. After that, the notary was brought into the room to witness as Madge signed the document.

Remy produced the dying declaration and offered it to the court as exhibit number one for the prosecution. Remy then turned Smith over to the defense for cross-examination.

Inman began with a series of questions about the preparation of the dying declaration, detail by detail.

"Now, you say that from day to day, from March 17 up to March 28, you went out to see and you talked with Madge Oberholtzer?" Inman asked.

"Yes, sir," replied Smith.

"At various times?"

"Yes, sir."

"And you say on various times she told you parts of the story?"

"Yes, sir."

"And you kept it in memory?"

"Yes, sir."

"And when the time came for you to piece it out and write it out and make notes of it and dictate it to the typewriters, to the stenographer, you dictated what you say, I believe, was the substance of what she told you from your memory, is that right?"

"No, I didn't say that."

"Do you recall saying to Mr. Remy a few minutes ago, 'I wrote the substance of what she said at my office?' "

"Yes."

" 'From my memory?' "

"I did."

"You said that?"

"Yes, sir."

"You wrote the first draft of this statement mentioned about three or four days before the 28th of March, did you?"

"No, sir."

"You didn't? Do you recall saying to Mr. Remy just a few minutes ago, this: 'I wrote it three or four days before the 28th of March'?"[11]

Inman used rapid-fire questions about Smith's every movement in preparing the declaration. If Inman could force Smith to trip over his own words in the witness box, making his testimony appear to be inconsistent, it might be possible to have the entire dying declaration declared inadmissible as evidence.[12]

The pummeling continued as the questions came faster and faster.

"So, on the 26th of March you dictated the statement first to the stenographer from the notes which you had prepared and from the notes which Miss Ermina Moore had prepared, is that right?" Inman asked.

"No sir, that is not right," Smith replied.

"What is it?"

"From the notes which Miss Ermina Moore had prepared and which I had prepared I wrote in longhand—in her presence and in the presence of Mr. Dean—the statement, and from what I had then written in longhand, I dictated to the stenographer."[13]

Smith managed to catch the tiny nuances that Inman was slipping into the questions. Smith knew that Inman's goal was to trip him, while his own goal was to stay upright.

"How many pages of the longhand were there as you first wrote it out with your hand?" Inman asked.

"I don't remember that," Smith replied.

"Was it written in pencil or ink?"

"Pencil."

"Pencil?"

"Yes."

"Was there anybody present when you wrote that out?"

"Now you are referring to the very first time?"

"Yes, the longhand copy?"

"Well, do you mean the copy of the statement I wrote on the 26th, or the notes I wrote before?"

"No, you said a while ago you first took the combination and wrote out the statement in longhand, now that is the only thing I am inquiring about."

"Oh, the question is, how many pages?"

"Yes?"

"Well, I don't remember."[14]

At one point, Inman took a hostile line with Smith, suggesting that he and Griffith Dean had gone to Stephenson's office to bribe him into a settlement. Smith had already admitted that he and Dean had tried to discuss payment of medical costs with Stephenson, but now Inman was attempting to make this sound like bribery.

"I will ask you if you did not go to the office of Mr. Stephenson in the Kresge Building and demand that he pay $100,000 to settle the matter?" said Inman.

"I did not," Smith replied.[15]

Inman then asked Smith the same question again, each time lowering the amount, from $50,000 to $25,000 to $10,000. Each time Smith denied it.

Then Inman asked Smith if it was true that he demanded $100,000 from Stephenson and that Stephenson had replied, "I have been blackmailed by experts, and amateurs can't get away with it." Smith also denied this.

Ralph Kane leapt up from the prosecution bench. "This is nothing but a piece of pettifogging!" he shouted. "I move that it be stricken from the record!" But Smith had already denied the statement, so the court let the question stand.[16]

Then Inman questioned Smith about who else was in Madge's bedroom when the dying declaration was read to Madge.

"You said awhile ago that you had a notary, who was that?" Inman asked.

"I don't know her name, but she was not present," Smith replied.

"Well, what part did she do?"

"After that statement was signed, the notary was called up and she acknowledged her signature to the affidavit which was prepared from a copy of that [the dying declaration], had been prepared."

"She [the notary] acknowledged her signature to the affidavit?"

"Yes, sir."

"Where is that affidavit?"

"I don't know."

"Do you know what became of it?"

"I turned it over to the state's attorney."

"When?"

"Oh when I turned that [dying declaration] over, I think it was."

"Did the notary public take the acknowledgment of the signature of Madge Oberholtzer to this statement?"

"No, sir."

"Why didn't you have her do that?"[17]

Remy objected to this question, and Judge Sparks sustained the objection.

Here was a tiny hole! Why didn't Smith—who had taken so many other elaborate precautions in preparing this declaration—have the notary's affidavit? And why couldn't he remember the woman's name? Wasn't it odd that a man who had kept such meticulous notes, locking copies away in safe-deposit boxes, had failed to get the name of the woman who notarized this all-important document?

"You don't know her name?" asked Inman.

"No, sir," Smith replied.

"Where did you get her?"

"She was friend of Miss Ermina Moore's."

"How much time elapsed between the signing of this document [the dying declaration] and the signing of the affidavit?"

"When she [Madge] signed that document, some one, I don't know whether I stepped to the door and called down stairs to the notary, and she came up and came in and she signed the—"

"Who had brought the notary?"

"I had."

"You had?"

"Yes, sir."

"Did you drive out and take her in your car?"

"I did."

Then Inman turned and asked, "Mr. Remy, will you be willing to let us see the affidavit?"

"I have not got it with me," Remy replied. "It is in Indianapolis."

"If you don't mind, will you bring it up?"

At this point, Judge Sparks interrupted, "The affidavit, I don't think, is proper testimony."[18]

Inman moved on to a line of questions about how Madge signed the dying declaration and whose pen she had used to sign it. Smith said she had used Griffith Dean's fountain pen.

"She wrote her name there without anybody holding her hand, I believe you said?" Inman asked.

"That is correct," said Smith.

"I notice just below her signature and down to the left, there are two words and two sets of figures as follows: 'Dated March 28, 1925' wrote?"

"Yes."

"Who wrote that?"

"I did."

"When did you write that?"

"As I remember now, I wrote that after I got back to the office. I am not sure. I told you in the bail bond hearing I was not sure, and I don't know, I don't remember."[19]

Inman had found another flaw in the declaration and was using it to make Smith squirm.

"I beg pardon," said Inman. "I am not inquiring about the bail hearing now; you think you wrote these words when you got back to the office?"

"I think that is it," Smith replied.

"Did you write those words with the same pen that Miss Oberholtzer used to sign her name?"

"I don't remember."

"Do you remember whether you used a fountain pen?"

"Yes."

"And whose pen was it?"

"I said I don't remember."

"You don't remember?"

"No, sir, I don't."[20]

Inman pulled out a transcript of Smith's testimony from the bail bond hearing in June and began to read from it. It was a section where Inman had asked Smith the same questions about how the date was written at the bottom of the declaration. In June, Smith had told the court that he had written the date on the document immediately after Madge signed it and while he was still at the Oberholtzers' house. Inman noted that Smith had just testified to having dated the document after he returned to his office. After dramatically pointing out this inconsistency to the jury, Inman turned to Smith.

"Now, Mr. Smith, are you sure, sir, that Madge Oberholtzer wrote that name?" Inman queried.

"Yes, sir, she did," answered Smith.

"I will ask you if this question was not asked you when you testified under oath on the bail hearing in this case, and if you didn't make this answer: 'Who dictated these words to the stenographer?' [Referring to the statement.] Answer: 'Mr. Dean and myself.'?"

Smith replied, "Yes, sir, I said that. It was not right."

Assistant prosecutor Ralph Kane sat up and said, "What was that?"

"I said I made that statement, it was not right," said Smith. "I mean he was present with me."[21]

With that, Inman said he had no further questions, and Smith stepped down from the witness stand. Inman had managed to point out some apparent lapses in Smith's otherwise thorough preparation of the case. The crucial question was whether any of this would cause the jury to doubt the prosecution's case against Stephenson.

The next witness for the prosecution was Ermina Moore. Her voice was quiet, and the people in the courtroom leaned forward to hear Madge's friend testify. Will Remy asked her to tell the jury how she and Madge came to be close friends.

Remy questioned her briefly about the preparation of the dying declaration. Moore's story matched Asa Smith's at every turn.

Inman took up the cross-examination more gently with Moore than he had done with Smith. Indiana juries, Inman knew, still did not look favorably on lawyers who browbeat young ladies on the witness stand.

Inman returned to the question of the date at the bottom of the declaration, asking Moore if she saw Smith actually write the date on the last page of the declaration. She replied that she had not.

Moore told how on March 15 she and Madge had gone out for a Sunday afternoon drive on March 15 on the road to Noblesville and back to Madge's home. Madge was going out that evening on a date with George Watson, a tall, well-built, blond car salesman whom Madge had introduced to Moore during the last session of the legislature. Moore also said that she had last seen Watson on the Fourth of July.

The next time Moore saw Madge was on Tuesday, when Madge had been brought back home beaten, bruised, and dying. From that day on, Moore went to see Madge every day, except for two, until Madge's death. With that, Inman excused Moore from the witness stand.[22]

The prosecution next called attorney Griffith Dean. Again, Remy asked questions to lend Dean's supporting testimony to Smith's account. After brief questioning, Remy turned Dean over to Inman for cross-examination.

Inman repeated the same line of hostile questioning he had used earlier on Smith.

"Did you call on Stephenson?" Inman asked.

"Yes," said Dean.

"Did you make a demand of him?"

"No."

"You didn't collect anything?"

"No."

"Did Smith go with you?"

"Yes."

"I'll ask you if you didn't demand $100,000, then $50,000, then $25,000, and then $10,000 and if Stephenson didn't tell you he had experts try to blackmail him and that amateurs couldn't get away with it?"

"No," said Dean. "I never did."[23]

With that, Inman dismissed Dean from the witness stand.

Remy attempted to have the dying declaration, exhibit number one, entered as evidence in the case. Immediately, Ira Holmes and the other defense lawyers began protesting loudly that the declaration should not be allowed as evidence.

The judge excused the jurors while the defense presented its reasons for banning the dying declaration. Floyd Christian outlined several reasons why the dying declaration should not be admitted as evidence. "If this was suicide, then it can't be homicide, for the two are diametrically opposed," he said. Christian claimed that Madge had taken the poison on her own and pointed out that in a number of Indiana cases, suicide had been ruled to be a complete defense against the charge of murder. Attorney Holmes then read the entire dying declaration, stopping at the end of each sentence that the defense wanted to have stricken from the record, and gave the defense counsel's reason for each objection. Attorneys Christian and John Kiplinger then offered a long list of citations from Indiana law books, which they claimed supported their point of view. The entire recital lasted an hour and forty-five minutes, which the newspapers declared was "a record in length of objections to a criminal court procedure."[24]

When the defense at last subsided, Judge Sparks addressed the counsel on both sides, saying that "there is no doubt but that the dying declaration should go in" as evidence in the case. He held, however, that parts of it might be deleted before it would be read to the jury and said that he would give a ruling the next day if he decided any parts should be stricken.

"Of course, the court can't rule on the matter now," Sparks explained. "I think some parts of the statement should go out. . . ."

Sparks said that, in deciding which parts of the dying declaration to strike, he "would not confine myself to the absolute rules of evidence as I would if the witness were right here." He said he had doubts about the admissibility of Madge's conversation with Shorty, the chauffeur, and said that "there are other things that should not go in."[25]

After this speech, Sparks announced that court would be held all day on Saturday and all day on the following Tuesday, election day.

Losing Ground

October 31–November 4, 1925

"STEPHENSON FORCES LOSE TILT" was the banner headline of the *Indianapolis Star* on Saturday morning, recounting Friday's battle of wits between the attorneys. "DYING DECLARATION OF GIRL WILL GO INTO EVIDENCE OF MURDER CASE UNDER RULING" was the paper's second headline.

Judge Sparks opened the morning session with his ruling on which parts of the dying declaration were admissible as evidence in the case. It was a victory for the prosecution. The judge left the statement almost completely intact. He struck only the sections that were declared legally incompetent—mostly sections that reported Madge's conversations with persons other than the defendants. But the context of the story remained intact. Following the judge's ruling, the dying declaration was admitted as evidence in the case, and Marion County prosecutor Will Remy read it to the jurors.[1]

As Horace Coats from the *Indianapolis Star* noticed, "Although the statement had been read in its entirety the previous afternoon by Mr. [Ira] Holmes, when the defense objections to the statement were outlined, a morbid interest in the contents of the declaration was confirmed by the large crowd waiting in the court room before court convened."[2]

The prosecution now began to run through a list of witnesses who would testify in support of the claims made by Madge in her dying declaration. The first was Ted Wilson, the night clerk from the Indiana Hotel in Hammond. Wilson, a pale young man in his early thirties, wore a dark suit and vest and combed his dark hair straight back over his head. He told the court how he had seen three people enter the hotel early in the morning on March 16. One of them signed the register as "Mr. and Mrs. W. B. Morgan, Franklin, Ind.," and the other signed as "Earl Gentry, Indianapolis." The couple was assigned to room 416, and Gentry was assigned to room 417.

"Are those men in the court room now?" Remy asked him.

"Yes," said Wilson. "If I could leave my seat I could pick them out." He walked over to where Stephenson and Gentry sat. He smacked his hand down hard on the table in front of Stephenson and said, "That's the man who registered as Mr. and Mrs. Morgan." Then he walked over to Gentry and quietly laid his hand on his shoulder.[3]

Inman cross-examined Wilson using the same tough grilling tactics he had used on Smith the day before. Focusing on the floor layout of the Indiana Hotel, Inman determined that no door connected the two rooms but that there were working telephones in both rooms. (This implied questions: Why hadn't Madge simply used one of the telephones to call for help while Stephenson slept? Why had she resorted to poison instead of the phone?)

The prosecution next called Lee Ayres, the day clerk of the hotel, who corroborated Wilson's testimony. A hotel maid, Lillian Reed, told how she was asked to bring up extra towels to the room. She told of cleaning up the rooms after the trio was gone, finding some gun bullets in a drawer, an empty whiskey bottle, a bottle of witch hazel, an empty milk bottle, and some oranges. She described the rooms as "torn up." Cross-examination by Inman was brief. Afterward, Judge Sparks declared a one-hour recess for lunch.[4]

In the afternoon session, James Hollins, a black man in his early thirties, was called to the stand. A bellhop at the Indiana Hotel, Hollins told how he had seen the trio as they walked into the lobby of the hotel. Then, as had Ayres and Wilson, Hollins pointed out Stephenson and Gentry at the defense bench.

Hollins had also delivered breakfast to room 416. Stephenson, he said, had answered the door and was in the midst of changing clothes. The woman, he said, was dressed and sitting on the right side of the bed.

"What, if anything, did you notice about the girl's appearance?" Remy asked.

"I noticed a red place on her cheek," said Hollins. He also said that the girl acted as if she had been drinking. Inman's cross-examination, again, was very brief.[5]

The fifth witness of the day was W. S. Porter, a conductor on the Pullman car that Stephenson's party had taken to Hammond. Porter identified Klinck as the man who had handed him the tickets for the trio on the train, then Porter identified Stephenson as one of the men who got off the train at Hammond.

Under cross-examination, Porter said he heard no disturbance aboard the train car that evening. Inman asked about the number and location of the buttons in each train compartment that can be used to summon the conductor. Porter confirmed that such buttons are in the sleeping compartments and the toilets of each drawing room. Again, Porter said he heard no outcry from any of his passengers.

The final witness of the day was Levi Thomas, a short black man in his forties with a receding hairline and a small moustache. Thomas was a porter on the Pullman car the night the trio went to Hammond. Inman asked Thomas if he had overheard any conversation between Stephenson and the woman who was with him.

"She said, 'Oh, dear, put the gun up, I am afraid of it,' " Thomas replied.[6]

"She said: 'Oh, dear'? Did she say anything else?" responded Inman.

Remy objected to the question, and Judge Sparks sustained the objection. The judge then added, "Here is the proposition: she said 'Oh, dear, put the gun up.' She might not have meant to address it to him; she might have addressed it with fear. That is not fair. Gentlemen, you can argue that before the jury; I don't know."

Christian rose to complain that it should be left to the jury to decide the meaning of the words.

"That is not for you gentlemen to assume; you may argue that before the jury," said the judge.[7]

Christian was preparing to make another objection to the judge's remarks when Sparks suddenly declared the court adjourned for the day.

Angered by this, the defense attorneys spoke to reporters immediately afterward, saying that they planned to file another motion to halt submission of evidence and dismiss the jury on Monday morning. Inman charged that the judge's remarks during Thomas's testimony, which were made in front of the jury, were prejudicial to the case and were grounds for declaring a mistrial.

Both sides declared the day's testimony a victory. The state's attorneys said they had established their case by positive identification of Stephenson and Gentry. The testimony of the hotel employees helped support the dying declaration. The defense attorneys also claimed victory, noting what they considered to be discrepancies that had been pointed out by the day's testimony. The case would continue Monday.[8]

On Sunday, the jurymen were escorted around Noblesville by bailiffs Fred Harger and Ingram Mallery. They went to Sunday services at the First Christian Church, then went back to the Houston Hotel for dinner. For exercise in the afternoon, they walked a mile west of the city along State Road 33 "and observed the wreck of the bridge over Cicero Creek, which collapsed a few days ago, one span falling into the stream."[9] In the evening, they attended another religious service. During the week, the local fraternal orders—the Elks, the Masons, and the Knights of Pythias—had agreed to give the jurors the use of their club rooms. Jurors who did not want to go to the clubs were taken to see movies. For the group of mostly farmers, this was truly living in style.

Stephenson passed the time in the jail, where Sheriff Charles Gooding and his wife gave him the run of the place. To show his appreciation for the kind treatment, Stephenson gave the sheriff a large sum of money, which Gooding supposedly used to pay off the mortgage on his house.[10] Stephenson was still living the good life—almost as if he were still living in the mansion in Irvington. Most of the time, he spent his evenings reading the reports of the trial in all the various newspapers.

He often had visitors. At one point, his former bodyguard, Court Asher, brought a briefcase full of money to Stephenson in the jail. The money—$17,000—had been collected by Stephenson's friends, Arthur Robinson and George Coffin, who each gave $5,000. They also collected $6,500 from Lawrence Cartwright, the Republican chairman for the Eighth Congressional District; and $500 from a Harry Hoffman in Muncie, Indiana.

But Stephenson was in a bad temper when Asher arrived with the cash. Stephenson was expecting more than $17,000, and he insinuated that Asher had stolen some of the money. Asher became angry and dumped out the briefcase. "I throwed it all over the jail," Asher recalled. "I throwed it in his face."[11]

November 2, 1925

The trial resumed Monday, November 2. The weather was still cool in the morning with frost and a morning fog surrounding the courthouse as the crowds began arriving. Newspaper coverage attracted more and more people to the trial each day. Spectators waited in the hall outside the court for their chance to go in and look at the former grand dragon and his men who were on trial. Several women's groups had become regulars at the trial—a church sewing group from Irvington, a group of Madge's sorority sisters, some female statehouse workers. Several of the women brought their lunches with them and stayed in their front-row seats to make sure they would not lose their places during the recess.

As promised at the close of Saturday's court session, the defense started the day with its second attempt to halt the trial, claiming that Judge Sparks's comments before the jury were prejudicial. But as he had done before, the judge overruled the motion, telling the defense attorneys that they could file a complaint after the trial.[12]

The first witness called for the prosecution was Jack Culbertson, the night desk clerk from the Hotel Washington in Indianapolis. Culbertson told the court that he had been on duty the night of March 15 and that he had received a call asking him to reserve a drawing room on a Pullman car on the Monon train to Hammond. He had made the reservations as requested, but he did not see who came to pick up the tickets at the hotel desk. Inman did not bother to cross-examine Culbertson.

The second witness was more significant—Madge's nurse, Beatrice Spratley. Remy's questions were similar to those he had asked her during the June bail bond hearing. Consulting the medical charts she had kept on the case, the British nurse gave a detailed account of Madge's exact physical condition.

After having Spratley describe the nature of the bruises and lacerations on Madge's body, Remy asked, "Did any of the lacerations you have described become infected?"

"The one on the left breast," she replied, but she could not say how long the infection had lasted. Some of the bruises were still visible at the time of Madge's death.[13]

In his cross-examination, Inman asked Spratley, wasn't it true that she had testified at the coroner's inquest that for two weeks during her treatment Madge's condition was "absolutely normal."

"If I did, I didn't mean that she was well," the nurse replied. "If she had been well, I would not have been there. I was working night and day. She was very sick. If I said 'normal' I must have been referring to her temperature."[14]

Consulting Spratley's chart, Inman asked if it was true that Madge had been given morphine injections twice on March 28 and several times on days thereafter? The nurse said this was true and that the dosage was a fourth of a grain of morphine in each injection. Who administered the morphine injection on the night of March 28? Kingsbury had given it, Spratley replied, explaining that she was sleeping at the time the injection was given. Inman was building his case—namely, that Madge had not been completely alert at the time the declaration was read to her and at the time she signed it.

After more than an hour on the stand, Spratley was finally dismissed, and the prosecution called Lt. Jesse McMurtry, a city detective with the Indianapolis Police Department. McMurtry testified about the arrest of Stephenson at the Hotel Washington, explaining how Stephenson tried to pass himself off to police as his own secretary, Fred Butler. McMurtry also told how Stephenson was carrying a .45-caliber automatic gun.

"He asked us why we had not called him by telephone and he would have come down to headquarters," McMurtry said. "He said we had nearly missed him, as he was getting ready to leave on a business trip for New York."[15] After McMurtry's testimony, the court adjourned for an hour and fifteen minutes for lunch.

In the afternoon, the state called Andrew Brown, a superintendent for Western Union's Indianapolis office. Brown had records of telegrams received at the office on March 16. Remy asked Brown to identify a telegram, which was then entered as evidence and read to the jury. The message read: "We are driving through to Chicago. Will take train back tonight. —Madge."[16]

The telegram was sent from Hammond, Indiana, at 8:51 A.M., March 16, 1925. The telegram had been read to Matilda Oberholtzer over the telephone, according to the marks on Brown's copy. Inman did not cross-examine Brown.

The last witness of the day was Dr. Virgil H. Moon, an instructor of pathology at the Indiana University School of Medicine. Moon had assisted with the autopsy and had done a microscopic examination of Madge's kidneys, liver, and lungs. Charles Cox handled the questioning for the state.[17]

Moon's testimony dealt what the newspapers called a "body blow" to the defense's arguments. The doctor testified that he had found that the damage done to the kidneys from the mercuric poisoning to have been almost healed.

Cox questioned Moon about his knowledge of mercuric poisoning.

"What is the fact, Doctor, as to whether there may be a recovery from bichloride of mercury poisoning when a quantity largely in excess of a fatal dose has been taken?"

"Very many such cases, where a quantity greatly in excess of the fatal dose has been taken have recovered," Moon replied.

"State whether bichloride of mercury poisoning is almost uniformly fatal."

"It isn't uniformly fatal, nor is it fatal in a high percentage of cases," Moon replied. He then listed a number of cases that occurred from 1879 to 1910 which showed that only 53 percent of mercuric poisoning cases were fatal. In cases occurring since 1910, the fatality rate had dropped to 25 percent, the doctor noted.

"You spoke of the post mortem examination disclosing an abscess in the lung," said attorney Cox. "Will you state the characteristic of that?"

"Microscopically, this abscess consisted of pus, as usually is found in abscesses; it [the abscess] also showed the presence of the germs which produced it, these were of the variety which we call staphylococci," replied Moon.

"Pus-forming germs?"

"Yes, sir."

Then Cox asked, "In this particular case of Madge Oberholtzer, did your post mortem examination disclose any injury to her body which might have been the cause of this infection?"

"I found only one area from which such an infection could probably have originated," said Moon.

"Tell what it was?"

"The lacerated and recently healed infection in the skin over one breast was the only one which I found from which such a pyemia [blood poisoning] as I have described could probably have resulted."

"Could such injuries as you discovered be infected by human teeth?"

"They could be, yes."

"I may have asked this before: Did any of these marks on the breast show evidence of an infection having been present?"

"One of them showed very unmistakably; the infected wound which had recently healed."

"Are wounds made by biting usually infected?"

"They are very apt to be infected."

Then Cox posed a long "hypothetical" question, reciting in the question everything that had happened to Madge Oberholtzer and recounting her physical condition as reported by the doctors. Cox ended this long question with a final query: "What, in your opinion, Doctor—she dying on the last of the twenty-ninth or the beginning of the thirtieth day—was the cause of her death?"

Moon replied, "In the hypothetical case, death resulted from a complication rather than from the direct effect of the mercuric chloride poisoning. . . . The nature of the complication is definitely indicated as that of a blood stream infection, with some pus-forming bacteria."

Question by question, Cox, with the help of Moon, was destroying the principal argument of the defense. According to Moon, Madge Oberholtzer did not die from mercuric poisoning. Her death was caused by blood poisoning—the result of Stephenson's savage attack on her during the night train ride to Hammond. The infection from the bites on her breasts had spread throughout her body so that it was not the mercury tablets that killed her but the staph infection.

If Moon was correct, then Madge's death was not suicide. It was murder. The tablets had not killed her. The murder weapons were Stephenson's own teeth.

November 3, 1925

Tuesday morning, November 3, was election day in Indiana. In Indianapolis, John Duvall was forecast as the easy winner of the state's largest mayoral election. As Duvall told his supporters two days before the election, "My policies have received the editorial endorsement of both of the leading newspapers of Indianapolis. My policies have received the indorsement [sic] of thousands of men and women who want to see Indianapolis continue to grow and prosper, to the end that Indianapolis may become known throughout the length and breadth of the land as 'the best governed city in all America.' "[18]

But for the time being, Indianapolis was chiefly known throughout the land for the murder trial of former Grand Dragon D. C. Stephenson. Papers from all over the country were running coverage of the trial in Noblesville. It was front-page news in New York, Cleveland, and Detroit. The newspapers in Chicago sent their own reporters down to cover the trial. Stories about the trial were even appearing in some European newspapers.[19]

The front page of the *Indianapolis Star* on election day ran a banner: "STATE GAINS IN MURDER TRIAL: STEPHENSON JURY TOLD WOUND WAS FACTOR IN DEATH." The prediction of clear skies, warm weather, and a heavy voter turnout was a secondary story on the front page. Ironically, the front page also carried a report of how slates had again been distributed by an election eve clothespin campaign—typical Klan work, even though Stephenson was behind bars. The story also noted that several groups had gone out on the streets and engaged in fistfights and brawls to stop the distributors of the clothespin slates. People were tiring of the Klan.

The election did nothing to reduce the size of the courtroom crowd—now over four hundred people. Several women came to the trial with infants in their arms. At one point during testimony, a baby began crying so loudly that the trial stopped. "I like children," said Judge Sparks, "but we can't hear." The disappointed mother was asked to leave.[20]

Testimony on Tuesday began with the continuation of Dr. Moon's cross-examination by Inman, who was trying desperately to get the jury's attention turned back to the bichloride of mercury tablets. Inman arranged a small demonstration to show how quickly mercury bichloride dissolves in water. Inman enlisted Moon's help to hold the glass of water. Then, like a stage magician, Inman dropped a tablet into the water and asked Moon to describe the speed with which the tablet dissolved.

"Now, Doctor, would you mind to shake that a little, without taking a chance?" Inman commanded. Moon tried to shake the glass, but it was too full of water and it splashed over. Inman poured a little of the water out into a cuspidor. "Now?"

"Yes, the foam is coming up and is giving the water a little greenish tinge," said Moon.

"So when you drop the tablet into the glass of water, and in the course of a few seconds, if you shake the glass, it colors the water green?"

"As soon as it gets into solution the water becomes green."

"So it takes, in fact, Doctor, but a very few seconds for it to dissolve in water?"

"The jury shall be the judge of the amount of time taken," Moon replied.

"Now, Doctor, assuming that you drop such a bichloride of mercury tablet into a glass of water, or say drop three of them into a glass of water at one time, and in the course of a few seconds shake it up, stir it up after the tablets have fallen to pieces and begin to scatter through the water and over the bottom of the glass; if you would drink that glass of water containing that dissolving tablet, these dissolving tablets, into your stomach, thereby throwing the whole mass into quick contact with the heat of the stomach, it would cause the dissolution to be accelerated, would it?"

"Probably would," said Moon.

Then Inman sprang back with: "What was the immediate cause of the death of Madge Oberholtzer?"

But Moon held his ground: "In my opinion, the immediate cause of death was an infection carried through the blood stream, localizing in the lung and in the kidney, particularly in the kidney. That was the immediate cause. There were other and contributing causes."[21]

"After she had lived twenty-five days from the time she took the poison, to-wit, until April 11, say, it is your view that she should have recovered if complications had not set in, is that right?" Inman asked.

"That is my opinion, sir," Moon replied.

A long discussion followed of how long it usually takes victims of mercuric poisoning to die. Moon testified that he had done considerable research into the effects of mercuric poisoning and that he had never found a case where the victim died after surviving twenty-five days. Therefore, he reasoned, Madge's death must have been caused by something other than mercuric poison—namely, the staph infections from the bite wounds.

Dr. J. A. MacDonald took the stand as the next medical witness for the prosecution and as one of the doctors who had been called by Dr. Kingsbury as a consultant for Madge's treatment.

MacDonald told the court he had been called to the Oberholtzer home twice—on April 6 and April 10. He testified that he had found one or two abrasions on Madge's chest, but by that time, the abrasions had nearly healed. On his second visit, Madge's condition was worse.

"How would the delay of twenty-four to twenty-six hours in giving medical aid affect the subject's chances of recovery?" Cox asked. If the defense mounted a successful argument against Dr. Moon's claim that death was caused by an infection from the bites, then the state would also argue that Stephenson's failure to find medical treatment for Madge contributed to her death.

The defense lawyers strongly objected to the question, pointing out that the defendants had given Madge a bottle of milk as an antidote and that the milk constituted "medical aid." The judge overruled the objection.

MacDonald said the delay in receiving medical aid would have affected her condition "adversely."[22]

Cox asked how the mercury bichloride would have affected Madge's mental state. The doctor replied that, given such a small dosage, it would have had no effect on the woman's mental condition or faculties.

On cross-examination, Inman began to ask questions about how large a dose of mercury bichloride would be needed to produce a fatal dosage.

"If a lady should take six tablets of bichloride of mercury containing seven and one-half grains in each tablet, a total of some forty-four grains, would the chances of absorption be greater than if five or six or ten grains had been taken?" Inman asked.

"Yes," said MacDonald.

Inman questioned MacDonald about possible antidotes for mercuric poisoning. The doctor named egg whites, flour or starch mixed with water, and emetics of mustard.

"If there were no food in the stomach, the power of attack of the poison on the walls of the stomach would be greater, would it not?" asked Inman. MacDonald agreed that it would.

Then, following another set of questions, MacDonald said that he felt the mercuric poisoning had caused the nephritis, which was partly responsible for Madge's death.[23]

In the afternoon, the prosecution called Dr. R. N. Harger, a professor of chemistry at the Indiana University School of Medicine who had assisted in Madge's autopsy. He told the court that he had found mercury in her liver and kidneys after the organs had been submitted to him for chemical analysis. He said he found one grain of the poison per pound of tissue in the liver and one-twentieth of a grain of mercury per pound of tissue in each of the kidneys.[24]

November 4, 1925

Wednesday morning, November 4, the papers trumpeted the victory of John L. Duvall, as predicted, by a margin of more than eight thousand votes over his Democratic opponent. The *Indianapolis Star* also noted that all five candidates running on the Klan-backed "United Protestant" school board slate had won; the Indianapolis public schools would now be in the hands of Klan-supported politicians.[25]

At his trial, Stephenson paid more attention to the election results in the newspapers than he did to the testimony. *Indianapolis Times* reporter John L. Niblack noted, "Stephenson read results of the Indianapolis election most of the morning, studying the returns carefully. Although his double chin is prominent after seven months in jail on a good diet, the ex–Klan leader these days is wearing as haggard a look as it is possible for a well-fed fat man to register."[26]

Dr. Harger continued his testimony on the witness stand in the morning session, the conclusion of cross-examination by Inman.

Cox, who handled all questioning of medical witnesses for the state, next called Dr. John H. Warvel, a pathologist from Methodist Hospital who had analyzed Madge's blood samples, and Dr. H. O. Mertz, an Indianapolis physician who had been called by Dr. Kingsbury as a consultant in treating Madge.

In turn, Cox asked both doctors the same hypothetical question he had posed to Drs. Moon and Harger the day before, each time ending with the question, what would have been the cause of death?

"In my opinion," said Warvel, "death was caused by some secondary infection superimposed on nephritis." Thus, he agreed with Moon's testimony that the infection from the bite wounds, not the poison, was the primary cause of death.[27]

Mertz's reply was that he thought the girl's death was caused by "an acute infection superimposed upon acute nephritis"—almost identical to the opinions of Drs. Warvel and Moon.

Warvel also concurred with Moon's finding of a congested area in the lungs filled with pus cells, again pointing to an infection, not the poison.

At 4:15 P.M., Remy stood and announced that the state was resting its case. After some procedural matters, the court adjourned for the day. In the morning, the defense would begin to present its case.

The Defense Takes Over

November 5–6, 1925

The defense attorneys began on a strangely subdued note at the opening of court on Thursday. Some reporters were expecting a dramatic opening statement from Eph Inman or Ira Holmes. Some thought that Stephenson himself might take the stand in his own defense.

Instead, the defense began with a motion asking that the jury be immediately instructed to return a verdict for the defense on the theory that the prosecution had not presented a sufficient case to establish guilt. This was a standard defense move and one which Judge Sparks immediately overruled.

The defense attorneys withdrew to a corner of the courtroom along with Stephenson, Klinck, and Gentry. They conferred in hushed tones for about fifteen minutes, apparently discussing their next move. At the end of the conference, Judge Sparks instructed the bailiffs to seat the jury.

Inman rose from his seat and, without further explanation, announced, "Your Honor, the defense waives an opening statement." This was a total surprise.[1]

After Cox's dramatic opening for the state with all its colorful talk of Madge's testimony from the grave and winged angels, most of the audience had been eagerly anticipating Inman's comeback speech that was sure to follow. But Stephenson's attorneys were mysteriously silent. Why?

Stories came out later that claimed Stephenson had tied his lawyers' hands before the trial began. He was afraid to let his attorneys defend him too aggressively. Fifteen years later, Stephenson claimed that his life had been threatened. He said that Robert F. McNay, a central Indiana grand titan from the Evans-Bossert Klan, had visited him in the Noblesville jail before the trial had even begun. "McNay came to the jail for the purpose of telling me what the klan would do to me if I revealed klan interest in my conviction," Stephenson said. "He said Dr. Evans had arranged for conviction, and that I could do nothing to acquit myself of the charge. McNay said klansmen would kill me if I attempted to testify on my own behalf, or permitted any witness to testify who revealed the klan conspiracy against me."[2]

There were other intimidations for his attorneys to worry about. On Monday of that same week, the newspapers had carried a story that quoted a member of the prosecution team. The reporter had asked a lawyer—probably Remy—how long the state would take to present its case. "In all, we are going to examine perhaps twenty or twenty-two witnesses. But we may use a hundred or more in rebuttal in the event the defense makes any attempt to attack the character of Miss Oberholtzer."[3] A hundred witnesses! Could the prosecutor be serious? Inman and Holmes knew that their clients were not spotless citizens; stories about Stephenson's wild parties and his ways with women were well known to the attorneys. This intimidating promise may have encouraged the defense lawyers to start the case less dramatically than they might have done otherwise.

The first witness for the defense was Dr. Orvill Smiley, an Indianapolis doctor and surgeon, who was offered as an expert witness. Smiley claimed to have treated, as Inman established in his opening questions, about thirty cases of mercuric poisoning during his medical career—three in the last six months.

"Bichloride of mercury is known to your profession as one of the most deadly poisons, is it not?" asked Inman.

"It is," said Smiley.

"What is regarded as a fatal dose?"

"The lowest minimum dose to be fatal is said to be about three grains, and it ranges up from that, depending on conditions."

"Suppose six tablets were dropped into a glass of water, and drunk by a person—would the absorption take place more readily because the tablets had been dissolved?"

"It would," said the doctor, who then went on to explain that the force would be greater if the poison were taken when there was no food in the stomach. Bichloride, he said, always affects the kidneys rapidly, usually within thirty minutes.

"If a large quantity of bichloride of mercury were taken into the stomach and later vomiting occurred and the substance vomited would fall on the naked skin, such as on the chest and abdomen, would it have the effect of inflaming and corroding the skin?" Inman asked.

"If allowed to remain on the skin for thirty minutes or an hour, it would," said Smiley. Without saying it in so many words, Inman was trying to use the doctor to suggest to the jury that those weren't really bite marks that everyone had seen on Madge's chest but merely splotches where the poison had touched her bare skin!

Then Inman used one of Cox's questioning techniques by stating a long "hypothetical" question, reciting all the facts of the case and ending with a question about what, in the doctor's opinion, was the cause of death. "Bichloride of mercury" was the answer.[4]

Cox cross-examined Smiley for the state. He began by asking the doctor if he knew the three defendants.

"I have seen Mr. Stephenson a few times," Smiley answered.

"Have you practiced in his house?"

"Yes. I have seen the gentleman out there a time or two," the doctor replied. He said he could not remember the name of the man he treated at Stephenson's house, but said that he had been there three or four times to see a patient who had the flu.

This was new! Inman had not brought out that Smiley knew Stephenson personally.

Then Cox began to question the doctor about how many cases of mercury poisoning he had treated. The doctor claimed he had treated thirty such cases. "Some, I think were very profound, and some were mild; most of them died," said the doctor.

"And how many of the thirty of your patients got well?" Cox asked.

"Most were vaginal cases, nearly all cases will get well if you get them early, before absorption takes place." (The "vaginal cases" refers to the fact that mercury bichloride, which was supposed to be used as a disinfectant, was sometimes used by women in a stronger dilution to abort pregnancies.)

Ralph Kane protested that the witness had not answered the question. Judge Sparks ordered the question repeated: how many of the thirty patients got well?

"I can't say definitely, but those that took it by the mouth, less than ten percent of them got well," Smiley said.

"How many of them took it by the mouth?" Cox asked.

"I don't remember."

"You have no recollection of that? Have you made any record of those cases?"

"Some of them I have a record of, and some of them I do not have."

"And you have no recollection—"

"Those were al—"

"—of how many bichloride poisoning cases you had where they took the poison through the mouth?" Cox asked.

"At least twenty."

"At least twenty?"

"Yes."

"And what percent of them got well?"

"Not more than ten percent of them."

"Not more than ten percent?"

"Two or three."

"Two or three of them got well?"

Cox had established several things for the jury with his questioning. The state had already presented evidence which showed that the odds of surviving mercuric poisoning were good with medical treatment. Yet Smiley admitted that he had lost 90 percent of his patients! Furthermore, Cox had shown that the doctor kept poor records of his patients. Did this man sound like an expert medical witness, let alone a competent physician?

Cox asked him, "Are you absolutely sure bichloride of mercury caused her death?"

"Reasonably sure."

"But you said a while ago that you were absolutely sure," Cox reminded him. "Are you still absolutely sure?"

"Yes."

"Where did you read that any of those cases was when the stomach was full, where did you?" Cox asked.

"Well, for instance, I read Blair, an English toxicologist, he is the—I read Solomon, I read Bosider and Wood."

"And did you read that in Witthouse?"

"Woods, Clark, Landers, another English toxicologist, Milt, etc., etc."

"You have read those within the past two or three weeks?"

"Not all of them."

"Most of them?"

"Yes."

Then Smiley claimed that one of his reference books, Blair's Toxicology, described a mercuric poisoning case where the victim had survived forty-one days before dying.

"Well, you were familiar with Witthouse's book?" Cox asked.

"No, I don't know anything about it," said Smiley.

"Oh, I thought you did."

"No, I didn't make that statement, I don't know any-thing—"

"You don't know anything about Witthouse's book at all?"

"No."

"Do you know whether Witthouse is a recognized authority on toxicology?"

"I don't know anything about it."

"And don't you know, Doctor, that that book reports five hundred sixty-five cases running from 1879 to 1910 which were treated in hospitals, well-authenticated cases, don't you know that?"

"I don't know whether Witthouse is a law book or some other kind of book, I don't know anything about it."

"And you say you don't know he reports five hundred sixty-five cases—?"

"That is what I said, three times," Smiley retorted.

"—And that three hundred and two of them only were fatal?" said Cox. Then pausing, he said, "You spoke of your familiarity with Blair?"

"Yes."

"How many cases of mercuric poisoning does Blair report, Doctor?"

"I believe thirty-six, I believe in the article I just referred to, in the chapter I referred to."

"Just thirty-six?" Cox seemed incredulous. "Have you any knowledge at all, Doctor, as to whether the percentage of fatalities as stated by Blair was ninety percent, more or less?"

"He says sixty-one percent, specific—no, one percent of what he—" Smiley was stumbling.

"How was that?" Cox asked.

"This paragraph merely dealt—that I have in mind, merely dealt with the time of death after taking the bichloride."

"And you are testifying here as an expert?" Cox almost laughed as he asked the last question. Smiley had crumbled on the stand.

"Theoretically—" said Smiley.

"And after losing ninety percent of your mercurial poisoning cases, you consider yourself an expert?" The audience in the courtroom laughed loudly at Cox's comment. Judge Sparks rapped his gavel and called for order.

"Circumstances—" Smiley started to say, but Cox cut him off.

"No further questions."

"Circumstances," the doctor continued lamely, "alter cases."[5]

Cox, the former Indiana Supreme Court justice, had proven that Inman was not the only lawyer in the courtroom who knew how to slice an expert witness to shreds on the witness stand. That Inman, Holmes, and the rest of Stephenson's attorneys abandoned an opening statement and chose to start with Smiley suggests that they were in complete disarray.

The second witness for the defense was Dr. Paul F. Robinson, the Marion County coroner who had presided over Madge Oberholtzer's autopsy. Inman began with the usual questions to identify Robinson and explain his qualifications to the jury. Then Inman asked, "Have you had occasion to come in contact with mercurial poisoning resulting in death?"

"A great many cases, running into the hundreds," Robinson replied.

"In the case of Madge Oberholtzer, did you designate some officer to conduct a post-mortem examination of the body?"

"Yes. Dr. Virgil H. Moon."

"Did you see the body of Madge Oberholtzer?" Inman asked, and Robinson replied that he had.

"Did you notice any bruises or wounds on her body?"

"None that attracted my attention," Robinson replied.

"Did you notice any abrasions on the breast?"

"No, I did not."

Was Robinson lying on the witness stand? Dr. Moon had noticed the bruises and marks and vividly described them to the court.

"You held the inquest in the case of the death of Madge Oberholtzer?" Inman asked.

Robinson said that he had, then Inman handed him a transcript of the coroner's inquest, which ended with the coroner's verdict on the cause of death: mercurial poisoning. Inman asked Robinson to verify the document. Robinson carefully read the last page, glanced over the first few pages, and said, "That is it."

"When you render a verdict as to the cause of death," Inman asked Robinson, "do you file it with the clerk of the court?" Robinson said that he did and that he had filed the verdict that Inman now held. Inman then tried to offer the coroner's verdict as evidence. Cox rose to protest, saying that the coroner's verdict was incompetent to prove any fact about the cause of Madge Oberholtzer's death. Judge Sparks also sustained this objection.

Inman then launched into another long hypothetical question, restating all the facts of the case as he had done with Smiley. This time, it took him forty-five minutes to go through the recitation. In the middle of this, Judge Sparks ordered a brief recess. Afterward, Inman returned, spoke for another fifteen minutes, then ended his "question" by saying, "Doctor, assuming the facts and conditions to have existed as I have described them, what, in your judgement, caused the death of Madge Oberholtzer?"

"I'd say death was due to mercurial poisoning, from taking bichloride of mercury," Robinson replied. With that, Inman concluded his direct examination.[6]

The last witness of the day was a Dr. J. D. Moschelle, an Indianapolis doctor who testified under Inman's questioning that he had served a year as an intern in the Indianapolis city dispensary. During his internship, Moschelle said he had treated several kinds of poison cases, including three where the poison was taken through the mouth. In one case a mixture of mercury and carbolic acid was spilled on a patient's skin; the poison was absorbed into the patient's body, and the patient died.

Then Inman repeated his long hypothetical question—this time in only thirty-five minutes—and the doctor replied that he believed Madge's death resulted from "nephritis caused by drinking bichloride of mercury."

Inman then asked if he felt that medical aid given to her after more than six hours would have helped her. Moschelle replied that he thought medical aid at that point would have done no good.

"Is there any certainty that medical aid would have even prolonged the patient's life?" Inman asked.

"There is no certainty, but I think the aid given her undoubtedly did prolong her life," the doctor replied. Moschelle was then turned over to Cox for cross-examination.[7]

"Dr. Moschelle, the character of the questions which the state will ask you may depend somewhat on your answer to the question I shall now ask you," said Cox. "Do you wish your testimony here to be regarded as that of an expert witness on bichloride of mercury poisoning or merely as that of a physician and surgeon engaged in the general practice?"

"I expect that to be merely as a physician and surgeon engaged in the general practice," Moschelle replied.

"You have no special claims to expert knowledge as a toxicologist, Doctor, as I understand it?"

"Not as a toxicologist, no."

"And while you know, of course, something about pathology, you make no claims to being an expert pathologist?"

"I do not."

Cox then proceeded with several simple, general questions about medicine, asking Moschelle to describe the differences between an abrasion and an incised wound. Eventually, Cox came back to the question of whether medical aid would have helped someone in Madge's condition: "And, Doctor, if they could have prolonged her life by giving her help—"

"They could have prolonged her life and they did prolong her life," Moschelle replied.

"And if that medical attention that she received after she got home had been given her twenty-four hours before, her life might have been still further prolonged, might it not, Doctor?"

"It may have," Moschelle conceded.

"And, Doctor, if the staphylococci infection was introduced into the patient's system by a bite of the man in the berth with her, and that staphylococci infection had caused the high temperature, the pus in the blood which the fighting soldiers of the blood were called into service to overcome, and which caused the abscess in the lower lobe of the lung, that might have been an instrument in shortening her life, might it not?"

"It might have, yes, sir."[8]

Cox had just managed to get the defense's own witness to admit two of the state's main contentions: that Madge's life could have been prolonged had Stephenson gotten her medical treatment sooner than he did, and that the staph infection from the bite wounds may have shortened her life.

With that piece of disappointing testimony, the first day of the defense's case came to a close—a bitter day for Stephenson's lawyers.

November 6, 1925

In spite of the previous day's losses, the defense attorneys resumed their case on Friday morning with yet another doctor's testimony. This time they called an Indianapolis physician, Dr. John W. Williams, who had spent nine months as an intern at the local Methodist Hospital. Williams tried to uphold the defense's position that Madge's death was caused by mercuric poisoning.

Inman recited the same hypothetical question he had put to the previous medical witnesses. Then he asked, "Assuming these things as I have related them to be true, what, in your opinion, caused the death of Madge Oberholtzer?"

"Bichloride of mercury," said Williams. Inman continued to question him from several different angles about bichloride of mercury, each time returning to the doctor's assertion that it was the poison—and therefore, not Stephenson—that must have caused her death.[9]

Cox cross-examined Williams. "Did you ever treat D. C. Stephenson for delirium tremens while you were at the Methodist Hospital?" Cox asked, unexpectedly changing course by alluding to Stephenson's problems with alcohol.

Before Williams could answer, the defense attorneys were on their feet raising objections to the question. Cox shouted back at them, and an argument erupted. Judge Sparks banged his gavel several times.

"Hereafter, if you have any remarks to make," the judge said, "address them to the court. Not that I want to be talked to, but if you can't talk to each other pleasantly, talk through me." He ended by approving the defense's objections to the question about delirium tremens.

Following the session with Williams, the defense called deputy sheriff James Carter of Marion County to the stand. His testimony was a change of pace for the defense—a first attempt to establish an alibi for Earl Klinck. Carter told the court that he knew Klinck as a fellow deputy sheriff. So far, Klinck had only two connections to the Oberholtzer case: he had given the train tickets to the Pullman porter at Union Station the night Madge was abducted and he had driven her back home on the morning of March 17. He had not taken the train ride to Hammond.

Carter said that he had seen Klinck at the county garage in the rear of the Marion County jail at about 9:30 A.M. on March 17, the same morning Klinck was supposed to have taken Madge home. Carter said they talked about Klinck's plans to "go on a fishing trip." He did not see Klinck again until about 11:00 or 11:30 A.M. the next day back at the jail.

Remy began cross-examining Carter with a series of specific questions about several dates, apparently trying to test Carter's memory on the witness stand. "On the 12th of March, did you and Klinck make an arrest?" he asked. For the first time on the stand, Carter opened a small notebook to check the date before answering, and Remy pounced: "Yet in your previous testimony concerning Klinck you have used only your memory? . . . Isn't it true that all these events have been recalled to your mind very particularly?" Carter answered yes to both questions.[10]

"And yet it took you three days to get Stephenson after the indictment was returned, didn't it?" Remy asked. The question was an attempt to link Carter to Stephenson in the jurors' minds. Carter replied that the indictment had not reached the sheriff's office for some time after it was issued by the court.

Remy's cross-examination was interrupted by a lunch recess, but Carter was returned to the witness stand immediately afterward and Remy continued his work.

"What did you do in the matter of arresting Stephenson?" Remy asked. The defense attorneys objected to this, but they were overruled by Judge Sparks. Carter answered that he first went to the Consolidated Building (where the trio was finally arrested after Sheriff Hawkins's two-day "search"). Remy asked a series of questions that suggested there had been a prearrangement made between the sheriff's department and the defendants about how the arrest should be carried out. Carter denied this vigorously.

Then suddenly Remy switched back to questions about other specific arrests, dates, and times. This tactic caught Carter off guard, and he began to make mistakes. Remy's unspoken question was, if Carter couldn't remember other cases, why was his memory of his "going fishing" conversation with Klinck so clear? Having brought a glimmer of doubt to the testimony, Remy summarily dismissed Carter.

Cox then called Dr. Smiley back to the witness stand to continue cross-examination of the defense's first expert witness. Cox began by asking Smiley if he had talked to anyone about his testimony in the case; Smiley denied this.[11]

"Don't you know Dr. John W. Williams?" Cox asked, referring to the first witness of the day. Smiley said he did not. "You mean to say you don't know him—never heard of him before?" Again Smiley denied it.

Then Cox asked him several questions about Blythe's *Works on Toxicology*, the book which Smiley had incorrectly identified as "Blair's" the day before. "Where did you get this book?" Cox asked.

Smiley's confidence suddenly fell: "Another doctor loaned it to me."

"Who was the other doctor?"

"I don't know who it belongs to."

"How long have you practiced medicine?" Cox asked.

"I was graduated in 1908," the doctor answered.

"Did you ever attend a veterinary school?"

"No, sir. I taught pharmaceutics and toxicology last year in Indiana Veterinary College . . ."

"You have some veterinary remedies?"

"No, I am not altogether a 'hoss' doctor."

"Did you ever have any connection with the Standard Veterinary Remedy Company?" Cox asked. Smiley admitted that he had. Then the prosecution presented an exhibit of a newspaper advertisement for the company's veterinary products. "I will ask you if that is one of your advertisements?" continued Cox.

Smiley admitted that the ad was one for the veterinary company, but he claimed that his only connection was a financial one and that he had nothing more to do with the company. The damage was done.

Cox continued to attack Smiley's "expert" status. "Again, let me ask you, Doctor, you spoke, if I remember correctly, of another authority on toxicology called 'Milt'? . . . When did you read that?"

"I have seen it every day for the last two years," Smiley replied.

"How large a book is it?"

"It is a book of about five hundred pages, I think."

"Is it standard?"

"Yes, sir, it is."

"And is it a human or domestic animal toxicology?"

"It is all the same," the doctor replied. "Does not matter whether it refers to human or animals. All experiments are done on animals. This happens to be a veterinary book."

By clever questioning, Cox had managed to make the defense's "expert" witness look like a quack by suggesting the taint of "veterinary work" in a courtroom filled with medical experts.

But Cox wasn't through yet. Now he was zeroing in on Stephenson, through Smiley, Stephenson's own witness.

"You told us yesterday, as I recall, that you never had treated the defendant Stephenson in his home in Irvington?" Cox asked.

"That is what I said, yes, sir," Smiley replied.

"But you said you had prescribed for him?"

"Yes, sir."

"Where?"

"At two or three of the hotels. And then one time—I have forgotten the address—it was on Meridian Street someplace . . ."

"Never at any hospital?"

"I saw him once at one hospital."

"Which hospital?"

"The Methodist Hospital."

Cox knew there would be a chorus of objections to his next question, so he asked it quickly: "How many different times did you treat him for delirium tremens or the effect of it?"

Stephenson's attorneys were on their feet in a moment, objecting. Judge Sparks sustained the objection, but Cox had again managed to get "delirium tremens," a condition associated with alcoholism, into the jurors' ears a second time in the same day. Now he backed up and went into the question again.

"What is the fact as to whether you ever did treat him for delirium tremens or alcoholism?"

Smiley hesitated, then said, "I can't say that I ever treated him for delirium tremens."

"Did you ever treat him or prescribe for him for alcoholism?"

In his weakest denial yet, Smiley replied, "Not alcoholism alone, no."

"For alcoholism in part?" Half an admission might be better than none at all.

"Yes, one time he was a little nervous and had been losing a lot of sleep, and he might have had a little alcohol, I don't know. . . . I didn't see him take any. . . ."

"You say 'not alone,' Doctor—what else?"

"Loss of sleep and overwork and exertion, et cetera— nervousness."[12]

After Smiley's second appearance on the witness stand, the defense returned to the work of presenting an alibi for Klinck. The next witness for the defense was Marion County deputy sheriff Frank Kempf, who was the turnkey in the county jail, responsible for receiving and discharging all prisoners.

Kempf testified that he had turned four prisoners over to Klinck at 6:30 A.M. on March 17—the same morning Klinck was supposed to have taken Madge Oberholtzer back to her house. Kempf said that Klinck had put the four in a sheriff's car and taken them to the Indiana State Farm in Putnamville. After returning from this trip, Kempf said that Klinck ate lunch at the jail, then left again. This time, he was assigned to go with a sheriff's matron and transport a female prisoner to the Indiana Women's Prison in Indianapolis. Returning in the afternoon, Klinck then went out to patrol for speeders and liquor law violators. Kempf produced the receipts for the prisoner transport assignments, and the defense entered these as evidence.

"When did you first see these [prisoner transportation] receipts?" Remy asked.

"On March 17," Kempf replied.

Remy asked why was it that, out of all the prisoner transportation receipts he handled at the jail, Kempf was able to remember this particular assignment so well? Kempf said it was because he got the receipts on March 17, St. Patrick's Day. The prisoners had been "kiddin' Klinck about the St. Patrick's Day parade" that day.[13]

Two more deputies followed Kempf on the witness stand. William Anderson and Leonard Koffel both supported Kempf's testimony. They had seen Klinck at the jail just before he left to transport the four prisoners and later, before he left for the women's prison.

Remy cross-examined both men briefly. He asked Koffel about the "search" for Stephenson that the sheriff's department made on April 20. Koffel told how they had looked for the three defendants at the Hotel Washington and the Seminole Hotel but couldn't find them. Remy asked if they had thought to look for the defendants at Stephenson's house in Irvington; Koffel admitted they had not.[14]

After the two deputies, a woman named Cora Householder was called to the witness stand. She was a mystery witness for the defense; no one knew why this small, plump housewife had been called to the trial.[15]

Householder took the stand and Holmes began the questioning. She told the court she lived at 5850 Beechwood Avenue, an Irvington address just a few blocks from the Oberholtzer home. Holmes asked if she was still living with her husband, and she replied that they were separated. Holmes asked if she knew Madge Oberholtzer, and Householder told the court that she had known Madge for several years.

"I will ask you to state to the jury whether you saw Madge Oberholtzer at any time at the police station building where your husband was employed?"

"Once," Householder replied, just as Remy stood up to object.

"The objection will be sustained," said Judge Sparks. "I don't understand how that would be competent."

"Well, it is preliminary, Your Honor," said Holmes. "And we think it is competent."

"If it goes to show character, it certainly would not be competent. You can't prove it by specific acts. I don't know—" the judge paused. "You can make your offer to prove. I am in the dark. . . . I don't know what it is."

Holmes turned back to Householder. "After you moved to Irvington . . . tell the jury whether your husband, at any time, lived at the Oberholtzer home," he asked.

"He did," she replied.

"And tell the jury what he did, if anything, with reference to keeping his automobile at the Oberholtzer home?"

"What has that got to do with this case?" Ralph Kane complained to the judge, who sustained the objection.

"How long did your husband live in the Oberholtzer home?" Holmes asked, trying a slightly different approach.

"We object to the question," said Kane, "as not being material or competent or tending to sustain any issues in this case." Again Judge Sparks sustained.

Holmes could see this was not going well for the defense. "State to the jury whether at any time you saw Madge Oberholtzer with your husband?" Again Kane objected, and again the judge sustained the objection. Holmes then made an offer to prove to the court—out of hearing of the jury—that the testimony he was attempting to get from the witness had a direct bearing on the case. The jurors were escorted out of the courtroom, and attorneys for both sides approached the bench. The judge held his gavel in midair, ready to put an end to the debate if it became too heated.

The jury left the room, but the reporters stayed and overheard everything that was said by the attorneys in their brief conference with the judge. As the *Indianapolis News* summarized it, "The defense offered to show that Mrs. Householder saw Madge Oberholtzer at police headquarters, where the husband of the witness worked, and talked with Miss Oberholtzer regarding her relations with Mr. Householder."[16]

Judge Sparks, however, could not be persuaded that character testimony of this sort could have anything to do with the murder trial before him.

Defense attorney Floyd Christian pleaded one last time with Judge Sparks. "If Your Honor please, we would like to present this question outside of the presence of the jury, briefly and not take very much time."

Cora Householder intended to testify that her estranged husband, Charles, had been having an affair with Madge shortly before her death. The defense hoped her testimony would prove that Madge was a woman of low character and not the sweet young martyr the prosecution had described at the beginning of the trial.

The state's attorneys had long suspected that Stephenson's attorneys might eventually use this tactic. For that reason, they had already gathered witnesses of their own with tales to tell about Stephenson's bizarre sexual encounters with other women. If the trial was to become a mudslinging contest, neither side intended to let the other walk away clean.

But Judge Sparks would allow no mudslinging in his court. He refused to permit any testimony of "inadmissible character" and cited several court cases to defend his position. If the defense attorneys hoped to build a case on Madge's indiscretions—what the judge called "specific acts"—they would have to find another judge who would allow it. With that, the jury was brought back into the courtroom, and the judge excused Cora Householder from the witness stand.

Outside the courtroom, a reporter for the *Indianapolis Times* caught up with Householder as she was leaving. Although her testimony was not given in court, she told it to the *Times* for the rest of the city to read about.[17] She told how she and Charles had been married for twenty years and how they had separated on Christmas Day, 1924. She said that her husband, a former city fireman who now worked for the police department, had known Madge for the past eighteen years. Following the Householders' separation, she said her husband had moved into the Oberholtzer home, where he was living as one of the Oberholtzers' boarders at the time Madge died. Cora Householder's last words to the reporter sounded a bit relieved; she said she had not wanted to be a witness in the trial because she sympathized with the Oberholtzer family.

The Cora Householder episode shows how Madge's martyrdom had raised her to a level where her personal conduct was simply above questioning. In the press and in the courtroom, she had been portrayed as "Madge Oberholtzer, clean of soul"— Cox's words from his opening statement. Nasty stories were somehow irrelevant, and the judge would not tolerate them in court— even if there was a possibility that those stories were true.

The second point worth noting is that, for the most part, the press seemed to agree with the judge. Only the *Times*—always regarded as the most sensational of the three local dailies— presented a detailed account of Cora Householder's story. The other papers followed the judge's sense of discretion and turned their eyes away. Although both the *Indianapolis Star* and the *Indianapolis News* mentioned her brief appearance, neither paper pursued the story beyond the courtroom.

What if the story had been pursued? What if Judge Sparks had permitted Householder's testimony? Would things have worked out any differently at the trial? Perhaps. Already highly charged, the trial might have become more vicious. The most important difference might have been in the public's perception that Madge was something less than a pure innocent and that she somehow had a greater responsibility for her own death than the prosecution was willing to admit. The public of 1925 was drawn to the story of the innocent young martyr. Would the public be equally drawn to the story of a lustful young opportunist whose romance with a political power broker backfired and led to her death?

Chapter Thirty

"The Old Man's" Friends

November 6–9, 1925

The sunlight was fading quickly by midafternoon on Friday when the defense called Dr. Vallery Ailstock, a dentist from Columbus, Indiana, to the witness stand.

Ira Holmes quickly established that Ailstock had been a Klan organizer in Bartholomew County during Stephenson's reign and that the dentist had known Stephenson for about three years. When questioned, Ailstock said that he had met Madge Oberholtzer one time when Stephenson brought her with him on a visit to Columbus, Indiana, in January 1925.

"Well, I was standing on the corner of Fifth and Washington streets, talking with Dr. Clawson, a friend of mine," said Ailstock. "And it happened that I lived in an apartment at that corner, and there was a large automobile drove by to the curb and somebody said, 'Well, hello, Doc!' We looked up. It was Mr. Stephenson. We stepped over to the curbing and down in the street by the side of the car where he had parked and shook hands with him, passed the time of day, and he says, 'Well, boys?' Then he introduced us to Miss Oberholtzer."[1]

The dentist started to recount the conversation, but he was interrupted by an objection from attorney Ralph Kane. Ailstock's testimony might contradict Madge's deathbed statements about having only gone out with Stephenson on four occasions; she had mentioned a couple of dinner parties but no long drives in his car.

The judge decided to overrule Kane's objections and allow Ailstock to continue with his story.

"Well, Mr. Stephenson turned the conversation then. . . . Well, I talked to Mr. Stephenson regarding the trip that he had made to Columbus once before, and I invited him down to go fishing and he said that he would come, and I walked around to the other side of the car to talk to Mr. Stephenson personally, and talked, I think, probably five minutes. And I heard Mr. Clawson say, 'Well, maybe Ailstock has some, I don't. I don't use it.' And on hearing my name, I says, 'What is that?' And Clawson said, 'Well, there was something said about alcohol and liquor and I told her that I didn't use it, being a chiropractor, but you, being a dentist, would probably have some.' And I says, 'No, I don't use it, my position does not allow it and I don't use alcohol in my practice. I don't even have an alcohol permit.' And Mr. Stephenson said, 'Well, that is enough of that, now.' He says, 'You are not feeling any too well this evening, anyway.' And that was the turn of the conversation. Something was said then in regard to—between Mr. Stephenson and I—about the purchase of the Indiana Dental College; I told him I had been approached by . . .'"

Holmes asked, "Did Miss Oberholtzer engage in that conversation?"

"She did. . . . She said that was strange, that I ought to have it, it would make good gin," said Ailstock.

"What are you referring to that you 'ought to have'?" Holmes asked.

"Alcohol," said Ailstock.

Holmes asked, "Did you see her any more after that?"

"I saw her once after that in Stephenson's office," replied Ailstock. "It was shortly after or just before that night. I don't know which. I was up there on the dental college matter. . . ."

"Where was Miss Oberholtzer?"

"She was sitting in the reception room."[2]

This was a different view of Madge Oberholtzer, indeed! Trying to get an illegal drink from a small-town doctor while in the company of Stephenson. Though not as potentially damaging as Cora Householder's testimony, it was another attempt by the defense to remove some of the glow from Madge's halo.

At 5:00 P.M., Judge Sparks interrupted the cross-examination and adjourned the court until the next day.

November 7, 1925

Rain was slapping against the courtroom windows when the trial convened at 9:00 A.M. Saturday morning. Outside a strong wind was blowing. The crowds again filled the courtroom, though there would only be a half day of testimony, with the court scheduled to adjourn at noon.

Ailstock was called back to the witness stand for cross-examination by Kane, who went carefully back over Ailstock's account of his talk with Stephenson and Madge Oberholtzer in Columbus.

Then Kane began to toughen up his questions. He began to probe Ailstock on his involvement with the Klan and his work as a field man for Stephenson. He started asking questions about Ailstock's personal life. Kane ended with a question that strongly implied that Ailstock was involved in an affair with a woman, which Ailstock strongly denied.[3]

The women in the courtroom audience, who disapproved of all witnesses for the defense, enjoyed Kane's rough treatment of Ailstock. At the questions about Ailstock's alleged affair, the audience burst into applause for Kane's questioning.

Judge Sparks rapped his gavel and delivered a short speech to the audience: "This is a solemn place, and it is a solemn business we are transacting. There should be no such demonstrations as that. No feeling or noise should be manifested in any way."[4]

Kane proceeded, asking more questions about Ailstock's Klan connections. At one point, the defense attorneys leapt up and objected to a question. Kane threw back an angry comment, and both sides erupted into an argument. Again, the judge was banging his gavel. This time, the lecture was delivered to the attorneys for both sides. "This kind of thing is beneath you," he scolded them. "You are all better lawyers than that."

The next witness was Mrs. E. B. Schultze, a housewife from Laurel, Indiana, who told an unusual story about a visit D. C. Stephenson had paid to her home in November 1924 accompanied by his guest, Madge Oberholtzer. (This is a full two months earlier than Madge's claim that she had met Stephenson at Governor Ed Jackson's inaugural ball in January 1925!)

"It was in the evening," said Schultze. "Mr. Stephenson and Miss Oberholtzer drove up to the house. He introduced the woman as Miss Oberholtzer. They came in and sat down. After we sat there a while, Mr. Stephenson said he wanted to wash his hands. He and Mr. Schultze left the room. When they came back, Mr. Stephenson played with the baby—got down on the floor and crept around. They stayed about an hour."[5]

"Did you hear Mr. Stephenson address her that night?" Holmes asked.

"Yes, he called her 'Madge.' "

Schultze said that, at one point, Madge remarked to Stephenson, "Hadn't we better be going, dear?" And on another occasion, Madge said, "The baby wants you to play with him again, Stevie."

Under cross-examination by Remy, Schultze explained that she knew Stephenson from his visits to talk with her husband, a local Klan organizer, about Klan business. She could not give a definite date of Stephenson's visit, but she said that it occurred sometime between the election day and Thanksgiving Day of the previous year.

Another witness for the defense, James H. Lambert, contradicted Madge Oberholtzer's deathbed statement. Lambert was the assistant manager of the Hotel Washington. He testified that he saw Madge the night of March 15 when he stepped outside the hotel to buy a newspaper. She had been sitting alone in the front seat of a car in front of the hotel.

"What occurred while she was in the auto in front of the hotel?" Remy asked.

"She nodded at me and said, 'Good evening.' I made a slight bow in return and also said, 'Good evening,' " replied Lambert.[6]

Remy grilled Lambert heavily during the cross-examination, but Lambert stuck tightly to his story. He was emphatic that he could easily identify Madge because he had seen her on several occasions when she called at the hotel to see Stephenson. Lambert was the last witness on the stand before the court adjourned at noon for the weekend.

The jurors spent a quiet Sunday attending church services in the morning. As always, they were accompanied by a bailiff. In the afternoon, they were escorted on a long walk outside Noblesville, then came back to their hotel and pitched horseshoes for an hour. One reporter noticed that all the jurors had fresh haircuts; he learned that one of them had requested permission to visit the barber, and the others decided to go along. Only one juror had been allowed to go home since the start of the trial. Cash Applegate received permission to look after his livestock, but he had been accompanied by a bailiff to his farm and back again.

November 9, 1925

Monday morning saw a parade of witnesses called to the stand for Stephenson's defense. A reporter for the *Indianapolis Star*, Herbert Eiler, was first on the stand. Eiler was one of several reporters who had attended the autopsy of Madge Oberholtzer. His testimony was brief: he had seen a small blue spot on the woman's body, just below the collarbone on the left side. The bruise was about the size of a penny. He had noticed no other bruises or marks on her body. Eiler was excused without cross-examination.[7]

Eiler was followed by Eugene J. "Jep" Cadou, a reporter for the *Indianapolis Times*, who had also attended the autopsy. Cadou told the court that he had seen no bruises at all on Madge's body, adding that he had not noticed the small bruise Eiler had mentioned. Cadou was briefly cross-examined and dismissed.

Two more reporters—Blythe Q. Hendricks, formerly of the *Indianapolis Times*, and C. Walter McCarthy, of the *Indianapolis News*—were called, but neither man was present.[8]

Ralph E. Rigdon, a Republican campaign solicitor for the Republican State Committee and a political friend of Stephenson's, was next on the stand. A stout, cocky political boss, Rigdon oozed smugly on the stand.

Rigdon said he had seen Madge Oberholtzer in Stephenson's offices in the Kresge Building several times during the 1925 session of the legislature and also with Stephenson in a room on the twelfth floor of the Hotel Washington.

"When you saw her in Stephenson's private office, what was she doing?" asked Holmes.[9]

"She was just sitting there," Rigdon replied, smiling.

He went on to tell how, on a visit to see Stephenson about personal business, he had been invited up to Stephenson's suite in the Hotel Washington. Madge was already in the room. The three of them talked for awhile, then they all drank a glass of gin. Stephenson and Madge remained in the room together after Rigdon left.

Kane took over the cross-examination, snapping like a bulldog at Rigdon's heels.

"Now when you got to the room, you say Madge Oberholtzer and Stephenson were in the room?" Kane asked.

"When I got there—yes," said Rigdon.

"And when you got in—"

"I had talked my business with Stephenson on the outside."

"But had no conversation about your business?"

"Not this particular business I went to see."

"After you went in you remember you took a drink of gin?"

"Yes, he offered—"

"Stephenson had a supply of gin?"

"There was a bottle of gin," said Rigdon. "I don't know whose it was."

"Well was he handling it?" asked Kane.

"No, I don't know as he was."

"Who suggested that you have that drink of gin?"

"I don't recall who made the suggestion."

"Did you see any bottle of gin before it was offered?"

"No, I don't recall . . ."

"Did you suggest you were a little dry and would like to have a drink?"

"No, I don't think I suggested that."

"But you are very positive that you took a glass of gin, and that Madge took a drink?"

"Yes, sir."

"Now don't you know there is not a word of truth in that—that you didn't see the girl at that hotel at all—" Kane began to lose his composure.

"To which the defendants object," said Ira Holmes.

"—And that the statement that the gin was drunk at that time is a plain lie, don't you know that!?" Kane ended with a shout.

"No, sir," said Rigdon.

"We object to that, Your Honor," Holmes chimed in again.

Before the judge could speak, Kane continued his harangue, "—And that you came here for the express purpose of committing perjury and that every thing you said on that subject is a lie!?"

Now Rigdon was angry, too. "You are not big enough to tell me that on the street!" he shouted.

Judge Sparks began to rap his gavel loudly on the bench. "Answer that question and you can do what you please on the street," the judge instructed Rigdon.

"Yes, I'll meet you on the street!" Kane shouted at the witness. The spectators were loving the show, and some began to clap.

The judge again directed Rigdon to answer the question, and the defense lawyers were up on their feet shouting a chorus of objections. "No!" Rigdon shouted back at the judge.

Inman started to make a formal objection to the bench about Kane's conduct, but Judge Sparks pounded the gavel firmly on the bench, and at that, the noise stopped abruptly. "Now, gentlemen," said the judge. "I want you to understand right now this is not a justice of the peace court. This is a place where you are going to have to conduct yourselves properly, and if you can't conduct yourselves properly on both sides, I am going to get somebody that will."

"It's not fair to me!" Rigdon started to protest.

"You keep still!" Judge Sparks glared at him. "I am not asking advice from you! I will run this by myself!"

This quieted Rigdon, who meekly replied, "I beg your pardon."

"I am addressing the audience," said the judge. "Go ahead and answer the questions, and keep still afterwards."

The fireworks subsided only briefly. Kane's next question to Rigdon was barbed, "You're a close friend of Stephenson, aren't you? And you came up here to help him out, in fact, you would go to any limit to help him out?"

Rigdon rose in his seat and leaned over the witness stand to look Kane squarely in the face. "No!" he shouted.

"You know you're telling a lie!" Kane shouted back.

Rigdon lunged as if he would leap on Kane, then stopped and shouted, "You're afraid to say that on the street!" Again the judge had to quiet attorneys on both sides, but this time he sustained the defense's objections. The rest of Rigdon's cross-examination was handled without any more outbursts. Kane had already accomplished what he wanted—namely, to make the defense's witness appear angry and threatening on the stand.[10]

The next witness was Maxine Elliott, an eighteen-year-old stenographer who had once worked in Stephenson's offices. Elliott told the court how she had seen Madge Oberholtzer in Stephenson's offices several times. Madge's visits were usually between 4:30 and 5:00 P.M. Elliott said she often saw Stephenson and Madge leave the office together and that sometimes Madge stayed in the office with him after the rest of the office staff went home. Elliott added that Madge's visits began in January 1925, and she was a frequent visitor during January and February.[11]

Raymond Donahew, a real estate agent who shared offices with Stephenson in the Kresge Building, testified that he had worked as an organizer for the Ku Klux Klan under Stephenson in Ohio, Minnesota, and Washington. Ira Holmes asked Donahew if he had ever seen Madge Oberholtzer around Stephenson's office. Donahew replied that she was "there frequently during the legislature."

"Was she there at any particular time?" Holmes asked.

"At all times of the day," Donahew answered.[12]

Lee Ayres, the Indiana Hotel clerk whose testimony had been heard the previous week, was returned briefly to the witness stand. Floyd Christian asked if it were true that in a conversation with a Samuel Rosen of Gary, Indiana, that Ayres had said he would "get plenty of money from the state for testifying that Stephenson and party were at the Indiana Hotel." Ayres denied this. Christian asked if it were true that Ayres had said that the "politicians of Indianapolis were putting up all the money to convict Stephenson." Ayres also denied having said this. Finally, Christian asked if Ayres had said that Stephenson and his lieutenants were not at the hotel but just a short man and a tall, heavyset man, who had been with Madge Oberholtzer. Again, Ayres denied having said this. At this, he was dismissed from the stand.[13]

The final witness of the day was Foster Strader, a former Stephenson office manager and courier.

"When did you first see Madge Oberholtzer?" Holmes asked.

"About a week after the general election of 1924," Strader replied.

"How often did you see her?"

"On an average of every three or four days at Stephenson's office, twice in the dining room of the Hotel Washington about the middle of the session of the 1925 legislature."

Strader testified that he was first introduced to Madge in Stephenson's private office but that on other occasions he had seen her in Stephenson's waiting room. After a brief cross-examination by Kane, Strader was dismissed. The court adjourned at 4:30 P.M., just as the sun was setting.[14]

If nothing else, the defense had managed to raise several questions about how honest Madge Oberholtzer had been in giving her deathbed statement. Several people had testified that they had seen her not on the few occasions that she had claimed but often and as a regular companion of Stephenson's. Had Stephenson and Gentry really held guns on her, as she claimed, or was she calmly waiting for them in the car, as the hotel manager claimed? The defense would continue to pursue these questions while attempting to raise others that might swing the jury away from a conviction.

November 10, 1925

On Tuesday morning, Ralph Kane, who had nearly come to blows with defense witness Ralph Rigdon the day before, appeared in court with large black bruise over his right eye. Remy and the other members of the prosecution team kidded him about the bruise. Kane claimed that he had bumped his head on a cellar door at his home the previous evening.[15]

The first witness of the morning was Dr. J. E. Sturdevant of Noblesville. Floyd Christian handled the direct examination for the defense, asking Sturdevant the usual hypothetical question about what might have caused the death of Madge Oberholtzer. Sturdevant replied that he did not feel that the wound on Madge's left breast would have had anything to do with the abscess that was found in her lung during the autopsy.[16]

As with the other medical witnesses in the case, Charles Cox cross-examined Sturdevant. Dr. Virgil Moon, who had appeared as a witness for the prosecution the previous week, was now seated at the table with the state's lawyers. Throughout the cross-examination, Moon prompted Cox on questions to ask the defense's witnesses.

At one point, Cox asked Sturdevant how much he was being paid for his appearance in court.

"I usually receive $100 a day," he replied.

"Answer the question," Cox said sharply.

"I told you—$100 a day."

"Isn't it true that you are receiving $1,000 a day?"

"No."[17]

Cox, using a technique more like Ralph Kane's, began arguing with the witness on the stand, and Judge Sparks had to halt the questioning to silence the two men.

Christian then asked the court to call Dr. L. R. Lingeman of Noblesville to the stand. The doctor testified that he had observed cases of mercury bichloride poisoning, influenza, nephritis, and other diseases.

Under questioning, Lingeman raised an important point. He said that it was possible for staphylococci bacteria to be introduced to the bladder during catheterization. (Kingsbury had ordered catheterization for Madge during her final illness.)[18]

"Is transfusion of blood sometimes the source of infection?" Christian asked.

"It may be," Lingeman replied. (Madge had also received several transfusions.)

He told the court how, in treating influenza cases, it was not uncommon to find complications such as abscesses in the lungs. (The court had earlier learned about the cases of flu that had gone through the Oberholtzer household a few weeks before Madge's disappearance.) He also stated that in cases of nephritis, the lungs may become waterlogged.

"What length of time have you known for a patient suffering from bichloride of mercury poisoning to live?" Christian asked.

"I have read of a case in which the patient, after taking bichloride of mercury, died on the forty-fifth day," replied Lingeman.

Christian then restated the long hypothetical question, which he ended by asking Lingeman if he felt the alleged wound on the woman's breast would have any connection with her death. The doctor replied that he felt it would not.

Cox began cross-examining Lingeman by asking more questions about the case Lingeman had cited in which the poisoning victim survived forty-five days. Lingeman said that the man had taken 105 grains of mercury bichloride and that he had died while undergoing a spinal puncture to relieve pressure on the spine.

"Isn't it possible that the patient might have died from the spinal puncture?" Cox asked.

"It might have caused the death," Lingeman replied.

A similar spinal puncture had been performed on Madge Oberholtzer just before her death. On redirect examination, Christian asked the doctor if this operation might have caused her death as well. Lingeman replied that it might have. He added that she had probably absorbed a fatal dose of poison during the six hours that elapsed from the time she took the tablets until she told the defendants that she had taken poison.

After Lingeman left the stand, the defense attorneys asked permission to be excused for a few minutes to hold a private conference. Judge Sparks said that this would be permitted, so the lawyers filed out of the courtroom. In five minutes they returned, and to the surprise of everyone in the court, Inman rose and announced, "Your Honor, the defense rests its case."[19]

Remy said that the defense's abrupt decision to rest its case had caught the state's attorneys unprepared. He requested an adjournment until 2:00 P.M., to give the state's rebuttal witnesses time to get to Noblesville. Judge Sparks said he would adjourn the court until 1:15 P.M., which should give sufficient time for the state's witnesses to arrive.

Dr. R. N. Harger, a toxicologist from Indiana University, was the first witness recalled by the state for rebuttal testimony. Under direct questioning by Cox, Harger discussed his knowledge of the medical literature on toxicology.

"Is there a toxicology by 'Milt'?" Cox asked, mentioning one of the references that had been cited by Dr. Smiley, the defense's "expert" medical witness.[20]

"I think not—quite sure of it, in fact," said Harger. He added that he had looked through "all the regular sources" and could not find so much as a treatise written by anyone named Milt.

"If witnesses have used these texts I have mentioned to support their statements," Cox asked, "what would you say about the authority of their testimony?" The defense attorneys objected to this, so Cox rephrased his question.

"Have you made a search for cases of poisoning, especially bichloride of mercury taken by mouth, where the patient lived although the poison was taken five hours or more before medical aid was rendered?" Cox asked.

"I have," said Harger.

"And cases where what should ordinarily be considered a fatal dose had been taken?"

"Yes, sir."

"How many such cases have you found?"

"In medical literature, eleven such cases," Harger replied. He added that he was prepared to give a list of the authorities he had found, but the defense lawyers objected that this did not constitute a rebuttal.

Cox turned to address the jury and the audience. "At least two medical witnesses for the defense stated that there were no instances of recovery of cases where fatal doses had been taken and no medical aid had been given until after five or six hours' lapse of time." Then Cox went on to have Harger testify about one of the cases he had discovered, in which the victim survived a twenty-two-grain dose of mercury bichloride and had gone two days before receiving medical treatment. Again, the defense objected that this was not a rebuttal of any defense testimony.[21]

On cross-examination, Inman began by turning his questions back to patients who had recovered from mercuric poisoning, asking, "You say these eleven cases got well?"

"Yes," said Harger.

"How many of the other cases died?"

Harger said that the 11 surviving cases had been reported in 9 different medical articles, then pointed out that out of 450 total cases, he believed that 40 had died.

"In any one of the eleven cases where the patient got well, how much of the poison was absorbed?" Inman asked.

"I don't know," said Harger. "I know the amount taken but not the amount absorbed."

"The largest factor would be the amount absorbed, would it not?" Inman asked.

Harger replied that the largest factor would be the treatment given to the patient.[22]

Following Harger's rebuttal testimony, the state next called Jeannie Brown, the wife of *Indianapolis News* publisher Hilton U. Brown. She had been ill in bed but had come to Noblesville for the trial to testify as a character witness for Madge. No sooner had Brown taken the stand, however, than the defense attorneys objected to her testimony. Character witnesses could not be admitted during rebuttal, they claimed, because no attack had been made on Madge's character by the defense. Remy insisted to the judge that, indeed, the dead woman's character had been attacked by innuendo used by the defense. Judge Sparks, however, ruled with the defense that Madge's character had never been called into question. Brown was dismissed.[23]

Next, the state called Dr. Cleon Nafe, superintendent of the Indianapolis City Hospital. Again, the defense counsel objected, noting that Nafe would not be rebutting earlier testimony but would, in fact, be delivering new testimony. Attorneys from both sides approached the bench, and a lengthy debate ensued. Finally, the judge announced that Nafe's testimony would not be allowed because it was not rebutting any testimony given by any other witness.[24]

With two of their main witnesses barred from testifying, the state's attorneys requested that court be adjourned until the next morning at nine o'clock. With that, the day's testimony came to a sudden end.[25]

That day's *Indianapolis News* announced that the jury costs for the Stephenson trial were expected to run as high as $2,500—more money than the jury cost for the trial of ex-Governor McCray. Sheriff Gooding told reporters that the lengthy search for jurors had cost more than $1,800 alone.[26]

November 11, 1925

The following morning, testimony began with two black prisoners, Pete Majors and Thomas Tuggie, and two white prisoners, Harry Mescall and Louis Brunner, from the Indiana State Farm in Putnam County. These were the four prisoners who were supposedly taken from the Marion County jail to the state farm by Earl Klinck on March 17. Majors told the court that he and the three other prisoners were driven to the farm by Red Koffel, a deputy sheriff, and a trustee from the jail. He was sure that Earl Klinck had not been in the car. Tuggie, Mescall, and Brunner all made similar claims.[27]

On cross-examination, Holmes demanded to know how it was that Majors so clearly remembered the exact day of the drive to Putnamville. Majors explained that it was exactly four days after the day he had been convicted—and that day had been Friday the 13th, he said with a grin. The prisoners were followed by Oren D. Williams and Orville Collins, both clerks at the state farm. They, too, corroborated the story told by state witnesses that removed Klinck's alibi. Williams was asked to identify a prisoner sign-in book from the state farm.

"Do you remember who brought these men to the farm?" Will Remy asked him.

"I recall faintly," Williams answered and went on to describe Koffel.

Remy stepped over to the table where Klinck sat and pointed a finger at the defendant. "This man did not come there with the prisoners that day, did he?"

"I do not recall him at all," said Williams.[28]

The courtroom action paused after Williams's testimony while Judge Sparks halted activity to announce his decision to ban smoking in the courtroom. Although circuit court rules prohibit smoking in the courtroom, Judge Sparks had leniently decided to overlook smoking during recesses—especially since attorneys on both sides were fond of their pipes and cigarettes, and the packed courtroom made it difficult for the lawyers to step out in the hall during recesses.

Now, however, there was a blue haze of smoke hanging thick in the air. "Hereafter at recess," the judge said, "we will have no smoking in the courtroom during recess. The room is crowded and perhaps not as well ventilated as it should be and smoking during recess causes the air to become foul. It is the general rule that smoking is prohibited in the courtroom and we will adhere to that. Men—and women, too—if they desire, must step from the courtroom to smoke." The audience laughed lightly at the reference to women smoking, a sight that was still considered mildly scandalous.[29]

The next rebuttal witness was Stanley C. Hill, one of Madge's former boyfriends. Hill was introduced to the court as now being involved in Florida real estate sales. Under questioning, he explained that he had known Madge since October 1923.[30]

"Were you at the Governor's banquet the night of January 13?" Ralph Kane asked.

"Yes, sir," said Hill. He explained that he was secretary of the Inaugural Committee and had been in charge of arranging the seating of guests at the banquet. Madge, he said, had assisted by placing name cards at each table. Hill told the court that he had introduced Madge to Stephenson that evening.

"State when—at what particular time—that introduction was made?" Kane asked.

"As the guests came in, they were shown to their seats or found their place cards, and, after going to our places, Madge and I pointed out the seats to the people as nearly as we could remember where we had placed the cards, and as I came over to the seat—we were sitting, as I said, directly across from Mr. Stephenson—and he introduced a Miss Meade, who was his guest, and I presented Miss Oberholtzer to Miss Meade and to Mr. Stephenson. . . ."

". . . Now, do you know whether Madge Oberholtzer had ever been introduced or had met Stephenson before that evening?" Kane asked.

"I am positive that she had not," Hill answered.

At this, the defense attorneys objected, and the court upheld their objection because Hill could not possibly know whether or not the two had met before that night.

On cross-examination, Inman tried to establish how close Hill was to Madge.

"As of the 13th of January, when this Governor's banquet took place, had you been constantly, every day and night, in the presence and company of Madge Oberholtzer?" Inman asked.

"With very few exceptions," Hill replied.[31]

The court recessed for lunch at noon and reconvened at 1:00 P.M. The state had to request another recess because its next witness had not yet arrived. The second recess lasted until 3:00 P.M., when the next rebuttal witness finally arrived.

Ralph Roudebush, a Noblesville poultry dealer, testified that he had been in Columbus, Indiana, on the January night that Stephenson supposedly drove through the town with a Madge at his side. Roudebush said that he had seen another man in the car with Stephenson, but no woman was there. Roudebush also said that Chester Clawson, who, according to Dr. Vallery Ailstock, had seen Stephenson there with Madge, had not been there on the street.

On cross-examination, Floyd Christian asked Roudebush if he had been connected with one of Stephenson's businesses. The witness answered that he had been a stockholder in a Stephenson organization called the "Cavalry Motion Picture Company," which was already defunct. (The company's correct name was Cavalier Motion Picture Company.)

Roudebush said that on the night he saw Stephenson in Columbus, he had asked Stephenson what stockholders could do to get back their money.

"What did Stephenson say?" Christian asked.

"He said, 'I am the law and have money behind me. There's nothing you can do,'" Roudebush answered.[32]

After Roudebush's testimony, the state announced that it was resting its rebuttal testimony. Now it was the defense attorneys' chance for rebuttal. Instead of advancing their case, however, the attorneys called a pair of witnesses whose testimony did nothing to help the defendants. Ira Holmes first recalled deputy

sheriff Frank Kempf, who was asked if he had taken any prisoners to the state farm in March. Kempf replied that he had not
and was excused from the witness stand.[33]

Deputy sheriff James Carter was called next and asked if
he and Klinck had made any arrests on the afternoon of March
near the Memorial Cemetery. He replied that they had. Holmes
asked if, in March, he had taken any prisoners to the state farm,
and Carter replied that he could not remember. With that, the
defense attorneys announced that they would have to wait for
the arrival of more witnesses in the morning and requested an
adjournment.[34]

"The Fairest Trial in History"

November 12–14, 1925

The defense's case ended on a weak note. A former Klan employee, Fred Stone, was called to the stand. He told the court how he had seen Stanley Hill with Madge Oberholtzer in Stephenson's offices discussing final plans for the governor's inaugural banquet three or four days before January 12. The testimony did little more than suggest that perhaps Madge had known Stephenson longer than she later claimed.

The next—and the last—rebuttal witness for the defense was Roscoe Carpenter. His testimony was to have something to do with Stephenson's Cavalier Motion Picture Company. But every question put to the witness by the defense attorneys brought an objection from the state's attorneys until, finally, Carpenter was excused without giving any significant testimony.

The defense attorneys called for Dr. Vallery Ailstock and Chester Clawson from Columbus, Indiana, to appear, but neither man arrived in time.

"Is that all, gentlemen?" Judge Sparks asked the defense attorneys.

"If the court will give us no more time . . ." Eph Inman started to say.

"Gentlemen, you have had plenty of time since last evening to get all your witnesses here," the judge said. "The arguments will then be started."

The order of closing arguments would be Will Remy first for the state, followed by Ira Holmes closing for the defense, then Charles Cox giving the state's second closing, and Floyd Christian with the defense's second closing argument. Eph Inman would deliver a final closing for the defense, and Ralph Kane would make the final closing argument for the state.

Remy rose and began to speak softly:

> We have had a fair trial and these defendants have had a fair
> trial. No one in the history of jurisprudence ever had a fairer
> trial.
>
> Gentlemen of the jury . . . Madge Oberholtzer is dead.
> She would be alive today if it was not for the unlawful acts of
> David C. Stephenson, Earl Klinck, and Earl Gentry. They de-
> stroyed her body. They tried to destroy her soul. And here in
> the past few days they have attempted to befoul her charac-
> ter. It's easy to understand that any man who had stooped to
> the crimes charged against the defendants would not hesi-
> tate to assassinate a character.
>
> Madge Oberholtzer was looking into the face of eternity
> when she made her statement. All the means that were em-
> ployed by the defense couldn't break it down. And so, they
> tried to make you think that Madge Oberholtzer was a bad
> girl! That is the most shameful page of the history of this
> case. They put their gang on the stand—I say gang advisedly,
> for these witnesses were part of the little coterie or organiza-
> tion of men who worked for or under Stephenson—some of
> whom were paid by him and who associated with him. They
> were put on the stand because they couldn't get anyone else!
> Her character still shines untarnished!
>
> But they were unable to break down her story. Through
> their maze of lies and artifices, her statement stands forth as
> the truth. . . . He said he was the law in Indiana, and gentle-
> men, sometimes I think he was not far from being the law in
> Indiana. Thank God he can't say he is the law in Hamilton
> County. [1]

Remy spoke for three hours. The courtroom was packed
with a quiet crowd that hung on every word. People were
crammed into the spaces between the rows of seats and the railing that separated the audience from the lawyers' tables. People
sat on the floor in the aisles of the courtroom. More people
spilled out into the hallway, listening through the doorway. Outside, a morning fog had given way to rain and thunderstorms.
The sound of rain beating against the windows punctuated the
pauses in Remy's speech.

Throughout the arguments, Stephenson sat at his desk
with his eyes fixed on papers spread before him, taking notes on
the state's closing arguments. Several times, he looked up,
yawned, then went back to his note writing. Klinck and Gentry
both sat quietly next to him with their eyes fixed on the speakers. Behind his bench, Judge Sparks sat, sometimes listening,
sometimes writing as he prepared his final instructions to the
jury.

"They did not go to Chicago," Remy said. "No! That would have meant crossing the state line, and it would have brought a charge in the federal court. Even Mr. Stephenson is afraid of that court. He does not claim to be the law in the United States. He limits himself to Indiana, I hope."

Remy was red-faced, shouting till his words rang in the courtroom, pointing his finger a few feet away from Stephenson's face.

"Stephenson said to her when he learned she had taken the poison: 'You'll have to have your stomach pumped out.' I don't know where he had the experience, but he knew her stomach should be washed out. As to experience, he told Gentry, 'I have been in tighter places than this, Gentry, but have always got out.' Wouldn't it be interesting to hear about some of those tighter places?" Remy paused to let these words sink in to the jurors.

"Then he offered to take her to a hospital where she could register as his wife. But she refused to do that. She refused, as any decent, self-respecting woman would, to pose as his wife.

"If Madge had been the kind of girl they would have you believe she was, she would have done as Stephenson suggested, gone to Crown Point and married him, or gone to a hospital and registered as his wife.

"The reason she did not was that she was a clean, decent, honorable, respectable girl, who had been trapped by these fiends. It is to her everlasting honor that she refused to do these things that Stephenson finally suggested after he became scared."

Madge's mother, Matilda Oberholtzer, sat with other members of her family on the west side of the courtroom, her face tense and drawn. She sat rigidly upright in her seat.

Remy continued: "The delay that elapsed from the time they learned she was suffering the pangs of death, the exposure and lack of care, hastened her death. It's the law of Indiana that although a person has been told by hundreds of doctors he is to die in six, twelve, or two hours, he has the right to the last ten minutes of his life, and any who fails to give the attention and care it is possible to give is guilty of murder."

Remy recalled for the jury the testimony of the state's medical witnesses who had described poisoning cases in which immediate treatment saved the victims' lives.

"This girl's life might have been saved. The defense says it could not, but there have been cases where the life of a person was saved under such conditions where the persons had gone for as many hours without treatment.

"But there was an abscess on her lung, brought on by the fangs of D. C. Stephenson. These doctors—the best that could be obtained—said that helped to cause her death."

Then Remy began to ridicule the witnesses who had been called for the defense, describing them all as members of "Stephenson's gang." He called Ralph Rigdon a "utility witness for the defense—he would testify to anything that the others would not." Then Remy pointed to the defense attorneys and shouted, "They did not produce a single witness outside of their own gang! Wasn't that a fine array of witnesses?"[2]

After a short lunch break, it was time for the defense's closing arguments. Ira Holmes began his argument by saying that he had served as defense attorney in many murder cases that had been prosecuted by Remy. "And I have yet to hear him give a witness for the defense any credit for telling the truth. Witnesses for the state are always truthful and the defense witnesses are lying, according to him."[3]

Holmes made a simple plea that the three men should be acquitted because there was simply no evidence to convict them. He went on to say that the prosecution of Stephenson and his friends was a form of political persecution.

Briefly reviewing the evidence, Holmes declared that it showed no other fact than that Madge Oberholtzer's death had been a "plain case of suicide." By describing how the defendants had gotten a bottle of milk for her, Holmes said, her own statement proved that Stephenson had tried to help her.

"Suicide is not a crime in Indiana," Holmes argued. "Therefore, to be an accessory before or after the fact would be no crime in Indiana."

Then Holmes tried to pick apart Madge's dying statement. "When I deny the truth of statements in this alleged dying declaration, I am not saying that Madge Oberholtzer lied," he said. "This statement did not originate with her. It originated in the mind of Asa Smith, with the aim of making money."

Holmes began to read through the declaration, pointing out inconsistencies. "Why didn't she make an outcry when she was taken through Union Station? . . . The statement says that after they were in Hammond, Madge Oberholtzer was forced to send a telegram dictated by Stephenson. Shortly afterward, she was allowed to go out alone to purchase a hat. She bought the hat and a little later went into a drug store, unguarded, and bought the poison. Couldn't she have sent another telegram refuting the one 'dictated' by Stephenson?" Such flaws, Holmes claimed, proved that the idea of a forced abduction was absurd.

"We have done nothing to blacken her character any more than the evidence of what she did during her life serves to blacken her character," Holmes said.

Holmes also noted that there could be no charge of first-degree murder because there was no premeditation, a necessity for a first-degree murder charge. "If you find Stephenson guilty of murder, you must find that he forced her to take poison and there was no evidence like that," Holmes concluded.[4]

By now it was four o'clock and still raining. Charles Cox, who had delivered the oratorical opening statement for the state, now rose to give the state's second closing argument.

"I know, gentlemen of the jury," Cox began, "that some of you would be reluctant, in the ordinary murder case—perhaps in any murder case—to vote to inflict the death penalty. But let me ask, if a degenerate sheep dog got into your fold and killed your ewe lambs, wouldn't you kill him? The law—your law and mine—gentlemen of the jury, says that if murder is committed in the act of committing a rape or by the administering of or causing poison to be administered, that one of the penalties shall be death.

"If these men—Stephenson, the sadist, the moral degenerate, and Klinck, the gorilla, the strong-arm man, and Gentry, who minister to distressed womanhood by sitting by and without protest seeing a woman ravished—if these men can take away a lady, entrap the one you love . . . and defile her and bite her and kill her by physical force or mental compulsion, those men should be killed by the law. . . .

"They did not intend to kill her, perhaps, but they are liable criminally. They are responsible to the law for everything that naturally and probably flowed from the things they did to her.

"Her name has not been assailed. It could not be. If it could have, these ghouls would have done it. Instead they tried to attack her name, her memory by insinuation and innuendo. They try in this way to lead you to believe Madge Oberholtzer was a bad woman.

"They killed her, murdered her, and now they would write the scarlet letter on her tomb." Cox pointed at Inman. "Are you going to let this painter of words, this man with the melodious voice, paint this letter on her tomb? He can't do it. But that is what it would mean if the verdict coming from you men is anything short of murder."

Cox spoke directly to the jurors. "These degenerates, these perverts, drunken with power, would go free to commit other outrages. But you won't let them do it. I think I know what is in the hearts of good men."[5]

At five o'clock, Judge Sparks rapped his gavel, interrupting Cox's closing argument to announce that the court would adjourn until the morning, when Cox could continue his closing.

November 13, 1925

Court resumed the next morning at 8:30 A.M., a half hour early to give the attorneys more time for closing arguments.

"I told you in my opening statement that Madge Oberholtzer would be the principal witness for the state and, gentlemen, she has been," Cox said when he resumed.[6]

"That morning in the garage of Stephenson's, she was so prostrate, so weak and helpless, she could not dress herself. Klinck, the beast, the gorilla, dressed her. No doubt her mind went back to the days when she was a lisping child at her mother's knee and she must have thought of the awful contrast of being dressed by her mother and there that morning having to attend her this beast, this Klinck.

"You remember that she went on that trip without coat or hat. Would that appear she went on this trip willingly? You know it's not true. If a woman of brazen character would not do a thing like this, you know a woman of good standing and reputation would not be a willing member of the party."

Cox turned from the jurors and looked out into the courtroom toward Madge's family. "There is a man and woman in this courtroom now, a broken father and mother who brought Madge Oberholtzer into this world, who rejoiced at her coming, who cared for her in her babyhood, in her infancy, in her childhood, their only little girl, their only ewe lamb. They are entitled to some consideration at your hands, gentlemen of the jury. They are entitled to ask you that all that human laws can do shall be done, and they do not ask it except they are justified by the evidence and the law, as they are.

"Madge Oberholtzer's brutal murder must be avenged by the law, and I ask you, gentlemen of the jury, in the name of the law, in the name of this sorrowing father and mother, in the name of virtuous girls, in the name of the daughters of us all, in the name of all good women everywhere, in the name of justice and in the name of the law, I ask you to write your verdict with a view of stopping the sort of thing that has been going on. Write it so that it will be impossible again for one, coming as this man came to the state of Indiana and the city of Indianapolis two or three years ago, and in two or three years boasting that he is the law and the government in Indiana, that he can commit crimes so detestable as this and get away with it because he has the power."[7]

Attorney Cox completed his closing shortly after 10:00 A.M. The court called a ten-minute recess, then reconvened for Floyd Christian's closing defense argument.

As Holmes had done earlier, Christian tried to attack the inconsistencies in the dying declaration.

"How did this girl know about bichloride of mercury?" Christian asked. "I don't know, but there must be some explanation. How did she take it? It hasn't been proved beyond a reasonable doubt that she did take it by mouth.

"Sometimes girls in our best families do things that are wrong. Why didn't she tell her mother first? Why was her mother and father barred from the room when Smith, Dean, and Kingsbury framed that dying statement?

"If a man went home and committed suicide because his banker refused to lend him money, you wouldn't hang the banker. It would be a plain case of suicide, as this is. Suicide can't be homicide and homicide can't be suicide. They are as different as black is from white."

Christian's oratory was interrupted by a commotion in the front row of the courtroom. An eighty-one-year-old spectator had suddenly fainted. Sheriff's deputies picked the woman up and carried her into the sheriff's office, where she was soon revived.

Christian concluded his remarks by urging the jury to "uphold true American principles and, with the courage of heroes, write a verdict on the evidence in the case, having in mind the definition of a reasonable doubt."[8]

The court took a one-hour recess for lunch at the conclusion of Christian's arguments, then reconvened at 1:15 P.M. to hear Eph Inman's closing for the defense.

Inman began with a grand flourish, the kind of courtroom speech for which he was well known. "There probably has been no case like this in the history of the American Union," he declared. "There has been none in the world, so far as I know."

Leaning over toward the jury, as if he was about to tell them a dark secret, Inman said, "It is no trouble for you men to see that there is some mysterious power in this state that is back of the persecution of these men—trying to send them to the electric chair. These men know it. D. C. Stephenson knows it. Some men are jingling the gold now of the enemies who seek their destruction.

"I would that you and I—the thirteen of us—could sit down and talk about this case, that you might ask questions of me, and we could clear this thing up.

"The attorneys for the prosecution were hired for money to get blood in this case," Inman said. "The state has drawn pictures not with brush and paint, but with brush and mud. Judge Cox said some of the most terrible things I ever heard said in a court room.

"I'm not here to blacken the character or the name of Madge Oberholtzer. I'm here to be of some service to you, if I can in my own feeble and humble way."

Inman looked toward the group of attorneys at the state's table, then stood in front of Stephenson and pointed to him. "They are trying to rush this man to the electric chair to get rid of him for his enemies!"

Stephenson's arrest and the murder charges against him, said Inman, were politically motivated.

Standing directly in front of state attorneys Cox and Kane, Inman charged, "You can't crush the truth! You may think you can, but it will travel along, take new life and rise again, regardless of the fact that lawyers hired for money will call it a lie."

Inman turned his attention to the dying declaration and to Asa Smith, the Oberholtzers' lawyer. "Did these men put a revolver in her face and say, 'You drink or we'll kill you'? Why, you'd think from that statement that there were sawed-off shotguns, .44s, and all kinds of firearms in that house, and all drawn on that woman to make her drink. Asa Smith ought to be ashamed of that fabrication the longest day of his life."

Inman denounced the state's attorneys for their attacks on the defense witnesses. According to the state's attorneys, Inman said, all the witnesses who dared to testify for the defense were perjurers.

"The prosecutor has accused us of 'falling back' on the suicide theory. This defense always has held to the theory of suicide. This prosecution has abandoned its theory of poison on which it started out. A new theory, that of infection, has been hatched up between the bail hearing last June and now."

Why was it, he asked the jury, that Madge had sent the first telegram to her mother saying that she was "driving through to Chicago" and not bothered to send a second telegram when her "captors" were not guarding her? She had ample opportunity to buy a hat with money she had borrowed from Stephenson while she was out. Why hadn't she sent a second telegram then, if the first one had been sent under duress? Inman exhibited the telegram to the jurors again, calling their attention to the "firm, round hand" of the signature, which gave no evidence of being written by a woman who was deadly frightened for her life.

"If she was the heroine you say she was, why did she condescend to take a cent of money from Stephenson. Why did she need a hat? Couldn't she commit suicide bareheaded?" Inman asked the state's attorneys.

"Why didn't she go to the druggist where she got this poison—the druggist in the hotel—and tell him of her plight and beg for the poison instead of condescending to take money from Stephenson? . . . Where is the milliner from Hammond? Where is the druggist? Why didn't they bring them here to testify? . . .

"There is not a lawyer in Indiana—not a lawyer in the nation—freed from prejudice and interest, who wouldn't say, and who doesn't say, that this prosecution for murder is entirely without justification and without precedent in the jurisprudence of the country. Not only that, but every cool-headed, every fair-minded, reasoning man you may meet upon the street—in public or private—feels and will say they might be guilty of something, even assuming the theory of the state and the story of its witnesses to be true—we don't know—but they are not guilty, and could not be guilty, of murder—or guilty of homicide, in any degree.

"The sole question presented here is: can suicide be murder? Can suicide be homicide? The law doesn't say it can be and never will say so. No man has ever said so—or ever will say so, unless he says it in contradiction of the law.

"If this so-called dying declaration declares anything, it is a dying declaration of suicide, not homicide. Why, she only told of how she committed suicide!

"She, by her own concealment of taking the poison for six hours, made medical aid of no avail. She, by her own willful act and conduct, made it impossible for these men to save her life.

"Has everybody lost his head? Pray, are we all insane? Must prejudice and passion submerge the world for the purpose of some particular case, leaving us, when it is over in a wild disorderly state—in mental bewilderment and anarchy in the heart's regret and the soul-sickness of remorse?

"The conviction of these men might satisfy the transient spirit of the mob for the moment being, but the mob itself, after the savage thrill of the triumph has passed, would learn that a fatal error has been made.

"These men have been made helpless for seven long months by fate unwarranted and cruel. . . . A jury of intelligent men, of sensible, thinking men, have been accepted to pass upon the question—a jury, which we have a right to feel will not be stampeded into doing violence to common sense and law."[9]

"Maybe someone feels that I say these things because I am engaged in the defense of these men. It is true that I am so engaged. But, after a long service in the great profession of the law—and, I pray, an honorable one—my heart gives utterance to this: That I have not, in all my professional life defended one for murder where I felt in my soul there was as complete absence of justification for such a charge as there is in this sad case."

Inman ended his speech with a benediction. "Gentlemen, I have done. I give this great issue, the safety of my clients to you. By the law of reason—by the law of courage—by the law of right—I feel that your consciences will not allow any harm to come to these men. They have already suffered much—too much—far too much. And I am grateful to heaven in the confidence that they are now approaching the end of it all. I thank each one of you for your patience—your infinite patience. And may there fall upon you the blessings of the Almighty God of us all."[10]

It took the entire afternoon for Inman to deliver his speech for his clients. He spoke in his grand oratorical style for four hours and forty-five minutes, until the court adjourned for the day at 5:00 P.M.

November 14, 1925

Ralph Kane continued closing arguments at 8:30 A.M. on Saturday, November 14. The courtroom was packed. Kane began with his voice raised to a shout. "In all the history of the middle ages, when feudal barons ruled with the mailed fists of despots, when there was no law but the law of force, and when outrages, the despoiling of women, were in the general course of events, there is no case to compare with the shameful character of this!" said Kane. "These defendants are as guilty of the murder of Madge Oberholtzer as though they had stabbed her with a knife![11]

"This has not only been a revolting offense against the law of the land, but it has been a terrible offense against the laws of the Creator!

"Inman consumed four hours in throwing a smoke screen over the facts in the case. He did not discuss a fact that had been introduced in evidence. . . . When Judge Cox told you yesterday that their witnesses were perjurers and members of a defense conspiracy to evade facts and give false testimony, he spoke the truth.

"Under the law that when these defendants unlawfully abducted Madge Oberholtzer from her home and unlawfully took her to Hammond and unlawfully attacked her, they were in commission of unlawful acts which held them responsible for the body of that girl and when by their acts they drove her to take poison they made themselves murderers as much as if they had stabbed her."

Kane told the jurors that he would "tear the mask" from Inman's face and show that the entire defense of Stephenson was a fraud and a deceit. "This man stood before you and talked about how he was so fair that he nearly leaned backward, he was trying to mislead you right there!" Kane shouted.

"Do you believe you are so credulous that you will believe their theory that this girl went along on that trip with those men willingly? Even a woman of evil virtue shows a little pride in a case like that—she does not start out on a long trip like that without making any preparation, without taking any lingerie with her. She would not have got into that Pullman compartment with Stephenson while this big pug ugly Gentry was with her.

"We can't bring Madge Oberholtzer back to life and restore her to her bereaved parents," said Kane. "But we can make an example of them for the protection of other daughters.

"Was Madge Oberholtzer a willing party to this outrage? Let's look into the evidence. Didn't that nurse tell you of the wounds all over her body? . . .

"And then, gentlemen, do you believe that this woman had not been attacked, assaulted, ravished, raped, humiliated, driven to despair and forced by these defendants to drink poison, because she had lost her jewels, she had lost that which she held dearer than her life—her chastity?

"They hop on Asa Smith. If any of these defendants or their attorneys, too, for that matter, enjoyed the character and reputation of Asa Smith, they would be most fortunate indeed. God bless Asa! He has the respect and confidence of every man and woman who know the facts in this case. I'll tell you why they have been bitter against Asa Smith. He took that dying statement from Madge Oberholtzer, which has been her testimony in this trial. He is the man who brought the evidence into this court that these defendants can't get away from. He is not only a hero of the nation for his services in the world war, but he is the hero in this case.

"Poor girl. She had been robbed of everything she held dear, of all that life had meant to her through twenty-eight short years, and knowing she was about to die, she called Asa Smith. And yet these criminal lawyers have come here, paid by the filthy dollars D. C. Stephenson got in the legislature, and have the nerve to attack the character of Asa Smith!

"The moment Madge Oberholtzer left her home and met Gentry, who had been sent as her escort, she was in the clutches of the tiger. He took her to Stephenson's home, the tiger's lair. Then Klinck came into the picture. They were all around her, and in the ride in the automobile, she told you Klinck and Gentry sat on each side of her.

"These criminal lawyers tell you she made no outcry. In the first place, Washington Street isn't a crowded thoroughfare at that hour of the night.

"And they bring in this hotel clerk, Lambert, a dirty, lying cur, to try to break down the story of this poor girl! His testimony on its face was a lie. He said that on that night, this girl, whom he had seen only twice before, was in an automobile in front of the Washington Hotel and she called to him and he spoke to her. This girl was a lady, a college girl, and she had no acquaintance with him.

"And then that poor fish came on the stand and told you he had never told a living soul of what he knew. In the name of God, how did Stephenson's . . . gang find out that Lambert would testify for him? It was a lie, made out of whole cloth and they knew it! But in the stress of their desperation they would try to make a jury of Hamilton county men believe this Lambert against the dying statement of this girl.

"The defense has made capital of the fact Stephenson suggested they go to Crown Point and be married. Why, Stephenson did not want to marry her because he loved her, because he wanted her to be his wife. He realized the terrible situation he was in, and offered to marry her so that he might escape exactly what he is facing now.

"If the prosecutor of Hamilton County has the nerve I think he has and the nerve he ought to have, he will have a grand jury empaneled and have those four deputy sheriffs indicted for perjury, and all other witnesses the defense has brought in here to swear to lies. That bunch of turnkeys who are more fit to be jail birds than keepers of prisoners."

Kane went on to call defense witness Ralph Rigdon a "loafing vagabond, who hung around the legislature and the foot of Stephenson and licked his boots for the few crumbs he could get.

"You are going to write into your verdict whether your daughter, my daughter, will be protected from the vandalism of the criminally inclined. That is the responsibility on you. Not only the eyes of this community but the eyes of the entire state and nation are on this courtroom scene.

"The people of this nation wish to know whether an Indiana jury will permit vagabonds to commit a fiendish crime of this sort. . . . I wish to know whether there's a man in this community who would sign a verdict to acquit this hideous monster who preys on the virtuous young daughters of our state!"

Kane's dramatic last speech of the trial lasted nearly two and a half hours. He concluded a few minutes before eleven o'clock.

Judge Sparks read his instructions to the jury, a twenty-five minute discussion of the grounds on which someone could be found guilty of murder in the first or second degree. Following lunch, the jurors began their deliberations. And at 5:21 P.M., the jurors, carrying their hats and coats, filed back into the courtroom to announce their verdict.[12]

The verdict: Stephenson was guilty of murder in the second degree; Klinck and Gentry were found not guilty.

A week later, Stephenson made the long trip up to Michigan City, Indiana, where he was to become Indiana State Prisoner Number 11148.

House of Cards

1925–27

Stephenson had kept his mouth shut all during his trial. Later he claimed this was because he feared for his life, that members of the Klan had threatened to kill him if he took the witness stand in Noblesville.[1] It is more likely that his lawyers feared that putting him on the witness stand would give the prosecution a chance to cross-exam Stephenson.

A third possibility—certainly a major one in Stephenson's mind—was that the outcome of the trial simply did not matter. Wasn't his good friend Ed Jackson now seated as governor of the state? And was it not within Jackson's power to issue a pardon for his friend Stephenson? Stephenson had only to keep quiet, play the part of a model prisoner for a few months—a year at the most—until the heat of the trial had dissipated, and then a pardon would be announced and he would walk out of prison a free man. He even bragged to reporters that the governor would issue a pardon soon.

And so Stephenson kept quiet all through December 1925 and January 1926. He was quiet all through the spring and summer. He worked in the prison laundry, and the days passed slowly.

By late summer, he was growing impatient. Life in the prison was too much like work for Stephenson. The laundry was a hot place to work, and during the summer months it was even hotter.

Why was it taking so long for his pardon to be issued? Perhaps his friend, the governor, had forgotten him? Perhaps if he talked to some reporters, the governor might remember that Stephenson knew a few things about how he had been elected?

But when Stephenson tried to arrange an interview with some reporters, he had a rude awakening. The prison warden, Walter Daly, would not allow him to be interviewed! Daly announced that only attorneys and relatives could interview prisoners. When Stephenson discovered that he was being confined without means of communication, he panicked.[2]

He went to his cell and began to write letters. He used his contacts inside the prison to smuggle the letters from the laundry to a cooperative guard. At 6:00 P.M. when the guards changed shifts, his contact guard would carry his letters outside the prison and deliver them to Martha Dickinson. Dickinson was a married woman from Spencer, Indiana, but she was also deeply attached to Stephenson. She had followed his case throughout the trial at Noblesville and afterward volunteered to serve as a courier for letters coming out of the prison. Dickinson would give the letters to Stephenson's former pilot and bodyguard, Court Asher. Asher, in turn, would take the letters to their final destinations.[3]

The first letters merely explained that Stephenson felt he was being held incommunicado and that he had things to tell that would be of interest to the readers of Indiana newspapers. This news piqued the interest of Thomas H. Adams, the conservative crusading editor of the *Vincennes Commercial.* Adams got together with some of his colleagues and formed a special committee—made up of members of the Indiana Republican Editors' Association—to investigate charges of political corruption within state government.[4]

Adams, a crusty editor of the old school, simply would not tolerate corruption—especially corruption within his own party. He went directly to Jackson, on behalf of the editors' committee, and asked that Jackson order a state investigation of the charges that Stephenson was making. Now it was Jackson's turn to panic. He replied that such an investigation "was unnecessary and would serve no good purpose."[5]

Adams would not be dismissed so easily. Working through Court Asher and reversing Stephenson's "mail" system, Adams sent a letter back inside the prison asking Stephenson to provide more concrete charges. On September 29, 1926, Adams got what he needed. It was a letter from Stephenson claiming he could prove that "a prominent Indiana politician" owed him $825,000 in campaign expenses and that the mayors of three major cities and forty smaller towns around Indiana were also indebted to him. To back this up, Stephenson authorized Asher to turn over a photographic copy of a "contract" that had been drawn up by Stephenson and signed by John L. Duvall, the mayor of Indianapolis. The February 12, 1925, contract read: "In return for the political support of D. C. Stephenson, in the event that I am elected Mayor of Indianapolis, Indiana, I promise not to appoint any person as a member of the board of public works without they first have the indorsement [sic] of D. C. Stephenson. I fully agree and promise to appoint Claude Worley chief of police and Earl Klinck as a captain."[6]

This was political dynamite of a most explosive kind. The editors were not fools. There had been charges made during the 1925 election that Stephenson was helping run Duvall's mayoral campaign. The charges became so loud that, just days before the election, Duvall had issued a public denial of the charges: "Statements that D. C. Stephenson, ex–Ku Klux Klan leader now on trial at Noblesville on a charge of murder, is connected in any way with the Republican City ticket is characterized as absolutely false by Mr. Duvall."[7] And who else but Jackson could be owing as much as $825,000 to Stephenson? The editors began to press Jackson harder for an open interview with Stephenson.

Duvall loudly denied the authenticity of the contract he had signed for Stephenson and filed a lawsuit on October 22, 1926, for $1 million against Adams and the newspapers that printed the copies of the contract.

Jackson tried to stop the editors' investigation, but things were rolling too quickly. It was too serious to laugh off, too big to ignore.

The *Indianapolis Times* began printing front-page editorials signed by the paper's new editor, Boyd Gurley, who had recently moved to Indianapolis from the *South Bend News-Times*. Gurley also wrote open letters to prominent officials, such as U.S. senators James Watson and Arthur Robinson, urging them to pressure Jackson into allowing Stephenson to speak.[8]

Finally on October 25, 1926, Tom Adams of the *Vincennes Commercial* was allowed to interview Stephenson inside the prison. When Adams came out, he wrote an editorial that ran on the front pages of newspapers all over the state. In it, he wrote that Indiana was facing "a cabal strong enough to prevent this man, facing an eternity in prison, from telling everything he knows. His every evasion was enough to prove to me the things we were trying to find out about. They are trying to control him, and by 'they' I mean the fellows who are guilty. It's simply a blockade. If these Stephenson contracts are destroyed, most certainly a deal was made with him. If the deal was made, what was it? . . . That man, criminal though he may be, surrounded by his former friends who are seeking to keep him in prison for an eternity, prevented from talking, a dictaphone in his solitary cell, paints a background which points clearly to the guilt of these men than if Stephenson were to tell his story."[9]

No sooner had the editorial appeared than the Indiana attorney general's office sent deputy prosecutor William H. Sheaffer to Michigan City, Indiana, to interview Stephenson. When Sheaffer got there, however, he discovered that Stephenson's attorneys John Kiplinger—Ed Jackson's close friend—and Lloyd Hill had gotten there first. As a result of his talks with his attorneys, Stephenson announced that he would have nothing more to say until after the November 2 election.[10]

By now, there were investigations going on at every level of government. The Marion County prosecutor's office was busy investigating charges of corruption within the Duvall administration. The Indiana attorney general's office was investigating the same charges at the state level. At the federal level, U.S. Senator James Reed had started an investigation of political corruption in Indiana and had sent investigators from the U.S. Department of Justice to conduct interviews. Specific attention—and publicity—was given to the fact that U.S. Senator Arthur Robinson had received considerable support from the Ku Klux Klan. U.S. Senator James Watson, a personal friend of Reed's, was treated a bit more kindly, although suggestions were also made during the investigation that Watson, too, had been closely associated with the Klan.

John Maroney, a federal investigator from the Department of Justice, was allowed into the prison to interview Stephenson. Nothing of what Stephenson told Maroney was revealed, but Stephenson gave no more interviews for several months after that.[11]

The next time Stephenson appeared in the newspapers was the spring of 1927. This time, however, the focus was not on political corruption in the state but on Stephenson's personal life. His first wife, Nettie Brehm of Oklahoma City, was in Indianapolis suing Stephenson for $10,600 in support payments for herself and her eleven-year-old daughter, Florence Catherine. On March 31, the warden refused to allow Stephenson to be brought to a Marion County court to testify in the support payments case.[12]

On April 8, 1927, Stephenson's former secretary, Fred Butler, testified in Marion County Superior Court that Stephenson had given a touring car to Jackson in January 1925 to use while campaigning for governor. Jackson, contacted by reporters, denied this claim.[13]

Meanwhile, the governor and the warden were unsuccessfully attempting to seal up Stephenson's leaks of information from the prison. Three guards were fired on April 13 for having helped smuggle Stephenson's letters out to the newspapers.[14]

On May 16, Stephenson requested a ninety-day parole from Governor Jackson through the prison's board of trustees. In his request, he claimed that he was the victim of a frame-up and needed time to prepare his appeal. He also filed charges with the State Board of Charities that he was being mistreated by prison officials. Jackson tried to muster some bravado when the reporters asked him for a response. He announced that he would not allow himself to be blackmailed into releasing Stephenson from prison. Clearly, Stephenson's last hopes of a governor's pardon had finally vanished.[15] (On July 1, the State Board of Charities rejected Stephenson's charges of mistreatment, and the prison trustees denied his request for parole.)

On May 17, charges were filed in Indianapolis against Duvall and his brother-in-law, city controller W. C. Buser, for conspiring to commit a felony and for violations of the corrupt practices act.

Stephenson continued to release damning information to the press. The politicians had been nervously laughing at his claims of having evidence to support his stories. He continually referred to "my little black boxes"—a reference to where he kept his incriminating evidence. Did the boxes really exist? And if they did, what did they contain? Reporters and court investigators were hot on the story, and results would soon be forthcoming.

On July 13, Stephenson produced thirty-one cancelled checks that had been drawn for Jackson's gubernatorial campaign in 1924. The largest of the checks was for $2,500. The governor, who had earlier claimed that he had never taken any money from Stephenson, suddenly "remembered" that he had sold a horse named Senator to Stephenson for $2,500. Efforts to locate the horse were unsuccessful, and reporters were told that Senator had choked on a corncob and died. Six days later, a Marion County grand jury was called to investigate charges of political corruption in the county.[16]

On July 24, the black boxes were finally uncovered, and they were loaded with trouble for the politicians who had been on Stephenson's payroll. Former *Indianapolis Times* reporter John L. Niblack, now holding a law degree and working as an assistant Marion County prosecutor, received the boxes in a secret meeting at a round barn near Lick Skillet, Indiana. Niblack was accompanied by a special deputy, attorney Emsley W. Johnson, Sr., and Johnson's son, Emsley Jr. It turned out that Stephenson had entrusted the boxes to his former business partner,

L. G. Julian of Evansville, Indiana, who had kept careful watch over them. Now, on Stephenson's request, Julian turned the boxes over to the grand jury.[17]

The next day, July 25, a story written by Frank Prince appeared in the *Indianapolis Times*. Prince was a thirty-nine-year-old ex-convict who had been released from the Indiana State Prison in 1925, after serving four years for fraudulent check writing. Using his network of prison contacts to get information, Prince reported about what else Stephenson might be able to tell investigators. The story detailed how, during Jackson's administration as secretary of state, he had attempted to bribe former Governor Warren McCray with an offer of ten thousand dollars and a promise of immunity from prosecution. Proof of the bribery rested with Stephenson, who admitted that he had helped plan the operation.

More indictments were filed on September 7, this time against John J. Collins, the purchasing agent for the city of Indianapolis, for bribery, and against Earl Garrett, the city's market master, for obtaining money under false pretenses. Both men had been key figures in the Indianapolis Klan organization as well as the Republican party machine. Six Republican Klan members of the Indianapolis City Council were also indicted for accepting bribes.[18]

Another round of charges from the Marion County investigation—and by far the most serious—was released the same day. Indictments were filed against Governor Ed Jackson, Marion County Republican chairman George V. "Cap" Coffin, and attorney Robert I. Marsh, charging them with conspiring to bribe former Governor Warren McCray.

Within less than a year of his conviction, Stephenson had managed to turn loose a flood of information that now threatened to topple most of the state's key political figures.

Duvall claimed innocence, but the jury didn't believe him. The signature on the contract with Stephenson was too real to deny. So on October 12, 1927, the jurors convicted the mayor of Indianapolis, sentenced him to jail for thirty days, and fined him one thousand dollars. He was also barred from holding a public office for four years from the time of his conviction. Duvall resigned from the mayor's office in November but filed an appeal. The verdict was ultimately upheld in 1931, and he was forced to serve his thirty-day sentence.[19]

The six city council members who were charged with accepting bribes pleaded guilty to minor charges, paid their fines, and resigned from the council. The president of the council, Boynton Moore, was found guilty of accepting a bribe, but Jackson immediately issued him a pardon.[20]

The way was clear for the trial of the governor. The indictment had charged Jackson, Marsh, and Coffin with conspiring "with one David C. Stephenson to feloniously bribe and offer to bribe one Warren T. McCray, then Governor of Indiana, by offering him $10,000 in lawful United States currency to appoint James E. McDonald as Prosecuting Attorney of Marion County." Ironically, if McCray had accepted the bribe and appointed McDonald—Stephenson's choice—as prosecutor, instead of Will Remy, no indictments might have ever been brought against Jackson and the others.[21]

The trial began on February 7, 1928. The three men were "arrested" by the sheriff, who called them by telephone and asked them to turn themselves in at the courthouse. All three complied quietly.

The chief prosecutor was Remy. The chief witnesses at the trial were to be Stephenson; former Governor McCray; James Noel, McCray's attorney; and Fred Robinson, McCray's 1920 campaign manager.

Stephenson was called as the state's first witness against the governor. His testimony began with a detailed account of his ordination as grand dragon of the Ku Klux Klan. But when the questions came around to the bribery incident, Jackson's defense attorneys began a long string of objections, chiefly around the point that Stephenson was a convict and, therefore, his testimony could not be trusted. Judge Charles McCabe called a recess to consider the objections and announced that the trial would continue the next morning.[22]

The following day, the judge declared that Stephenson's testimony would be allowed. But suddenly, the witness announced, "Your Honor, I refuse to answer the question on the grounds it might incriminate me." The prosecution's star witness—eager to testify the day before—had just taken the Fifth Amendment![23]

The jurors were excused from the courtroom, and a private conference was held between the prosecuting attorneys, the judge, and Stephenson. He told how he had been visited in the Marion County jail—where he was being held during the trial—by a powerful attorney from Muncie, Indiana, who was connected with the Klan. The attorney had warned him not to testify against Jackson. "It is a matter of life and death with me. I fear the consequences if I tell the story of the alleged bribe," Stephenson told the judge. Finally, the judge gave up, excused Stephenson from the courtroom, and ordered the prosecutor to call his next witness.[24]

The trial proceeded. The jurors heard Robinson, a former state purchasing agent, describe how he had been instructed to deliver a satchel with ten thousand dollars in it to McCray and how the governor had refused to accept the money. They heard McCray's attorney, James Noel, describe how, once McCray had refused the bribe, the offer was repeated to him. Finally, McCray himself took the stand and told his version of the story.

The prosecutor had to prove that the bribe offer had been made and that it had been concealed by the defendants. However, the judge ruled that too many people were aware of the bribe in order for it to be considered a case of concealment. On February 16, the judge instructed the jury to find the defendants "proved, but not guilty." He reasoned that no concealment was proven and the felony charge had occurred more than four years ago. This meant that it was outside a two-year statute of limitations and, therefore, the defendants could not be convicted. Jackson and his cohorts escaped—but only by a technicality.[25]

After the trial, Jackson's political career was ended. Many people pressured him to resign, but he refused and went on to serve out the rest of his term. Upon leaving the governor's office, the Republicans wanted nothing more to do with him. He was an outcast from his party.

———————————

If Stephenson's stories were ending some careers, they were also helping launch a strange career. The ex-convict reporter, Frank Prince, who had written some of the major stories about Stephenson's prison allegations, found himself the center of attention in the city's social circles.[26]

Helen Orr English, the attractive widow of one of the city's wealthiest men, announced a series of awards would be given on her behalf for "outstanding newspaper reporting." The "contest" was announced on January 16, 1928. Three weeks later, on February 7, she announced that the winner was Frank Prince. He would receive one thousand dollars for "clarifying the political atmosphere of Indiana." Prince promptly quit his job with the *Indianapolis Times* and went to work as a publicist for a Klan investigator and presidential hopeful, Senator James Reed.

Coincidentally, Prince and Helen English discovered they were in love. On March 24, Prince and English announced their

engagement. The marriage took place on April 10 at an Episcopal church in Baltimore, Maryland, and the pair honeymooned
in Atlantic City, New Jersey.

A few days later, on May 8, the headlines of the *Indianapolis Times* trumpeted the news that the newspaper had been
awarded a Pulitzer prize, one of journalism's top honors, for
"meritorious public service" in reporting about political corruption. Nowhere in the paper was Prince's name mentioned. But by
that time, he was enjoying his share of his new bride's fortune.

Their happiness did not last long. Helen English Prince filed
for divorce on October 25, 1929, citing grounds of cruelty and
incompatibility. She kept Prince's name, however, and shortly after divorcing him, she remarried him. On June 16, 1932, she
took a massive overdose of sleeping pills in her room at the Bilt-
more Hotel in Los Angeles, California. Prince brought her back
to Indianapolis to be buried at Crown Hill Cemetery on June 22.
Eight days later, on June 30, the Indianapolis papers announced
that Prince had just come into a fortune of fifty thousand dollars
plus a summer home called "Heart's Ease By The Lake" in Le-
land, Michigan. He had also been named a director of the English Foundation, the city's major philanthropic organization.

Prince's fame continued to skyrocket. He left Indianapolis,
went to St. Louis, Missouri, and became affiliated with the Universal Match Company. Under his direction, the company blos-
somed and grew from a small maker of book matches into a
pioneering manufacturer of automated vending machines. By
1960, when he was seventy-one years old, Prince's Universal
Match Company held more than $40 million in assets. Prince
himself was a millionaire several times over and was turning his
interests to philanthropy.

In 1960, Theodore Link, an investigative reporter for the
St. Louis Post-Dispatch, discovered that Prince was an ex-
convict. Questioned about his past, Prince readily admitted that
he had served more than nine years in prisons in Indiana and
Illinois for grand larceny, forgery, and fraudulent check writing.
The paper ran the story, and Prince was disgraced. Ironically, the
editor of the *Post-Dispatch* at the time was Joseph Pulitzer, Jr.,
son of the man whose namesake award Prince had helped win—
without credit—for the *Indianapolis Times.*

———————————

After Jackson's trial, Stephenson's life in prison began to settle
down into a routine that would last for many years, and through

several governors' terms. He began filing a long list of petitions and appeals to have his 1925 conviction reversed. He began to study law behind bars and ultimately became a well-versed jailhouse lawyer. He would eventually present more than forty appeals to the state—not one of which would be granted. He hired, fired, and rehired lawyers at a blinding clip.

On February 28, 1930, Stephenson's attorneys filed a request for a clemency hearing based on his claims that Madge Oberholtzer had been poisoned by an illegal abortion. According to Stephenson, Madge had been having an affair with Charles Householder, the retired fireman who had taken a room with the Oberholtzer family. Stephenson claimed that Madge was pregnant and that he had taken her to Gary, Indiana, to have the abortion performed. "I shall refrain from referring to the details of relations between the deceased [Oberholtzer] and Householder, other than to say they were such as might easily have called for the services of a Dr. Faulds," Stephenson wrote.

The application for clemency was based on an affidavit by Dr. Mabel Faulds, who claimed that a woman who matched Madge Oberholtzer's description had come to the doctor's Gary office for a "criminal operation" [abortion] on the same day that Madge had been taken by train to Hammond.

This was Stephenson's first attempt at an alibi. Could there have been any truth to it? The courts never bothered to investigate his claim.

In 1939, another major appeal was mounted, this time by a Noblesville law firm, Cloe & Campbell. The case was publicized by a former investigative reporter for the *Indianapolis News*, Robert A. Butler, who produced a book about the Stephenson case in hopes of raising public support for Stephenson. A red paperback edition of the book sold for one dollar per copy. By this time, Stephenson had been in prison for fourteen years and was long past his fear of the Ku Klux Klan. Most of the book was given over to a long dissertation by Stephenson, which gave his account of what "really" happened to Madge Oberholtzer. The book presented allegations that the signature on Madge's deathbed statement was a carefully drawn forgery. Photographic enlargements of Madge's signature claimed to "prove" how the forgery was made.

But the elaborate promotional work held no sway with the courts. In its January 1940 term, the Hamilton County Circuit Court rejected Stephenson's latest petition and specifically mentioned the Butler book. The Indiana attorney general, Omer Jackson, asked in his reply, "Does petitioner sponsor or approve such methods and practices while his petition is under consideration by this court?" In other words, Stephenson shouldn't be allowing his friends to circulate books that claimed he was framed while his case was still under appeal.[27]

Many people began to refer to Stephenson as a political prisoner of the state of Indiana. Certainly this was Stephenson's view of his own predicament. "The press has frequently indicted me with the charge of bad political practice," said Stephenson. "My answer is that I am very probably more guilty of the charge than their wildest fancy may suppose, but I was not playing a game of solitaire in politics, and I have not been tried for political activity. I was allegedly tried because a middle-aged woman—twenty-nine years old [sic]—committed suicide. The political importance of this charge lies in the widely discussed feature that the politicians who were the sole beneficiaries of my political activity are the same politicians who so vehemently oppose a fair trial of the alleged murder charge."[28]

After the 1939 petition, Stephenson claimed that he was financially destitute and unable to pay attorneys to represent him. So he began to handle his own case, acting as his own attorney. He spent his time in prison reading the law books in the prison library and writing copious notes to support his case. In March 1945, Stephenson was back in the newspapers as he attempted to plead for a new trial. A photograph showed Stephenson, now fifty-one years old and looking more like a history professor than a convicted murderer, standing in front of a stack of law books in the Hamilton County Circuit Court.[29]

His voice was clear and confident, though he frequently sipped water from a glass as he spoke. "I hope the court will be patient with me. I must do this job alone and I haven't the skill of the learned gentlemen representing the State of Indiana," he told Judge Cassius M. Gentry.

"Mr. Stephenson," the judge replied, "I am saying to you now that you can have all the time you want to present your case. In fact, I think the court can learn from you."

"That's a beautiful compliment, Your Honor."[30]

Beautiful compliment or not, it did not work. The Indiana Supreme Court quickly issued a writ of prohibition against Judge Gentry, forbidding him from continuing Stephenson's plea. The case was closed, and Stephenson was again taken back to prison.[31]

In 1950, Governor Henry Schricker granted Stephenson a St. Patrick's Day parole from prison on the condition that he take a job in Illinois and stay there. Instead, he first went to

Tulsa, Oklahoma, to live with his daughter. He stayed only a few weeks, then sought permission from the parole authorities to go to Cairo, Illinois, to take a job with an advertising agency. In September, however, he failed to appear for a meeting with his parole officer and was reported as a parole violator. Investigators found him in Robbinsdale, Minnesota, a suburb of Minneapolis, working in a print shop. He was arrested on November 15 for parole violation. On November 23, the Minnesota Supreme Court ordered him sent back to Indiana to be returned to prison.[32]

Six more years went by. Another governor, George N. Craig, gave Stephenson a complete discharge from prison on December 20, 1956. The discharge was a surprise. Only a week before he was released, Hugh P. O'Brien, chairman of the State Correction Board, had told a reporter that Stephenson was unsuitable for parole because of his inability to cope with the outside world. But Governor Craig thought differently. He decided to extend executive clemency to sixty prisoners a few days before Christmas. "I think it was the right thing to do," the governor told reporters. "He has served longer than anyone I know of for the commission of second-degree murder." Suddenly, O'Brien changed his mind about the matter: "I don't see why Stephenson won't be able to cope with life. He's mentally all right." And so, Stephenson was released.[33]

Stephenson moved to Seymour, Indiana, where he married his third wife, Martha Dickinson, the widow who had helped smuggle his letters out of prison thirty years earlier.

By the time he was released, he was no longer the charismatic charmer he had been in the 1920s. Now he was a round, pudgy old man with watery eyes that peered out from behind a thick pair of glasses. His hair, always thin, was now much thinner—nearly bald on top. He had finally become an "old man"—living up to the nickname he had used more than thirty years earlier. Ed Jackson was dead now. So was Earl Gentry. Earl Klinck had simply disappeared. The man who had called himself "the law in Indiana" was now very unimposing.

On November 16, 1961—five years after his release—Stephenson was arrested in Independence, Missouri, on a charge of attempting to molest a sixteen-year-old girl. She claimed he had tried to force her into his car, but she broke away from him. The judge issued a three hundred dollar fine—which Stephenson paid out of his pocket—and ordered him to leave the state.[34]

Stephenson went back home to Martha in Seymour, Indiana. But within a year, they had separated. Sometime in 1962, Stephenson left Indiana and was never seen in the state again.

In the end, Stephenson died far from the public limelight he had lived in for so many years. He died in Jonesboro, Tennessee, June 28, 1966, in the arms of a woman who believed she was his wife.[35]

He arrived in Jonesboro in 1963 to be treated at the veterans' hospital there. Shortly after he was released, he went to work as a writer and printer at the *Jonesboro Herald and Tribune*. He was back at the trade he had learned long ago in Oklahoma, before the Klan, before prison—he was back in the newspaper business.

Stephenson met a widow in Jonesboro, a Presbyterian Sunday school teacher—Martha Murray Sutton—whom he married in 1964. She was 55 and he was 74. She did not realize that he was still legally married to Martha Dickinson Stephenson of Seymour, Indiana. Stephenson spent the last two years of his life selling a type-cleaning machine that he had invented.

Gordon Englehart, an Indianapolis-based staff writer for the *Louisville Courier-Journal*, learned about Stephenson's death in 1978, after a three-month search across six states. He interviewed Stephenson's Tennessee widow. She had no idea of her late husband's flamboyant past or of his other wife, whom he had left behind in Indiana. She remembered him only as a kindly gentleman who had a fondness for children and often bought ice cream cones for the neighborhood children—blacks as well as whites.

Stephenson died on a hot summer's day while carrying a basket of fruit into the house from the car. He collapsed, clutching his chest. His heart stopped beating, and he died in his wife's arms. "I knew nothing of his background," his widow told Englehart. "Except that I loved him very much and we were married. He was a very wonderful person."

Englehart went to the Veterans Administration cemetery where Stephenson was buried and photographed the small marble slab that bears the inscription:

DAVID C STEPHENSON
TEXAS
2D LT CO D 36 INFANTRY
WORLD WAR I
AUG 21 1891   JUNE 28 1966

Was Stephenson Framed?

For twelve years, I studied the puzzling case of D. C. Stephenson, poring over archives looking for answers to sixty-year-old questions. Whenever I discussed the case with colleagues, they would inevitably ask the question, "Well . . . what do you think? Was he framed or wasn't he?"

During the long research process, I found many questions that appeared to have been deliberately avoided by the trial court. There were questions that Stephenson's attorneys could have raised in court which might have helped his case. They did not raise the questions. Were they simply unaware of the questions? Were they afraid of the answers? I looked for answers on a trail that has been cold for sixty years. For the most part, all I found were more questions.

Was he framed? I don't believe he was. There is some evidence that suggests he might have been. There is also ample evidence to suggest that he was not framed, that simple justice was done at Noblesville, and that he paid the price the law demanded. At least there were many powerful people who had motives to see him put in prison, and Madge Oberholtzer's death provided them with an opportunity to keep him there.

Did he cause Madge Oberholtzer to commit suicide? That, after all, was the official reason he was sent to prison. I feel that he was probably guilty of rape but not murder. My belief is that Madge committed suicide by taking poison in a larger dose than she had intended in an attempt to strike back at a man who had rejected her. At the very least, I do not believe that she was the innocent young girl that the state's attorneys depicted for the farmers who sat on the Noblesville jury.

Did he deserve to serve thirty-one years in prison? All the evidence suggests that, as Stephenson himself claimed, he was kept a political prisoner of the state for many years longer than he should have been. Other men of that time who committed first-degree murder and received life sentences served less time than he did on a charge of second-degree murder. Even if he was guilty of causing Madge's death, he served much longer than any "average murderer" of his day should have served. Incredible efforts were made to keep Stephenson in prison—long after most of his political cronies and enemies were either retired from public office or dead.

Unanswered Questions from the Trial

Consider the oddities of the case with what occurred immediately before and during the original trial in 1925.

The oddest piece of the puzzle is Madge Oberholtzer's dying declaration, which her attorney, Asa Smith, pieced together as she lay dying at her parent's home in Irvington.

Among the puzzling points:

• *The disappearance of the notary public who signed the dying declaration.* The woman, whom Asa Smith took with him to the Oberholtzer home, was never identified and never found. Smith and his partner, Griffith Dean, testified that they simply could not recall the woman's name. This is doubly mystifying in light of all the other elaborate precautions they took in obtaining and securing the declaration.

• *Madge's explanation of how she obtained the mercury bichloride poison.* She claimed that she had been abducted from her home in Irvington and raped during the train ride to Hammond. Yet her supposed "captors" allowed her to leave the hotel room the following morning to go buy a hat. Not only that, but her "guard" let her enter first a millinery shop—alone—and then a pharmacy—again, alone—while he waited outside each time. Common sense says that a kidnapper would not allow his victim this kind of freedom. Common sense also says that the victim, given this much opportunity, could surely have whispered a word to a hat shop clerk or a druggist and brought a squad of policemen descending on the kidnappers in an instant. Instead, Madge merely used the opportunity to purchase poison, which she took back to the hotel to consume later.

• *Madge's unusual choice of suicide weapons.* Given the wide selection of things you could buy to kill yourself at the average drugstore of 1925, it is extremely odd that Madge chose mercury bichloride to do herself in. Rat poison. Sleeping pills. Pain pills. Razor blades. Rope. She bypassed all these choices and, instead, bought a chemical that was intended to be used in greatly diluted quantities as a disinfectant.

But why mercury bichloride? I put that question to Frank Campbell, an attorney in Noblesville who worked with his father on Stephenson's case in 1939 and 1940 when Stephenson was attempting to win a new trial. After thinking about the question for several moments, Campbell replied, "I wish somebody had thought to ask that about the mercury bichloride forty years ago. I never did."[1]

I began to investigate other possible uses for mercury bichloride and discovered that in the 1920s it was sometimes used by women to induce an abortion. The chemical, slightly diluted and applied directly to the vaginal area, would sometimes bring an abrupt end to an unwanted pregnancy. (Used in too high a concentration, the chemical would also result in mercuric poisoning—one reason for the frequency of mercuric poisoning cases.) Stephenson later claimed that Madge was pregnant and that he lent her his car to take the trip to Hammond to get an abortion. Did she try to take matters in her own hands and, instead, make a terrible mistake?

• *The notion that Madge would kill herself because she had been raped.* This idea seems particularly ancient nowadays. But it was also out-of-date in the 1920s. Still, the state's attorneys played the theme of "lost innocence" to the rural jurors, representing Madge as a virginal child who was shocked into suicide by a brutal rape attack. It might have been believable for an inexperienced teenager who, perhaps, feared her parents' wrath and shame. It is less believable in the case of a twenty-eight-year-old woman. Rape might have provoked her to seek revenge against her attacker. It is less likely that rape would have led her to commit suicide.

• *The curious unwillingness of the court to allow any testimony that might question Madge's character.* Judge Sparks, perhaps revealing the code of honor of a man of his times, stoutly denied the defense attorneys the opportunity to introduce testimony into the trial that would call into question Madge's personal conduct. The attorneys had been prepared to bring Cora Householder to the witness stand to offer testimony that her husband, Charles, from whom she was getting a divorce, had been having an affair with Madge in the months before her death. Indeed, Cora Householder appeared in the courtroom. Judge Sparks quickly silenced her testimony and removed her from the stand at the first hint of where her testimony was leading. She later talked to reporters outside the courtroom, but this, of course, was not heard by the jurors. No other witnesses were allowed who might have revealed other "unpleasant" possibilities about Madge's personal conduct.

None of these questions were voiced during the trial, so Stephenson went to prison to serve his sentence.

Stephenson's Versions of What Happened

Throughout his time in prison, Stephenson maintained that he was not guilty of murdering Madge Oberholtzer. Over the years, he offered several versions of what "actually" happened during the train ride to Chicago.[2]

Among his explanations:

• He was traveling on the train, not with Madge Oberholtzer, but with the wife of a "prominent Hoosier politician." His claim: that he was trying to help the woman settle an argument with her husband. The politician, according to Stephenson, was Lieutenant Governor Harold Van Orman, and the woman was Van Orman's wife, Susie. His attorneys tried several times to get the Van Ormans to sign an affidavit to this effect; they never did.

• He claimed that Madge Oberholtzer had become pregnant, that Madge was going to Gary to get an abortion, and that he merely lent her the use of his car and his chauffeur, Shorty DeFriese, to "take her anywhere she wanted to go."

To back up this claim, Stephenson's attorneys secured a statement from Dr. G. B. Jackson, a gynecological specialist. Jackson said that he had been called to the Oberholtzer home by Dr. Kingsbury to perform an examination of Madge Oberholtzer on the evening of April 6, 1925, to determine if she showed any signs of having recently undergone an abortion. Jackson said his exam did not uncover signs of an abortion, but that he told Kingsbury if an abortion had been performed two weeks earlier, she would have had time to heal. Jackson was never called for testimony by either side during the original trial.

Stephenson also obtained an affidavit from a Dr. Mabel Faulds from Gary, Indiana, who claimed that she had performed an "illegal operation"—a euphemism for abortions in that time—on a woman who matched Madge's description. But this information was also ignored.

In 1980, I decided to try to follow this thread. I learned there indeed was a Dr. Mabel C. Lawrence Faulds who was practicing medicine in Gary, Indiana, in 1925. Born in 1881, she was a graduate of the Dearborn Medical College in Chicago. She kept an office at 708 Broadway on the second floor of a two-story building that also housed the People's Trust & Savings Bank. She died in 1962.

During her years of practice, Faulds's state medical license was revoked twice. The first time was in 1948, when it was revoked in August for non-payment of registration fees and reinstated in October of that same year. The second revocation came in May 1954 when Faulds was 74 years old. She had just been convicted of performing abortions and was sentenced to three to fourteen years at the Indiana State Women's Prison and fined $100. Her 78-year-old partner, Dr. Flavia M. Doty, was also convicted of performing abortions and sentenced to a term in the Indiana Women's Prison. That she was convicted of performing abortions 24 years after Stephenson first mentioned her name in public testimony suggests that there might have been some truth to his story. But no one in the Indiana legal system bothered to check out the story. The State Board of Trustees denied Stephenson's clemency application.

These claims—all made by Stephenson in the late 1930s and 1940s when he was attempting to win a new trial—were never fully investigated. Though he filed many petitions for a new trial—more than 40 petitions in 31 years—the courts simply rejected the petitions, and Stephenson remained imprisoned.

If he knew all this in 1925, the question begs for an answer, why didn't he bring this information into his original trial, take the witness stand, and let his lawyers call for testimony from the people who could have provided him an alibi?

Stephenson always claimed that it was fear for his life that kept him from testifying. He claimed that he had been visited in his Noblesville jail cell by Robert F. McNay, a member of the Walter Bossert faction of the Klan, before the trial began. He said that McNay had warned that if Stephenson took the witness stand to testify in his own defense, the Klan would see that he was murdered there in the courtroom.[3]

McNay was the manager of the Red Star League, a political unit of the Ku Klux Klan and a great titan of the Klan under Grand Dragon Walter Bossert. McNay was friends with another important klansman, Robert W. Lyons, an attorney, who was treasurer of the organization under Bossert. Lyons had been an assistant of Stephenson's but later switched to Bossert's side.

Could McNay or Lyons have actually issued or carried out a death threat?

Stephenson alleged that they already had.

A Second Murder—Unsolved

Early on the morning of July 3, 1925, a Noblesville man, Harry Lowe, discovered a young woman lying on the roadside near a bridge. The woman had been badly beaten. Her face was mutilated, and blood was caked on her body and clothes. Lowe put the woman, who was still breathing, in his car and took her to the hospital at Noblesville. She died there at 8:00 A.M.[4]

The woman's name was Edith Irene Dean, a twenty-five-year-old secretary of the Young Women's Republican Club in Indianapolis. No arrests were ever made in connection with her death.

Stephenson claimed, however, that he knew who was responsible and collected affidavits from witnesses to support his accusation. He even had an affidavit, taken from Dean in his own jail cell only a few hours before she was murdered.

According to Stephenson, Dean came to visit him in the Noblesville jail at 6:00 P.M. on the evening of July 2. She came to tell him that two Ku Klux Klan officials, Robert McNay and Robert Lyons, had tried on three occasions during that week to persuade her to sign a statement similar to the "dying declaration" of Madge Oberholtzer. The statement, she said, was similar in all respects to the Oberholtzer statement—a story about how Stephenson had abducted her and raped her—except that all the events were to have taken place in Louisville, Kentucky, instead of Hammond, Indiana. She claimed that McNay and Lyons offered her fifty thousand dollars to sign the statement that would be used "to smear the reputation of D. C. Stephenson." She told them she would consider their offer. Then she drove to Noblesville to report what had happened to Stephenson and his attorneys.

Dean left the Noblesville jail at about 10:00 P.M. that evening. Her car was followed, according to Stephenson, by a car carrying McNay, Klan organizer Ray Huffington, and another man. They forced her car off the road, then made her get into a Buick sedan that belonged to Lyons. They took her to a dairy barn west of the White River in Hamilton County where they questioned her and beat her for an hour and a half, trying to find out everything she had told Stephenson.

Around midnight, Robert J. Wadsworth was driving his automobile from the town of Carmel in Hamilton County to his home in Castleton. Along the way, he had a flat tire and stopped near the Eller's Bridge over the White River to fix it.

Wadsworth later told Stephenson that he could see another car parked at the side of the road about two hundred yards ahead of his car. He started to walk toward the car. As he approached the car, he heard a woman scream twice. Two men were holding a woman up against the back of the car, and one of the men was viciously beating her. Her hair was covered with blood, and her head was bleeding profusely.

"Don't kill her, McNay," Wadsworth heard one of the men say. And the man addressed as McNay replied, "Why not? That's what Bob Lyons wants us to do, ain't it?"

Wadsworth did not interfere with the beating but slipped back to his car and drove away. He drove all the way home on the flat tire, afraid that McNay might pursue him and kill him, too. Wadsworth went to the Noblesville jail two days later, on July 5, and told D. C. Stephenson and his attorneys what he had seen and heard, and filled out an affidavit describing it all.

The next morning, Edith Dean's body was examined by Charles Coaltrin, the coroner of Hamilton County. He declared that she had died as the result of a ruptured spleen, which she had received during the beating. No one was ever arrested for her murder.

Nearly all of Stephenson's story checks out. Indeed, a young Indianapolis woman, Edith Dean, was murdered in Hamilton County early in the morning on July 3, 1925. And no one was ever arrested in the case.

McNay was later convicted in Terre Haute, Indiana, in another case, the molesting of a fourteen-year-old girl. He was also tried on federal charges for participation in an interstate crime ring and served time in the federal penitentiary at Ft. Leavenworth, Kansas.

The story goes a good distance toward explaining why Stephenson then, in August, was capable of being threatened out of testifying in his own defense. If McNay had truly carried out such a brutal act against so minor a character as Dean, at what limit would the Klan stop to silence Stephenson?

Of course, the story also has some obvious problems. If Wadsworth saw what he described to Stephenson, why didn't he tell the story to Sheriff Gooding and testify against McNay and Lyons?

Stephenson said that he had warned Wadsworth to say nothing about what he had seen and heard to anyone or else he might become a murderer's target, too. Only twenty years (to the day) after Edith Dean was last seen alive, on July 2, 1945, did Wadsworth put his story down on paper in an affidavit that Stephenson used to try to convince the courts to grant him a new trial.

Stephenson included these charges in a petition for *writ of error coram nobis* in the Hamilton County Circuit Court in 1945. Indiana Attorney General James A. Emmert filed a petition for writ of prohibition with the Indiana Supreme Court to block Stephenson's writ. The attorney general dismissed Stephenson's tale of Edith Dean's death as a "weird tale of intrigue . . . the 'criminal history' of various parties not directly connected with the issues of the case." And that was as far as Stephenson's story ever got. His claims were never investigated by the state.

Robert Lyons:
A Missing Link in the Stephenson Story?

But who, exactly, was Robert W. Lyons? And was Lyons really powerful enough to keep Stephenson in prison? Perhaps so.

Robert Lyons was the son of a Presbyterian minister, a veteran of World War I who served as an army field clerk. He graduated from Earlham College and was studying law at the University of Chicago when the war interrupted his studies. After the war, he returned to Indiana and got a job as a furniture salesman.

This was about the time he first met D. C. Stephenson. Stephenson liked Lyons and offered him a job with the Ku Klux Klan, canvassing for new members in the upper Midwest. A super-patriot himself, Lyons was attracted by the strong nationalism of the Klan.

Lyons went up into Wisconsin and Minnesota to recruit klansmen. But he soon discovered that there were too many foreign-born Norwegians and Swedes. They were enthusiastic about celebrating their new citizenship by joining the flag-waving Klan, but the matter of their birth made them ineligible for membership. So Lyons proposed the formation of a special auxiliary organization that would allow "acceptable" foreign-born people to enter a group based on Klan principles. This idea caught on, and memberships in Wisconsin and Minnesota began to grow.

By the time Lyons returned to Indiana, Stephenson was out of the Klan and Walter Bossert was the new grand dragon. Lyons signed on with Bossert's organization and eventually became treasurer of the Klan for Indiana.

In 1927, Lyons received his law degree from Indiana University. He applied for membership in the Indianapolis Bar Association but was denied membership because of his prominent Klan connections. This was only the first time that Lyons's Klan background would hinder his career.

He became a powerful Indiana lobbyist and represented a national chain of grocery stores before the General Assembly. He was elected executive vice president of the National Chain Store Association in 1927. He became a specialist in tax law and began to practice law in Washington, D.C.

Lyons continued to live in Indianapolis. Throughout the 1930s and 1940s he lived in magnificent style on the north side of Indianapolis, much as Stephenson had once lived in Irvington. Lyons bought an impressive collection of valuable paintings. He kept a suite of offices in the prestigious, Republican-dominated Columbia Club on Monument Circle. Lyons and his family vacationed at a winter home in St. Petersburg, Florida. Some believed that he was a millionaire. As Irving Leibowitz of the *Indianapolis Times* put it, "If he was not a millionaire, he lived like one."[5]

But money alone was not enough to help Lyons shake his past connections with the Ku Klux Klan. His involvement with the organization in the 1920s marked him for life.

In the late 1930s, he became active in American Legion activities and began campaigning to become the Indiana member of the legion's national executive committee. Opponents reminded legion members of Lyons's Klan connections, and his supporters faded away.

He went on to become an important "behind the scenes" leader in the Republican party. The *Indianapolis Times* described him as a "kingmaker in Indiana politics."[6]

In 1944, Lyons was selected to serve as a Republican national committeeman to represent Indiana. The newspapers remembered, however, that he had once been a prominent klansman. Editorials appeared in Indiana newspapers from Indianapolis, Richmond, South Bend, and Michigan City, urging the state's Republican leaders to rethink this idea. Under enormous pressure from the state's Republican leaders, Lyons resigned from the national post June 13, 1944, eleven days after he was elected.

This reaction, of course, was based merely on the knowledge that Lyons had once been the treasurer of the Ku Klux Klan.

What would the reaction have been if Stephenson had been allowed out of prison to establish his claim that Lyons was linked to the murder of Edith Dean?

"Observers of Lyons thought perhaps his passion for secrecy may have dated back to the Ku Klux Klan era in Indiana," claimed one 1949 newspaper profile of Lyons.

Lyons died in 1949 of a heart attack in a Washington, D.C., hotel room. He was fifty-three years old. In obituaries of Lyons, all three Indianapolis newspapers referred to him as a "mystery man" of Indiana politics.

"He made occasional trips back to Indianapolis," wrote Ralph L. Brooks for the *Indianapolis Star*'s front-page obituary of Lyons. "What he did, whom he talked with on those return trips was known to few—only those whom he contacted—although at times word ran like a prairie fire among politicians that 'Bob' Lyons was in town. But Lyons usually had transacted his business and quietly gone back to Washington or down to Florida by the time word got around. And only a few persons had seen him."[7]

Certainly Lyons had both the possible motive and, because of his political connections, the opportunity to keep Stephenson behind bars indefinitely.

Perhaps the most curious aspect of the Lyons connection is the proximity of his death—on February 3, 1949—to Stephenson's parole from prison on March 17, 1950. With Lyons gone, it wouldn't have mattered anymore what Stephenson might have said about him. Stephenson was no longer a political liability, just a relic.

The story of Lyons's involvement may be, as the attorney general called it, only a "maniacal dissertation." It may have been only one more of Stephenson's neatly constructed lies, built to fit a certain set of facts. The most difficult part of sifting through Stephenson's life is that he told so many lies and so often that it is difficult to know when he was telling the truth and when he was lying. But still the possibility lingers: was this one time when he was telling the truth?

The most popular view among most Hoosiers who are familiar with the case is that Stephenson got what he deserved—even if it was not precisely for the crime he was alleged to have committed. He was responsible for bringing the Klan to an incredible level of power. He was guilty of invading the legislature and buying politicians around the state. While he did not invent corrupt politics in Indiana, he certainly did as much as he could to take advantage of it.

Stephenson's last word on his own guilt or innocence was provided in a letter he wrote to an Indianapolis newspaper: "I should have been put in jail for my political activities, but I am not guilty of murder."

In his book, *So They Framed Stephenson*, Robert Butler quoted former Indiana Governor Harry G. Leslie, one of the many governors who refused to grant clemency to Stephenson. As Leslie explained it, "Ninety percent of them [the prisoners in Michigan City] are serving time for things they did not do, because they should be where they are for the things they did do. Stephenson is one of the ninety percent."[8]

When asked, several years after the trial in Noblesville, if he believed that Stephenson was guilty, Will Remy replied tersely, "Well, a jury and seventeen courts, both Federal and State, have said he was guilty. That's good enough for me."[9]

Notes

Chapter One ■ The Closing Door

1. *Indianapolis News,* November 14, 1925, 1–3.
2. *Indianapolis Times,* November 16, 1926, 1.
3. *Indianapolis Star,* November 15, 1925, 1–10.
4. *Indianapolis Star,* November 16, 1925, 1.
5. Unpublished memoirs of William H. Remy, in the D. C. Stephenson Collection, Indiana Historical Society, Indianapolis, Indiana, 258.
6. *Indianapolis Star,* November 17, 1925, 1–8.
7. *Indianapolis Star,* November 22, 1925, 1.

Chapter Two ■ A Nobody from Nowhere

1. Harold Zink, "A Case Study of a Political Boss," *Psychiatry: Journal of the Biology and Pathology of Interpersonal Relations* 1 (November 1938): 527–33. Zink credited Stephenson's quote to "associates of Stephenson" (most likely Court Asher).
2. Scraps of Stephenson's fake biography are found in many of the pre-1925 articles that were written about him. The best is an interview with Stephenson by Ned McIntosh of the *New York World,* August 14, 1924, from which these examples are taken.
3. William G. Shepherd, "Indiana's Mystery Man," *Collier's,* January 8, 1927, 8.
4. The "real" account of Stephenson's early years is compiled from three principal sources: Edgar Allen Booth, *The Mad Mullah of America* (Columbus, Ohio: Boyd Ellison, 1927); Zink, "Case Study" (cited above); and the notes of newspaper reporter Harold C. Feightner, collected in the Indiana Division, Indiana State Library, Indianapolis, Indiana, and the Franklin College Library, Franklin, Indiana. The Booth book is a rambling, often-vindictive account of Stephenson's rise to power in the Klan, written shortly after his fall. The author claimed to be a close associate of Stephenson's, but the name "Edgar Allen Booth" does not appear on the membership lists for that time period nor did I find mention of that name in other Klan documents. I believe that "Edgar Allen Booth" is most likely a pseudonym. Many of Booth's comments on Stephenson's early years are supported by similar accounts in the more academic work of Zink, who cited as his sources "early associates of Stephenson in Oklahoma." The material in the Feightner files comes from his years of writing about Stephenson and the apparent preparation of an unfinished book about the Stephenson case. The

collection of Feightner papers at Franklin College is included as part of the collection of Roger Branigin, Feightner's good friend and former Indiana governor.

5. What was Stephenson's father's real name? This is a good example of just how much of a mystery man Stephenson really was. Sources do not even agree on his parents' names! Booth (cited above) refers to Stephenson's father as "Arizona D. Stephenson." Feightner, however, says that Stephenson's brother's name was Arizona. A source within Booth's book, however, indicates that after Stephenson grew up and left home, his parents moved to Manhattan, Kansas, where his father died some years later. A check of the city files in Manhattan turned up the name "Andrew Monroe Stephenson," who died September 17, 1923, at the age of eighty-four. His date of birth was September 15, 1839, and he was a native of Missouri. His age corresponds with that of D. C. Stephenson's father—fifty-two years old when his son was born in 1891. For these reasons, I suggest that this was most likely Stephenson's real father. D. C. himself was absolutely no help at all in settling the matter. In a May 17, 1965, application for a burial allowance from the Veterans Administration, he listed his mother's name as "Blanche Bennett" and his father as "Howard R. Stephenson." Howard and Blanche Bennett were Stephenson's bodyguard and housekeeper at his home in Indianapolis.

6. The historical background of the Maysville, Oklahoma, area is constructed from interviews conducted by the author in 1981 with several residents of the area, a few of whom had memories of the pre-statehood days of Maysville.

7. The track of Stephenson's newspaper career is derived from material in Booth's *Mad Mullah* and Feightner's papers, Indiana State Library (both cited above).

8. Material on farmer/publisher John Cooper was supplied by his son, Walter Cooper, in an interview with the author, 1981.

9. Joseph E. and Jessamine S. Kallenbach, *American State Governors, 1776–1976, Volume 1, Electoral and Personal Data* (Dobbs Ferry, N.Y.: Oceana Publications, 1977), 476.

10. Oscar Ameringer, *If You Don't Weaken: The Autobiography of Oscar Ameringer* (New York: Henry Holt and Company, 1940), 271.

11. Ibid., 274–75.

12. Booth's *Mad Mullah* and Feightner's papers, Indiana State Library (both cited above).

13. Feightner papers, Indiana State Library (cited above).

14. Certified copy of marriage license of D. C. Stephenson and Nettie Hamilton, Johnston County, Oklahoma, March 26, 1915.

15. "Woman and Child in Action for Support," *Indianapolis News*, March 18, 1925, 1.

16. Divorce papers, *Violet M. Stephenson v. David C. Stephenson*, Court of Domestic Relations, Summit County, Akron, Ohio, February 28, 1924, D. C. Stephenson Collection (cited above).

17. Ibid.

18. Booth, *Mad Mullah*, 10.

Chapter Three ■ The Early Days in Evansville

1. Statistical material on Evansville is from two sources: "Facts About Evansville Worth Remembering," *Evansville City Directory*, 1922,

29–30, and John E. Iglehart, ed., *An Account of Vanderburgh County from Its Organization*, included in Logan Esarey, *History of Indiana from Its Exploration to 1922* (Dayton, Ohio: Dayton Historical Publishing Company, 1923), 215–17, 259–65.

2. The Vendome Hotel served as Stephenson's base of operations during his year-and-a-half stay in Evansville. All his business mail was sent to the hotel, and he used it as a return address on his outgoing mail as well. See correspondence in the D. C. Stephenson Collection (cited above).

3. "Mayor Proposes Improvements of Local Highways," *Evansville Journal-News*, January 5, 1920, 1.

4. Stephenson's exaggerations of his military record are covered in Booth's *Mad Mullah*, Shepherd's "Indiana's Mystery Man," and Zink's "Case Study" (all cited above).

5. Julian's titles are taken from the 1922 *Evansville City Directory*. Julian was one of the few who kept faith with Stephenson. Even after Stephenson was in prison, Julian continued to work diligently for his release, always believing that Stephenson was innocent.

6. Stephenson's attempts to start a veterans organization are outlined in the Reverend V. W. Blair's pamphlet, "The Stephenson Case" (privately printed, 1940), under the heading "Statement of D. C. Stephenson to his attorneys." Private collection.

7. The list of Evansville fraternal groups is taken from the 1922 *Evansville City Directory*.

8. David M. Chalmers, *Hooded Americanism: The First Century of the Ku Klux Klan: 1865 to the Present* (Garden City, N.Y.: Doubleday & Company, 1965), 29.

9. William G. Shepherd, "How I Put Over the Klan," interview with William J. Simmons, *Collier's*, July 14, 1928. This article was the first of a three-part interview with Simmons. Subsequent interviews appeared July 21 and July 28, 1928.

10. McIntosh interview with Stephenson, *New York World*, August 14, 1924.

11. Booth, *Mad Mullah*, 13–14.

Chapter Four ■ The Klan Reborn

1. One of the most readable modern sources of information on the Klan's history is David M. Chalmers's *Hooded Americanism* (cited above). His book provided much of the information on the early Klan. A newer work, Wyn Craig Wade's *The Fiery Cross: The Ku Klux Klan in America* (New York: Simon and Schuster, 1987), includes some historical background on the early Klan but focuses more closely on the modern Klans. For a more in-depth treatment of the Klan in the Midwest, see Norman Frederic Weaver's "The Knights of the Ku Klux Klan in Wisconsin, Indiana, Ohio and Michigan," Ph.D. diss., University of Wisconsin, 1954. A more recent work—Frank M. Cates, "The Ku Klux Klan in Indiana Politics: 1920–1925," Ph.D. diss., Indiana University, 1971—focuses even more closely on Stephenson's political organization.

2. Curiously, there seems to be a slight resemblance between Stephenson's story and the fictional hero of Thomas Dixon, Jr.'s *The Leopard's Spots* (though only to a certain point). It is easy to imagine that Simmons might have presented Stephenson with a copy of the book, since it is known that Simmons had read it himself. The book might have fed some of Stephenson's egomaniacal dreams.

3. The best original source of information on the Klan's revival and Simmons's role is Shepherd's three-part interview with Simmons that appeared in July 1928 issues of *Collier's* (cited above). These include details of how Simmons eventually lost control of the organization.

4. Mike Royko, *Boss* (New York: Signet Books, New American Library, 1971), 35–38. This is a biography of former Chicago Mayor Richard J. Dailey.

5. John Higham, *Strangers in the Land: Patterns of American Nativism, 1860–1925* (New Brunswick, N.J.: Rutgers University Press, 1967), 229–32.

6. William G. Shepherd, "Ku Klux Koin," *Collier's*, July 21, 1928, 38–39.

7. The Klan language and the list of Klan questions are from Robert Coughlan's article "Konklave in Kokomo," reprinted in *The Aspirin Age, 1919–1941*, Isabel Leighton, ed. (New York: Simon and Schuster, 1949; New York: Simon and Schuster, Touchstone Books, 1976), 118–19.

8. Stephenson's trip to Atlanta is mentioned in several sources, including Chalmers's *Hooded Americanism* and Zink's "Case Study" (both cited above). Stephenson alludes to this visit in a statement to his lawyers in the pamphlet "The Stephenson Case" (also cited above).

9. Kenneth T. Jackson, *The Ku Klux Klan in the City* (New York: Oxford University Press, 1967; New York: Oxford University Press, 1977), 145.

10. *New York World*, September 1921.

11. William J. Simmons was quoted by William G. Shepherd in "Ku Klux Koin" (cited above): "Certain newspapers also aided us by inducing Congress to investigate us. The result was that Congress gave us the best advertising we ever got. Congress made us."

12. Calvin D. Linton, *The American Almanac* (Nashville, Tenn.: Thomas Nelson, Inc., 1977), 303.

13. Jackson, *Klan in the City*, 146–47.

Chapter Five ■ The Klansman and the Mayor

1. Court Asher quoted in William G. Shepherd's "Indiana's Mystery Man," *Collier's*, January 8, 1927, 9.

2. *Evansville Courier* eulogy and biographical information on Mayor Benjamin Bosse are from John E. Iglehart, ed., "An Account of Vanderburgh County from Its Organization" (cited above), 504–7.

3. This incident is taken from the unpublished manuscript "*Courier* History (as told to Karl K. Knecht by Col. William J. Rogers, Oct. 25, 1956)." This piece is contained in historical files of the *Evansville Courier*, Evansville, Indiana, 4.

4. Louis Francis Budenz, "There's Mud on Indiana's White Robes," *The Nation*, July 27, 1927, 81.

5. Zink, "Case Study," 528–29.

6. Blair, "The Stephenson Case" (cited above).

7. *Evansville Journal*, March 26, 1922, 1.

8. *Evansville Journal*, March 27, 1922, 1.

9. *Evansville Journal*, March 29, 1922, 1.

10. Election results from the *Indianapolis Star*, May, 5, 1922, 1.

11. Divorce papers, *Violet M. Stephenson v. David C. Stephenson,* Court of Domestic Relations, Summit County, Akron, Ohio, February 28, 1924. A copy is found in the D. C. Stephenson Collection, Indiana Historical Society, Indianapolis, Indiana.

12. Booth, *Mad Mullah,* 35.

Chapter Six ■ Citizens of No Mean City

1. Booth Tarkington, *The Magnificent Ambersons* (New York: Doubleday, Page and Company, 1918), 389.

2. *Violet M. Stephenson v. David C. Stephenson,* State of Ohio, Summit County Court of Common Pleas, No. 47872. A copy of the transcript of the divorce hearing is found in the D. C. Stephenson Collection (cited above).

3. Descriptions of Stephenson's office are found in John Niblack's *The Life and Times of a Hoosier Judge* (self-published, no date), 194–95; John B. Martin's *Indiana: An Interpretation* (New York: Alfred A. Knopf, 1947), 193–95; and Booth's *Mad Mullah,* 36–38.

4. John A. Davis, "The Ku Klux Klan in Indiana, 1920–1930: An Historical Study," Ph.D. diss., Northwestern University, 1966, 326.

5. Leonard J. Moore, "White Protestant Nationalism in the 1920's: The Ku Klux Klan in Indiana," Ph.D. diss., University of California at Los Angeles, 1985, 17.

6. Lowell Mellett, "Klan and Church," *The Atlantic Monthly* 132, no. 5 (November 1923): 588.

7. *Papers Read at the Meeting of the Grand Dragons, Knights of the Ku Klux Klan at Their First Annual Meeting held at Asheville, North Carolina, July 1923* (no publishing information), author's personal collection, 127.

8. Jacob Piatt Dunn, *Greater Indianapolis, Vol. 1* (Chicago: Lewis Publishing Company, 1910), 433.

9. *Indianapolis News,* August 24, 1927, and August 29, 1927, clippings in the Indiana Biographical Files, Indiana Division, Indiana State Library, Indianapolis, Indiana.

10. Paul Brown, ed., *Indianapolis Men of Affairs* (Indianapolis, Ind.: American Biographical Society, 1923), 476–77.

11. *Papers Read at the Meeting of the Grand Dragons* (cited above), 25, 29.

Chapter Seven ■ The Art of the Double-cross

1. Material on the National Horse Thief Detective Association is taken from the *Journal of the National Horse Thief Detective Association, 1922,* from a private collection.

2. William E. Wilson, "Long, Hot Summer in Indiana," *American Heritage* 16, no. 5 (August 1965): 56.

3. Davis, "Ku Klux Klan in Indiana," 134.

4. Simmons's vacation is mentioned in Jackson's *Klan in the City,* 13.

5. A catalog of Clarke's problems is found in Robert L. Duffus's "Salesmen of Hate: The Ku Klux Klan," in *World's Work,* 1923.

6. The account of how Simmons was deposed is written combining accounts that appeared in William G. Shepherd's "The Fiery Double-Cross," *Collier's,* July 28, 1928, 9, 47–49; and Chalmers's *Hooded Americanism,* 100–105.

Chapter Eight ■ The Start of a New Regime

1. Indiana membership figures are from an audit report of the Indiana Klan by the accounting firm Ernst & Ernst, found in the D. C. Stephenson Collection, Indiana Historical Society, Indianapolis, Indiana.

2. Moore, "White Protestant Nationalism," 10–12. Moore also questions whether or not Stephenson was really as effective a Klan leader as others supposed him to be. "While Stephenson carved out a sensational public image, in general he accomplished little as leader of Indiana's massive Klan movement. . . . Aside from establishing his own political base . . . Stephenson did little to elevate the Klan's ideals above mere rhetoric."

3. List of Stephenson's personnel is from various sources, primarily the material in the D. C. Stephenson Collection (cited above).

4. Martin, *Indiana: An Interpretation*, 205.

5. Robert S. Lynd and Helen Merrell Lynd, *Middletown: A Study in Modern American Culture* (New York: Harcourt, Brace & World, Inc., 1929; New York: Harcourt, Brace & Jovanovich, Inc., Harvest/HBJ, 1956), 482.

Chapter Nine ■ The Rising Opposition

1. Elmer Davis, *Show Window* (New York: The John Day Company, 1927), 191.

2. Chalmers, *Hooded Americanism*, 50–55.

3. Joseph Michael White, "The Ku Klux Klan in Indiana in the 1920's as Viewed by the Indiana Catholic and Record," Master's thesis, Butler University, 1974, 27–53. This exhaustive paper, which includes much more information about the struggles between the Klan and the Catholics in Indianapolis, is in the collection of the Catholic Archdiocese, Indianapolis, Indiana.

4. Ibid., 36.

5. *Tolerance*, Chicago, Illinois, March 18–September 9, 1923. Available on microfilm in the Indiana State Library, Indianapolis, Indiana.

6. Ernst & Ernst audit report, D. C. Stephenson Collection (cited above).

7. Davis, "The Ku Klux Klan in Indiana, 1920–1930," 137–46.

Chapter Ten ■ "Americanism Gone a Little Sour"

1. Robert L. Duffus, "Salesmen of Hate: The Ku Klux Klan," *World's Work*, 46 (1923): 31–38.

2. Booth, *Mad Mullah*, 70–72.

3. Testimony of D. C. Stephenson before a Marion County grand jury, October 1927, on microfilm in the Indiana State Library, Indianapolis, Indiana.

4. Dale's story is reprinted in *Tolerance*, June 24, 1923, 8–10. Also, the *Winchester Democrat*, June 7, 1923, 8; and June 14, 1923, 1. Both are available on microfilm in the Indiana State Library, Indianapolis, Indiana.

5. *Winchester Journal-Herald*, June 27, 1923, 1.

6. Robert Coughlan, "Konklave in Kokomo," reprinted in *The Aspirin Age, 1919–1941*, Isabel Leighton, ed., (New York: Simon and Schuster, 1949; New York: Simon and Schuster, Touchstone Books, 1976), 105–29.

Chapter Eleven ■ Kokomo, Indiana

1. Court Asher talked to William G. Shepherd about his airplane flights with Stephenson in "Indiana's Mystery Man," *Collier's*, January 8, 1927, 8. Also see John B. Martin, *Indiana: An Interpretation* (New York: Alfred A. Knopf, 1947), 184–216.

2. Detailed accounts of the traffic problems caused by the Klan rally and stories about the rally were carried in the July 4, 1923, issues of the *Indianapolis Times* and *Indianapolis News*; also the July 5, 1923, issues of the *Indianapolis Star* and the *Kokomo Dispatch*.

3. The near-accident with the airplane was mentioned only in the July 5, 1923, *Indianapolis Star* front-page account of the rally.

4. Descriptions of the rally are taken from the newspaper editions cited in note 2 above and from the Klan's own newspaper, the *Fiery Cross*, July 6, 1923. Available on microfilm from the Indiana State Library, Indianapolis, Indiana.

5. Niblack, *The Life and Times of a Hoosier Judge* (self-published, no date), 194–96. Niblack's version of the rally is both witty and readable.

6. The full text of this most interesting Stephenson speech is found in the *Fiery Cross*, July 6, 1923, 1.

7. Niblack, *Life and Times of a Hoosier Judge*, 196.

8. Interview by the author with a Howard County farmer and his wife, August 1984.

9. Robert Coughlan, "Konklave in Kokomo" (cited above), 110.

Chapter Twelve ■ The Ladies' Man

1. Details of Stephenson's house and its history come from my interviews with the home's present owner, Robert Van Buskirk, who had done extensive research on its history. The sale to Stephenson is documented in papers among the D. C. Stephenson Collection in the Indiana Historical Society, Indianapolis, Indiana. Details of the home's renovation are also contained in that collection.

2. The figures are from an audit of the Indiana Klan conducted by Ernst & Ernst public accountants. The study was done by the firm's Atlanta office, commissioned by Imperial Wizard Evans. The full report is found in the D. C. Stephenson Collection (cited above).

3. The details of Stephenson's cars, staff, and personal property come from various sources, including the 1928 Indiana attorney general's investigation, Indiana State Library, Indianapolis, Indiana; the D. C. Stephenson Collection (cited above); testimony of Court Asher to the 1927 Marion County grand jury, also in the D. C. Stephenson Collection; and the Harold C. Feightner papers, Indiana Division, Indiana State Library, Indianapolis, Indiana.

4. A technical report on the Reomar II is contained in the D. C. Stephenson Collection (cited above).

5. The reports on Stephenson's involvement with women come from two primary sources. The first is the D. C. Stephenson Collection (cited above), which includes attorneys' notes and police investigation records that were gathered for the 1925 murder trial. Among these are the statements of three women who knew Stephenson. These are quoted without reference to names, since at least one of the three women was still living and did not wish to have her name associated with any book on Stephenson. The second source is the tribunal of the Evansville,

Indiana, Klan of 1924, which officially removed Stephenson from the national organization. Part of the tribunal focused on his "immoral acts" with women. Included in the tribunal is the account of his arrests in Columbus, Ohio, and depositions from the witnesses. A copy of the tribunal report is in the Feightner papers (cited above).

Chapter Thirteen ■ Brief Glory

1. Kenneth T. Jackson, *The Ku Klux Klan in the City, 1915–1930* (New York: Oxford University Press, 1967; New York: Oxford University Press, 1977), 151.

2. An ad for the Buckeye Lake, Ohio, klonvocation appeared in the *Fiery Cross*, July 6, 1923, with lists of supporting Ohio klaverns.

3. Russ Walters, interview with the author, October 1981.

4. Charles Essex, interview with the author, October 1981.

5. *Fiery Cross*, July 20, 1923, 1.

6. This account is taken from the tribunal of the Evansville Klan of 1924 and is included in the Feightner papers, Indiana State Library (cited above).

7. Emerson H. Loucks, *The Ku Klux Klan in Pennsylvania: A Study in Nativism* (Harrisburg, Pa.: The Telegraph Press, 1936), 52–62.

8. Ibid., 49.

9. Booth, *Mad Mullah*, 44–45.

10. Hiram Wesley Evans, letter to D. C. Stephenson, August 2, 1923, D. C. Stephenson Collection (cited above).

11. Audit report of the Indiana Klan by the accounting firm Ernst & Ernst, D. C. Stephenson Collection (cited above).

12. D. C. Stephenson, letter to Hiram Wesley Evans, October 12, 1928, D. C. Stephenson Collection (cited above).

13. D. C. Stephenson, letter to Walter Bossert and others, September 27, 1923, D. C. Stephenson Collection (cited above).

14. Booth, *Mad Mullah*, 131–32.

15. Ibid.

Chapter Fourteen ■ "The Law in Indiana"

1. W. H. Settle, quoted in the *Indianapolis News*, December 30, 1925, 1.

2. David M. Chalmers, *Hooded Americanism: The First Century of the Ku Klux Klan: 1865 to the Present* (Garden City, N.Y.: Doubleday and Company, 1965), 143–44, 167. Max Bentley, "The Ku Klux Klan in Indiana," *McClure's Magazine*, May 1924, 23–32.

3. Bentley, "Ku Klux Klan in Indiana," 31.

4. Ibid., 30–31. Also see "The Kluxing of Politics in Indiana," *Tolerance*, May 27, 1923, 16. Written by an unnamed Kansas City reporter, the story was first published in the Bellingham, Washington, *Herald* and reprinted in *Tolerance*. A much closer investigation of the Klan's political involvements is contained in Frank M. Cates's "The Ku Klux Klan in Indiana Politics: 1920–1925," Ph.D. diss., Indiana University, 1971. These are the sources for information on the Klan in the 1922 primaries.

5. Bentley, "Ku Klux Klan in Indiana," 29.

6. *The State of Indiana v. The Knights of the Ku Klux Klan, et al.*, Marion County Circuit Court, 41769 (1925–29), Indianapolis, Indiana, papers of Attorney General Arthur Gilliom (microfilm), Indiana State Library, Indianapolis, Indiana.

7. Biographical information on Walter Bossert is from obituaries in the Richmond, Indiana, *Palladium-Item*, January 15, 1946. and the *Indianapolis Star*, January 15, 1946. Material was also gathered from Bossert's sister-in-law, Thelma Bossert, in an interview with the author November 15, 1981.

8. Robert S. Lynd and Helen Merrell Lynd, *Middletown: A Study in Modern American Culture* (New York: Harcourt, Brace & World, Inc., 1929; New York: Harcourt, Brace & Jovanovich, Inc., Harvest/HBJ, 1956), 484.

Chapter Fifteen ■ The Man Who Would Be Governor

1. Horace M. Coats, "Jackson's Life Story Is Rise from Factory to Statehouse," *Indianapolis Star*, January 12, 1925, Indiana Biographical Files, Indiana Division, Indiana State Library, Indianapolis, Indiana.

2. The rift between McCray and Jackson over the Klan is referred to in "The Kluxing of Politics in Indiana," *Tolerance*, May 27, 1923, 16 (cited above).

3. *Tolerance*, April 15, 1923, 1–2, 15.

4. *Indianapolis Times*, April 13, 1923, 1.

5. The gifts between Stephenson and Jackson are mentioned in several sources, including *The State of Indiana v. The Knights of the Ku Klux Klan, et al.*, papers of Arthur Gilliom (cited above); also Walter W. Watson's " 'Senator,' $2,500 Horse, Is Dead; Choked On Corn Cob, Report," *Indianapolis News*, July 15, 1927, 1.

6. The account of McCray's troubles is detailed in John L. Niblack's *The Life and Times of a Hoosier Judge* (self-published, no date), 163–86, 252–58.

7. Ibid., 253.

Chapter Sixteen ■ The Feuding Klans

1. *Fiery Cross*, December 29, 1922, 1; and December 28, 1923, 1.

2. Kenneth T. Jackson, *The Ku Klux Klan in the City, 1915–1930* (New York: Oxford University Press, 1967; New York: Oxford University Press, 1977), 16.

3. William G. Shepherd, "The Fiery Double Cross," *Collier's*, July 28, 1928, 48.

4. Material from Stephenson's trial before the Evansville, Indiana, Klan tribunal, June 23, 1924, 15. In the Harold C. Feightner papers, Indiana Division, Indiana State Library, Indianapolis, Indiana.

5. Booth, *Mad Mullah*, 110.

6. Divorce papers, *Violet M. Stephenson v. David Curtis Stephenson*, Court of Domestic Relations, Summit County, Akron, Ohio, February 28, 1924, D. C. Stephenson Collection, Indiana Historical Society, Indianapolis, Indiana.

7. Testimony of Samuel Bemenderfer, *The State of Indiana v. The Knights of the Ku Klux Klan, et al.*, papers of Arthur Gilliom (cited above).

8. Jackson, *Klan in the City*, 154.

9. *Indianapolis Star*, April 30, 1924, 1.

10. Jackson, *Klan in the City*, 152.

11. *Indianapolis News*, May 9, 1924, 1.

12. Ibid.

13. *Indianapolis News*, May 13, 1924, 3.

14. *Indianapolis News*, May 9, 1924, 1.

15. *Indianapolis News*, May 12, 1924, 1.

16. Ibid.

17. Gene Gladson, *Indianapolis Theatres from A to Z* (Indianapolis, Ind.: Gladson Publications, 1976), 13.

18. *Tolerance*, April 8, 1923.

19. *Tolerance*, July 19, 1923; and August 9, 1923.

20. *Indianapolis News*, May 13, 1924, 1.

21. Ibid.

22. "The Old Man's Answer to the Hate Vendors" is reproduced in the Evansville, Indiana, Klan tribunal proceedings, Feightner papers, Indiana State Library (cited above). A copy of the broadsheet is found in *The State of Indiana v. The Knights of the Ku Klux Klan, et al.*, papers of Arthur Gilliom (cited above).

23. Ibid.

24. Ibid.

25. Ibid.

26. Testimony of Chauncey Manning, Evansville, Indiana, Klan tribunal proceedings, Feightner papers (cited above), 39.

27. Ibid., 40.

28. *Indianapolis News*, May 13, 1924, 4.

29. Evansville, Indiana, Klan tribunal, Feightner papers (cited above), 40–41.

30. Jackson, *Klan in the City*, 155.

31. *Indianapolis News*, May 14, 1924, 3.

32. Ibid.

33. *Indianapolis News*, May 14, 1924, 3.

34. Ibid.

35. *Indianapolis News*, May 15, 1924, 1.

36. Ibid.

37. Ibid.

38. *Indianapolis News*, May 15, 1924, 1.

39. Ibid.

40. Elizabeth Dales and Katherine Edsall, *A Brief History of South Bend, Indiana, 1820–1960* (South Bend, Ind.: South Bend Public Library and South Bend Community School Corporation, 1970), 15.

41. Jill Suzanne Nevel, "Fiery Crosses and Tempers: The Ku Klux Klan in South Bend, Indiana, 1923–1926," senior history thesis, Princeton University, 1977, 66. A bound copy of this excellent paper is found in the Indiana State Library, Indianapolis, Indiana.

42. Stephenson's deposition, *The State of Indiana v. The Knights of the Ku Ku Klan, et al.*, papers of Arthur Gilliom (cited above).

43. Ibid.

44. Accounts of the riot are compiled from Nevel's "Fiery Crosses and Tempers" (cited above), 79–89; the *South Bend Tribune*, May 18, 1924, 1; and the *Fiery Cross*, May 23, 1924, 1.

Chapter Seventeen ■ On the Campaign Trail

1. References to the Stephenson Klan trial are from "Trial Before Tribunal," the booklet produced by the Evansville, Indiana, Klan after the 1924 tribunal. In the Harold C. Feightner papers (cited above).

2. Robert A. Butler, *So They Framed Stephenson* (Huntington, Ind.: self-published, 1940), 16.

3. Booth, *Mad Mullah*, 88.

4. David M. Chalmers, *Hooded Americanism: The First Century of the Ku Klux Klan: 1865 to the Present* (Garden City, N.Y.: Doubleday & Co., 1965), 202.

5. *Time*, June 23, 1924, 6.

6. Ibid.

7. Ibid.

8. Booth, *Mad Mullah*, 88–89.

9. A collection of clippings from various newspapers on the explosion of the Reomar II is in the D. C. Stephenson collection (cited above).

10. John L. Niblack, *The Life and Times of a Hoosier Judge* (self-published, no date), 196–97.

11. *Indianapolis News*, May 12, 1924, 1.

12. *Indianapolis Star*, January 12, 1925, 1.

13. Ibid.

14. *Indiana Year Book* (Indianapolis, Ind.: Indiana General Assembly, 1924), 48–51.

Chapter Eighteen ■ A Plan for the Statehouse

1. Booth, *Mad Mullah*, 52.

2. The various Klan bills were all detailed in newspaper articles in the *Indianapolis Star*, *Indianapolis News*, and *Indianapolis Times* throughout the months of January, February, and March 1925. A few of these for the bills mentioned are as follows: "Religious Garb Bill Killed," *Indianapolis Star*, January 22, 1925, 8; "Senate Kills Bible Reading Bill," Indianapolis Star, January 22, 1925, 1, 10; "Senate Kills 3rd Klan Bill" (on teacher qualification), *Indianapolis Star*, January 24, 1925, 10; "Bible Education Bill Passes in Senate," *Indianapolis Star*, January 29, 1925, 1, 8; "Klan Measure to Limit Teachers in Public Schools to Public School Grads," *Indianapolis Times*, January 23, 1925, 1; "Parochial School Bill Passes House," *Indianapolis Star*, February 26, 1925, 1, 11; "Movie Censorship Bill Dies in House," *Indianapolis News*, January 30, 1925, 10. These are only a tiny sample of the dozens of articles that appeared in the newspapers, often as lead stories, during this period.

3. Several newspaper articles in the major dailies during the 1925 General Assembly outline the divisions between pro-Klan and anti-Klan forces. One of the best, and one which identified George W. Sims as part of the pro-Klan faction, is "Religious Garb Bill Killed," *Indianapolis Star*, January 22, 1925, 8.

4. "Senate Committee Appointment; Anti-Klan Controls the Education Committee," *Indianapolis Star*, January 14, 1925, 1.

5. "Old Age Pension Bill," *Indianapolis Star*, February 20, 1925, 1–2.

6. Investigation of Alleged Political Corruption, transcript of the Marion County Grand Jury, October 12–14, 1926, D. C. Stephenson Collection (cited above).

7. "Governor Jackson Pledges Fearless Discharge of Duty," *Indianapolis Star*, January 13, 1925, 1.

8. "Text of Inaugural Address," *Indianapolis Star*, January 13, 1925, 10.

9. "List of House Committees," *Indianapolis Star*, January 13, 1925, 3.

10. Details of what happened at the inaugural ball are from the Stephenson murder trial testimony of Stanley Hill, quoted in "Stephenson Case Nears Close," *Indianapolis Star*, November 12, 1925, 7.

11. "Fashionable Athletic Club Dinner Ends Inaugural Day," *Indianapolis Star*, January 13, 1925, 1.

Chapter Nineteen ■ The Law Makers

1. Vital statistics are from burial records at Memorial Park Cemetery, Indianapolis, Indiana. Other family historical information was supplied by Mrs. Melvin R. Oberholtzer, interview with the author, 1978.

2. Church records of Irvington Methodist Church, Indianapolis, Indiana.

3. Jean Brown Wagoner, interview with the author, 1979.

4. Lena Pavey Morrow, Butler College Class of 1917, interview with the author, 1979.

5. Ibid.

6. *The Drift* yearbook, 1917, Butler University archives, Indianapolis, Indiana, 65.

7. Asa J. Smith, bound transcript of oral history, Indiana Division, Indiana State Library, Indianapolis, Indiana.

8. Madge Oberholtzer's job titles are from the *Indianapolis City Directory* (Indianapolis, Ind.: R. L. Polk & Company) for the years indicated.

9. Asa J. Smith, oral history (cited above).

10. Testimony of Matilda Oberholtzer, with transcripts of testimony drawn from the *Indianapolis Star, Indianapolis News*, and *Indianapolis Times*, October 1925.

11. Testimony of Stanley C. Hill, November 11, 1925, quoted in the *Indianapolis Star*, November 12, 1925; and the *Indianapolis News* and *Indianapolis Times*, November 11, 1925, issues.

12. Deathbed statement of Madge A. Oberholtzer, *Indiana v. Stephenson*, 1925, a copy of which is in the D. C. Stephenson Collection (cited above).

13. From an Historic Landmark file on the Hotel Washington. Copies available from the Indiana State Museum, Indianapolis, Indiana.

14. Deathbed statement of Madge Oberholtzer, D. C. Stephenson Collection (cited above).

15. Testimony of Court Asher, Marion County Grand Jury, October 13, 1926, D. C. Stephenson Collection (cited above).

16. Unpublished memoirs of William H. Remy, manuscript copy, D. C. Stephenson Collection (cited above), 244.

17. *Indianapolis Times*, January 7, 1925, 5.

18. *Indianapolis Times*, January 8, 1925, 5.

19. *Indianapolis Times*, January 2, 1925, 1; and January 6, 1925, 1.

20. *Indianapolis News*, January 8, 1925; and January 9, 1925; *Indianapolis Star*, January 9, 1925.

21. *Indianapolis Times*, January 14, 1925, 1.

22. *Indianapolis Star*, January 22, 1925, 8.

23. Voting records are taken from the *Indianapolis Star*, January 22, 1925; January 23, 1925; and January 24, 1925.

24. Voting records are taken from the *Indianapolis Star,* February 18, 1925; February 26, 1925; and March 4, 1925.

Chapter Twenty ■ Stephenson's Triumph

1. *Indianapolis News,* February 5, 1925, 18.

2. Ibid.

3. *Indianapolis Times,* February 26, 1925, 1; and February 27, 1925, 1.

4. *Indianapolis Times,* February 27, 1925, 1.

5. Ibid.

6. Ibid.

7. *Indianapolis News,* February 12, 1925, 1. Also testimony of Court Asher, Marion County Grand Jury, October 13, 1926, D. C. Stephenson Collection (cited above).

8. *Laws of the State of Indiana, 1925* (Indianapolis, Ind.: William B. Burford, 1925), 270.

9. The publishing company is named in a James E. Farmer "That Reminds Me" column from the *Indianapolis Star,* July 8, 1950.

10. Testimony of Court Asher, D. C. Stephenson Collection (cited above).

11. Ibid.

12. *Indianapolis Star,* February 19, 1925, 1.

13. *Indianapolis Star,* March 5, 1925, 1; March 7, 1925, 1; March 9, 1925, 1; and March 10, 1925, 1. Series of stories on the Highway Department corruption investigation and the "road ripper" bill.

14. John L. Duvall, letter to the editor, *Indianapolis Star,* April 25, 1955.

15. Testimony of D. C. Stephenson, Marion County Grand Jury, October 1926, D. C. Stephenson Collection (cited above).

16. Ibid.

17. Duvall letter (cited above).

18. Testimony of Court Asher, D. C. Stephenson Collection (cited above).

19. Testimony of Matilda Oberholtzer (cited above).

20. Deathbed statement of Madge Oberholtzer, D. C. Stephenson Collection (cited above).

21. Testimony of Matilda Oberholtzer, D. C. Stephenson Collection (cited above).

Chapter Twenty-one ■ Madge Oberholtzer Comes Home

1. Asa J. Smith, "Facts Concerning Evidence," a fourteen-page manuscript in the D. C. Stephenson Collection (cited above). This amazing first-person account was apparently written by Smith shortly after the incidents of March and April 1925 in anticipation of the trial against Stephenson. Direct quotations in this chapter which are attributed to Smith or the people he talked with are taken from this document. For additional information on Smith, see the bound transcript of his oral history, Indiana Division, Indiana State Library, Indianapolis, Indiana.

2. George E. Oberholtzer, formal complaint against D. C. Stephenson for kidnapping Madge Oberholtzer, D. C. Stephenson Collection (cited above).

3. Testimony of Eunice Schultz, with transcripts of testimony drawn from the front-page stories appearing in the *Indianapolis Star, Indianapolis News,* and *Indianapolis Times* during October 1925.
4. Ibid.
5. Statement of Dr. John K. Kingsbury, attending physician of Madge Oberholtzer at the time of her death, April 15, 1925, in the D. C. Stephenson Collection (cited above).
6. Ibid.
7. Ibid.

Chapter Twenty-two ■ A Dying Woman's Statement

1. Smith, "Facts Concerning Evidence," D. C. Stephenson Collection (cited above), 5.
2. Biographical data from Dr. John K. Kingsbury's obituary, *Indianapolis Star,* January 18, 1972.
3. Smith, "Facts Concerning Evidence" (cited above), 5.
4. Biographical data from Griffith D. Dean's obituary, *Indianapolis Star,* November 4, 1938.
5. Smith, "Facts Concerning Evidence" (cited above), 5–6.
6. Ibid., 9.
7. Ibid., 12.
8. Ibid., 14.

Chapter Twenty-three ■ A Death in Irvington

1. Asa J. Smith, "Facts Concerning Evidence." Also see the unpublished memoirs of William H. Remy. Both are located in the D. C. Stephenson Collection (cited above).
2. *Indianapolis Star,* April 3, 1925, 1.
3. Ibid.
4. *Indianapolis Times,* December 12, 1942, clipping in the Indiana Biographical Files, Indiana Division, Indiana State Library, Indianapolis, Indiana.
5. Unpublished memoirs of William H. Remy, D. C. Stephenson Collection (cited above), 242–44.
6. Ibid., 243.
7. Ibid., 244.
8. Leroy New, telephone interview with the author, November 1980.
9. *Indianapolis Star,* April 5, 1925, 1.
10. John L. Niblack, *The Life and Times of a Hoosier Judge* (self-published, no date), 209.
11. *Indianapolis Star,* April 3, 1925, 1.
12. *Indianapolis Star,* April 6, 1925, 1.
13. Ibid.
14. The reports are from the *Indianapolis Star* for the dates indicated in the paragraph. All stories mentioned are found on page 1.
15. *Indianapolis Star,* April 15, 1925, 1.
16. Ibid.
17. *Indianapolis Star,* March 19, 1925, 9.
18. *Indianapolis Star,* April 17, 1925, 1.
19. *Indianapolis Star,* April 20, 1925, 1.
20. *Indianapolis Star,* April 21, 1925, 1.

Chapter Twenty-four ■ An Investigation Begins

1. *Indianapolis Star*, June 10, 1931, clipping in the Indiana Biographical Files, Indiana Division, Indiana State Library, Indianapolis, Indiana.

2. Ibid.

3. Detective Jerry E. Kinney's notes are among the papers in the D. C. Stephenson Collection (cited above).

4. Ibid.

5. Ibid.

6. Ibid.

7. Ibid.

8. Statements of Levi Thomas, D. C. Stephenson Collection (cited above).

9. The coroner's report is in the D. C. Stephenson Collection (cited above).

10. Statement of Jack Culbertson, D. C. Stephenson Collection (cited above).

11. *Indianapolis Star*, April 26, 1925, 1.

12. Ibid.

13. *Indianapolis Star*, May 5, 1925, 1. Also *Indianapolis Times*, May 16, 1925, 1.

14. *Indianapolis Star*, May 16, 1925, 1.

15. Ibid.

Chapter Twenty-five ■ The Trial Before the Trial

1. *Indianapolis Times*, May 25, 1925, 1.

2. *Indianapolis Times*, May 23, 1925, 1.

3. *Indianapolis Star*, February 9, 1935, clipping in Indiana Biographical Files (cited above).

4. *Indianapolis Star*, May 14, 1925, 13.

5. *Indianapolis Star*, May 16, 1954, clipping in Indiana Biographical Files (cited above).

6. *Indianapolis Star*, May 26, 1925, 1.

7. Ibid.

8. Ibid.

9. A partial transcript of the bail bond hearing is contained in the D. C. Stephenson Collection (cited above). This material has been augmented by reports of the hearing written by Horace M. Coats for the *Indianapolis Star*, June 13–July 7, 1925.

10. *Indianapolis Star*, June 17, 1925, 8.

11. Ibid.

12. *Indianapolis Star*, July 30, 1925, 1.

13. *Indianapolis Star*, August 11, 1925, 1.

Chapter Twenty-six ■ A New Judge Arrives

1. *Indianapolis Star*, August 12, 1925, 1.

2. The account of how Judge Will Sparks received the phone call from Judge Fred Hines is based on an account given by Sparks's friend, Alan Nolan, interview with the author, September 1981.

3. Biographical information on Judge Will Sparks is taken from biographical files supplied by the judge's nephew, James Foster, during an interview with the author, November 15, 1981.

4. Ibid.

5. *Indianapolis Star,* August 12, 1925, 1.

6. Clippings on the Klan parade, private collection of Thelma Bossert, sister-in-law of Walter Bossert, and an interview of her by the author, November 15, 1981.

7. Robert A. Butler, *So They Framed Stephenson* (Huntington, Ind.: self-published, 1940), 23–25.

8. Ibid.

9. Accounts of the jury selection process are taken primarily from the stories written by Horace A. Coats for the *Indianapolis Star,* October 12–29, 1925, all appearing on page 1.

10. *New York World,* October 16, 1925, a clipping from the biographical files on Judge Will Sparks (cited above).

11. Ibid.

12. *Indianapolis Star,* October 29, 1925, 1.

13. Ibid.

Chapter Twenty-seven ■ The Opening Gambit

1. *Indianapolis News,* October 29, 1925, 1.

2. Ibid., 12.

3. Ibid.

4. Ibid.

5. *Indianapolis News,* October 30, 1925, 20.

6. *Indianapolis News,* October 30, 1925, 20–21.

7. Ibid.

8. *Indianapolis Star,* October 31, 1925, 9.

9. Ibid.

10. Asher L. Cornelius, *The Cross Examination of Witnesses: Rules, Principles and Illustrations* (Indianapolis, Ind.: The Bobbs-Merrill Company, 1929), 534–36.

11. Ibid.

12. Ibid.

13. Ibid.

14. Ibid, 539–40.

15. *Indianapolis News,* October 30, 1925, 1.

16. Ibid.

17. Cornelius, *Cross Examination of Witnesses,* 543.

18. Ibid., 545.

19. Ibid., 546–47.

20. Ibid.

21. Ibid., 549–50.

22. *Indianapolis Star,* October 30, 1925, 9.

23. Ibid.

24. Ibid.

25. Ibid.

Chapter Twenty-eight ■ Losing Ground

1. *Indianapolis Star,* November 1, 1925, 5.

2. Ibid.

3. Ibid.

4. Ibid.

5. Ibid.

6. Ibid.

7. Ibid.

8. Ibid.

9. *Indianapolis Star*, November 2, 1925, 3.

10. Testimony of Court Asher, Marion Co. Grand Jury, October 13, 1926, D. C. Stephenson Collection (cited above).

11. Ibid.

12. *Indianapolis News*, November 2, 1925, 1.

13. Ibid., 4.

14. Ibid.

15. Ibid.

16. *Indianapolis Star*, November 3, 1923, 8.

17. Cornelius, *Cross Examination of Witnesses*, 558–60.

18. *Indianapolis Star*, November 1, 1925, 1.

19. Biographical files of Judge Sparks, supplied by the judge's nephew, James Foster, during an interview with the author, November 15, 1981.

20. *Indianapolis News*, November 3, 1925, 1.

21. Cornelius, *Cross Examination of Witnesses*, 562–64.

22. *Indianapolis Star*, November 4, 1925, 9.

23. Ibid.

24. Ibid.

25. *Indianapolis Star*, November 4, 1925, 1.

26. *Indianapolis Times*, November 4, 1925, 2.

27. *Indianapolis Star*, November 5, 1925, 1.

Chapter Twenty-nine ■ The Defense Takes Over

1. *Indianapolis News*, November 5, 1925, 1.

2. Robert A. Butler, *So They Framed Stephenson* (Huntington, Ind.: self-published, 1940), 26–27.

3. *Indianapolis Star*, November 2, 1925, 3.

4. *Indianapolis News*, November 5, 1925, 1.

5. *Indianapolis Star*, November 6, 1925, 2.

6. Ibid.

7. Cornelius, *Cross Examination of Witnesses*, 587–89.

8. Ibid.

9. *Indianapolis Star*, November 7, 1925, 3.

10. Ibid.

11. Cornelius, *Cross Examination of Witnesses*, 580–87.

12. *Indianapolis News*, November 7, 1925, 3.

13. *Indianapolis Star*, November 7, 1925, 3.

14. Ibid.

15. *Indianapolis News*, November 7, 1925, 1–2.

16. Ibid.

17. Ibid., 2.

Chapter Thirty ■ "The Old Man's" Friends

1. *Indianapolis Star*, November 7, 1925, 3.

2. Ibid.

3. *Indianapolis News*, November 7, 1925, 3.

4. *Indianapolis Star*, November 8, 1925, 6.

5. Ibid.

6. Ibid.
7. *Indianapolis News,* November 9, 1925, 4.
8. Ibid.
9. *Indianapolis Star,* November 10, 1925, 1.
10. Ibid.
11. *Indianapolis News,* November 9, 1925, 1–4.
12. *Indianapolis Star,* November 10, 1925, 10.
13. Ibid.
14. Ibid.
15. *Indianapolis News,* November 10, 1925, 1.
16. *Indianapolis Star,* November 11, 1925, 11.
17. Ibid.
18. Ibid.
19. Ibid.
20. Ibid.
21. Ibid.
22. Ibid.
23. Ibid., 1.
24. Ibid., 11.
25. Ibid.
26. *Indianapolis News,* November 10, 1925, 14.
27. *Indianapolis News,* November 11, 1925, 24.
28. Ibid.
29. Ibid.
30. Ibid., 1.
31. Ibid., 24.
32. Ibid.
33. *Indianapolis News,* November 12, 1925, 22.
34. Ibid.

Chapter Thirty-one ■ "The Fairest Trial in History"

1. *Indianapolis News,* November 12, 1925, 1–15. Also *Indianapolis Star,* November 13, 1925, 1–3.
2. *Indianapolis News,* November 12, 1925, 1–15.
3. *Indianapolis News,* November 13, 1925, 16.
4. *Indianapolis Star,* November 13, 1925, 1–3.
5. *Indianapolis News,* November 13, 1925, 25.
6. Ibid.
7. Ibid.
8. Ibid.
9. *Indianapolis Star,* November 14, 1925, 1–3.
10. Ibid., 3.
11. *Indianapolis News,* November 14, 1925, 1–3.
12. *Indianapolis Star,* November 15, 1925, 1.

Chapter Thirty-two ■ House of Cards

1. Robert A. Butler, *So They Framed Stephenson* (Huntington, Ind.: self-published, 1940), 29.
2. John L. Niblack, *The Life and Times of a Hoosier Judge* (self-published, no date), 218–19.
3. Testimony of Court Asher, Marion County Grand Jury, October 13, 1926, D. C. Stephenson Collection (cited above).
4. "Notes on Stephenson Case," from Harold C. Feightner's papers, in the Roger Branigin Collection, Franklin College, Franklin, Indiana.

5. Ibid.

6. Ibid.

7. *Indianapolis Star,* October 30, 1925, 1.

8. *Indianapolis Times,* October 5, 1926.

9. "Notes on Stephenson Case," Feightner papers, Roger Branigin Collection (cited above).

10. Ibid.

11. Ibid.

12. Ibid.

13. Ibid.

14. Ibid.

15. Ibid.

16. Niblack, *Life and Times of a Hoosier Judge,* 221.

17. Ibid., 224.

18. Ibid.

19. Ibid.

20. Ibid., 249.

21. Ibid., 251.

22. Ibid., 252.

23. Ibid.

24. Ibid., 257.

25. Information on Frank Prince comes from several sources, including the files on Mrs. William English in the English Foundation, Indianapolis, Indiana; articles in the *St. Louis Post-Dispatch,* February 7, 1960, and February 9, 1960; and records of the Indiana State Prison at Michigan City, Indiana.

26. Response of the State of Indiana to the Petitioner's Statement, in the Hamilton Circuit Court, Noblesville, Indiana. Private collection.

27. Statement of D. C. Stephenson, October 27, 1939. Private collection.

28. *Indianapolis Star,* March 6, 1945.

29. Ibid.

30. *Indianapolis Star,* March 29, 1945.

31. *Indianapolis News,* November 23, 1951.

32. *Indianapolis Star,* December 22, 1956. Also *Indianapolis Times,* December 30, 1956

33. Irving Leibowitz, *My Indiana* (Englewood Cliffs, N.J.: Prentice-Hall, 1964), 224–25.

34. *Louisville Courier-Journal,* September 17, 1978, 1.

Epilogue ■ Was Stephenson Framed?

1. Attorney Frank Campbell, interview with the author, Noblesville, Indiana, 1979.

2. Private collection. Also, Butler, *So They Framed Stephenson,* 12–52.

3. Butler, *So They Framed Stephenson,* 26–28.

4. Private collection.

5. Leibowitz, *My Indiana,* 219.

6. *Indianapolis Times,* February 4, 1949, 1.

7. *Indianapolis Star,* February 4, 1949, 1.

8. Butler, *So They Framed Stephenson,* 133.

9. Niblack, *Life and Times of a Hoosier Judge,* 218.

Sources

Alexander, Charles C. "Kleagles and Cash: The Ku Klux Klan as a Business Organization, 1915–1930." *Business History Review* 39 (Autumn 1965).

Ameringer, Oscar. *If You Don't Weaken: The Autobiography of Oscar Ameringer.* New York: Henry Holt and Company, 1940.

Baritz, Loren. *The Culture of the Twenties.* Indianapolis, Ind.: The Bobbs-Merrill Company, 1970.

Bentley, Max. "The Ku Klux Klan in Indiana." *McClure's Magazine,* May 1924.

Blair, The Reverend V. W. "The Stephenson Case." Privately printed, 1940.

Bohn, Frank. "The Ku Klux Klan Interpreted." *The American Journal of Sociology* 30, no. 4 (January 1925).

Booth, Edgar Allen. *The Mad Mullah of America.* Columbus, Ohio: Boyd Ellison, 1927.

Bosler, Monsignor Raymond. Interview with author. 1980.

Bossert, Thelma. Interview with author. November 15, 1981.

Breeden, B. J. Interview with author. 1980.

Brockway, Chance "Sonny." Interview with author. October 1981.

Brown, Paul, ed. *Indianapolis Men of Affairs.* Indianapolis, Ind.: American Biographical Society, 1923.

Broyles, Kenton H. Interviews with author. 1984–85.

Budenz, Louis Francis. "Scandals of 1927: Indiana." *The Nation,* October 25, 1927.

——— . "There's Mud on Indiana's White Robes." *The Nation,* July 27, 1927.

Busch, Francis X. *Guilty or Not Guilty?* Indianapolis, Ind.: The Bobbs-Merrill Company, 1952.

Butler, Robert A. *So They Framed Stephenson.* Huntington, Ind.: self-published, 1940.

Cameron, James. *A Time of Terror.* Milwaukee, Wisc.: T/D Publications, 1980.

Camp, Vashti. Interview with author. January 1980.

Campbell, Frank W. Interview with author. 1979.

Campbell, Frank S. *The Story of Hamilton County.* Noblesville, Ind.: self-published, 1962.

Carlton, A. L. Interview with author. January 1980.

Cates, Frank M. "The Ku Klux Klan in Indiana Politics: 1920–1925." Ph.D. diss., Indiana University, 1971.

Chalmers, David M. *Hooded Americanism: The First Century of the Ku Klux Klan, 1865 to the Present.* Garden City, N.Y.: Doubleday & Co., 1965.

Cooper, Walter. Interview with author. January 1980.

Cornelius, Asher L. *The Cross Examination of Witnesses: Rules, Principles and Illustrations.* Indianapolis, Ind.: The Bobbs-Merrill Company, 1929.

"*Courier* History (as told to Karl K. Knecht by Col. William J. Rogers, Oct. 25, 1956)." *Evansville Courier* historical files, Evansville, Ind.

Craig, George N. Interview with author. February 1980.

Dales, Elizabeth, and Katherine Edsall. *A Brief History of South Bend, Indiana, 1820–1960.* South Bend, Ind.: South Bend Public Library and South Bend Community School Corporation, 1970.

David, Maurice A. Interview with author. 1980.

Davis, Elmer. "Have Faith in Indiana." In *Show Window.* New York: The John Day Company, 1927.

Davis, John A. "The Ku Klux Klan in Indiana, 1920–1930: An Historical Study." Ph.D. diss., Northwestern University, 1966.

Devricks, Ermina Moore. Interview with author. 1980.

Dixon, Thomas, Jr. *The Leopard's Spots: A Romance of the White Man's Burden.* New York: A. Wessels Company, 1906.

Doyle, Monsignor John. Interview with author. 1980.

The Drift (Butler College yearbook, 1917). Indianapolis, Ind.: Assembled and published by the Class of 1918, Butler College.

Duffus, Robert L. "Salesmen of Hate: The Ku Klux Klan." *World's Work* 46 (1923).

Dunn, Jacob Piatt. *Greater Indianapolis.* Vol. 1. Chicago: Lewis Publishing Company, 1910.

Duvall, Leslie. Interview with author. 1982.

Elrod, French. Interview with author. 1980.

Esarey, Logan, ed. *History of Indiana from Its Exploration to 1922.* Vol. 3, *An Account of Vanderburgh County from Its Organization,* edited by John E. Iglehart. Dayton, Ohio: Dayton Historical Publishing Company, 1923.

———. *History of Indiana from Its Exploration to 1922.* Vol. 4, *An Ac-*

count of Indianapolis and Marion County, edited by Kate Milner Robb and William Herschell. Dayton, Ohio: Dayton Historical Publishing Company, 1924.

Evansville City Directory. 1922.

Evansville Courier. Evansville, Ind., 1921.

Evansville Journal-News. Evansville, Ind., 1920–21.

Farmer, James E., ed. Dateline: Indiana. Indianapolis, Ind.: Indianapolis Press Club, August 1958.

——— . In Memorium: Asa Jessup Smith, Lawyer, Patriot, Wit, 1894–1973. Indianapolis, Ind.: Robert G. Moorhead and the Central Publishing Company, 1988.

Feightner, Harold. Personal Papers. Indiana Division, Indiana State Library, Indianapolis, Ind.; and Franklin College Library, Franklin, Ind.

Fiery Cross. Indianapolis, Ind., 1923–24.

Foland, John A. Remembrances. Noblesville, Ind.: Self-published, 1976.

Foster, James. Interview with author. November 15, 1981.

Garrigus, Ross H. Interview with author. August 1982.

Gladson, Gene. Indianapolis Theatres from A to Z. Indianapolis, Ind.: Gladson Publications, 1976.

Hadden, Briton, and Henry R. Luce. Time Capsule/1925. New York: Time-Life Books, 1968.

Harrison, Morton. "Gentlemen from Indiana." Atlantic Monthly, May 1928.

High, Winston. Interview with author. January 1980.

Higham, John. Strangers in the Land: Patterns of American Nativism, 1860–1925. New Brunswick, N.J.: Rutgers University Press, 1967.

Hoffer, Eric. The True Believer: Thoughts on the Nature of Mass Movements. New York: Harper & Row, Perennial Library, 1951.

Hoover, Robert. Interview with author. 1979.

Indiana Biographical Index. Indiana Division, Indiana State Library, Indianapolis, Ind.

Indianapolis News. Indianapolis, Ind., 1921–25.

Indianapolis Recorder. Indianapolis, Ind., 1921–25.

Indianapolis Star. Indianapolis, Ind., 1921–25.

Indianapolis Times. Indianapolis, Ind., 1921–25.

Indiana State Prison. Prison Records. Michigan City, Ind.

Indiana Women's Prison. Prison Records. Indianapolis, Ind.

Indiana Year Book. Indianapolis, Ind.: Indiana General Assembly, 1924.

Irvington Methodist Church. Church Records. Indianapolis, Ind.

Jackson, Kenneth T. The Ku Klux Klan in the City. New York: Oxford University Press, 1967.

Jacobs, Judge Andrew, Sr. Interview with author. 1979.

Jones, Col. Winfield. *Knights of the Ku Klux Klan.* No publishing information, circa 1942.

Journal of the National Horse Thief Detective Association, 1922. Sixty-third Annual Session, Columbus, Ind., October 2–3, 1923.

Kallenbach, Joseph E., and Jessamine S. Kallenbach. *American State Governors, 1776–1976, Volume 1, Electoral and Personal Data.* Dobbs Ferry, N.Y.: Oceana Publications, 1977.

"A Klan Senator from Indiana." *Literary Digest,* November 14, 1925.

Kokomo Dispatch. Kokomo, Ind., July 5, 1925.

"Ku Klux Klan Kleveland Konvention." *Time* magazine, June 23, 1924.

LaFollette, Gerry. Interview with author. 1978.

Langland, James, ed. "Indianapolis Times Almanac and Year-Book, 1926." In *The National Almanac and Year-Book, 1926.* Cook County, Ill.: Chicago Daily News Company.

Laws of the State of Indiana, 1925. Indianapolis, Ind.: William B. Burford, 1925.

Leary, Edward. *Indianapolis: The Story of a City.* Indianapolis, Ind.: The Bobbs-Merrill Company, 1971.

Leibowitz, Irving. *My Indiana.* Englewood Cliffs, N.J.: Prentice-Hall, 1964.

Leighton, Isabel, ed. *The Aspirin Age, 1919–1941.* New York: Simon and Schuster, 1949; New York: Simon and Schuster, Touchstone Books, 1976.

Lester, J. C., and D. L. Wilson. *Ku Klux Klan: Its Origin, Growth and Disbandment.* 1905. Reprint. New York: AMS Press, 1971.

Linton, Calvin D. *The American Almanac.* Nashville, Tenn.: Thomas Nelson, 1977.

Loucks, Emerson H. *The Ku Klux Klan in Pennsylvania: A Study in Nativism.* Harrisburg, Pa.: The Telegraph Press, 1936.

Louisville Courier-Journal. Louisville, Ky., September 17, 1978.

Lynd, Robert S., and Helen Merrell Lynd. *Middletown: A Study in Modern American Culture.* New York: Harcourt, Brace & World, 1929; New York: Harcourt, Brace & Jovanovich, Harvest/HBJ, 1956.

Madison, James H. *Indiana through Transition and Change.* Indianapolis, Ind.: Indiana Historical Society, 1982.

Martin, John Bartlow. *Indiana: An Interpretation.* New York: Alfred A. Knopf, 1947.

Maysville News. Maysville, Okla., February 11, 1910–June 25, 1914.

Mellett, Lowell. "Klan and Church." *Atlantic Monthly* 132, no. 5.

Memorial Park Cemetery. Cemetery Records. Indianapolis, Ind.

"Mr. X." Interviews with author. 1983–84.

Moore, Leonard J. "White Protestant Nationalism in the 1920s: The Ku Klux Klan in Indiana." Ph.D. diss., University of California at Los Angeles, 1985.

Morris, Richard. Interview with author. 1979.

Morrow, Lena Pavey. Interview with author. 1979.

Municipal Code of the City of Indianapolis, 1925. Indianapolis, Ind.: William B. Burford, 1925.

Nevel, Jill Suzanne. "Fiery Crosses and Tempers: The Ku Klux Klan in South Bend, Indiana, 1923–1926." Senior history thesis, Princeton University, 1977.

New, Leroy. Interview with author. November 1980.

New York World. New York, 1921–24; and October 16, 1925.

Niblack, John L. Interviews with author. 1978–82.

——— . *The Life and Times of a Hoosier Judge.* Washington, Ind.: self-published, no date.

——— . Personal Papers. Indiana Historical Society, Indianapolis, Ind.

Nicholson, Meredith. *The Hoosiers.* New York: MacMillan Company, 1900.

Nolan, Alan. Interview with author. September 1981.

Nolan, Jeannette Covert. *Hoosier City: The Story of Indianapolis.* New York: Julian Messner Co., 1943.

Nussbaum, Lowell. Interview with author. 1979.

Oberholtzer, Mrs. Melvin R. Interview with author. 1978.

Palladium-Item. Richmond, Ind., January 15, 1946.

Papers Read at the Meeting of the Grand Dragons, Knights of the Ku Klux Klan at Their First Annual Meeting held at Asheville, North Carolina, July 1923. No publishing information.

Pelham, Ruth. Interview with author. 1981.

Royko, Mike. *Boss.* New York: Signet Books, New American Library, 1971.

St. Louis Post-Dispatch. St. Louis, Mo., February 7 and February 9, 1960.

Sann, Paul. *The Lawless Decade: A Pictorial History of the Twenties.* New York: Crown Publishers, 1957.

Schultze, Edward Burch. Interview with author. 1980.

Shepherd, William G. "How I Put Over the Klan." *Collier's,* July 14, 1928.

——— . "Indiana's Mystery Man." *Collier's,* January 8, 1927.

——— . "Ku Klux Koin." *Collier's,* July 21, 1928.

Smith, Asa J. Oral History. Bound Transcript. Indiana Division, Indiana State Library, Indianapolis, Ind.

Snyder, Louis L., and Richard B. Morris. *A Treasury of Great Reporting.* New York: Simon and Schuster, 1949, 1962.

South Bend Tribune. South Bend, Ind., May 1924.

State of Indiana v. The Knights of the Ku Klux Klan, et al. Marion County Circuit Court, 41769 (1925–29). Papers of Arthur Gilliom. Microfilm. Indiana State Library, Indianapolis, Ind.

Stephenson, Andrew Monroe. Death Certificate. September 17, 1923. Department of Health and Bureau of Registration, Topeka, Kans.

Stephenson, D. C., and Nettie Hamilton. Certified Copy of Marriage License. March 26, 1915. Johnston County, Okla.

Stephenson, D. C. Testimony before a Marion County grand jury. October 1927. Microfilm. Indiana State Library, Indianapolis, Ind.

Stewart, George. Interview with author. 1979.

Stewart, Marcus. Interview with author. 1979.

Tarkington, Booth. *The Magnificent Ambersons.* New York: Doubleday, Page and Company, 1918.

Taylor, Alva W. "What the Klan Did in Indiana." *The New Republic,* November 16, 1927.

Tolerance. Chicago, Ill., March 18–September 9, 1923.

U.S. Weather Bureau. Meterological Conditions Archives. University of Indianapolis Library, Indianapolis, Ind.

Van Buskirk, Robert. Interviews with author. 1980–89.

Wade, Wyn Craig. *The Fiery Cross: The Ku Klux Klan in America.* New York: Simon and Schuster, Touchstone Books, 1988.

Wagoner, Jean Brown. Interview with author. 1979.

Walters, Russ. Interview with author. October 1981.

Watson, James E. *As I Knew Them: Memoirs of James E. Watson.* Indianapolis, Ind.: The Bobbs-Merrill Company, 1936.

Weaver, Norman F. "The Knights of the Ku Klux Klan in Wisconsin, Indiana, Ohio, and Michigan." Ph.D. diss., University of Wisconsin, 1954.

White, Joseph Michael. "The Ku Klux Klan in Indiana in the 1920's as Viewed by the Indiana Catholic and Record." Master's thesis, Butler University, 1974.

Wilson, William E. *Indiana: A History.* Bloomington, Ind.: Indiana University Press, 1966.

———. "Long, Hot Summer in Indiana." *American Heritage* 16, no. 5 (August 1965).

Winchester Democrat. Winchester, Ind., June 7 and 14, 1923.

Zink, Harold. "A Case Study of a Political Boss." *Psychiatry: Journal of the Biology and Pathology of Interpersonal Relations* 1, no. 4 (November 1938).

Index